GOING
UP

Frederic Raphael

GOING UP

To Cambridge and beyond
– A Writer's Memoir

The Robson Press

First published in Great Britain in 2015 by
The Robson Press (an imprint of Biteback Publishing Ltd)
Westminster Tower
3 Albert Embankment
London SE1 7SP
Copyright © Frederic Raphael 2015

ISBN 978-1-84954-870-0

10 9 8 7 6 5 4 3 2 1

A CIP catalogue record for this book is available from the British Library.

Set in Bulmer

Printed and bound in Great Britain by
CPI Group (UK) Ltd, Croydon CR0 4YY

MIX
Paper from
responsible sources
FSC® C020471

For Beetle

CONTENTS

I

THE MANAGER'S NAME was Love. His first-floor flat was diagonally across the private road and the rose beds from ours. Each weekday morning, at eight fifteen, he hooked open his lattice-paned bedroom window and did exercises, in a white sleeveless vest and white drawers. Inhaling at length to expand his narrow chest, he flexed blanched arms, then bent and straightened unseen knees, five times. His physical jerks had the timeliness of a figure in some medieval German clock. On the hour of nine, he issued forth, at ground level, in black coat and striped trousers, in order to walk his briefcase to his bungalow office, opposite the green main gates and porters' lodge of Manor Fields. Tall and thin, head rounded off with a bowler hat and hanging forward on an elongated neck, he resembled an ambulant question mark. His first name was Bernard, but he was spoken of only as Mr Love.

Manor Fields consisted of several blocks of red-brick Key flats, disposed among lawns and nice trees in what was once the rural estate of Lord North. Built at the top of Putney Hill in the 1930s, they were designed to appeal to ascendant members of the middle class. Each set of three entrances – apart from the one labelled 'Harvard' – was named after an Oxford or Cambridge college, although few tenants were likely to have attended one. Perhaps out of secular tact, none of the blocks bore the names of sainted colleges. Our first-floor flat was 12 Balliol House. My father had been at St John's, Oxford, neighbour to Balliol, which was known to those next door as 'Bloody Belial'. One of Cedric's friends had tried to take a running jump from one college to the other and was impaled on the spikes atop an intervening wall.

In my teens, during the late 1940s, most of the lock-up garages in the back lot of Manor Fields stood empty. Early in the war, my parents had renounced their black Standard 8, EYR 332, with an enamel Union Jack on its bonnet device. Not until 1953 did they buy a patriotic, under-powered, fawn-coloured Morris. During the Blitz, Manor Fields' cavernous underground garage served as a communal air-raid shelter. On holiday from boarding school, I looked forward to the ululating air-raid siren. The threat of German bombs promised a late night, sweetened by communal cocoa and Huntley & Palmers biscuits and loud with ack-ack fire from a sand-bagged battery on Putney Heath. The moan of the all-clear was an unwelcome relief: it signalled bedtime.

No trace remained of the eighteenth-century mansion of the Prime Minister whose indecision had lost Britain its American colonies. However, when strange scents were sniffed in the first-floor flat rented by John and Adie Tutin, in Somerville House, which stood on the site of the great house, Adie – a short, permanently waved, blonde, breathless, one-eyed Yorkshire woman – was sure that the perfume emanated from the ghosts of conscience-stricken aristocrats. On the telephone to my mother, the gush of gossip from what I called 'Radio Tutin' was audible from my parents' bedroom door.

The Tutin flat featured a white telephone, concealed under the crinoline of a ceramic Madame Pompadour. It also sported a heavy collection of blue bound copies of the *New Yorker*, for which I had an exile's appetite. Central Park West, where I had lived until I was six years old, was my equivalent of the Old Country. In early adolescence, I embarrassed Adie by taking pointed pleasure in the Peter Arno cartoon of a businessman saying to the barman, as he indicated the scantily dressed floozy on the stool beside him, 'Fill 'er up.'

During summer holidays, I played tennis with the Tutins' neat, pretty brunette daughter, Dorothy. She had a freckled nose and a penetrating cross-court forehand. After a spell as a flautist, under the tutelage of the conductor of the Metropolitan Police band, Maestro Barsotti, Dotty gained entrance to RADA, borne on the wind of her mother's ambition. Adie seemed to have been born to impersonate Noël Coward's Mrs Worthington. Dorothy proved, in due time, that there was an escape from suburbia, along the yellow-brick road that led to the distant West End. Her favourite record, played on the family's wind-up gramophone, was 'My Heart belongs to Daddy'. I preferred another number in the Tutins' brittle collection: 'She had to go and lose it at the Astor'. The twist was that what the singer had lost was not her virginity but her mother's sable coat.

By the time I left Charterhouse, Dotty had her first professional part, as a pageboy (blackface, can it have been?) in some Shakespearian drama. She spoke no lines, but one of the reviews was headed 'THE TUTIN GIG-GLE'. After she was cast in Graham Greene's *The Living Room*, with Eric Portman, who fidgeted with eye-catching effect when anyone else on stage seemed to be attracting the audience's attention, Dotty never looked back. One day, I thought, I would write her a play and earn myself a one-way ticket out of Mr Love's enclosure.

Dr John Tutin was a tall, square-shouldered naval engineer. He had a dipsomaniac's careful step. Having gained pre-war fame by designing a revolutionary propeller for the *Queen Mary*, he went up to Piccadilly most days, after the morning rush, in black overcoat with velvet facings, and homburg hat. During the war, he had an office in Lower Regent Street, where he had been commissioned to work on 'The Tutin Safety Hatch'. It would assist submariners to avoid the fate of the sailors who, in June 1939, had been trapped, and drowned, in Liverpool Bay in HMS *Thetis*. When HMG ceased to pay his rent, Dr Tutin installed himself in the reading room of the Piccadilly Hotel, where he made seigneurial use of the stationery and other amenities. His velvet-faced comportment won salutes from the doorman and immunity from managerial question.

On the odd occasion, he joined Dotty and me for weekend tennis on one of the two *en-tout-cas* courts on the garage roof. Wearing jaundiced flannels and dainty gym shoes, he would pause and then serve with an abrupt dab of the racket that imparted a high, slow, unreachable bounce to the ball. John was sometimes partnered by the exophthalmic George Coulouris, an English actor with a Greek father. In New York, he had been a member of Orson Welles's Group Theatre and played the part of Walter P. Thatcher in *Citizen Kane*.

I was never more wholeheartedly British than in the last month of 1949, when, having finished my scholarship exams in snowy Cambridge, I stopped off at Manor Fields to await my results. Who could guess that, in 1938, I had been transported, an honest-to-God American kid, from New York City to England? As a result, I had been untimely ripped from Ethical Culture School, on Central Park West, and subjected to an English classical education, first at Copthorne, a Sussex prep school evacuated for the duration of the war to north Devon, and then at Charterhouse, near Godalming, Surrey.

I was alone in my parents' flat when, late in the afternoon and with waning hopes, I received a telegram from R. L. Howland, the senior tutor of St John's, congratulating me on having been elected to a Major Scholarship in Classics. A florin persuaded the telegraph boy to stay and share my pleasure with a glass of sherry. My joy derived less from the opportunity for advanced study of Latin and Greek than from triumph over George C. Turner, the headmaster of Charterhouse.

Obliged to return to Godalming for the rump of the Oration Quarter, I put on the fawn, zip-fronted trousers, without turn-ups, which I had acquired the previous summer, while on a visit to Kansas City, my mother's home town. Over my demonstratively transatlantic Arrow shirt, with button-down collar, I wore a Fair Isle sweater of many colours, knitted – on several simultaneous, curved needles – by my mother's agile young fingers (Irene was not yet forty).

I refrained from flaunting one of the hand-painted, kipper-wide ties that a salesman had wished on me in K. C. after I had promised that I was all right for socks. Even a modest sartorial declaration of independence would stand out against the herringbone-tweedy, house-tied uniformity of fly-buttoned Carthusians who had yet to complete their penitential sentences.

My sixth-form masters, I. F. 'Gibbo' Gibson and V. S. H. 'Sniffy' Russell were quick with congratulations. I received none from the headmaster. Some months earlier, George Turner had barred me from the shortlist of candidates for the Holford Scholarship, which offered one Carthusian per annum privileged access to Christ Church, Oxford. My candidature was proscribed because of a letter I had written to the Provost of Guildford. During a Sunday night sermon in chapel, he had invited the congregation to imagine young Jesus going to sell his handiwork as a carpenter to a Nazareth shopkeeper. 'And the shopkeeper,' he declared, '*being a Jew*, would give him as little for it as possible.'

Had I, at that point, ventured from the sixth-form stalls and strode down the long nave of the Giles Gilbert Scott Memorial Chapel and unlatched one of the big, echoing doors and gone out into the night, my time at the school might have been summarily curtailed; but it would have been a far, far better thing than I dared to do. I sat still. Later, closeted in my study, I wrote a sardonic letter to the Provost. He did not reply directly. He forwarded my callow philippic to George Turner, adding that he would never have said what he did if he had known that there were any Jews in the chapel. Turner, a short man, summoned me to his presence and accused me of bad manners towards a guest of the school. It was my duty to write and apologise. Brimming with unworthy tears, I refused. The headmaster then declared that my discourtesy rendered me ineligible to be included on the shortlist of candidates for Christ Church.

It was a Carthusian tradition that anyone who had won a major Oxbridge award was commissioned to carry the good news, on a card written by the headmaster, from classroom to classroom. The announcement that he had won an extra half-holiday for the whole school procured brief popularity for a clever boy. Carthusian slang labelled scholars 'hash pros', no deferential designation. In 1940s England, to be a professional implied that you did things because, unlike a gentleman, you needed the money. George Turner gave the rank and file no occasion to put their hands together for me. Nor did I receive the leaving prize of £40 in books regularly given to those who had won major laurels.

In the envoi appended to my last report, Turner hoped that my success would encourage me to abate my resentments and take pleasure in 'the adventure of ideas', a phrase lifted from the title of a book by Alfred North Whitehead, the co-author, with his quondam pupil Bertrand Russell, of *Principia Mathematica*. Russell's Whiggish accents were familiar from his contributions to *The Brains Trust* on the radio. Turner was advising me to renounce my mission to reproach the Christian world for iniquities visited on the Jews; I should do better to lose myself in the higher culture to which I was fortunate enough to have been offered access. I had every wish to do so.

To buy the blue Pelican edition of Whitehead's elegant book, I went to W. H. Smith's, in Putney High Street. A varnished board hung from two brass chains over the foyer of the shop displaying – in appropriate shades of blue – the winners of the University Boat Race each year since its inception in 1856. With instant new pride, I observed that Cambridge had won more races than Oxford. My vision of Cambridge promptly displaced that of Oxford. I imagined a Great Good Place, where wit procured eminence and where there was neither Jew nor Gentile.

Smith's had a lending library on the first floor. Monica Dickens, Agatha Christie, Georgette Heyer, Angela Thirkell and Daphne du Maurier were the authors most in demand by south London *literatae*. Suburban solitude made me bookish rather than scholarly. To learn about the world, one did not look or listen, one read. Until 1948, we had no television in 12 Balliol House; nor was there ever a gramophone. In 1925, partnering Phyllis Haylor, my father had been amateur dancing champion of the world. He always loved to dance. His favourite venues were downstairs at Hatchett's, adjacent to the Berkeley Hotel in Piccadilly, Quaglino's in Bury Street and, more rarely, the Savoy Hotel. It had an elevated dance floor and bespectacled, soft-voiced Carroll Gibbons's sucrose orchestra. What counted for Cedric was the beat, not the music.

We never went to concerts, rarely to the theatre. Our Philco radio was seldom turned on except to listen to the nine o'clock news (read, most often, by Alan Liddell or Bruce Belfrage), Tommy Handley's *ITMA* ('Well, if it isn't Poppy Poo-pah!') and Ronnie Waldman's *Monday Night at Eight*. It featured a weekly 'deliberate mistake', which listeners were incited to detect, and an encapsulated thriller, *Meet Dr Morelle*. On Christmas Day, we tuned in to the king's speech in good time to sympathise with brave royal pauses. My father and I stood at attention for the national anthem, enacting moral rectitude. My mother, being American, was exempt.

In the 1940s, I had no way of learning about sex except through print. Although a measure of information came with the kit, a solitary boy had to imagine how his bit might fit into hers and, more difficult, why she might care to brook such an invasion. I had neither brothers nor sisters. Since both my parents were only children, I also lacked first cousins. All my relatives were old. By the time I left Charterhouse, when I was eighteen, I had yet to see an unclothed female in the flesh.

At the age of eleven, I had been enlightened, by chance, about what men and women did in the course of what Somerset Maugham, when I came to read him, called 'sexual congress'. During a school holiday, while on a bicycle ride with a Dartmouth cadet who lived in the next entrance of Balliol House, I chanced on an unofficial exhibition of black and white photographs pronged on the barbed wire around the pond on Wimbledon Common. A congeries of tallowy men and Rubensesque women were disporting themselves with hirsute abandon. One or two were smiling at the camera. We looked and we looked, Martin and I, and then we pedalled home.

When I returned, alone, to do some revision ('boning up' might be an apt modern usage), the photographs had disappeared. I had to satisfy myself with the breasts of the single naked woman available, for one and sixpence, in the monthly *Lilliput*. The space between her legs was blanched and uncleft. I looked to Picasso for hairier information. *Lilliput* also carried the adventures of 'That Naughty Girl Myrtle'. She was advertised as being no better than she should be. Her chronicler never disclosed details of what precise naughtiness she got up to. I was much taken by a Reprint Society novel in which the heroine was revealed, by her overall tan, to have sunbathed in the nude. Art and literature supplied what suburban life concealed or was fudged by editorial discretion.

When I was fifteen, and my mother was quarantined with mumps, I had no recourse, between attending to her, but to sit alone and read. I happened on *Of Human Bondage* in my parents' shelves (two long rows, low under the bay window). Somerset Maugham's orphaned hero, Philip Carey, was bullied at school because he had a club foot. His guardian was a Church of England vicar, as the author's had been. Accused of a want of Christian charity, he retorted (perhaps more self-mockingly than his ward recognised) that parsons were 'paid to preach, not to practise'. Maugham's decorous eroticism was piquant enough to inflame adolescent desires. His young hero was dismayed, and all but dismasted, by Miss Wilkinson's pragmatic stays and undergarments. The Literary Guild's illustration of her, in booted *demi-déshabillé*, furnished my dreams and stiffened my ambitions.

Unlike the patrician elaborations of Osbert Sitwell's autobiography *Left Hand! Right Hand!*, which I tried to admire, in the Reprint Society edition, Maugham's unadorned ironies seemed by no means inimitable. Why not recapitulate juvenile sorrows with the vengeful accuracy that had made him a bestseller? He too had been translated as a small boy from one culture to another in which he both was and was not at home. Born in France, never quite at ease in England, he made a virtue of duplicity. Since Maugham was, as he later said himself, 'three-quarters queer', his doubleness was greater than it occurred to me to guess in the 1940s. Many years later, Jocelyn Rickards, the stage-designer wife of the film director Clive Donner and sometime mistress of, among others, Graham Greene and Freddie Ayer, told me that, in Australia at the same period, 'everyone' knew that Maugham was queer. Wagga Wagga, NSW, was evidently closer to informed circles than Putney, SW15.

Maugham's notebooks and prefaces acknowledged a debt to French models, especially to the short stories of Guy de Maupassant. I added the Penguin *Boule de Suif* to the three white shelves of my bedroom library. With the Anglocentricity primed by Churchill's 'finest hour', it did not occur to me that it would be better to read French, or any other writers – unless Latin or Greek – in their original language. Except for a fortnight in the early summer of 1939, when we went for a holiday in Knokke-le-Zoute (its attraction for my parents was its casino), I had never been to the Continent. During the war, Europe was defined as a place teeming with 'starving millions', any one of whom would have been grateful for my prep school menu of parsley potatoes and boiled cod, roly-poly pudding, watered treacle and the thick outside leaves of lettuce. The lure of 'the Continent' grew bright as I read Maugham's account of Philip Carey's anguished life as a young painter. To be poor and bohemian in Paris seemed very heaven.

Soon after reading *Of Human Bondage*, I won the third prize in the Charterhouse school painting competition. My true prize was the pursed displeasure on my housemaster's face. Harry 'HAM' March had excluded my landscape from the Lockites' official entry. I had been hung in the equivalent of the *Salle des Refusés*. At least as far back as the sixth century BC, when the Parian poet Archilochus shafted the family of the beautiful Neobule, who had dumped him, art and revenge have overlapped. The bearded judge, Claude Rogers of the Camden Town School, detected vestiges of 'significant form' in my suburban oil-on-canvas-paper. Dreams of Paris and its liberties came a shade closer.

In my teens, eager to get out of 12 Balliol House, I went regularly on the 14 bus to the second-hand shelves in the Charing Cross Road. From the diagonal rack beside the entrance to Joseph's cavernous bookshop, I picked up the works of Byron and Tennyson, in green boards, for sixpence each, and the Nonesuch edition of Hazlitt's essays for a shilling. I also acquired a prize copy of the often lauded Jeremy Taylor's 1651 *Holy Living*, with the front board detached, for thruppence. I bought it to see why Somerset Maugham had scoffed at it.

Having paid dawdling dues to English literature, I went up the street to Foyle's. There I passed not too quickly from history and fiction to the medical section, where it was possible to scan a few pages of Dr Van der Velde's *Perfect Marriage* before one's presence stuck out. The text informed me that, in the right position ('see fig. opposite'), the female genitals could be raised or lowered for more penetrating pleasure. A couple's clinching rapture was to arrive at simultaneous orgasm. It appeared to take a bit of doing, but practice made for perfection, after which what Jeremy Taylor called 'mutual endearment' would contrive a permanent bond.

The anatomical diagrams in *Perfect Marriage* were as salacious as the London Underground map, but they served to make me glad to be wearing my blue mackintosh as I walked past shady, half-curtained premises that sold Damarrhoids and trusses, to Leicester Square Tube station. During the long ride to Putney Bridge station, detumescence was assisted by *Idylls of the King*, though they too carried an erotic charge. What did not?

I quit Charterhouse without regret or gratitude. I had gone there, in the autumn of 1945, as a last resort. Earlier that year, midway between VE Day and the Japanese surrender, I sat the Winchester scholarship exam with a prep school friend, Richard Bird. A couple of months younger than me, Richard had spent most of the war years in America. After all the papers had been evaluated, I was fourth in the number of gross marks, Richard eleventh. Our prep school headmaster, 'Skete' Workman, promised that, even after the examiners had allowed 'weight for age', I was odds on to receive one of the twelve scholarships on offer. I set about learning Wykehamist slang. There was, I discovered, one way into the school grounds known as 'Non Licet Gate', because it was not lawful for boys to pass through it. I could hardly wait not to use it.

After the examiners' final conclave, I was seen to have descended from fourth to thirteenth in the published roll. Relegated to *proxime accessit* (a free translation, in the modern style, would be 'close but no cigar'), there was to be no place for me at Winchester. Richard had risen to sixth. He was in; I was out. My abiding suspicion is that the headmaster, Spencer Stottesbury Leeson, a canon of the Church of England and later Bishop of Peterborough, put his heavy, although not yet episcopal, hand on the scales, thus adding disqualifying weight to my age. During my interview with him and his formidable colleagues, Leeson had asked how I felt about going to chapel. I gave an honest trimmer's response: going to chapel had never bothered me at Copthorne School and would not bother me at Winchester. The sideways twitch of his mouth might have become a smile but it snagged into a wince.

Old Wykehamists have denied that my elimination could have had anything to do with anti-Semitism. Nothing excites charges of paranoia more quickly than the evidence of an accurate memory. Who will now believe that in the summer of 1945, after the recent discovery of the German concentration camps, a great English school was inflected by a policy which echoed, however discreetly, that of the defeated Nazis? In fact, in 1945, Winchester's rival, Eton College, announced its intention to operate a *numerus clausus*. My father's old school, St Paul's, with its long tradition of admitting any number of Jews, followed suit. *Non licet sed perpaucis Judaeis* (none but a very few Jews allowed) was the new slogan on their gates. Protests led by the Old Etonian A. J. Ayer, a leading Oxford philosopher (and ex-Guards officer), and by Isaiah Berlin, an Old Pauline of equal academic and social distinction, impelled both schools publicly to rescind the proposed measures. It would be nice to suppose that they ceased to operate them. Life in old England was dominated by those who composed not only its small print but also, if pressed, its invisible writing.

By the time Skete Workman learned of my rejection by Winchester, Charterhouse was the only major school whose scholarship examinations had not yet taken place. Despite blurring tears, I did my educated stuff and was given a £100-a-year scholarship. Two years later, it was increased by another £40 when I gained a 'senior scholarship' at the same time as taking the despised 'School Cert'. Arrogance and submission were the clever boy's systole and diastole. Part of the English education was to learn, by indirection, of the link between brains and money; a first-class degree gave a man access to enviable emoluments, but one must never talk about them and certainly not wave one's hands around while doing so. By the age of eighteen, I had been laced into the ways and manners of the middle of the English middle class towards the end of the last season of its high opinion of itself. The British and their king-emperor had been sent victorious by a manifestly Anglophile Almighty. Even if He seemed to specialise in close-run things, few doubted that He was still in His heaven.

Austerity and rationing were the outward and visible signs of patriotic taxes that had to be paid for post-war Britain to stay on top. Life under Clement Attlee's trustworthy, pipe-smoking, thin-voiced chairmanship was a grey vale of warnings and prohibitions. From her desk in the Home Office, the stern daughter of the voice of God warned us to 'Keep Death Off the Roads' and proclaimed 'Clean Living the Only Real Safeguard' against the unspeakable ills conveyed by the fell initials V. D. There were few activities about which we should not feel guilty. Good citizens were warned that 'Coughs and Sneezes Spread Diseases'; we should 'Trap Them in Our Handkercheases'. The traveller might still find himself sitting under a sign asking 'Is Your Journey Really Necessary?' Civilians of the 1940s were consigned to patriotic immobility.

According to John Raymond, a *New Statesman* pundit, post-war England was 'on the anvil'. The drama of the Berlin air-lift had proved that our
1948 and George Orwell's 1984 were distinguished only by a quirk of the
pen. Russia had replaced Germany as the heavy hammer that threatened to
come down on everything that the civilised world held dear. The war was
over, but hostilities might begin again at any time. Why else did Carthusians blanco belts and burnish brasses before parading in the Junior Training
Corps? In the second lustrum of the 1940s, I spent every Tuesday afternoon
'doing Corps'. I was neither keen nor slack; I conformed. I was conscious,
at the same time, that conformity entailed an element of irreconcilable difference. Was that why I bit my nails?

In my third year at Charterhouse, the JTC's commanding officer, Major
Morris, alias 'Magger Mo', announced a 'promotions exam'. With the com-
petitive docility that a good education fostered, I dealt with the questions set
before me as well as I could: I rehearsed the infantryman's mantra, 'Down,
Crawl, Observe, Sights, Fire!'; I defined an 'O-group' and its duties; my
sketch map was complete with 'church with steeple' and 'bushy-topped
tree', and I inserted an unambiguous arrow to indicate the proper line of
march; I was even practical enough to dismantle and reassemble a Bren
gun (real soldiers were said to do it blindfold) before jumping up and
standing to attention. If a condition for promotion had been that I should
itemise the details of the Sullan constitution, I should have done it with
equal zeal. There were no hurdles like English hurdles. What counted
was to clear them cleanly, never mind whether they led to anywhere one
really wanted to go.

As a result of gaining good marks, I leapfrogged from private to 'acting-
corporal'. The Napoleon of Godalming Hill was launched on his unlikely
ascent. Shortly afterwards, command of the Lockite house platoon was
wished on me by the incoming head monitor, Jeremy Atkinson, the other
senior scholar in the house (if only a natural scientist). Jeremy, whose

naval officer father had been killed in action off Singapore in 1941, had more urgent administrative things to do than to 'play soldiers'. He later became head of the school and was awarded the Holford Scholarship to Christ Church the year before I was disqualified from presenting myself as a candidate.

Leadership, I discovered, was akin to acting: imposture was easier, and more enjoyable, to sustain than sincerity. With calculated riskiness, I invited an unenthusiastic platoon to relish the comedy of excelling at something that neither they nor I wanted to do. My Tuesday afternoon squaddies responded with eager complicity: pretending to be keen turned conformity into performance. In my last Quarter, seconded by Sergeant James Cellan-Jones, I marched 'Lockites' into a tie with 'Robinites' for first place in the school drill competition. Which of the adjudicating officers could guess that our snappy uniformity carried a stamp of irony?

Promoted to under officer, I joined the only other Carthusian of the same rank, David Vansittart, a curly-haired, blond, blue-eyed Robinite. We two alone were entitled to wear officer's uniform, carry a leather-encased swagger stick and sport a Sam Browne belt. We also had the exalted right to parade in brown rather than black boots, a privilege I lacked the means to exercise. I could, however, look forward with some confidence to selection as an officer when the time came to do National Service. My khaki future was postponed by a government ordinance that allowed scholars first to go to university. It must have been intended to increase the military intake of young men with serviceable degrees in subjects such as engineering, medicine and current foreign languages.

Although competence in Latin and Greek was likely to be of small utility on the battlefield, one band of classicists was known to have played a notably gallant part in the war. A visiting lecturer had told us how knowledge of ancient Greek had qualified Stanley 'Billy' Moss, Patrick 'Paddy' Leigh Fermor, C. M. 'Monty' Woodhouse and Xan Fielding to lead guerrilla operations in Crete and on the Greek mainland. Seen from a distance, the adventures of those latter-day philhellenes furnished one of the few romantic episodes of the Second World War.

While at Charterhouse, Stanley Moss had been the fag-master of my friend Peter Green, probably the greatest, certainly the most versatile, of modern classical scholars. In 1950, Moss published the bestseller *Ill Met by Moonlight*. A film version, in which Leigh Fermor was played by Dirk Bogarde, embellished its real-life hero's Byronic renown. Moss himself, a Jew who was Leigh Fermor's 2 i/c in the great adventure of kidnapping the German general Heinrich Kreipe, derived little kudos or satisfaction from his success. 'Paddy', on the other hand, acquired iconic standing in Greece, and an elevated literary reputation in England, for the rest of his long life. He had been at the same school, King's Canterbury, as Somerset Maugham. Common Old Boyishness may explain how come, as a guest at the Villa Mauresque, Leigh Fermor offended his host by daring to tell a funny story about someone with a very b–bad s–stammer.

Moss was never at ease in the post-war world. In Peter Green's words:

> Bill was a charmer *de luxe*: very handsome, enormous natural grace. But he was also the absolutely classic example of the romantic Mediterranean expat with a Peter Pan psyche ... he simply couldn't, wouldn't grow old, or indeed up. Billy was the one who actually married his Polish countess, but drank himself to death at about the same age as Dylan Thomas.

Perhaps Moss, the rolling stone, could never forget the hundreds of Cretan hostages who were shot in reprisal for his and Paddy's audacious, award-winning exploit.

For non-combatants, the transcendent quality of *literae humaniores* was illustrated in the story of how, as his kidnappers led him through the Cretan mountains, General Kreipe glanced at snow-capped Mount Ida and then, perhaps in order to pull educated rank on his captors, recited the opening lines of Horace's Ode 9, Book One:

Vides ut alta stet nive candidum

Soracte, nec iam sustineant onus…

When Kreipe hesitated over the next phrase, Leigh Fermor took the cue and continued, without pause, to the end of the poem. The general looked at him and said, '*Ach so, Herr Major!*' Who would not wish to have been as superbly prompt as 'Paddy' at that moment? I wonder with what eyes Billy Moss, whatever kind of a Jew he was, observed this time-out-of-war exchange between his commanding officer and a *Wehrmacht* general.

I had been as diligent and house-spirited a Lockite as dread and ambition could contrive. When in office as a house monitor, I called my colleagues by their first names, but after what had happened a year or so earlier, I trusted none of them, even those innocent of overt malice. The version of myself seen or heard in public was carefully edited. I learned from Jeremy Atkinson how to tighten the lips in order to instil dread in the lower deck, as it were; but I was careful not to reveal to him, or to anyone else, anything that might be used against me. I kept a straight enough face to seem to be one of them, and a straight enough bat to get my house colours; but I walked alone, myself and my double.

Cicero's favourite *clausula* carried the concluding phrase '*esse videatur*', which we construed as 'that he may seem to be', whether one thing or another. While appearing to be a proper Carthusian, I was primed by Mr Maugham to take unforgiving note of my fellows' forms of speech and personal habits. I did so in a wide spiral notebook, ruled feint, that I had bought in New York City. *A Writer's Notebook* had shown me how neatly and surreptitiously a man might can his beans before opportunity came to spill them.

I I

DURING HOLIDAYS FROM Charterhouse, I had contrived to kiss a few girls, on unparted lips. English girls furnished a passive and interminable assault course: one got as far as one could, in a given time, before being stalled. Mona had the biggest, most enticing breasts. I never surmounted them. Two New York girls I dated during ten days in their city in the summer of 1949 were more accessible. Necking in the American style had its limits, but they were elastic. I sailed for England, on the *Queen Mary*, convinced that I was passionately in love with freckled Mary Jane, whom I had kissed deep into the early hours.

After I had returned to my Carthusian monastery, Mary Jane wrote me scented letters, in pale blue ink, on petalled paper, promising full-length proximities when we met again. In the interim, I convinced myself that my true love was the pretty Hilary Phillips, whom I had met, when we were sixteen, at the Liberal Jewish synagogue in St John's Wood. In a surge of ancestral allegiance, my father had sent me to be prepared for 'Confirmation', an anglicised form of Bar Mitzvah, appropriate for assimilated Jews. No Hebrew was required, apart from the ritual *Shema Yisroel*. More ardent in pursuit of Hilary than of hereditary solidarity, I had learned only with disappointment, in 1948, of the foundation of the state of Israel. Hilary's family celebration of the end of 2,000 years of Jewish homelessness obliged her to cancel a date on which I was hoping to proceed a button or two lower down the front of her nicely frilled, and filled, blouse.

My parents had chosen to live in SW15 not least because they did not care to be identified with 'north London'. Golders Green, with its Jewish connotations, stood for everything from which they wished to be discrete. My father neither denied his Jewishness nor was he at pains to declare it. He flinched when called 'Rayfle', a pronunciation that he took to insinuate that he was an alien. He insisted on our Raphael being said in the same way as the name of the Renaissance painter and the anglicised archangel. Out in Putney, we did not celebrate the foundation of the state of Israel. Zionism made no call on my father, although he would be pleased when, in 1952, his friend Sir Frank Evans was named British ambassador to Israel. My parents had met Frank and Mary in the 1930s, when Evans was British consul-general in New York. Mary was what my mother called a 'character'. At a post-war reception at the UN, she was being presented to the guest of honour when her pants fell down. She stepped out of them, handed them, between thumb and forefinger, to her husband – 'Here, Frank!' – and proceeded with the polite formalities.

My brunette mother was beautiful enough not to be taken for what she did not deny that she was but would as soon not be called. Irene (the final 'e' silent, as in *Goodnight, Irene*) never lost her American accent, but she showed little nostalgia for New York, still less for Kansas City, where her mother continued to live until the mid-1960s. In an access of daughterly loyalty, Irene then persuaded Fanny to cross the Atlantic and spend her remaining years, of which there turned out to be more than a few, at 12 Balliol House.

In 1930s New York, my mother's bankrupt father, Max, had separated from his wife and come to live in our spare room at 30 W 70th St. Cedric never complained then, nor did he when his deaf mother-in-law moved into the back bedroom that I had vacated in 12 Balliol House. She often took offence at what she thought she had overheard. My father nicknamed her 'Canasta-puss' on account of her addiction to the game, which she had played regularly with 'the girls' back in K. C. In exile, the skeletal Fanny smoked incessantly; but even in her nineties she would jump up when I came to the flat. 'Want a cup of coffee?' She made quantities of wide, flat, nutty and delicious cookies, in accordance with an allegedly Lithuanian recipe that existed only in her head.

Cedric hated cigarette smoke. Yet he treated Fanny with implacable politeness. Was his self-restraint a form of penance? As we were sailing back to England from New York, when I was already eighteen years old, my mother disclosed that, in his dancing twenties, Cedric had fathered a daughter on a certain Molly Hall, who had been a member of the Baltic Exchange, a rare distinction for a woman in those days. Molly had promised her lounge-lizard lover that she could not have children. A few months later, she informed him that she was pregnant. Cedric's father Ellis paid for her to go away, less because of the shame of the imminent bastard than because its mother was not Jewish. At some stage during the war, Molly opened a hairdressing salon in Surbiton called *Chez Raphael*. After 1945, she emigrated to British Columbia with her daughter, Sheila, and took the name Raphael-Hall. I have no clear idea why Irene waited so long to break the seal on that previously well-kept secret.

In 1929, Cedric went, on an immigrant's visa, to sell Shell gas in northern Illinois. He did so with career-enhancing success, although his Oxford accent was not an immediate plus among the area's filling station managers, many of them Irish. Before catching the boat-train to Liverpool, Cedric had promised his parents, with implacable gratitude, that he would marry the first Jewish girl he met who had a good figure, a pretty face and no moustache. The nineteen-year-old Irene Rose Mauser, who was working as secretary to an architect in Chicago, qualified on all counts.

Though he never thought well of her dancing, Cedric was always proud of Irene's smartness, in both transatlantic senses, and of her long-lasting good looks. They met, on a blind date, on a very cold Chicago Christmas Eve, at the Edgewater Beach Hotel. My mother promised that it was love at first sight. She did, however, discover – not long after they were married, in 1930 – that Cedric was still writing love letters to his old dancing partner, Phyllis Haylor. 'Phyll' had since turned professional and again won the World Dancing Championship, with a new partner. In old age, when Cedric was broken by ill health, she visited him several times in the Royal Hospital and Home for Incurables. Phyll's lover, the bisexual film critic and memoirist Nerina Marshall, was then living in Manor Fields. She became more friendly with my mother than my mother did with her.

When I was sixteen, my father sent me to the parquet-floored basement of a Knightsbridge Hotel, near Raphael Street, where Miss Haylor and Josephine Bradley and Charles Scrimshaw (a red carnation always in the button-hole of his black tailcoat) taught the waltz, the tango, the quickstep and the foxtrot, quite as if the 1920s had never come to an end. I soon despaired of winning pretty girls by the nimbleness of my chassis-reverse.

My father's old friend Victor Silvester (whom Cedric called 'Ginger') and his 'ballroom orchestra' became middle-class household names in the 1940s and 1950s. His strict-tempo slogan – 'slow, slow, quick, quick, slow' – applied as much to the nation as to its ballroom dancers: England might be dancing to the music of time, but it was in no great hurry. My father had been invited to become Ginger's manager when he first assembled his musicians, but he declined; perhaps because it was too risky, probably because the music business was no place for a gentleman. Despite his 'investments', a term he applied both to buying shares and to backing horses, Cedric never again had the opportunity to make any unusual money. He had to rely on his salary from Shell. Irene had an eye for bargains and managed always to be dressed fashionably. Since she never threw anything away, she was able, over the years, to retrieve and refurbish what had gone out of style as soon as its turn came round again. When she died, in 2010, at the age of 100, her wardrobe for all seasons included pairs of double-A I. Miller shoes that she had bought at Saks Fifth Avenue more than seventy years before, all in well-heeled condition.

Despite his steady devotion to Irene (or, when patiently displeased, 'Reen'), Cedric told me, late in his life, that he did not think that it mattered very much whom one married. Was his indifference the result of being a Stoic, a world champion, a Jew or an English gentleman? He never alluded to his triumphs on the dance floor, but his posture to the world came, I suspect, of what it pleased him to keep to himself: once a champion always a champion, but one must never advertise the fact. Modesty was his only conceit.

Cedric could read Hebrew, but understood little. He made no attempt to teach me or to have me taught. He referred to Gentiles only as 'the Christians'. Disdain and deference were on equal terms. In his hagiography of Virginia Woolf, Quentin Bell suggested that, when young, Leonard Woolf, an Old Paulined, spoke of Gentiles as 'goyim'. I doubt whether any well-educated English Jewish family of the time used that term. In his film *The Hours*, Stephen Daldry portrayed an exasperated Leonard Woolf shouting at Virginia, in broad daylight, on the platform of Richmond station. It is inconceivable that, in the period concerned, he would have raised his voice to his wife, in public, at any hour. The scene would have played better in a whisper anyway.

My father would have considered it outlandish to cleave to a kosher diet, but he did arrive home, now and again, with slices of bread-crumbed cold fried fish that could have come only from an East End delicatessen. He laughed, somewhat, at Jewish jokes, but he seldom told one and he never put on a supposedly Jewish accent. In New York, he had admired Jack Benny but deplored Eddie Cantor. In post-war London, he loved Bud Flanagan, suffered Vic Oliver, ignored Max Miller and liked Sid Field, whom we went to see in *Piccadilly Hayride* and in *Harvey*, in which he played a hallucinating drunk, unfortunately to the life.

The first Jewish story I ever heard, in New York, when I was five or six years old, was told by Seymour Wallace, one of the racier of my parents' crowd. It concerned the inevitable Itzig, who, time and again, when his best friend had tickets for the Giants, told him, 'Shelley, I'd love to come but I can't; Levinsky's playing.' Finally, Sheldon asks Itzig does he really have to love music that much. 'Music, shmusic!' Itzig says. Sheldon says, 'So how come it matters so much when Levinksy's playing?' 'Vot he plays,' Itzig says, 'who cares? *Vere* he plays, who cares? But *ven* he plays...! I sleep vit his vife.' Another overheard joke, of a similar low order, asked how you play strip poker in a nudist colony. The answer was 'Mit de tweezers'. That was as near the gutter as I came. A later slightly naughty number must also, I think, predate our passage of the Atlantic: 'The bee is such a busy soul / He has no time for birth control / And that is why today one sees / So very many sons-of-bees.' The last line sounds uniquely American; in the 1940s, 'son-of-a-bitch' had no current British usage.

Happy to pass for a New Yorker in the 1930s, complete with seersucker suit and panama hat in the summer, Cedric looked no less at home as a conventional 1940s Londoner. In chalk-striped Adamson's suit, white shirt with cuff-links and detachable collar, bowler hat, leather gloves and silk-sleeved umbrella, he waited each weekday morning at Putney Southern Railway station for the 9.08 to Waterloo. He was pleased to seem not to differ from other City-bound suburban gentlemen; that was the difference between them. They included our Somerville House neighbour Jack Piesse, who might nod at Cedric, but – from Monday to Friday – never said good morning. Yet Jack and his wife Margaret played after-dinner bridge with my parents every Saturday night, at alternating venues.

The handsome Jack was a solicitor for Esso Petroleum. He had had a brave war, from Alamein to Berlin, as a tank commander in the King's Own Scottish Borderers. In the week before Germany surrendered, a *Wehrmacht* soldier swung an unloaded rifle at his head in a dark cellar as Major Piesse was bent double, feeling with his dirk for trip-wires across the concrete steps. The German's rifle butt crashed against the wall, just past where

Jack's head should have been. Jack riposted with an upward thrust of his dirk. It was the only time on the long way from Sicily to Berlin when he knew for certain that he had killed someone.

Jack, an Old Tonbridgian, drove a Mark 5 Jaguar and played golf at Royal Wimbledon, where the entry form for new members demanded 'Name of father, if changed'. My Old Pauline father went by Underground to play at the adjacent Wimbledon Park golf club, which was not so inquisitive. It even admitted Variety actors such as Jeremy Hawk, Sid Field's straight man in his famous golfing sketch ('Address the ball', 'Dear Ball', etc.). Hawk wore light-blue golfing attire and a light-blue cap, in which he dazzled female members. My father played regularly with a Jewish businessman called Alec Nathan who was a director of the pharmaceutical company Glaxo. He urged Cedric to buy its shares while they were cheap, but he failed to do so.

On summer days, when the sun shone, Jack Piesse would take his deck-chair onto the lawn below the Manor Fields rose beds and render himself a darker shade of brown, an alien form of narcissism in those blanched, insular days. Stephen Potter's 1952 manual of *One-Upmanship* peddled a put-down to apply to smug, bronzed persons: 'Mediterranean type!' If anyone approached him with neighbourly overtures, Jack closed his eyes. On winter evenings, he sometimes invited me to Somerville House to play the board game *L'Attaque*. He had an antique set from his childhood. The pieces wore uniforms from the Napoleonic wars, except for the spy, who had a cloak, a slouch hat and a two-faced Continental moustache.

Once aboard the 9.08, Jack and other commuters would open *The Times*, with its eight columns of personal advertisements encrypted in small print across the front page, or the *Daily Telegraph*, as a prophylactic screen against encroaching conversationalists. After their arrival at Waterloo, 'the Drainpipe' shuttled the City men, like reticent sardines, to the Bank. A Stock Exchange joke of the period told of a woman crossing Threadneedle Street and being all but sandwiched between two buses coming in opposite directions. All of her clothes were ripped off in the process and she passed out cold. As she lay naked in the street, a chivalrous broker stepped out and covered her private parts with his bowler hat. When the ambulance arrived, its crew looked carefully for signs of injury; then one said to the other, 'Better get the man out first.' In his diaries, Evelyn Waugh alludes to a certain Enid Raphael who, so he reported, once said, 'I don't know why they're called "private parts", mine aren't private.' I could wish, but cannot believe, that she was some kind of a relation of mine.

My father walked down Threadneedle Street to 5 St Mary Axe, where a wooden lift worked by a rope pulley in the hands of the punctual, waist-coated Len carried him up to his office. The letters, of three single-spaced paragraphs, that he posted to me when I was at school, first in Devon, then at Godalming, were dictated to his secretary and typed on paper as blanched and flimsy as £5 notes (so rare they often had to be signed before a shop would accept them). Cedric's hieroglyphic signature was the only personal mark on the page. My mother wrote fluently in pen on blue headed station-ery. She signed herself 'Mummy', during my childhood, or 'Ma', once I was married. Only in the 1980s, after overhearing my American-Armenian agent, Ron Mardigian, call his mother 'Alice', did I adopt the habit of calling my mother 'Irene'. I never called my father by his first name.

Shell Oil had been founded by Marcus Samuel, the first Lord Bearsted. A posse of Jews figured in its original executive complement. My father joined the company just too late to be of their number. The company secretary was Alfred Engel, with whom Cedric had been at Oxford. Engel's son George was an outstanding classicist at Charterhouse a generation before me. The sixth-form master, A. L. 'The Uncle' Irvine, a Mr Chips who said goodbye just before I could profit from his exacting tuition, dispensed young Engel, once he had won his Oxford scholarship, from the diurnal drudgery of composing Latin and Greek proses and verses. Instead, he encouraged his prodigy to become an expert on Corinthian black-figure vases. Since I would have nine months between leaving school and going up to Cambridge, my father, while shaving one morning, in sleeveless aertex vest, commodious underpants and silk socks stretched to transparency by American-style suspenders, advised me to emulate young George. Arcane expertise could cut a key to distinction. As he spoke sound sense, I noticed that my father had a thickened and opaque left big toenail. Some twenty-five years after the reminder that winning scholarships was not identical with being a scholar, I was asked to review George Cawkwell's *Philip of Macedon*, an academic work of more diligence than wit. In it, George Engel was gratefully acknowledged as editor. There were some negligible flaws, which I did not neglect, and one passage of entirely scrambled print. Printers can do things, after proofs have been corrected, that even a punctilious editor has no chance to put right. Would I have cited Engel in my review had an antique splinter of envy not been lodged in my psyche? My less-than-pretty conduct is worth mentioning only because there must be thousands of such uncharted pettinesses in every life. Biography is not a science, but a branch of taxidermy. The autobiographer alone has the privilege of stuffing himself. I now have an opaque left big toenail.

During my years at Charterhouse, contact with the opposite sex was limited to epistolary exchanges with Hilary Phillips; mine more passionate (and purposeful) than hers. Her sister, Diana – who had an unfortunate eye – had gone to Oxford. Her parents were keen that Hilary should follow her. My licence to be alone, for an hour or more, with their daughter on the sitting room sofa in Portman Mansions, off the Marylebone Road, required me to improve Hilary's ability to construe Livy's provincial Latin prose. Her admission to Oxford depended on achieving that now obsolete competence. My path to a rewarding session of deep kisses passed through the Caudine Forks, in which, on Livy's account, a Roman legion was trapped by their Samnite enemies and obliged to ignominious surrender; which Hilary never was. As Latinist and as lover, my darling was of the Fabian persuasion. Had I been able to shape her into Oxford material, my ardour might have been capped by her grateful subjugation. That achievement was beyond me and so, therefore, was her Non Licet Gate.

Hilary did concede that French kisses were 'oddly satisfying', but when I promised that there were things that were more satisfying still, she cited the creed that marriageable men did not want a slice from a cut cake. She greeted my Cambridge scholarship with dismayed congratulations. Quick to calculate that she would be at least twenty-one by the time I graduated, Hilary then added on the two years in which I could expect to be doing National Service. She would be twenty-three, and adjacent to senility, before she could hope to have that ring on her finger. With whatever regret, I had to be deleted from the roll of suitable suitors. I had a suspicion that there was already a candidate for Hilary's favours, an off-stage Charles, of whom she spoke with teasing warmth.

My parents' friends often asked me what I 'wanted to do'. Cedric was keen that I qualify as a solicitor or an accountant, or both. Such people were rarely out of work. My uncle Lionel had been a barrister whose *mots* embellished the family anthology. Can he truly have been the first person to say in court, 'I deny the allegation and defy the alligator'? On solitary walks through rainy London, I often sought shelter by climbing the many stone steps to the public gallery in the law courts. I listened with emulous appetite to the silky Mr Fox-Andrews making his pitch for damages after improperly loaded barrels had rolled off a brewer's dray and done his client a thumping mischief. He displayed a neat wooden model on which he pointed out to his lordship how the barrels should have been ranged, and wedged, and how, in practice, they had been.

I could not understand why Mr Fox-Andrews spoke so slowly until I matched the spacing of his phrases with the movement of the judge's fist across a stiff page of his red, leather-bound ledger. I presumed that I, like Cicero in most of his cases, should appear for the defence. Although it was an article of faith in the system of British justice that a jury's verdict on the facts be deemed infallible (otherwise how should the death penalty remain unquestionable?), it appeared to have required advocates of rare resource to save any number of defendants from being wrongly convicted.

Since a first-class degree in Latin and Greek promised access to enviable eminences, I resolved to do my bit of Tacitus or Thucydides, Homer or Virgil, every day until October of the New Year, 1950, when I was due to go up to Cambridge. Meanwhile, how could I earn enough money to take some new girl to dinner in Soho and to a movie, preferably Italian or French, but not with Fernandel in it, at the Academy Cinema, or to the theatre (Jean Anouilh rather than Terence Rattigan)? As a result of his being put in charge of press relations for Shell, my father seemed well placed to help me find newspaper work. He treated influential City journalists, such as the *Daily Express*'s Fred Ellis and *The Economist*'s Rowland Bird, to informative lunches at the Berkeley Hotel in Piccadilly. Apprentices – such as the young William Rees-Mogg, later editor of *The Times* – qualified only for Le Perroquet in Leicester Square.

For all its convivial perks, Cedric's post-war office was a comedown. In 1945, he had been invited to return to New York, to take up the bigger and better-paid job that he had renounced, for patriotic reasons, at the outbreak of war. To his superiors' displeasure, he declined to go back to Rockefeller Center. He told me that his decision was due to his wish not to rupture my ascent on the British academic *cursus honorum*. I did, however, remember him saying, when I was a small boy, 'Never forget, you come third in this family.' Perhaps it was fourth: Cedric's mother Amy was a valetudinarian who contrived to move an inch nearer to death's door whenever her wishes were not honoured. She was determined that her son not escape across the water for a second time.

My father was never again offered work worthy of his qualities. When I saw him sitting at our Macy's dining room table, almost lipless with repressed fury, as he made itemised retorts, a), b) and c), to some chiding memo from a boss, Trevor Powell, who took pleasure in putting down someone cleverer than himself, I determined never to work in an office nor, if I could help it, to have a boss; better an unranked artist, preferably in Paris, than the second, or third, or umpteenth, businessman in London.

With Cedric on hand, the widowed Amelia Sophia excelled in coercive helplessness. For another dozen years my grandmother, attended by the sisters Winifred and Ada Stanley (pious subscribers to *The Watchtower*), played the supine tyrant in her eau de Cologne-scented flat, 12a Dorset House, overlooking Dorset Square. Whether her intermittent crises were due to heart attacks, as Winifred claimed, or to a surfeit of Maison Lyons violet chocolates, as Dr Cove-Smith hinted, Amy wanted Cedric (named after Little Lord Fauntleroy) to be on hand, whatever his American wife might wish. Ex-England and British Lions rugger captain Ronald Cove-Smith asked Amy, on one occasion, whether she had had a particular condition before. When she said she had, he said, 'Well, you've got it again.' Diagnosis and diplomacy went together at a guinea a visit.

Although Amy and my mother were barely, and rarely, civil to each other, Irene claimed that she was happy to have stayed in England. On the last occasion when she saw her 22-year-old kid cousin, Lieutenant Irvin Weintraub USAAF, before he and his glider crew and their GI passengers were massacred by the SS, after skilfully crash-landing at Arnhem, he said to her: 'For a Kansas City girl, you sure have come a long way.' Irene's uncle, Max's brother Fritz, died fighting for the Kaiser in the Great War.

My father blamed Winifred, who referred to him always as 'Mr Cedric', for the rift between Amy and his wife. In practice, it suited both women not to see or even to have to inquire about each other. Irene Rose Mauser had been a clever girl. Denied a college education by the bankruptcy of her father, Max, she went alone, in 1929, to work in Chicago when she was eighteen years old. Out of office hours, she kept company with the Second City's West Side bohemians. One of them – Herman, was it, or Mitchell?

– papered his living room, walls and ceiling, with silver paper. She had many followers but, I am pretty sure, no lovers. Buddy Cadison brought home an illicit, plain-wrapped copy of James Joyce's *Ulysses* from Paris and allowed her to walk down State Street with it under her arm. During the war, he came, in uniform, with gifts from the PX, to see her at 12 Balliol House.

Irene was quick-witted, sharp-eyed and methodical enough to run a business. My father, who was almost eleven years older, preferred that she remain in the tidy flat. 12 Balliol House never needed as much daily help as Irene was given. Mrs Garrod's thrice-weekly hoovering seemed to me, shut in my little bedroom at the end of the corridor, to moan for hours. Even in her thirties, my mother took an afternoon rest on her chaise longue, under a hand-knitted blue cover.

Now and again she went on the 14, 30 or 74 bus, with Adie Tutin, to Knightsbridge and a tour of Harrods. For a change, they would take the Underground to Kensington High Street and scan the merchandise at Derry & Toms or Barkers ('Going up,' the button-capped liftboys said, 'going up!'), rarely Ponting's, which had the low ceilings symptomatic of bargain basements. A congeries of overhead wires flew hermetic canisters of cash, with a pneumatic gasp, to a remote, inaccessible central till.

My mother had charge accounts, never a chequebook. Cedric gave her an allowance, but no access to his bank account. So far as I knew, in London she never set out to meet a man who was not her husband. In New York, she had had an admirer, a photographer called Vollmer, who took her picture with me in a sailor suit looking at a big book. Cedric had told her that he would divorce her if he ever caught her with another man. In hapless old age, sequestered in an olive-green hospital room, he told visitors that she had left him for a younger man.

During my teens, Irene's most congenial daytime companion in Balliol House was a slim, grey-haired young woman from Baton Rouge, Louisiana. Caroline Stewart lived directly below us and was literally on tap to come on up.

She and Irene drank noon Scotch, with plenty of water, and plenty of Scotch. Caroline's Southern voice was charmingly cracked. Her husband Max worked for Esso petroleum. On Sunday mornings, he and I played tennis on the garage roof against Jack and Margaret Piesse, who lived in the ground-floor flat below Mr Love. One box of Dunlop balls would last us at least a month. In the summer, my mother bought them, at three and six for six after they had been used, for nine games, at the Wimbledon tournament. When they got dirty, Jack Piesse shampooed them and ranged them on the radiator to grow fluffy again.

Margaret, a pretty young Yorkshire woman (he called her 'Tyko'), had been Jack's secretary when he returned from the war. After discovering himself to be Weybridge's most decorated cuckold, he retrieved his self-esteem by becoming the husband of a good-looking younger woman. Margaret had an excellent forehand and a bouncy figure. Her fiancé, an RAF fighter pilot called Budge, had been killed soon after he went on active service in 1941. She and Jack had compatible reasons to settle for second best.

Once I had left Charterhouse, I was eager for exercise and suggested that Margaret and I play singles on a weekday afternoon. We did so only once. Jack embargoed any further encounters. In my innocence, I could not imagine why. On New Year's Eve 1949, coming back to Balliol House from a dinner dance in the Manor Fields restaurant, Caroline Stewart, out on the grass in her nylon feet, silver high-heeled sandals in one hand, grabbed me to avoid falling over and kissed me, thoroughly, on the lips. I tasted the whisky on her tongue, and the heat, but I was too proper an inhabitant of Mr Love's domain to take advantage of the opportunity; or even to see it as one, although Max was in the States on business and I had been reading *Le Rouge et le Noir*, in the red Penguin translation.

Like Stendhal's Madame de Rênal, Caroline was approaching thirty. Max, she indicated, was no eager lover, but – despite those inviting silken feet – I was never any sort of stand-in for Julien Sorel. It was unthinkable to try anything with a married woman, especially when she was known to my parents.

My long conviction was that 'the Christians' always behaved with propriety; it would require only some small infringement of their rules for a Jew to be revealed for what he really was and then to be pitched into the abyss.

One of my father's Oxford friends was the *Daily Mail* journalist Guy Ramsey. He was married, *en deuxièmes noces*, as he was liable to put it, to the novelist Celia Dale. Her father James Dale was for many years Dr Dale in the morning radio serial *Mrs Dale's Diary*. An Old Harrovian, Guy had stayed only one year at Oxford. He then repaired to Princeton, where he claimed to have taken physical exercise for the last time. Playing soccer for a college team, soon after his midday meal, he ran in at over-full speed and scored a brave goal, after which he threw up. His exploit was headlined in the college magazine: 'FRESHMAN SHOOTS GOAL, THEN LUNCH'.

Guy had the manners, if neither the pedigree nor the means, of a literary grandee. When, after he had signed a cheque, a shopkeeper insisted that Guy prove his identity, the man was instructed to remember which side of the counter he was on. Guy's claim to a fourteen-point Fleet Street byline was founded on his having scooped the story of where Rudolf Hess was held, incommunicado, after his 1941 solo flight to Scotland. Hess had hoped to please his Fuhrer by conducting negotiations, through the good offices of the 14th Duke of Hamilton, with a view to a German alliance with Great Britain against the USSR.

Such an arrangement might have appealed to more members of the upper class than patriotic histories care to recall. Bolsheviks and Jews (with small distinction between them) were anathema to members of *The Right Book Club*, to which my middle-of-the-road parents had subscribed when we first came to England. Taking 'right' to mean correct rather than Fascist, they were treated to books such as Alistair Reed's *Spanish Arena*, in which Francisco Franco featured as a Christian gentleman. Among *The Right Book Club*'s selectors was Captain Archibald Ramsay. His anti-Semitism reached great, but never rare, heights of apocalyptic mania. My parents soon cancelled their subscription.

Shortly after landing, Hitler's deputy was driven south and secreted in a rural hideaway in Norfolk. Prompt propaganda advantage was taken of what was said to be his panicky desertion of a losing cause that, at the time, displayed few symptoms of imminent defeat. No hint was published of Hess's not unprecedented proposal for an Anglo-Saxon alliance. Hitler's racism was not likely to be a deal-breaker. 'Bendor', the Duke of Westminster, was hardly alone in blaming the Jews for the outbreak of war.

Polyvalent exegetes, with an eye on top tables, have sought to exempt T. S. Eliot from anti-Semitism by making out that he showed untypical symptoms of it only as a result of some temporary aberration. In fact, his attitude chimed harmoniously with that of the High Churchmen among whom he was so eager a recruit, as well as with that of the President of Harvard, under whose aegis he had studied before the Great War. In the 1930s, the hierarchy of the Anglican Church had voted to exclude Jewish refugees from England. The Archbishop of York was alone in raising his hand, if never a loud voice, against the embargo. Anti-Semitism was a popular social attitude until, supposedly, it was not; prejudice can be less a deep psychic trait than a smart button-hole.

After some bounty-hunting official tipped the *Daily Mail* the wink, Guy – who claimed to have local knowledge – was despatched to East Anglia to hound out the exact whereabouts of the fugitive Nazi bigshot. In truth, Guy had been to Norfolk only once before: as a young reporter, he was sent to cover a pre-war trial in which a rustic was accused of having carnal knowledge of a sheep. Returning in the LNER train, an old Fleet Street hand told the young Guy that he was disappointed by the crudeness of the case: he had hoped that the defence would take a romantic line and claim that the rustic had truly *loved* the woolly beast.

Having contacted the *Daily Mail*'s informant, no doubt with prompt cash in hand, Guy was given the address of the castle in which Hess had been secreted. He fattened whatever skimpy intelligence or gossip he could glean into a dramatic lead story that trumped the rest of Fleet Street. Hess's

sortie came early enough in the war to save his neck at the 1945 Nurem-
berg trial of the leading Nazis. He was sentenced to life imprisonment, even
though he had been closer to Hitler than Joachim von Ribbentrop, who
was condemned to death for planning aggressive war. Guy observed that
Ribbentrop was more properly *contemned* to death: the one-time champagne salesman's social climbing in pre-war London society (and the now
embarrassing memory of how welcome he had been) denied him reprieve.
I sensed a whiff of Ribbentrop in the anti-hero of Thomas Mann's last, unfin-
ished novel, *The Confessions of Felix Krull, Confidence Man*. The quality of
the champagne that Krull peddles declines as the decoration of the bottles
becomes more and more elaborately gilded.

Julius Streicher, editor of the Jew-baiting *Der Stürmer*, was also put
to death in 1945. He was crude and loudmouthed, but his anti-Semitic
sentiments closely resembled those of the nicely spoken Rothermeres, Lon-
donderrys, Lord Redesdale, Lady Astor and who all else among Britain's
eminent appeasers. In his 1937 bestseller *I Know These Dictators*, G. Ward
Price, Guy's colleague on the Rothermeres' *Daily Mail*, promised his readers that Hitler and Mussolini were more necessary than evil. It is routine for
journalists to find agreeable things to say about those to whom they have
privileged access. Dorothy Thompson was one of the few who, in the early
1930s, dared to portray Hitler, accurately, as an uncomely person of defec-
tive intelligence. She then made the clever, civilised mistake of supposing
that this would impede his ascent.

Philo-Semitism did not inhibit Guy from observing that Hitler had succeeded in making the world Jew-conscious. As well as covering big stories
(he was adept at empurpling his prose for royal occasions), Guy contributed brief book reviews to the *Daily Mail*. In the six- or eight-page 1940s
newspapers, literature rarely commanded more than half a page. Reviewers
were expected to cover four or five books in a few hundred words. Although
literary journalism was poorly paid, pristine review copies could be sold,

for tax-free cash, at a bookshop adjacent to the Cheddar Cheese, just off Fleet Street, for half their cover price.

If Guy liked books, he loved bridge. 'The pasteboards' were Celia's only competitor for his attention. He played at Crockford's, where the desk porter could cash cheques of up to £30 without asking questions. Guy wrote frequent, rarely paid-for articles in bridge magazines in which advocates of Acol and the Vienna Club illustrated the merits of their bidding systems with mutually accusatory instances from hands played in recent tournaments.

English post-war bridge circles were riven by the partisans of Terence Reese and of M. Harrison-Gray. Gray's colourful *Country Life* articles were longer, and more elegantly phrased, than Reese's laconic, black and white offerings in the *Evening Standard*. The rivals clashed vociferously at meetings of the British Bridge League. So graceless were their exchanges that Guy said that he always favoured whichever of the parties had not spoken last.

Guy's fondest affectation was to appropriate S. J. 'Skid' Simon's linguistic shorthand: 'Give tube', for example, when soliciting a cigarette. Skid may have been inimitable, but Guy could no more resist imitating him than he could that 'one last rubber', although he knew that Celia would be tight-lipped when he arrived late, yet again, for the supper she had cooked and which I was sometimes invited to share. Guy named their only son Simon.

Skid's Semitic provenance – his unabridged surname was Skidelsky – had not barred him from representing Great Britain in the 1938 Bridge Olympiad. He distinguished himself in the match against Germany by his flair and sportsmanship. The aristocratic captain of the German team told 'Skid' that he wished that he could introduce him to Adolf Hitler. The Fuhrer would surely then abandon his absurd Judaeophobia.

Simon died in 1949, aged forty-four. His influence on the bridge world persists both in legend and in his books. *Design for Bidding* and *Why You Lose at Bridge* are probably the clearest, certainly the wittiest, guides to commonsensical play. The latter volume ends with a chapter in which an archetypal quartet of bridge players – the Unlucky Expert, Mr Smug, Futile Willy and Mrs Guggenheim – is depicted in instructive combat. One meets their descendants at more tables than even their creator ever played at. In collaboration with the journalist and theatre critic Caryl Brahms, who long outlived him, Skid also wrote a series of brazenly facetious novels. The skittishness of *No Bed for Bacon* prefigured the movie *Shakespeare in Love*. In the couple's best literary number, *A Bullet in the Ballet*, the victim was a leading dancer. A footnote, unmistakably Skid's, was appended to his name: 'Don't feel too sorry for him; his Petrushka was lousy.' Skid's wife died, at the age of forty, a few months after him.

The Ramseys were kind enough to appear unsurprised by my ambition to be a writer. They lived in a small, ground-floor flat in Well Road, Hampstead, and had a roster of local friends with whom they held play-readings. Among the supporting cast (Guy and Celia were the Alfred Lunt and Lynn Fontanne of NW3) was their doctor, whom I was startled to hear them call 'Johnny'. My parents never called our Putney GP anything but Dr Millis. The star figures of the Ramseys' coterie were E. Arnot Robertson, the film critic, and Marghanita Laski, whose physiognomy gave her voice a singular warp. Arnot wrote several novels (including *Ordinary Families*), but is best remembered for her verses about a name-dropper that began, 'As I said to Dickie Mountbatten…'

The scholarly and political renown of Marghanita's family heightened her hauteur as a TV panellist on *What's My Line?* She also composed segments for the *Dictionary of National Biography*. Her 1949 novel *Little Boy Lost* was one of the few that, at the time, alluded directly, if mutedly, to what was not yet called the Holocaust. She lived, with a husband who was never mentioned, in *Capo di Monte*, a grand house on the top of Windmill Hill. Celia referred to Marghanita and Arnot with complacent sorority. They were the three Fates of Hampstead artistic society.

Guy said of himself that he had a journalist's skill for putting everything he knew in the shop window. Unlike my twelve-handicap father, the mature Guy took no exercise other than cutting and dealing the cards. He did, however, retail a golfing clerihew that I have never seen quoted elsewhere:

> The Earl of Chatham, William Pitt,
> Upon the eighteenth green fell, in an apoplectic fit;
> And all around enjoyed the joke
> As Fox murmured, 'Beaten, by a stroke!'

While he rejoiced in familiarity with the bridge world's top-class company, Guy was conscious that he never quite belonged in it. His book *Aces All* is a durable tribute to the great contemporary names – Reese, Harrison-Gray, Lederer, Kenneth Konstam, Jack Marx – against whom I came to play, as my patient father's impatient partner, in duplicate competitions. Although he published only one work of fiction, a Fleet Street thriller entitled *The Spike* (on which the bitch-victim is found impaled), Guy relished the role of literary musketeer. Topcoat slung, with Gasconesque swagger, around his shoulders, he sported the lippy diction and plump pinkness of Robert Morley, the actor and author of *Edward, My Son*, who enjoyed wattled Shaftesbury Avenue fame in the 1940s and 1950s. Mistaken for Mr Morley in West End restaurants, Guy was in no hurry to disclaim preferential treatment, even if it meant tipping the staff more than he could afford in order to sustain the grand illusion.

When Guy read my first jejune short stories, he was generous enough to deplore only gently the unsurprising surprises with which I chose to twist their tails. Celia was less diplomatic, especially when it came to clichés: 'Cut, cut, cut' was all her wise and trenchant advice. Mr Maugham had led me to think that familiar phrases made the reader feel at home: his characters found things as easy as falling off a log and were known to cut a long story short. In my lust to be eligible for print, I sent for a book of hints from the *Evening Standard*. One of them was to avoid static descriptions (for instance, 'he had black hair'); better to blend them with the action ('he ran his fingers through his black hair'). I ran corrective fingers through my stories, but they continued to be rejected by the evening papers and by *Argosy*. I was callow enough to read *With the Editor's Compliments* as an expression of encouragement.

Dinners at 3 Well Road, when I had the Ramseys' undivided attention, gave me a taste of the literary life never available in SW15. Guy's aptitude for fanciful imposture led him to cast himself as Gustave Flaubert to my Guy de Maupassant. He would, he assured me, notify me when I had written my *Boule de Suif* and was ripe for publication. Guy rivalled Bartlett in the cosmopolitan repertoire of his quotations. When in north Africa for the *Daily Mail*, he had found himself, like other British journalists, denied access to General de Gaulle. He contrived to send de Gaulle a message, in his fine calligraphy, in which he refurbished Thomas Jefferson's remark to Lafayette, '*Chaque homme a deux pays, le sien et la France.*' *Et voilà*: the general's door was opened to him. None of Guy's stock of apophthegms was more liberating than Robert Walpole's (as quoted by Boswell, quoting Johnson) 'Let us talk bawdy, then all may join in.'

He rejoiced in jokes not current in Mr Love's Manor Fields. For instance, there was the one about the different responses to sex to be heard on post-coital female lips: the French woman said, 'Jean-Paul is better'; the Italian woman said, 'What will you tell your wife?'; the German woman said, 'Can vee eat now?'; the Spanish woman said, 'Do it again or I keel you'; and the English woman said, 'Feeling better, George?' Another risqué number required Guy to write it out, in his elegant script, like a cryptogram: 'Fun. Fun. Fun worry worry worry'. Which, being read aloud, yielded 'Fun Period Fun Period Fun no period worry worry worry'; a not uncommon sequence in the days before the pill.

Guy's style was his content; he endorsed the view of the aloof pundit

Terence Reese that, in life as in bridge, a self-assured posture supplemented the effectiveness of the cards in his hand. Reese had been awarded a First in Greats and had a good measure of Oxonian *morgue*. Guy reported that while Terence was playing bridge at Crockford's during the Blitz, a panicked member burst into the ten-shilling room to announce that the Germans had just hit the War Office with their latest stick of bombs. Terence said, 'Not on purpose, surely.'

At the table, Reese was a renowned master of 'squeeze' plays. When, improbably, he got married, his regular bridge partner, Boris Schapiro, put it about that, after playing cards all evening, Terence went reluctantly to bed with his bride. 'Halfway through, everything stopped. Mrs Reese said, "Something wrong, darling?" Reese said, "I've just realised: if I'd only ducked the first diamond, I could have squeezed East and made that six no trumps."' The wall-eyed, long-lived Boris was a renowned *coureur de femmes*. In *Aces All*, Guy reports that, on being introduced to a good-looking woman, Schapiro's standard opening bid was 'How about a spot of adultery?' While dining with an ostentatiously *décolletée* woman, he passed his knife across the table to her neighbour and said, 'Cut me a slice.' Also a redoubtable horseman, Boris lived dangerously and continued to be cavalier well into his nineties.

Guy was forever playing the part of someone better-known and better-heeled than he was. He made commonplace phrases more trenchant by initialising some of the words: if he thought you were right, he would say, 'I couldn't A with you M.' In another register, he referred to Jesus as 'The late J. Christ esquire'. With her thick-lensed, circular and wire-rimmed spectacles, Celia was no beauty; yet there was an attractive contrast between her prim, often dowdy, appearance and her naughty giggle. Her tongue carried an accurate sting: a friend's chubby son was said to resemble 'the bacon-slicer at the Co-op'. She wrote with affectionate, pitiless familiarity about the lower middle class. Her mother showed people to their seats in the Apollo Theatre and brought them tea and biscuits at matinées. Celia had been the editor Arthur Christiansen's secretary in the great days of the *Daily Express*. Its master of the subtle arts, James Agate, spoke well of her youthful fiction, under a 26-point headline.

In his heyday, Agate was a feared, egotistic, homosexual literary and theatrical critic. Michael Ayrton told me how, when he was nineteen and had just designed John Gielgud's production of *Hamlet*, he met Agate, in the Underground. Agate saluted the young genius and tested the waters by saying, 'I don't know whether you would be interested, but I have a pair of Edmund Kean's nail-scissors in my flat, if you'd care to come up and see them.' The incurably heterosexual Michael declined the invitation.

I am sure that Guy – after a sorry first marriage with a German lady – was never unfaithful to Celia; but he gave the impression of knowing his way around women. Soon after I left Charterhouse, he advised me never to forget that, as Zola had dared to imply in *Nana*, the tongue could be a more durable organ for satisfying a woman than the penis. Her fellow courtesan Satin offered Nana practical proof. A Fleet Street joke of the period gave as an example of a physical impossibility 'two Lesbians whistling while they work'.

My father never offered anatomical advice; nor did he read foreign novels. His fictional reading was limited to the monthly selections of the Reprint Society. I do, however, recall him giving me Edmond Fleg's *Why I am a Jew*, on which he made no comment. When Cedric was in agony, from yet another attempt to cure the stricture in his urethra, Pat Cotter prescribed C. S. Lewis's *The Problem of Pain*, which he took with a glass of Robinson's lemon and barley water. It failed to convert him to Christianity. At Oxford, my father had belonged to the society for the destruction of Keble: they extracted bricks from its ugly, blushing walls. Cotter was the eighth-form Classics teacher at St Paul's, a croquet international and the *Financial Times* bridge correspondent. My father said that he was 'almost the nicest man in the world'.

My parents brought with them from New York a complete set of the works of Charles Dickens, bound in tooled leather, the voluminous red and black fruit of a special offer in the *Herald Tribune*. At Christmas, Cedric paid tribute to *A Christmas Carol* or to *The Pickwick Papers*, rather as he did, less regularly, to the Day of Atonement by fasting. He considered nothing funnier than Tracy Tupman's call of 'Fire, fire' after Mr Pickwick had fallen into the pond while skating on thin ice. I smiled, but I did not laugh. Mr Micawber's philosophy did not amuse me any more than Betsey Trotwood's cry of 'Donkeys'. Dickens's padded and buttoned prose recalled the heavy brown furniture in my great-aunt Minnie's Oakwood Court drawing room. Dickens may be the stuffy British idea of ingenious fun, but I have never quite forgotten that Fagin was part of it.

Apart from Mr Maugham (how long before I met one of those shameless women of his who were ready to 'pop into bed'?), the English-language novelists I favoured were Sinclair Lewis and Ernest Hemingway, both available for a few shillings in orange Penguin editions. I learned from 'Red' Lewis (nicknamed for the colour of his hair, not of his politics) how dialogue could catch the spirit of a character and convey tones and attitudes without additional prosaic verbiage. Although we had left St Louis when I was three years old, I recognised the inhabitants of *Main Street* as if I had spent many dull years in Gopher Prairie. I have never laughed at P. G. Wodehouse.

During my protracted adolescence, I carried a book wherever I went. I got through *War and Peace* as I walked between sixth-form classes at Charterhouse (Skid Simon and Guy Ramsey made a habit of reading while crossing the road). Books offered ticketless escape from what Byron called 'the tight little island'. The red-covered Penguin translations of Balzac, Stendhal, Dostoyevsky, Tolstoy, Turgenev allowed me to emigrate spiritually before I could afford a practical ticket. In the months before I went up to Cambridge, Jean-Paul Sartre was my magic carpet to Paris. Although I cannot spell out why existentialism was a humanism, as Sartre claimed, I shall never forget that one of his female characters had a triangle of red pubic hair.

Maugham declared, in *The Summing Up*, that he achieved literary success thanks, in particular, to a talent for dialogue; so too had Dumas *père*. I suspect that Willie's stammer made him a good, and retentive, listener. Later, alone, his fingers were quietly but unhesitatingly chatty. Facility for clever dialogue may owe more to a keen ear than to literary refinement. As Maugham had proved, the theatre – where dialogue was king – was a living, and a good one. The mind's eye furnishes a scene, but the mind's ear brings its performers to life. Maugham first came to England when he was eight years old. French was his first language, as American was mine. The need to assimilate obliged an alien to be a quick learner when it came to vowel sounds and vocabulary if he wished to avoid the scorn (or solicit the applause) of the natives. Conformity and mimicry, emulation and duplicity go easily together, irony their likeliest solvent.

Among my parents' books was *Play Parade*, a compendium of Noël Coward's plays, including *Private Lives*, *Design for Living* and *Cavalcade*. I noted how few words there had to be on the playwright's page and how few pages could constitute a play. In our early teens, Dorothy Tutin and I alleviated the flatness of our suburban lives by reading the parts of Elyot and Amanda, Coward's enviably cosmopolitan lovers. Side by side on my parents' American three-seater couch, we rehearsed chaste sophistication. Coward's skittish licence offered no cue for serious kissing.

In the last weeks of 1949, I knew no better means of allaying suburban solitude than taking the 74 bus to go to a drama group at the Liberal Jewish Synagogue in St John's Wood. My parents' piety was limited to paying their subscription. In return they received the monthly newsletter and the right to be buried in Willesden Cemetery, in a part of north London where they would never have considered living. The Alumni Drama Group was amateurish, even to an amateur whose greatest credit was to have played Osric in the

Charterhouse school play, in which I persuaded my fellow Lockite, Robin Jordan, to play Hamlet. Soon afterwards, he was the successful candidate for the Holford Scholarship to Christ Church that I had hoped for. There were several girls, of varying charm and dimensions, among the synagogue alumnae.

Before long, I asked the well-made daughter of a Golders Green dentist to come to see Hermione Gingold and Hermione Baddeley in Coward's *Fallen Angels*. Pat arrived in the foyer wearing a flounced skirt (her legs were not her best point) and a Tyrolean blouse, its laces criss-crossed over the proud constriction of her cleavage. When she failed to be amused by the clowning of the two Hermiones (she clicked her tongue, three times, in ritual disapproval), I lost my appetite for her undoing. The Master himself was, it had been reported, displeased by the Hermiones' mugging, quite as if his camp comedy had been travestied by their shamelessness, rather than rendered more hilarious than even he could ever have imagined. The most memorable moment was when la Gingold took off one of her high-heeled shoes, plunged it to cool in the champagne bucket, and then limped around the stage in absurdly dignified disequilibrium.

I returned to the drama group in the hope of better pickings. Its leader was a large, lively, bespectacled female (too grown-up to be a girl) called Jacqueline Weiss, a PhD in clinical biology. I described her as being dressed in 'loose covers', which I liked to presume amused her. The group was planning to do a production of Coward's *Hay Fever*. I was allotted the part of Simon. We were about to begin a read-through when a slim, dark-haired, black-eyed, beautiful girl in a green mackintosh and flat black shoes came into the rehearsal room. She had not attended previous meetings and was not known to the company. Her name was Betty Glatt and when she smiled – although it was not, at that moment, at me – so did I.

III

I N THE 1950s, the lure of amateur dramatics lay in the hope of rehearsing kisses more passionate than were likely in everyday practice. Since Betty and I were cast as brother and sister in Coward's play, that opportunity was denied me with her, for a while; but we soon found time to talk, at length. I had never met a girl at once so sure of herself, so bright and so lacking in conceit or caution. She appeared to have no problem in enjoying life. When she asked whether I was going to university, modesty did not forbid me to tell her of my award. Her eyebrows gave a lift of surprise and interest. She had just graduated from London University. Now at secretarial college, she had been a scholar in history at Westfield. They had wanted her to stay and do research, but she chose to be a woman. Her parents had a drapery shop in Marylebone High Street. Sylvia Betty was born in the flat upstairs. They now lived in Willesden. She told me that she had never been to the synagogue before. Like me, she was looking for company, not for God. She had long legs, lustrous black hair, full and lovely lips and those willingly amused dark eyes. We left rehearsals together.

Because I was playing the part of Simon Bliss in *Hay Fever* and because I did not like being called Freddie, Betty continued to call me Simon offstage.

When I told her that I meant to be a novelist, she asked to see something I had written. It did not occur to me to wonder whether she had a boyfriend. She did: a Welshman who later became a well-known newsreader on ITV. In my vanity and proximity, I never considered him a rival. I asked Betty whether everyone she knew called her Betty, even though her first name was Sylvia. On the whole, yes, they did; but her dentist brother-in-law Arthur did have a nickname for her. I promised not to use it if she would tell me what it was. All right, it was 'Beetle'; because she had that glistening black hair. I have rarely called her anything else; never Betty, though sometimes 'Bett'.

When I brought her my brown spiral notebook, she read a page, turned to the next, and read on. After a while she looked at me in a way that made me want to kiss her. She made no objection. She was at least three years older than I was and she had artistic friends in Tite Street, Chelsea. Years later, she told me that what convinced her that I would be a writer was a talent for standing back from events and describing them with seemingly impersonal accuracy. I learned from Maugham what he had from the Goncourts.

One night, after rehearsal, we walked down Lisson Grove and turned into a dark alley where there was a row of garages behind a petrol station. We kissed and kissed, until we were breathless, against a brick wall. After a while, but not before she had said, 'I love you, Simon,' we heard the sirens of a police car in the distance. A few minutes later, a van turned, on shrill tyres, into the alley, its lights went dark, and it was driven into the petrol station's big garage. The slatted door of the entrance slithered down like a portcullis.

A blaring police car flashed past, going on up Lisson Grove. We might have been in a gangster movie. We found a telephone booth around the corner. I dialled 999. The operator thanked me for my information and we went back to the alley to wait for further excitements. We waited and waited. Nothing happened. Could it be that there were crimes that the police elected not to solve? It was too late to resume our embraces that night, but we soon did so elsewhere. I was learning at last, and fast, that it was possible to be happy.

Early in the New Year, my father's connections in Fleet Street secured me an interview with the news editor of the *Sunday Express*, the bestselling popular Sunday newspaper that was not the *News of the World*. Close behind it in sales were *The People* and the *Sunday Despatch*, which was serialising *Forever Amber*. Kathleen Winsor's novel featured an off-the-shoulder restoration heroine not unlike Moll Flanders, though never so explicitly gamey.

John Gordon, the editor of the *Sunday Express*, responded with columns in which he deplored cleavage and similar threats to what had made Britain great. His pomposity provoked Graham Greene and his film producer, socialite friend John Sutro to announce the foundation of the John Gordon Society, an organisation devoted to endorsing the editor's moral code. They would be no more than vice-presidents. The presidential chair, with a pin under its cushion, was reserved for Mr Gordon. The editor boxed clever enough to take their irony straight; he took their garland of nettles as if it smelt of roses. John Sutro was a friend not only of Graham Greene but also of Somerset Maugham. When, many years later, I wrote a biographical sketch of Willie, Sutro sent me a handwritten letter of congratulation, which was folded in a sumptuous envelope with an inner lining of purple tissue paper. Graham Greene might have been a suitable chairman for the 'Some of my Best Friends Society'; his comity with Sutro did not inhibit him from portraying Jews, in his pre-war novels, with saleable malice.

The offices of Beaverbrook Newspapers were encased in a curvaceous modern black glass building. Its opaque ground-floor windows reflected a pub called the Hole in the Wall on the far side of Fleet Street. The *Sunday Express* news editor, Stanley Head, was an indoor man. Sallow and slumped in his tipped-back chair, unbrushed ash on the bulge of his misbuttoned cardigan, he had seen it all and liked little of it. The last thing he needed under his weary wing was a green apprentice who had not even worked on a local paper. However, my father's frequent lunchtime guest Alan Brock-bank, the paper's diplomatic, political, naval and industrial correspondent, had undertaken to supervise my novitiate, should I be admitted to the news-room. Stanley Head proposed, with a sigh, that I go and find a news story and write some copy. He would then see what he could do, or not.

Having spent a decade mimicking the orotund Cicero and the tersely sarcastic Tacitus, how could it be beyond my powers to compose winning paragraphs of penny-a-lining journalese? A composition was a composi-tion. I had done hundreds of them in Latin, Greek and English, verse and prose: show me the metre and I would finish the job. Having written my audition piece in what I took to be a suitably low style, I thought it wise to show it to Guy Ramsey, in case he had any suggestions. He did. The first was that I should tear it up and start again. He then spelt out the simple rules for any composition that stood a chance of passing muster in the Bea-verbrook press. Ideally, no story should be longer than three paragraphs, no paragraph longer than three sentences, and no sentence much longer than three words. As in Henry Luce's *Time* magazine, the Beaver's model for all seasons, a news story had to be front-loaded, the reader incited to read on by the urgency of the opening phrase. My draft disqualified itself on inspection: it contained several semi-colons and a few words of three syllables. With sub-editorial dexterity, Guy abbreviated my verbosity in line with Beaverbrook practice. Stripped of adjectives, adverbs or florid punc-tuation, the story became lean, vivid and presentable.

I took it into Stanley Head's office and put it on his desk, as if it were all my own work (the title attached to Leslie Grimes's daily cartoon in the *Evening Star*). He sighed and pulled the piece towards him. I stood there as he glanced through it. He sighed again, looked up, brushed ash from his sad knitwear, and said, 'If Brocky agrees, you can come in Tuesday. I can't pay you anything but expenses, if you're ever authorised to have any. Not bad for a beginner, this, not bad at all.'

Reporters in the 1950s lacked mechanical means to record what was said in an interview. The only way to validate a quotation was to produce shorthand notes. Before turning up for work in Fleet Street, I enrolled for evening classes at the Pitman Shorthand school in Wimbledon. The well-attended college was in a red-brick Victorian Gothic building in unsmart lower Wimbledon. Our grey teacher was a dedicated Pitman pietist. Having taught the Method for many years, she still gloried in the codified deftness with which whole syllables could be collapsed into a single stroke, light or heavy, up above or below or along the line on the page. She talked, with apostolic zeal, of the beautiful symbols and inescapable speeds that a true initiate could achieve. No accelerating speaker could ever get away from a fully armed, 200-words-a-minute Pitman graduate.

We sat at scholarly desks in a classroom. The hieroglyphs were chalked, in all their loopy elegance, on a wide blackboard. The quick clatter of trainee typists came from an adjacent room. I should have been wise to acquire their skill, but the girls (90 per cent of the tiros were female) sounded dauntingly fast as they translated the teacher's dictation onto keyboards masked, by a wooden panel, from visual inspection. The school brochure promised that a Pitman secretary could produce a page of flawless text in pitch darkness. I have never taught myself to type with more than three or four fingers; two usually suffice. Nor did I assimilate a full range of calligraphic elegance from the shorthand course. However, I did leave with enough of the curves and straights of the now archaic notation to be equipped to play the part of the Beaver's Johnny-on-the-spot.

Alan 'Brocky' Brockbank was a tall, sandy-haired balding man in his early fifties. In the war he had worked his way up from the lower deck to become a lieutenant-commander in the 'wavy navy' (the RNVR). With his notepad braced open at the due page by two rubber bands, he transcribed and composed his copy at speed, in 2B pencil, onto sheets of foolscap, no more than nine lines on a page, four or five words on a line. The corrected version was hammered out, double-spaced, on a heavy Royal Sovereign. A copy-boy then passed it to Bernard Drew, the garter-sleeved chief sub. He sat, scissor-fingered, at a long table in the middle of the wide, low-ceilinged newsroom.

The one thing reporters dreaded was that Bernard should scan their copy, look at the low, green ceiling, and then impale it on one of the two spikes in the centre of the table. If the piece survived to be allotted to a sub, his business was to eliminate symptoms of individual style. Even if its author merited a byline, as Brocky sometimes did, every text had to be trimmed in the house style so that it spoke in the accents only of the paper and of its proprietor.

The subs were the Beaver's military police. Guy Ramsey told me how Randolph Churchill, who wrote a column for the *Evening Standard*, had come into the office one day, loaded with a liquid lunch at White's, and abused one of the secretaries for making a mess of his copy. When she was reduced to tears, one of the subs turned to Randolph and said, in his oikish treble, 'Know your trouble, Churchill? Your name begins with C, H in *Who's Who* and S, H in what's what.'

The core staff of the *Sunday Express* was composed of men (there were no females in the newsroom) of a kind I had never met before. In 1950, popular journalism was an activity for artisans, rarely for graduates, never for first-class minds. Brocky and Bernard Harris, the sandy, blue-eyed, pipe-smoking chief feature writer, supplied most of the copy that bulked out the dummy edition of the paper, which grew fatter as the week progressed. Many-hatted in his roles as diplomatic correspondent, industrial correspondent, naval correspondent or *Sunday Express* reporters (the plural suggested that the Beaver had unlimited, ubiquitous resources), Brocky rarely stayed long in the office. He had no use for cyclostyled hand-outs from ministries or advertisers.

We were regularly on our way by taxi to confront politicians or businessmen. While other journalists waited in the proper place for the man of the moment, Brocky found his way to the back door and whoever might be coming out of it. Few escaped his mild, prehensile greeting, 'Oh, Sir Bernard … Alan Brockbank, *Sunday Express*…' The Sir Bernard most regularly in the news in the 1950s was Sir Bernard Docker, the chairman of both BSA and Daimler motors. He and his ex-showgirl wife Norah were notorious, but not wholly unpopular, for flaunting their wealth in a time of austerity. Their Daimler was covered with gold stars and was said to have gold bumpers. The couple's flagrant ability to gild lilies was at once scandalous and entertaining. While his lady revelled in her notoriety, Sir Bernard was never seen to smile.

Persistent but never nasty, Brocky was adept at accompanying whatever absconding mogul it might be to his waiting black Humber or Armstrong Siddeley Sapphire (the cad's Rolls-Royce, deemed luxurious on account of its 'fluid flywheel', whatever that was). Brocky could hold open a car door, with implacable courtesy, in such a way that his victim could not contrive to get inside before he had answered just a couple of questions. He always had a small point he wanted to clarify and, oh, one very last thing he wanted to be sure he had got right. After the publication of an annual report with one or two things in it that Brocky didn't quite follow, we surprised Billy Butlin, the holiday camp king, at the back exit from one of the Nissen huts that augmented the BEA terminal at Heathrow. In the face of my master's gentle inquisition, little Billy spilled enough beans to furnish us with an exclusive.

We had liquid sessions in a pub near Transport House with Herbert Morrison, another little man, at once cocky and shifty, his glass eye less elusive than the good one. What I heard from his lips was enough to rend from end to end my naïve notions of socialist solidarity, but memory's sieve has not retained exactly what he said about Stafford Cripps or 'Nye' or the recently retired Ernie Bevin, whose post as Foreign Secretary Morrison occupied long enough only to establish his incompetence to hold it.

Bevin's reputation has been glorified by his civil service mandarins. The lecherous Ernie's working-class anti-Semitism was an easy fit with that of The Office's 'camel corps' of Arabists. The dockers' leader took easily to *ex officio* presumption: Lady Diana Cooper reported, without surprise or outrage, how Bevin had pressed fat kisses on her at an embasssy reception in Paris. Morrison's great achievement was domestic: he was the prime mover of the Festival of Britain. He urged us to go and have a look at what was happening on the South Bank.

Since the Beaver was not known to be dogmatically hostile to the Festival of Britain, Brocky deputed me to visit the dusty site. One of the press people described how the roof on the half-finished Festival Hall had been prefabricated in several large, hooped pieces. I could come and see if I was interested. Of course I was. 'No inside access yet, unfortunately.' He led me to a 70-foot wooden ladder attached, halfway up the building, to a girder, to which another ladder of the same length was tied, at a reverse angle. 'Once you're halfway up, all you have to do is swing yourself round and onto the other ladder and on you go.' I invited him to lead the way. 'Lean away from the ladder,' he called down to me, 'otherwise you bump your knees and block yourself.' However shakily, what had to be done was done. At length, I swung myself over the parapet of the roof, took a deep breath, and showed interest in the metal tracks along which the sections of the roof were due to be rolled.

While we smoked our Woodbines, my guide told me the then new joke about the worker who went out of the gate every day with a wheelbarrow with waste paper in it. The security man checked it for stolen goods (there was no shortage of pilfering on any building site) but never found anything. After several weeks, the guard said, 'I know you're nicking something and I promise not to do anything about it, but what the hell is it?' The worker said, 'Wheelbarrows.'

With a long look at London's flat, often still flattened, horizons, I climbed over the parapet and onto the first of the two pliable ladders. Back at the office, I wrote up the details of the revolutionary roof. Bernard Drew stabbed my work onto the spike without hesitation.

The sad-countenanced John Prebble was the Beaver's house intellectual. In his mid-thirties, he smoked a straight pipe, lit with proletarian Swan Vesta matches, wore serious glasses and did not mix with the artisans. Having served in the Royal Artillery during the war, he owed his job, to some degree, to the fact that, like the Beaver, he had been raised in Canada. Prebble had his own small office. Its tight window opened only onto the newsroom, whence I could see him frowning over sources from which to cull material that would pass muster with the Beaver. Even a junior reporter could recognise a man who had hoped to have better things to do than try to wrest readers from Kathleen Winsor. I did not know at the time that Prebble was an ex-Communist. It amused the Beaver to employ left-wingers such as Michael Foot and, in due time, Alan Taylor, whom he could massage, with praise and money, into becoming right-handed, as it were. Prebble left Fleet Street after writing a 1956 bestseller, about the Tay Bridge disaster of 1879, and found a new allegiance in Scottish nationalism.

The other feature writer with an office (and a page) of his own was Logan Gourlay, a tall, narrow, dandified and equally unsmiling Scot who covered show business and reviewed movies. With an elastic expense account, he could afford not to acknowledge the engine room crew even when we shared the lift with him. Not long after I joined the paper, he was found guilty of padding his expenses and dismissed. He later edited a book entitled *The Beaverbrook I Knew*.

Although His Lordship never came up to the office from Cherkley Court, his manor in the Surrey countryside, the proprietor kept a long-sighted eye on his publications. Fear (and vain hope) of a 'call from the country' procured adherence to his foibles. One of the loftiest of his courtiers, George Malcolm Thomson, was said to have told another journalist that, when alone with Max, he felt like Napoleon's Marshal Ney. To which the other replied (or said he had): 'Surely you mean Marshal Yea.'

It was mandatory to deny the existence of the Beaver's blacklist. All the same, I soon learned, as if by osmosis, never to speak well of Lord Louis Mountbatten. In the Beaver's inferno, 'Dickie' had an irredeemable place in the deepest circle of the damned: too vain to take expert military advice, Mountbatten had been responsible for sending a large contingent of ill-supported, under-trained Canadian commandos to their doom in the 1942 raid on Dieppe. To compound the scandal, he had, as the last Viceroy, given away India. Even the Beaver did not go so far below the belt as to publish what was loudly whispered in grand circles: that Mountbatten's wife, Edwina, had a more than diplomatic affair with Pandit Nehru, and that her husband was more than somewhat complaisant.

The proprietor's anathema extended to anyone who advocated joining the prototype of the European Union. Britain's affiliation with the benighted continent would clash with the policy of Imperial Preference, the Beaver's economic panacea. His opposition to the incipient Franco-German *entente* was embodied in the Crusader *couchant*, with lance and shield, in a niche at the top right-hand corner of our front page. To defer to the Beaver's prejudices came as easily as the imitation of Ciceronian irony or Ovid's metrical cynicism. Any party line, I realised, was liable to be as infectious as the common cold. Anyone could become an apparatchik, if duly salaried. There was secret comedy in honouring any creed that offered status and conferred privileges.

My St John's College contemporary the historian John Erickson was the first to remark how, during Stalin's Terror, those rounded up and accused of capital crimes appeared before 'grinning judges'. Both the victims and those who condemned them to a slow or a quick death knew the whole thing to be an inescapable and bloody farce. To play the ambitious clerk required neither sincerity nor belief. Like Castiglione's courtier, a journalist can remain free within his servility by knowing – but never, ever saying – how absurd it is, and how furtively delicious, to conform to the wishes of a tyrant who has favours to offer.

Brocky was gallant enough to act quite as if he needed a green bag-carrier. He often took me to the pubs where trades union leaders sighed with mild and bitter regret at Clem Attlee's lack of socialist steam. Like *ITMA*'s Colonel Chinstrap, when offered another tongue-loosening glass, they never minded if they did. Brocky maintained that the key moment in British post-war history came when the National Union of Mineworkers refused the offer of a seat, or seats, on the newly nationalised Coal Board. By declining directorial responsibility, the NUM left the power where, in truth, they preferred it to be: in the hands of the middle-class managers whom they chose to denounce rather than to supplant.

As the days went by, I was entrusted with less minor errands and inquiries. It was surprising to discover how easily people were flattered when approached by a cozening apprentice and how willing, often eager, to disclose petty secrets. My initiation into the means by which our foreign news coverage seemed to be ubiquitous came when one of the subs approached me, one Saturday morning, with a flimsy print-out, on pink paper, from the *Agence France-Presse*. 'Doing anything, Fred?'

'No. Rather not.'

'Write this up for me then, old son, would you, as if you were in Peking?'

As soon as I sat down at a vacant Royal Sovereign, I was looking out over the Forbidden City. In almost no time my Chinese meal was ready to go to the subs' table. The capacity for fluent imposture supplied one of the reasons for the central role of the Classics in English establishment life. Like satire and snobbery, parody and docility are never incompatible: the satirist is often a toady with two sets of teeth: one snarls at the privileged, the other smiles when offered preferment. Sir David Frost and Sir Jonathan Miller came to prove the point.

Outstanding in the Beaver's spectrum of hates was the annual British Industries Fair. This apparently benign and patriotic enterprise incurred his displeasure because exhibiting industrialists were encouraged, by the Labour government, to make deals with Europe rather than with the Empire. Brocky sent me down to Olympia to see what I could root out in the way of a story. If it was to make the paper, it would have to show that the BIF was doing a disservice to This Country.

The press officers at Olympia were busy handing out cyclostyled cheer that trumpeted record agreements to supply British products to all sorts of foreign markets. That sort of happy news was not what I was there to unearth. Then an aggrieved salesman told me that undercover agents from German industrialists, although officially proscribed, were on the prowl, like the spy in *L'Attaque*, with offers to undercut British prices. As a result, orders were being taken away from Our People by the resurgent Hun.

Fuelled with pay-dirt, I hurried back to the office, sat down at a spare typewriter and beavered away at a mostly monosyllabic exposé of Teutonic subterfuge. As he scanned my draft, I saw Bernard Drew's brow lose its suspicious crevices. He looked up at me and said, 'You couldn't bulk it out a bit, could you, Fred?' Of course I could. When my piece made the Scottish edition of the paper that Saturday, under the byline 'By *Sunday Express* Reporters', the Bernards, Drew and Harris, came across to show me the page hot off the stone. The *novillero* had made his first kill.

The word came down from Stanley Head that I should file my expenses. I asked Brocky what might count as legitimate apart from my bus fare to Olympia. 'Bus? I told you to take a taxi. And those salesmen you talked to, you did buy them a few rounds of drinks, I hope, didn't you? Go and do some clever arithmetic. Only, Fred, remember: no round numbers.'

After the paper had gone to bed, generous solidarity led the old hands to escort me to the Hole in the Wall for a celebratory drink. As our platoon of Expressmen came in, a solitary hack at the bar called out, 'Here come the Beaverbrook lackeys.' William Barclay, the Scotsman who wrote the 'Crossbencher' column (in which His Lordship's likes and dislikes among politicians were praised and pilloried), responded, 'Dirrty old *News of the Worruld!*'

I was shocked and liberated to find that the only morality in journalism was that the story came first. By the time I took the bus to north London to find out more about a man called Raven who, the Press Association reported, had taken his baby daughter and fled to Paris, I was Joseph Conrad's Verloc, a secret purveyor of bombshells seated among leisurely citizens.

Raven and his family lived in Royalty Court, a block of 1930s flats regal only in name. A huddle of journalists and cameramen were loitering under the stiff canopy over the front door, hoping for a tearful statement from the abandoned wife. The Fleet Street code of conduct required that reporters 'fill in' any member of the fraternity who was late on the case. Even though I came from 'the bloody *Sunday Express*', I was suffered to fish in the common pool. There was little in it but tiddlers. My colleagues outside Royalty Court were content to spend their morning in paid patience. As soon as it was opening time, they took it in turns to go, in small groups, to the nearest pub.

As a pupil in Brocky's school, it occurred to me that there had to be a back entrance to the Ravens' second-floor flat. I walked round the block and found the narrow backstairs that allowed dustmen to collect and tote the tenants' rubbish to their van. I went up cold concrete steps to the second floor and tried the appropriate door. I almost hoped that it would be locked. It was not. There I was in the small, empty kitchen of the beleaguered family. I looked at the used breakfast things, cosied teapot, United Dairies bottle (with a cardboard top, not gold foil, like our *Express* full-cream milk) and dented cornflake packet and I felt the triumph and shame of the debutant double-dealer. As I coughed and turned to go, a young woman came in from the hallway and said, 'What the hell's going on? Who the hell are you?'

I said, 'I'm awfully sorry. Raphael. *Sunday Express*. The door was open.'

'Press? You're not supposed to be in here, press.'

'Are you the mother, possibly, Mrs Raven, of the– the–?'

'What if I am?'

'I wonder if you'd care to tell me your side of the story. Very sorry about what happened. It must be terrible for you.'

It was not difficult to adopt the tone and syntax of a Job's comforter. The woman was so desperate that she seemed reluctant to have me leave. 'What do you want me to tell you? He's gone, Derek, and never said a word to anyone.' More embarrassed than ruthless, I hardly knew what I did want to know.

'Um, your little boy,' I said, 'what's his name and how old is he exactly?'

'Little girl.'

'Of course.'

'Jennifer. Two. Three in October.' She told me how crowded her parents' flat was for all of them, including the baby, and how her husband didn't always get on with her mother.

I was touched and disappointed: nothing she was telling me, of domestic and financial strains, was likely to warrant buttressing my expenses. I lacked the heartlessness to ask whether her husband had another woman or enough money to stay in France. I said that perhaps he would be back soon. 'Do you think?' She sat, elbows on the table, chin on the heels of her hands. Our Readers might be shocked by the husband who took his child to The Continent, but by the next weekend, the bloodless kidnap would no longer be news. Forty years later, it furnished an episode in my novel and TV series *After the War*.

Clement Attlee's Labour government was reaching the end of its lease. In February 1950, his thin voice called for a general election. Brocky and I took the train to Plymouth to attend a rally to be addressed by Winston

Churchill on behalf of his son. When recruited to Parliament in 1943, during a wartime by-election, Randolph had had a walkover. Now that the
inter-party truce was over, the war hero and cuckold, whose wife, Pamela,
had had a notoriously public affair with the millionaire American Averell
Harriman, was opposed by Michael Foot, who had been editor of Beaverbrook's *Evening Standard* when he was twenty-eight.

Unlike Randolph, Foot had no prestigious war record, but he had been
born in the constituency. He was rejected from the army on medical grounds.
Foot had, however, been one of the cross-party troika (with Frank Owen
and Peter Howard) who – under the pseudonym 'Cato' – composed the
bestselling 1940 pamphlet *Guilty Men*. Published by Victor Gollancz, it
pilloried selected appeasers, almost all Tories, who were accused of selling the pass and leaving Britain too weak to confront Hitler in good time.
The troika's *nom de plume* was oddly chosen: in ancient Rome, both the
famous Catos were bywords for intransigent conservatism. Quentin Hogg,
the MP for Oxford University, who had been among Neville Chamberlain's
more durable friends, responded with a polemic entitled *The Left Was
Never Right*. Although it cited chapter and verse in exposing the unpatriotic
delinquencies of pre-war Labour politicians and their opposition to rearma-
ment, Hogg's overheated book never achieved the classic status of Cato's.

We arrived in Plymouth by the early train and were taken in hand by the
local Tory apparat. A marquee big enough for a society wedding had been
rigged to receive the press, who were present in large, soon bibulous, numbers. The word must have passed in Fleet Street that the hospitality would
be worth the journey. Long, white-sheeted trestle tables were heaped with
sandwiches and pies. More important for old, outstretched hands, cases of
beer and spirits were stacked behind the buffet.

In mid-afternoon we heard that Churchill's train was going to be a little late; and then that it was going to be later than that; and then very late
indeed. Glasses were refilled, and refilled again. The first, and likeliest,

version of the story was that the hold-up was due to a farmer having stalled his tractor on a level crossing. In trying to haul it free, some yokels had managed to tip the silly thing on its side. It seemed hardly the kind of story to garnish the front page, even of the Scottish edition. After glasses had again been freshened, someone suggested that there might be a sinister side to the accident. What if it had been part of a left-wing scheme to sabotage Winston's campaign to get his son elected? Michael Foot's chums on the left-wing Bevanite *Tribune* were the fancied suspects, but it would make a better story if it had something to do with the Communists: RED PLOT TO DERAIL WINNIE was the right line to spruce up the northern edition.

The great man did eventually arrive, but not before the stacks of beer, gin and brandy had been thoroughly broached. It was too late for his speech to be any use even for the London edition. I doubt whether Brocky and I stayed to hear it. It had no effect on the result: Randolph was defeated by Michael Foot, who retained the seat until he decamped to Ebbw Vale in order to take on the mantle of Aneurin Bevan, of whom he wrote a two-volume hagiography.

When the results of the general election were announced, Attlee's majority was seen to have shrivelled but not vanished. Since honour still had some place in politics, it was possible that the Prime Minister would feel sufficiently rebuffed to be obliged to resign. During the interregnum, Brocky and I were able to walk up to 10 Downing Street, without being quizzed or frisked.

Attlee was standing, in his signature funereal rig, on the front doorstep, a polite huddle of attendant journalists and a few cameramen below him. His emaciated voice announced that he had yet to consult his colleagues and assess the results in full. The British reporters were inclined to respect the Prime Minister's temporising. Then an American voice was heard to call out, 'Make up your mind, Mr Attlee, you going or staying?' Attlee was constrained to be decisive. 'We shall carry on,' he said, in a modest voice that was never going to inspire anyone to fight on the beaches. The outspoken impatience of his American inquisitor announced that the leading Western power was no longer Great Britain. It was rare to hear someone who was not in fee to the British habit of deference.

My colleagues had few illusions about the merits or morals of our betters, but they were never openly disrespectful; nor, in my hearing, foul-mouthed. Effing and blinding was not yet the journalistic habit. Perhaps John Gordon's Calvinist editorship served to moderate his underlings' vocabulary. The only modest 'dirty' joke I remember hearing in the newsroom came in the form of the innocent question 'Where is the smallest airfield in the world?' Ever the eager candidate, I was quick with the innocent answer: 'Athens'. 'No,' said Bernard Harris, 'under a Scotman's kilt: just room for two hangers and a night-fighter.' Somewhat akin to this was the phrase, said to be the sub-editors' regimental motto: 'Snip, snip and Bob's your auntie!'

Expressmen were content to have bylines, discreetly imaginative, untaxed expenses and a word of praise from someone higher up the chain of command. The penultimate accolade was a congratulatory word from The Country; the ultimate was to be summoned to the Beaver's presence. The clearest intimation of favour on such an occasion was for the newsman to be asked what kind of a car he drove. It was prudent to name a modest motor, after which, one was licensed to hope, the Old Man would say, 'Someone in your position, Mr X, ought to be driving a Wolseley.' Mythology promised that one executive took modesty to a hopeful extreme by responding that he didn't actually run a car at all. 'Very wise,' said the Beaver, 'nasty, expensive things, automobiles, and they're always going wrong. So … keep up the good work, Mr Y, keep up the good work.'

At the weekend, the skeletal staff of the *Sunday Express* was swollen by the influx of 'Saturday men': jobbing journalists who worked for the daily press during the week and came in to fatten our news and sports pages. I became friendly with a *Daily Telegraph* reporter called Ray Foxall. He had a neat brown moustache and swift shorthand. Since he lived in Putney, we took the Tube home together after the paper had been put to bed. It was a sumptuous privilege to sit with a copy of the next day's paper and open it wide before the other passengers' civilian eyes.

One evening when I went to dine with Guy and Celia Ramsey in Well Road, I found them in anxious mood. The new editor of the *Daily Mail*, pressed to economise by Vere Harmsworth, had decided to dispense with Guy's services. The previous one, Frank Owen, had been a good journalist but a laggard leader: it was said of him, 'The editor's indecision is final.' Guy had been confident that something else would come along soon, but it did not. The following Saturday night, as Ray Foxall and I changed trains at Earl's Court, he told me that the *Daily Telegraph* was taking on new staff. The following morning, before I went to play tennis with Jack and Margaret Piesse and Max Stewart, I called Guy and repeated what Ray had told me. The Ramseys always stayed in bed till noon on Sunday, reading Lord Astor's *Observer* and Lord Kemsley's *Sunday Times*, but my interruption was not unwelcome. A week later, the *Telegraph* hired Guy as a feature writer and deputy drama critic. He was also to fill in as deputy chief reviewer on the literary pages. In the latter capacity, he must have been one of the last people ever to use the word 'limn' in the popular press. I had to go and look it up. Later, the *Telegraph* bridge correspondent died and Guy was appointed in his stead. Thanks to Ray Foxall, I had been able to do Guy a good turn, at last.

IV

BEETLE AND I watched the 1950 election results as they were flashed on big screens in Trafalgar Square. I had considered myself a socialist ever since 1945, though my vision of socialism involved scarcely more than the abolition of privilege and racial discrimination. As a historian, Beetle had been an admirer of Peel and Palmerston, but she had no urgent contemporary opinions. Her beautiful four-years-older sister Joan was married to a Communist and appeared to go along with his convictions. Baron Moss had grown up in the East End. His father owned a cinema in the Mile End Road. He had witnessed Mosley's marches and heard the chant of 'We've gotta get rid of the Yids'. A neighbour's twelve-year-old daughter had been thrown through a plate glass window by the Fascists. Such episodes, and the revelation that the British Union of Fascists was subsidised by Mussolini, have done little to impede the myth, propounded left and right, by Michael Foot and Enoch Powell, that Oswald Mosley was the 'lost leader' who might have restored Britain's greatness.

Having been a Bevin Boy during the war, Baron became a layout man on the staff of the *Daily Worker*. He spent long hours in the office and was paid £6 a week. When we visited him and Joan in their narrow, semi-detached house in Wembley, I was impressed, if never convinced or converted, by his faith in the coming of the classless society exemplified by Stalin's Soviet Union. Experience underground in the Nottinghamshire coal-field lent practical force to Baron's beliefs. My ideas came only from books.

In the early 1940s, *Guilty Men* had convinced me that the Tories were the vessels of reaction and anti-Semitism. More recently, I had read *The God That Failed*, in which Arthur Koestler, Stephen Spender and others announced their disillusionment with the party. George Orwell's *Homage to Catalonia*, primed by his naïve decision to join the Trotskyite POUM, had the merit of recounting specific personal disgust with the Communist Party's murderous machinations in the Spanish Civil War. Although he claimed merely to have signed up with the first available outfit, Orwell seems to have had some instinct never to line up with the big battalions. Nevertheless, he assumed it to be right to be on the left, in whatever undefined niche.

Baron relied on Karl Marx's long-distance clock, and Joe Stalin's rewinding of it, to vindicate the party's wriggling line. If Baron made me feel slightly ashamed to be working for the capitalist press, it was a proud moment when I was put on salary ('But not a word to the NUJ, Fred'). My weekly small brown envelope contained £4.10s, fattened by the unround number of my expenses. The Beaver's pennies enabled me to take Beetle to the cinema or to the gallery in the theatre. Terence Rattigan's *Adventure Story* had a memorable *coup de théâtre* when Basil Sydney, as Alexander the Great's friend 'Black Cleitus', came in from backstage, staggered forward almost to the footlights, and then fell on his face to reveal the seven-foot lance in his back, planted there by the drunken master who had saved his life at the Battle of the Granicus.

We also saw Laurence Olivier give a mannered performance in Christopher Fry's *Venus Observed*; Paul Scofield playing twins (one of them Frédéric) in *Ring Round the Moon*, with the beautiful young Claire Bloom; Ralph Richardson as *Cyrano de Bergerac* (autumn leaves fell on the New

Theatre stage). I imagined writing plays of similarly elaborate elegance as we had dinner after the show in old, chaste Soho. Goulash at the Hungarian Czardas cost three and sixpence. I dreaded the wine waiter. We drank water.

We first made nervous love, in my parents' absence on holiday, on my narrow bed in the Balliol House back room, which looked out on the hazy view that had won me third prize in the Charterhouse painting competition. Unlike Hilary Phillips, Beetle seemed unfazed by the prospect of my going up to Cambridge. Since I could not imagine better, I assumed we were together for good. I never thought about marriage; nor, so it seemed, did she. Having grown up in a large Jewish family, she had none of my sense of woeful isolation. She was both clever and athletic: she had been in the gym team and almost beat me when we raced for a bus. As a St Paul's first XI bowler, she once took five wickets for eight runs.

On bank holiday Monday, we sat on a slatted bench in the Large Mound stand at Lord's to watch Middlesex play Sussex. Hoping, in vain, for Compton and Edrich to repeat their record exploits of the 1947 season, we rented fat, rectangular-buttoned plastic cushions for threepence. I never saw Denis make more than thirteen runs; nor did I suspect that he did not wear a cap because he was under contract to Brylcreem.

We did see Bill Edrich bowl his slinging zingers fast enough, despite his bad shoulder, to oblige Denis's wicket-keeping big brother Leslie to stand well back, which he did not always do to the serviceable Laurie Gray. I was luckier and happier than I had ever imagined possible. Then came a small, but growing, summer cloud: in June, North Korea invaded the South. If there was full-scale war with the Communists, whose universal solidarity I never doubted, I was, I imagined, certain to be called up. I might never get to Cambridge. Ambition makes more cowards than conscience.

However British I was now pleased to be, America had a tenacious hold, especially the smart wit I associated with the *New Yorker* and the Algonquin Round Table. Beetle endured my descriptions of Thurber's cartoons and the relish with which I recounted the tag in *The Secret Life of Walter Mitty* 'What a dumb moll I picked!' I was glad to discover that she felt the lure of America: she had considered going to the States to work. Never had I met anyone who embraced life so gladly and so fearlessly. She seemed even to enjoy being a solicitor's secretary. We used to meet in the Strand for the one and tenpenny buffet lunch at Quality Inn. In the evening, I waited for her under the clock at Swan & Edgar's in Piccadilly. As she came up to me, she was always smiling, head slightly on one side. Since she was a Paulina (as well as good to look at and a good dancer), she and my father were quite easy with each other. My mother, not yet forty, was no more than polite. Like Judith, the *prima donna* in *Hay Fever*, Irene was never wholly pleased if anyone else's happiness distracted the attention from her.

Beetle's mother was neither jealous nor critical. Rachel, whom her three daughters called Ray or Rooky, was the oldest of twelve siblings who had grown up in Brick Lane and whose surrogate mother she had been. Her parents had eloped from Odessa before the Great War. Her grandfather was said to have cursed the runaways and prayed that their progeny would die. Their first two children did indeed die, but their subsequent children lived, and many prospered. They spilled out of the East End into shops and businesses in less cramped parts of London. Happy to be English, they felt no call to be assimilated to the point of being indistinguishable. Most kept kosher; some married out, others did not. They were what they were.

Beetle's father, Hyman Glatt, had come from Poland when he was fourteen, after working from the age of ten in a match factory. He was dark-eyed and handsome and, although shy, charming enough to attract a regular female clientele to his ladies' clothing shop in Marylebone High Street. Ray subscribed to *Vogue* and kept herself, unpretentiously, if never inexpensively, in fashion. She was too busy and too sociable to worry about what Beetle and I might be doing when left alone on Saturday afternoons in 84 Mount Pleasant Road. After we had made enough love for a while, we

played cricket in the narrow garden and then there was Fuller's walnut cake
for tea. We often went to the movies at the cavernous Kilburn State Cinema.
It sported a luminous cinema organ that rose stridently from the pit during
the interval. After the movie, I took some alien bus to Hyde Park Corner
and changed to the familiar 74, which took me to the top of Putney Hill.
On one such trip, I left my yellow Everyman Nietzsche on the seat beside
me, Zarathustra's funambulist halfway across the void.

Fleet Street gave me exhilaratingly disillusioned access to what I took to
be the real world; but I left the *Sunday Express*, after my nineteenth birthday
in August of 1950, with small ambition to return to journalism. I resumed
my study of the Classics, in accordance with Mr Howland's explicit suggestions about darning the holes in my reading. The Korean War made no
call on my services and little on my attention. The condition of 'only child-
ishness' makes a man both old before his time and forever, in his own mind,
too young for the demands of maturity.

In early October, I packed my old school trunk and sent it PLA (Passenger Luggage in Advance) to St John's College, Cambridge. My father's only
advice was that I should not push myself forward; better to wait for others
to 'beat a path to my door'. A Jew was wise to leave it to 'the Christians' to
bid him join their company. Cedric gave me £6 pocket money for the term
and warned me not to run up bills. His income at Shell was just too great
to warrant any financial supplement from the 'state scholarship' for which
I had qualified, *en passant*, by my Cambridge success. He undertook to
pay my buttery bill, but my allowance had to cover any books I wanted to
buy. Doubtless he assumed that I should have access to excellent libraries,
but perhaps it said something about the priorities of 1920s Oxford that he
was more willing to furnish my larder than my mind.

When I caught the train from King's Cross in early October, I sported
an army surplus duffel coat and dark-green corduroy trousers. I wore my
long blue and pink striped Charterhouse scarf, not for any nostalgic reason

but because I had been told that freshmen were not entitled to wear college scarves. Thanks to Beetle, I was some kind of a man, but I was also a new boy, at once apprehensive and confident that I merited the place that I had been denied at Winchester. My secret regret was that, unlike Oxford, Cambridge did not require scholars to wear longer gowns than commoners. I was a socialist eager for distinction.

My sense of election led me to ask a fair-haired young man who shared my third-class compartment what college he was going to. When he replied 'King's', in an American accent, I felt a surge of protective affinity. How long had he been in England? 'Not too long.' And what was his name? 'George Plimpton.' My mother had given me half a bottle of Scotch in case I needed to do some sophisticated entertaining. Taking him to be a stranger in a strange land, I invited Plimpton to come and visit me in St John's, not too far away from King's. I wished him luck, in the British style, as we walked along the long platform at Cambridge station. On my way to catch the bus, I saw him standing at ease in the taxi queue. He wore a pork-pie hat and a Burberry raincoat with tartan lining and carried a two-handled soft leather valise.

I had quit a London that still bore brave scars. Buildings sliced open in the Blitz had yet to be torn down or repaired. Empty lots ('SECOND FRONT NOW' still faintly visible on their low brick walls) were flagged with wild flowers. Cambridge was at once antique and pristine. Privileged pre-war England was still there. It warranted the assumption that the inalienable grace of scholarship lay in access to beautiful places and in the company of those who measured each other only by their intelligence.

My first smug pleasure was to buy a gown. Without my knowing, its shiny purchase betrayed the arriviste. A frayed, time-worn, slightly empurpled heirloom gown was the hallmark of those who had had to try less hard to get at least as far. I carried my new brown-paper parcel down Trinity Street to the red-brick gateway of St John's. The head porter, in top hat, black coat and striped trousers, directed me to E staircase in Third Court. The college was crowded enough for many freshmen to have to share rooms or to be despatched to live in 'licensed digs'. Scholars, however, were allotted a set of their own.

RAPHAEL, F. M. was inscribed in white letters on a black panel at the entrance to my staircase. I climbed six flights of steep, narrow wooden stairs (past the first-floor set belonging to DR DANIEL) and up to the gabled garret that doubled for heaven. There was a sitting room, with a metered gas fire, a chapped, narrow sofa and a low-bottomed armchair. The slim desk in the window overlooked the green, uncreased waters of the Cam. When I leaned out and looked to the right, there was the Bridge of Sighs. From the mansard bedroom window, I could see across the Backs towards King's. I put my portable typewriter and my notebook on the table and a few textbooks on the empty shelves and wondered what my neighbours, BECHER, R. A. and WILSON, D. M. might be like, and whether they were scholars.

I paraded, in my new black gown, to Chapel Court to pay the obligatory call on my tutor. A queue of freshmen dressed the stairs up to R. L. Howland's door. Behind and below me stood a short, dark-haired, round-faced person who told me, in a singsong accent that I had never heard before, that his name was Sullivan. John Patrick was also a major scholar in Classics. He had taken the examination a year earlier than I, but had chosen to do his National Service (he emerged as a sergeant in the Education Corps) before coming up. The son of a docker, he had attended the Francis Xavier Jesuit school in Liverpool. Latin and Greek grammar had been beaten into him by sacerdotal teachers as dedicated as they were merciless in the application of the tawse.

Mr Howland was known to his colleagues as 'Bede'. He had been effortlessly learned for as long as anyone could remember. He was also an Olympic athlete (he put the shot for Britain in Berlin in 1936) and a soccer blue. Although a noted Aristotelian, he was no intellectual. When

I was a scholarship candidate, my interview with him had been more about Shrewsbury versus Charterhouse football than about the subtle arts. He now welcomed me with a large smile, as if my award had been a credit to both of us. He suggested no particular lecturers whom I should favour, but he assigned me, for Latin composition, to a certain Professor Anderson, who had rooms in Second Court, and for Greek to Mr Crook, whose rooms could be found under the arch between Second Court and New Court. More housemaster than tutor, Howland expected me to get a First because that was what scholars were supposed to do; it required diligence, not originality. I was there to be a credit to the college and, he dared to advise me, have a good time. His genial style was at once unfeigned and a cover for the astute assessment of others. Although I knew nothing of it at the time, he was a trusted recruiter for the British intelligence services.

Sullivan and I scanned the list of lecturers and composed a menu that began at nine in the morning with Mr Lee on Latin verse, followed by F. E. Adcock, a lisping epigrammatist, for ancient history. John Patrick had escaped from a Merseyside back-to-back and from Roman Catholicism. He had no nostalgia for working-class life, none of Baron Moss's revolutionary solidarity, small appetite for the candle-lighting angst of Graham Greene (who was, John told me, known in France as 'Grim Grin'). He had three years in which to sharpen his excellence and arm himself for the steep climb to the academic high ground. I was more dismayed than stimulated by his single-mindedness. Who but a perfectionist would choose to read *Advanced Greek Prose Composition*? I preferred *The Magic Mountain* and *Manhattan Transfer*.

Early in our first year, Sullivan set himself to practise a skill that I have never acquired. He wrote to famous people in a way that at once quizzed and flattered them. By doing so, he insinuated himself into their train. I am told that, early in his career, a famous modern historian spent the first two hours of his day writing sincere letters of praise to persons who might later be useful to him. Proust and Henry James were no less effusive; the latter's letter of sympathy over the death of a friend's pooch is a masterpiece of careful, only slightly camp, condolence. Sullivan's first mark was Ezra Pound, whose *Homage to Sextus Propertius* had piqued his purposeful interest.

Robert Graves was already known to have mocked Pound's errors, not least in translating '*minas*' – in Latin the accusative plural of a noun meaning 'threats' – as 'mines', of the Welsh variety. Graves was a self-consciously vatic poet, of a kind viewed with suspicion in the Cambridge English faculty, a brave soldier in the Great War, a classical scholar and the bestselling author of *I, Claudius* and *Claudius the God*, which were based on Suetonius's lascivious gossip, not least about the emperor's delectable, nymphomaniac wife, Messalina, who enjoyed a night job as a common prostitute. Although Suetonius had had privileged access to imperial records, he was regarded by classicists as uncanonical on account of his journalistic vulgarity, none of it improbable when read in a modern light.

Graves was also a copious translator with too keen a philological conscience for him to indulge in Poundian glosses. As an ex-frontline soldier, he may not have been as indifferent as Eliot and company to Pound's siding with our recent enemies. His younger brother, Charles, was a popular journalist and *bon vivant*. My father had been in officers' training camp with him, on Wimbledon Common, at the end of the Great War, and was a contemporary of Robert's at St John's College, Oxford. Robert was an Old Carthusian, whose *Goodbye to All That* was the measure of his small enthusiasm for the school. William Makepeace Thackeray had already called our old school 'Slaughterhouse'. There are few grateful literary Old Carthusians. Simon Raven wrote sentimentally only about his days playing cricket on Green, with Peter May and Jim Prior. He regretted his expulsion most keenly because it had robbed him of one more season as a flannelled fool.

With regard to accuracy in translation, Sullivan might have been expected to side with Graves, but he found something exemplary in

Pound's innovative *arrivisme*. I never imagined that Pound would reply to an unknown correspondent, but John had phrased his letter with specific interrogative applause. Edward Shils, an eminent sociologist, isolated what he called 'Vitamin P', a prescription guaranteed to have an uplifting effect on recipients. The 'P' stood for praise. No one was known to be allergic to it. A few weeks later, John was pleased to show me the two green, typewritten pages on which Pound responded thoroughly, and almost gratefully, to his queries.

The ribbon on Pound's typewriter was of a pale, unusual, pinky-brown hue. I regarded Ole Ez's green signature with a mixture of nausea and envy (of its recipient). By procuring the Bollingen Prize for him in 1949, T. S. Eliot and his friends had purged Pound of the iniquity surrounding his virulent wartime broadcasts in favour of Fascism. Was there a tinge of 'there but for the grace of God' in the great Tom's endorsement of the prize committee's decision? It implied that it was uncomely to disqualify someone who had done nothing worse than incite the physical elimination of all Jews. The reputation of Karl Shapiro, a good poet and a combat veteran, never recovered from his pronounced dissent from the majority of the Bollingen Prize committee's decision to drape Ole Ez with redeeming laurels.

Mr Eliot benefited, in post-war literary circles, from the modernisation of the fourth-century BC Athenian law against *mnesikakein* (recalling attention to previous misdeeds). It continues to be said that he was not an 'anti-Semite', as if this were a condition similar to being diabetic, rather than a fashionable vanity to be paraded in pre-war company and abandoned, overtly at least, when no longer marketable. Between 1945 and 1960, the murder of six million Jews had no specific name and was rarely mentioned. Pound did later apologise, grudgingly, for his embrace of what he chose to call the 'suburban prejudice', but only on the grounds that anti-Semitism had deformed his overgrown *magnum opus*. He showed no genuine shame at having aligned himself with mass murderers. His post-war poem 'Pull down thy vanity' sounded like some kind of recantation; but it was addressed to those who dared to criticise genius.

Sullivan had landed a difficult fish with the easy bait of inquisitive admiration. Equipped with the insurgent nerve and sourced intelligence that would mark his professorial career, John was pleased to be both rigorous and heterodox. Having learned some German while he was in the Intelligence Corps, perhaps in the knowledge that it would be needed to read the footnotes in scholarly texts and to garnish his own, *Weltschmerz* and *Stimmung* figured in his apprentice, quasi-parodic scholarship. The *zeitgeist* was, of course, omnipresent in post-war Cambridge. It spoke, very often, in the moderated tones of a cosmic sergeant-major: 'Get some service in, son'; 'You've got two chances: a dog's chance and fuck all chance'; 'When I say move, I want you to move like shit off a shovel, MOVE!'

In the hope of being in the swim, at whatever shallow end, I went to Bowes & Bowes and bought Pound's *Seventy Cantos*. I wrote F. M. Raphael on the fly-leaf; stranger to myself. If I had somewhat hoped to find Pound's work despicable, it held me in its serpentine coils like Laocoön. 'Fish-scale roofs' was a masterly phrase; but I did wonder why the arcane adjective 'swart' had to feature twice in the first Canto. Pound's Chinese character Kung had the same name as a Brighton and Hove hotelier's son, first name Freddie, who was in my house at Charterhouse. In a time of rationing, he received enviable, unshared food parcels. He was attractive and 'spo-ey' (sportive) enough to be immune to accusations of meanness.

Howland distributed printed forms with the names of canonical authors at the top of large white spaces. We were expected to fill the blanks with the specific works that we had read. Did he assume that we would have the wit to find our way in the libraries and explore their catalogued riches? I hardly knew where to start. I read a great deal, but without system. There seemed to be little difference between the Latin and Greek compositions I was set to do, while preparing for Part One in the Classical Tripos, and those I had done at Charterhouse. I found myself in a glorified school distinguished by less discipline and, though I had yet to see any, a few girls. Where were the scintillating souls in whose company I dreamed of shining?

My neighbours at the top of E staircase in Third Court were also freshmen. Like Sullivan, Tony Becher had done his National Service before coming up. He had been at Cheltenham College and was then a second lieutenant in the army. His father was a colonel in the Indian Army. I was rather too pleased to discover that, although he too had a scholarship, it was only 'minor' and in mathematics. David Wilson was a large, jolly, provincial person with no scholarly distinction. Tony and I were not unkind to him, but he seemed not quite to be of our public school *genre*. He neither drank alcohol nor played poker. He had come up to read Archaeology, hence his proximity to Glyn Daniel, whose rooms were two floors below ours.

In quite short order, David Wilson abandoned his teetotal regime and became a first-class archaeologist. Like George Engel, he chose an academically untenanted topic in which to specialise: in his case, the Vikings. He ended his career as the director of the British Museum, in which role he defended the retention of the Elgin Marbles. He responded to hectoring Hellenists, Melina Mercouri the most voluble, with the unflinching good humour that he had displayed as my neighbour. His achievements were capped with a knighthood and an honorary fellowship of St John's.

As college steward, Glyn Daniel was in charge of the wine cellar. His oenological prescience had procured a fine store of the great vintage of 1945. We gulped youthful Château Lynch-Bages at three and six a bottle with ignorant enthusiasm. When I went up, Glyn was a remote, if never ineffectual, don with whom I shared an address. Two years later, he was nationally famous as the question-master of the TV panel game *Animal, Vegetable, Mineral*, in which distinguished archaeologists competed in identifying artefacts and fragments recovered from recondite ditches. Sir Mortimer Wheeler was the most charismatic. The first telly don to grace academia with erotic cachet, he had a cavalier moustache, an unearthly instinct for where to dig victoriously and a predator's eye for the ladies. Glyn Daniel was warily indulgent of his pulling presence.

David Wilson declined an invitation to broach my half-bottle of whisky. I opened it for George Plimpton, when he came to call. I had no soda water and there was no ice. He soon dispelled my notion that he was a lonely transatlantic stranger. Already a Harvard graduate, he let me know that he had been a member of the Hasty Pudding and Porcellian clubs, not that I had any notion of how distinguished these affiliations made him. Having made it clear that he did not lack elevated connections in King's, he sipped my spare tooth-glass dry and walked out of my door and my life.

A few years after I saw him for that second and last time, Plimpton founded the *Paris Review*, a straight-faced derivative of the *Harvard Lampoon*, in which he had had an editorial hand. The epitome of the daring young man willing to swing on any publicised trapeze, he made an ostentatious career of playing sports with those much better than himself. Merely getting into the ring with Archie Moore was an act of gallant folly. As a gentleman sportsman who ate his helpings of humble pie with a silver spoon, Plimpton tricked foolhardiness into an expression of arrogance. While taking every opportunity to acquire Corinthian kudos, he could never be accused of social climbing; there were no higher rungs for him to reach. The *Paris Review* was funded by his well-heeled friends. Its rare fame was secured by the fact that it never sold many copies. To be selected for interview might glorify the writer who was put to the question; it certainly elevated the selector, Mr Plimpton himself, into being the literary taste-master of his time. Social climbing downwards, he proved how refined his intellectual palate was by patronising the *gratin*.

Johnians were divided into Hearties and Arties, never into oiks and toffs: few ever wore the flat caps that distinguished members of the Pitt Club, a pillared outpost, so its members liked to suppose, of White's or Brooks'.

Hearties predominated in St John's on account of the Lady Margaret Boat Club, which supplied six of the members of the victorious Cambridge crew of my first year. LMBC launched thirteen crews in the bumping races, twice as many as any other college club, including First and Third Trinity. What became of Second Trinity remains a mystery.

As promptly public-spirited as Cimon the Athenian aristocrat, who dismounted from his high horse in order to pull an oar alongside *tous pollous* in a trireme, the scholarly Sullivan and Becher signed on like commoners and went down to the river to do their 'tubbing'. Trainees had to sit in a concrete stall locked to the river bank and pull an oar without getting anywhere. My only sporting show of collegiate spirit was to volunteer to play hockey. When I was selected for the second XI's away match against my father's old college, we were driven to Oxford in the usual high charabanc. We sat with our hosts all afternoon while rain blackened the waterlogged pitch. We had dark-blue tea and were then driven back to Cambridge. After I declared myself no longer available for selection, there was no loud call for me to withdraw my resignation. I do not remember talking to anyone in our team apart from someone called Ian Telfer and a tall second-year man by the name of Mike Littleboy, for whom the very attractive Joan Rowlands (later Bakewell) had an early passion.

My pigeon-hole in the Junior Combination Room was stiff with invitations to join all sorts of societies, political, recreational, dramatic, athletic, religious and ethnic (I had never before seen the word 'Majlis'). Contending versions of Christianity – SCM and CICCU – promised to redeem me, but I did not feel the vocation; nor had I any wish to seek out other Jews in Cambridge. I did play bridge several times in a school that included Peter R., a Trinity PhD student who claimed my company as if I had no right to withhold it. He had dark curly hair and a blanched complexion and a habit, in serious conversation, of thrusting his right hand deep inside the front of his trousers, where it would remain for a few seconds before he extracted it and took his perfumed fingers to his nose. His shamelessness was appalling and liberating: here was a Jew who didn't give a damn what people thought. I never sought his company, but seldom refused it.

One fine Saturday afternoon, after we had failed to find anyone else who wanted to play bridge, he suggested that we take a punt on the Cam. Once launched, Peter steered with clumsy purpose towards where a punt with two young women in it was moored.

'Which one do you want?'

'Peter, really, listen – I—'

'You can have the one with the striped hat on.'

I was looking the other way when we bumped against them.

Peter said, 'Hullo, girls, are you waiting for us by any chance?'

Maud and Gwen were teachers up from Southampton for the weekend. We accompanied them to Grantchester, where we had tea. For the return journey, Maud joined me in one punt; Gwen and Peter took the other. Maud was fair and nicely made and looked pretty enough as she sprawled amidships while I poled the punt towards The Mill. When we had disembarked, after returning to Silver Street Bridge, Peter and Gwen went off together and I took Maud back to my rooms, where we were soon kissing keenly enough for me to pause and sport my oak.

I did what she would allow me to do, top half only, and she sighed and smiled and, although she avoided meeting my tongue with hers, she settled down to have a good time. I made no serious attempt to go 'all the way', as John O'Hara put it, in *Appointment in Samarra*. It is nice to suppose that, while I took mean sensual pleasures where I could, my fidelity to Beetle was never in question. Had my school teacher been experienced, and desirous enough, would I have declined to take her to bed? In another of O'Hara's expressions, it would have depended more on whether I had a 'thing' available than on sentimental loyalty.

Maud and I met up for something to eat with Peter and Gwen, who seemed content to be together. After spaghetti in Rose Crescent, we checked in the current *Varsity* for some social occasion to attend. The only dance advertised for that night was a Caledonian Ball, in a hall adjacent to the Catholic Church. We went to change (dinner jackets and long dresses were obligatory) and then joined the kilted and tartaned company.

Inside the temporary Highlands, we stood to one side while clansmen, with upraised hands, pranced over the bright blades of claymores, if that is what they were, laid on the parquet. We spoke to no one; no one spoke to us. I suppose that, since we had paid the pipers, we danced for a while and then we left. On the way back to her hotel, I embraced Maud again, and pressed her against the evidence of my desire, which she seemed to appreciate. I suggested that she come to my rooms in St John's for breakfast before she and Gwen caught their train. After tea and cornflakes, we did some more kissing and then she looked at her watch. I took her in the bus to the station, bought a penny platform ticket and accompanied her to where Gwen was waiting and then I walked back to college.

The next time I saw Peter, he said, 'How far did you get with her?'

I cannot remember what I said; nor did I probe him for confessional boasts. I ducked further invitations to go fishing, but I did accompany him to an advertised meeting of the (ultra left-wing) Socialist Club. No cadres from the central committee were there to sign up the three postulants, who dispersed without saying anything comradely to each other. My appetite for the Red Dawn had to be sated by reading the *Daily Worker* in the Junior Combination Room, although I never contributed to Walter Holmes's fighting fund nor did I believe its story that America was using germ warfare in Korea. Along with most liberals, however, I assumed the *Manchester Guardian* to be right when it insisted that Joe McCarthy was conducting a 'witch-hunt'.

Resentment of American post-war hegemony soon led the liberal press to assume the innocence of the Rosenbergs and of Alger Hiss, Harry Dexter

White and other palpably guilty tools of Soviet intelligence. Distinguished Hollywood fugitives from McCarthy's inquisition found sympathetic refuge in England. Flourishing in the light of their presumed martyrdom, Joe Losey and Jules Dassin were later idolised by *Les Cahiers du Cinéma*. 'Julie' Dassin had directed the excellent 1948 movie, *Naked City*; Losey nothing better than *The Prowler* (1951) or more overtly red than *The Boy with Green Hair* (1948). No good liberal repeated Billy Wilder's remark about the so-called 'unfriendly witnesses' who were brought before the Senate committee and sanctified, in liberal opinion, as the (innocent) Hollywood Ten: 'Two of them were talented,' Billy said, 'the others were just unfriendly.'

I did join the Union, but lacked the nerve to speak at its debates, even though I was not impressed by the playground politicians who jostled for office on those mock-solemn, black-tied occasions: among them, Geoffrey Howe, Douglas Hurd, Percy Cradock and Tam Dalyell, who was otherwise known as 'the Turd Man'. The last, although an Old Etonian laird, liked to prove his earthy saltiness by referring to his honest agricultural labours. Many years later, I debated at the Union with Geoffrey Howe. He told that he should much have preferred to be a movie director than a Cabinet minister. Percy Cradock, who became a diplomatic sinologist, cultivated a mandarin manner even as an undergraduate. He happened to be in the university library when Mr Khrushchev was scheduled to pay it a visit. He and his companion were obliged to abandon their seats while the secret service checked for dangerous devices. Cradock was heard to say, 'What time is it by your bomb, Douglas?'

While in Fleet Street, I had been behind the scenes, however briefly, with several of the metropolitan politicos whose favours Union presidents solicited by inviting them to speak at the debates. Celebrities of all kinds were recruited: Donald Soper did his smocked, sincere, low churchy stuff and so did a Jesuit who, when proposing a motion that Divorce Was A Bad Thing (or opposing one that claimed it was not), made bold with the phrase

'Change of life means change of wife', quite as if it would rally at least a good number of his juvenile audience to the principle of lifelong fidelity. There was not yet anything shameful in the notion of growing up, or old, or even of honouring one's vows.

The Union's premises were a few yards away across St John's Street, behind the Round Church. There was a snooker table and a large library, including many chapped *en regard* Loeb editions of the classics. I read them, rather too quickly, in order to be able, with some sort of honesty, to fill in the blank spaces in Howland's form. Without the dedicated classicist's tolerance for dust, I lacked John Sullivan's systematic resolve. His lecture notes were thorough and legible; mine sporadic and hard to decipher for revisionary purposes. Bluff played no big part in John Patrick's game. Keen to shine, I was averse to sustained polishing or boning up (I used to put a gleam on my corps boots by working on the toe-caps with the handle of an obsolete tooth-brush).

When I took my verses and proses to Professor Anderson, the old Latinist covered them with red annotations. He pointed, with a quivering nib, to one of my phrases and said, 'Where did you get that from?' I said, 'I made it up, sir.' He said, 'We don't do that.' Compositions worthy of a scholar were patchworks of certified phrases; no marks for originality. I consoled myself with the thought that Catullus, if he happened to walk that way, would not have been spared Professor Anderson's querulous quill. I was more interested in ancient history than in irregular verbs, in anthropology (George Thomson's irreverent Marxism was much to my taste) than in the correct inscription of Greek accents. I continued to distribute *perispomena* and *proparoxytones* with wanton inaccuracy.

Quite early in my first year, Ian Mackay, the combative *News Chronicle* industrial correspondent, and his mistress and colleague Margaret Stewart, called on me in my rooms, perhaps as the sequel to a lunch at the Berkeley with my father. They took me to a big house somewhere behind Sidgwick

Avenue where Sunday tea was poured by a famous Cambridge *salonnière* whose name I failed to catch. There were rows of hard chairs, as if for a conference, facing a dais on which I presumed that our hostess and her familiars were going to instigate a sophisticated causerie to match Goldsworthy Lowes Dickinson's *Modern Symposium*. I sat there until the place filled, teacups were issued, and the proceedings proceeded. I have no idea who the platform performers were nor what topics they broached. I did not exchange a word with any of those who sat near me. As a social climber, I have no head for heights.

I did consider going for an audition at the élite Amateur Dramatic Club, which had its own theatre in Park Street, but I so dreaded rejection that I never even reached the door at which Peter Hall did not hesitate to knock on his way to taking command of the Cambridge stage. I signed up for the second team by joining the CU Mummers, whose presiding committee set no high hurdles for spear-carriers. The Footlights Club was famous for its satire, which (having read Addison and Juvenal and S. J. Perelman) I did not think beyond me, but again I funked an audition, lest I be asked to sing.

When I went to the offices of *Varsity*, the undergraduate newspaper, in the hope that professional experience would earn me a prompt byline, my Fleet Street credentials more alarmed than impressed the editors. I then made contact with the 'Young Writers Group', which was presided over (Cambridge brimmed with presidents of various denominations) by a Johnian called Donald Rudd. A small, clerically cut third-year man, he published the first thing of mine, apart from those anonymous contributions to the *Sunday Express*, to appear in print. It was a wan poem, in free verse, about the smoky view across London from the same Manor Fields back bedroom window which had primed the painting that earned me that third prize from Claude Rogers.

The only club I joined with confidence was the CU Bridge Club. I had learned the game by watching Irene and Cedric playing with his parents before and during the war. My skill was the small dividend of being an only child. After the war, I went with my father, on wet weekends, to Mrs Mac's club, in South Kensington, where we played for sixpence a hundred. Once I left Charterhouse, Cedric licensed me to play in the Crockford's two-shilling room. At such elevated stakes, no money passed. At the end of a rubber, one 'took' one of the opposing pair and entered his or her name, and the number of points won or lost, on a printed card. Accounts were rendered monthly. Cedric allowed me a generous 'float' of £6. If I lost more than that I had to go home.

On an early occasion, I cut Jeremy Tatham, a junior international, as my partner. After our opponents had bid a vulnerable small slam, while missing two necessary aces, Tatham made a bored discard, late in the play, which was almost immediately revealed to be a revoke. It procured no illicit trick for our side, but our opponents had the right to demand two penalty tricks and did so. As a result, they won a twenty-point rubber. I had to go home almost as soon as I had arrived. Tatham took his pipe from his mouth only to tell me that it was my fault for not saying, 'Having no more clubs, part-ner?' He was quite right; but I still rejoiced when the ascendant Jeremy Flint dropped the other Jeremy as his partner. Flint had the habit, if I cut him as partner, of reading the *Evening Standard* when, by some mischance, I rather than he happened to become declarer. When the last trick had been played, he would look up from the racing page and say, 'How did you get on?'

I was opportunist enough to drop the names of Flint and Terence Reece to Peter Swinnerton-Dyer, a young Trinity mathematics don who had played for England and reigned as the godfather of the CU Bridge Club. Exercis-ing his right to *triage*, he divided suppliant members, with drawling Old Etonian *morgue* (he was heir to a baronetcy), into 'Probables, Possibles and Awful Warnings'. Mention of my friendship with Guy Ramsey put me, pro-visionally, in the first category.

Among others in that rank I discovered Richard Bird, my prep school friend. After four superior years as a Wykehamist colleger, he had won a major scholarship in Modern Languages at Clare. We fell together as bridge partners and invited each other, alternately, to tea in our rooms. Fitzbillies, across the street from Mill Lane, where I went to Guy Lee's lectures on mornings when I woke up in time, sold very short shortbreads dipped thickly at each end in chocolate, and Chelsea buns, sticky with succulent raisins. Richard and I were among the worst losers in the bridge club, but we did well enough, often enough, in duplicate competitions to win Swinnerton-Dyer's baleful favour.

Richard had not only taken what I thought of as my place at Winchester; he had, before that, spent the war in the US. He was, in those enviable respects, what I might have been. We must have found things to talk about apart from the Acol bidding system and the gnathous anatomy of Swinnerton-Dyer, whose glistening gums gloved his teeth except for the last tenth of an inch, but our topics never included sex and had little intellectual content. A very conventional pair, we never lent each other books nor, despite Richard's linguistic scope, did we discuss going abroad.

Johnian scholars were privileged to read the long Latin grace before we all sat down to the evening meal in Hall. I had no crisis of faith before reciting '*Oculi omnium in te sperant, domine, et tu das illis cibum in tempore...*' nor in concluding '*per Christum Jesum Dominum Nostrum*'. It was nice to suppose that Jewishness was no longer of significance, to me or to others.

We had to wear gowns at lectures, when dining in Hall and whenever we went into the streets at night. To be spotted improperly dressed led to the proctors unleashing their attendant, bowler-hatted 'Bulldogs' in pursuit. College porters doubled as proctorial sidekicks in order to earn a little extra money. They were rarely zealous or fleet of foot. I was too pleased to merit a gown ever to go out without mine. However, having stayed for too many last rubbers at the bridge table, without being forearmed with a late pass, meant that I sometimes had to climb over the New Court gate. I have a coin-shaped scar in my left calf where a spike went in.

Guy Fawkes Night was a traditional occasion for festive misbehaviour. In the later 1940s, the undergraduate population had included ex-soldiers who had seen active service. Some had had access to the means for creating nostalgic explosions. Lamp-posts were uprooted and used to torpedo shop windows, for the fun of the crash, never for loot. In the 1950s, 5 November remained an inverted saturnalia during which the privileged indulged in playful vandalism, but no loud damage was done. The police suffered to have their helmets knocked off and sometimes purloined (to be returned the following day). While glass was broken and happy louts cheered, I was reminded of *Kristallnacht*, another November night, in 1938, when Nazi mobs were licensed to smash Jewish shops. During my first year, I never heard anyone use the word Jew abusively. I imagined that that kind of nonsense was forever behind me. The Provost of Guildford remained an *ex officio* figure on the panel of my superego: I wanted, at all costs, not to honour his idea of a Jew. On pub crawls, I made a habit of buying an early round, in order not to seem to have dodged the column. I bought cigarettes (Players No. 3, one and tenpence for twenty) less because I liked the smoke – the brown smell on the side of my index finger was more delectable – than in order to be equipped to pass them round. My cigarettes went on the buttery bill and were paid for by my father, unlike the copy of T. S. Eliot's *Four Quartets* that I bought at Bowes & Bowes. Alone in my happy attic, frowning to mime seriousness, I found that *Burnt Norton* emitted no evocative perfume. What were *The Dry Salvages* to me?

I tried sporting a pipe, as Sullivan did, but it was difficult to keep alight and scorched my throat. Out on pub crawls, I was impressed by Tony Becher's and Sullivan's capacity for drinking pint after pint and by their ability to get up the next morning in time for a nine o'clock lecture. Living at the top of E staircase made me wary of overfilling my bladder. To get to the lavatories, we had to go down six flights of stairs, cross the courtyard and go into the clammy canyon of the communal facilities. The Rabelaisian solution was to do as David Gore-Lloyd did during our poker games (in which one could lose as much as three shillings on a catastrophic evening): he opened my mansard window and pissed directly into the Cam.

David's family manufactured Wills Gold Flake cigarettes. Before the war, they owned a steam yacht with a crew of eight. No sort of a scholar, he was a Roman Catholic from, he indicated, an old recusant family. Until publication of the Kinsey Report, he went regularly to the Catholic church; its large, ornate black and white clock jutted over the Regent Street pavement. The discovery that almost all priests were statistically determined to have sexual outlets (Kinsey's 'scientific' term) did not torpedo David's faith, but it did precipitate a slide from ancestral credulity. No critic of the time doubted that Kinsey's 'research' had been scientific. It was unthinkable that his whole statistical apparatus could have been, as it proved, wilfully warped. Who could have guessed, in those days, that the whole exercise might have had the unacknowledged motive of seeking to normalise Kinsey's own bisexual proclivities? His allegedly scrupulous method had no place for qualitative distinctions: in Kinsey's book, when quantifiable man went into the bedroom, love was never made; quotas were filled. Robert Graves's 'meum-tuum sense' had no place in them. Thanks to Kinsey, seconded by a sprinkle of sophistry from me, David Gore-Lloyd's antique Christianity fell away. The Church lost the antique lustre, advertised with euphuistic elaboration, in *Brideshead Revisited*, which had been recently Penguinised in a tributary ten-pack of Evelyn Waugh's works.

To supplement college food, Tony Becher and I frequented the Taj Mahal, in the paved enclave, opposite St John's main gate. For two and sixpence, we ate heaped brown plates of food while looking out at the entrance to Whewell's Court, Trinity, where Wittgenstein (of whom I heard my first whisper from a young don called Renford Bambrough) had had his austere rooms before he left them to go and die, of prostate cancer, in Dr Bevan's house. As for William Whewell, the quondam Master of Trinity and an important philosopher in his day, who was he compared to his late tenant? Yet Sidney Smith had said of him, 'Science is his forte and omniscience is his foible.'

Sullivan and Becher had learned the vocabulary of the barrack room. They spoke of 'bints' and the need for a shag with a squaddy's unashamed and unselective appetite. When frustrated, Tony threatened to have 'the screaming ab-dabs'; masturbation was 'bashing your bishop', perhaps because the erect penis, plus foreskin, looks like a mitred bishop on a chess-board. Fingers were known, at vexed moments, as 'cunt-hooks'. According to Tony, 'Up your gonger!' was an Other Ranks commonplace. The recom-mended destination was, in the context, unmistakable but I have never seen the phrase reproduced in reminiscent print. If a woman had the curse, she was said to have 'the jam rags up'. National Service was a march on the wild side. I knew only one man, in my fourth year, who had actually done any fighting. He had been a tank commander in Korea. Quick thinking under Chinese fire enabled him to get his tank literally back on track and saved his crew. He received the MC but I cannot remember his name. He sang nicely in the Footlights.

Whatever Philip Larkin may have said about the cultural divide between repressed pre-1963 England and Swinging London, the 1940s and 1950s were enriched by a sexual vocabulary, and a certain common experience, that derived from National Service. Ex-sergeant Sullivan recounted how he had first got his end away, under some Liverpool pier, as the result of a 'knee-trembler' with an older girl. In the Education Corps, he widened his carnal knowledge by tumbling his sergeant-major's wife while on the move in the back of a three-hundredweight lorry. He had been sweetly surprised by the dexterity with which another older woman had climaxed their sexual bout by reaching beneath and between her legs to caress his balls. Being an officer and a gentleman may have postponed Tony Becher's *dépucelage*, but his language had lost its virginity during his thirteen weeks of 'basic training'. Tony did not do so in person until the Christmas vac of 1950, while on a holiday in South Africa. He returned to tell us about it and also about avocado pears, which none of us had ever tasted. He had picked up the habit of calling black children 'piccanins'.

Sex was neither a priority nor an obsession with Sullivan, nor did it leave a sentimental afterglow. *Mutatis mutandis*, he aped Macbeth: if 'twere done, 'twere best it be done quickly. I listened and smiled and said little. Love for, and pride in, Beetle kept me reticent. When she first came up for the weekend, we spent an anxious night in my narrow bed, with my oak sported. Had we been discovered, or betrayed, I should certainly have been sent down. I introduced her to my friends only when we happened to bump into them. She was a happy secret I was not keen to share. In her absence, I wrote her long letters and she wrote back as promptly and as unguardedly. I was smiling as soon as I saw her envelope in my pigeon-hole.

Why then did I ask Hilary Phillips to visit me in Cambridge? I went to meet her on the long platform when she arrived one Saturday morning in the spring term. She wore a garden-party hat and carried a candy-striped umbrella. I greeted her as if I were again an awkward adolescent. I doubt if I kissed her hullo; pretty as ever, those heels, that skirt, and especially the hat did not belong in Cambridge. I conducted her with more embarrassment than ostentation through the courts of St John's and up the wooden stairs to my proud garret. I fear that I invited her to come up at least partly so that I could make it clear how wide the gap now was between us.

I was eager to establish my well-read emancipation from religious belief and from what D. H. Lawrence called 'the beastly bourgeoisie'. Having recently been swept away by A. J. Ayer's *Language, Truth and Logic*, I enlightened her on the literal nonsensicality of metaphysics, which included the existence of God and the apparatus of transcendental morality. As

I offered Fitzbillies cakes and pressed her to a glistening Chelsea bun, I paraded all the jejune sophistication of a smiling intellectual bully. If my one-time darling had been more calculating, she might have smiled and sighed and offered me her lips, to start with; but she did not. My well-sourced repudiation of suburban morality made her sigh and look at her little watch.

I lacked the ruthlessness, if not quite the desire, to make a more virile assault on her than I had ever attempted in Portman Mansions. Certain that she would never do it, and not at all certain that I wanted her to, I asked her to have another Chelsea bun and stay with me that night. She declined to do either. The not wholly unwelcome effect of my rhetoric was to hasten her return to the station. Not long afterwards, I heard of her engagement to someone called Gerald.

My thespian reputation was not enhanced when I was cast in the salty part of Poseidon in a clumsy Mummers production of Jean Giraudoux's *The Trojan War Will Not Take Place*. I had no idea that the play, written in 1935, was designed as propaganda for Franco-German *rapprochement* or that Giraudoux had been an enthusiastic member of the Vichy government. Throughout that first year I was too content with Beetle to venture any bold step on the ladder to Cambridge advancement, intellectual or social. I never went to meetings of the Classical Society. No one reproached me for my sporadic attendance at lectures. Ovid wrote my report: *Video meliora proboque, deteriora sequor.*

Nevertheless, I was shocked when, during a discussion of Book Lambda of Aristotle's *Metaphysics*, Howland advised us not to bother with several chunks of text on which, *experto credite*, we should never get a question, because no one had any clear idea what they meant, perhaps not even Aristotle. Glad to be spared having to construe the inexplicable paragraphs, I was enough of a humbug to think that scholars should have been required to puzzle over them. 'Bede' did me too much honour: assuming that I was enough of a scholar, it did not occur to him, who had found things so easy, to play more literally the role of 'director of studies' and oblige me to ordered diligence.

So far as the Classical Tripos went, the Golden and Silver Ages of Greece and Rome furnished texts and cruxes enough to abbreviate any curiosity about, for instance, the Hellenistic world. After the ignominious death of the city's greatest orator, Athens was said to have had no stylist worth emulating. The rhetoric of the great Demosthenes had been directed against Alexander the Great's father, King Philip II of Macedon. He dwelt, with conspicuous disdain, on the alien provenance of the pretender who affected to be the ruler of all the Greeks. In fact, Demosthenes's style was more admirable than his character: he was a self-glorifying, sometimes corrupt, politician. In 1950, he was still depicted as a prototypical Winston Churchill, fulminating against tyranny and denouncing appeasers and collaborators, such as Aeschines and Isocrates. With the loss of its independence and its empire, Pericles's exemplary *polis* dwindled into a provincial university city under foreign patronage, first Macedonian then Roman. In the 1960s, Harold Macmillan would propose that Britain stand to Jack Kennedy's USA in the wise role that the Greeks, supposedly, had with the Romans who supplanted their place in the sun. In the early 1950s, however, Britannia appeared to retain a ruling role in the world's order. If one wanted time to stand still, Cambridge was the place to be.

V

PLAYING BRIDGE WAS my regular drug. Among those often available to make up a four was Ivan Idelson, a chess Blue, who was doing a PhD in some abstruse department of mathematics. Brown-eyed and black-haired and, I assumed, of Russian origin (he called himself Ivahn, although later in life he anglicised the pronunciation as Eye-v'n), he rented a room at 5 Jordan's Yard, a mews of decrepit terraced houses across from the side gate of St John's. I would find him wearing a claret-coloured smoking jacket and, quite often, playing Chopin on the black overstrung piano in the front room. He lived with a buxom, horsey, boss-eyed girl called Sonya. I accompanied her, because she asked me, to a point-to-point at Cottenham, a village near enough to Cambridge to be reached by bicycle. We watched the races and were spattered with mud from the loud hoofs and then we pedalled home. I went up the sagging stairs with her to the room she shared with Ivan and she told me, hugging her knees as she rocked on the bed where I was sitting, that she had taught him everything he knew about sex. I was not tempted to take the course.

One day, looking for a Saturday afternoon game of bridge, I was walking across King's Bridge and met a Leavisite research student against whom

I had played a few times. He was unavailable, he said, because his 'woman' was coming up from London. As he talked, he removed the little plastic lid from his pipe and, while it dangled on a short lace, applied a Swan Vesta match to the tamped tobacco. His frown was deepened by wanting to know something that he hoped I might be able help him with: not to put too fine a point on it, female anatomy. His woman seemed willing to go to bed with him but he was unsure how he could know exactly when, that is where, it would be right to, well, I knew what he meant. I was a little pleased to be able to tell him that, provided the female disposed herself amiably, the way in would be available to firm pressure. If he had time to consult it, I told him, there was a book called *Perfect Marriage* that carried clarifying diagrams. He sighed, put a new match to his pipe, and – between puffs – said that he would go back and read *Women in Love* again. The followers of Dr Frank Leavis, like those of Ludwig Wittgenstein, were a clan of believers whose fidelity to their leader allowed no deviant reading. D. H. Lawrence was Leavis's guide to 'mature' sexual practice. My bridge-playing friend's name was Hitchcock.

The lease of 5 Jordan's Yard was held by a shiny-headed ballistics boffin with white eyelashes over blue, unblinking eyes. John Brickell did secret government work in a laboratory on the outskirts of the city. We knew no more than that it was well paid. His tenants could do as they pleased as long as they pleased him. With no woman of his own, he relished the sight of comely Scandinavian females. Ilse (whom Brickell called 'Nutty slack'), Monika ('Monik / She's a tonic / She's Supersonic / Our Monika', according to Tony Becher) and Anna (the actor Tony White's pneumatic mistress) had only to sanction his seigneurial presence while they dressed and, preferably, undressed. Tony White was Peter Hall's regular, very handsome, leading man at the ADC. He would disappoint his director by declining to become a professional actor. In the mid-1970s, he got wind of the fact that I had portrayed him, as Dan Bradley, in *The Glittering Prizes*, but died of septicaemia, after breaking his leg in a casual football game, before he could see what I made of him. When John Sullivan was dying, in 1993, he asked me to send him the tapes of the same TV series, in which he was lightly disguised as Bill Bourne.

Swollen with bohemian tenants, 5 Jordan's Yard seemed to be held together only by its thin, papered walls. The pretty Danish Brigitte shared one of the upstairs bedrooms with Rijn Van Dyck, a Dutch research student with a charming smile and a pale, rumpled, no longer young face. A Yugoslav émigré, Poznan Mirosevic-Sorgo, lodged in another upstairs corner. Michael Jurgens, the son of a Netherlands margarine magnate, was a frequent caller. He told us that margarine was colourless until jaundiced by chemical means. He was so pale that he might have been made of it. He admired Beetle.

The narrow staircase sagged as you climbed the two steep flights to where Gordon Pask had filled the wide attic rafters with rows of batteries and valves linked by a nexus of wires to the panel from which he controlled their interplay. Gordon was small, wore a selection of old clothes, and had curly metallic hair. Of no manifest age, he had large, pale grey, unblinking eyes and unhappy teeth. It was painful to see him smile. An early pioneer in computer technology, he was said to have begun his PhD thesis with the words 'As I have said before'. His current project was the construction of a musical typewriter. Gnome and gnomic, he was at once a parody of an eccentric genius and, as his electronic innovations were to prove, the genuine article.

Gordon lived with a large, plain Communist called Elizabeth. When, after a number of years, they had a child, he referred to it as 'the gadget'. With his dwarfish other-worldliness, he seemed to have more things on his mind than he was ever going to have time to unpack. While taking breaks from assembling machinery of unfathomable complexity, featuring something called 'negative feedback', he composed elongated, dark-figured murals on the walls of the downstairs room where Ivan Idelson mooned over his piano.

John Brickell found me amusing enough to be given a seat at the Sunday lunches that he cooked and loaded onto a wide, black centrally pedestalled round table in the ground-floor room. He expressed 'be gone' to unwanted postulants merely by looking at them. His stare could have a forbidding steadiness; those on whom it was fastened rarely came back. When I told him that Beetle and I were nervous of spending another night in my rooms, he offered his kitchen floor. There was a camping mattress we could borrow. Who would ever know or care that I had not been in my Third Court garret all night?

5 Jordan's Yard became our weekend home from home. Our nights were interrupted only by Gordon Pask. He would crepitate down the yielding stairs and then appear, fuzzy-haired, in the doorway. 'Don't disturb yourselves, my dears…' Since the natural span of the day was too short for his complicated work, Gordon had a chronometry of his own: each of the days of his ten-day week lasted thirty-six hours. As a result, he sometimes needed sustenance in the early hours. He would step over us in order to take a pot of Oxford marmalade from the cupboard. He consumed several spoonsful, wincing, and then filled a glass of water with which he washed down a number of aspirin tablets shaken from a bottle in his pocket. He winced because the marmalade had found the cavities in his teeth. Aspirin was more readily accessible than dentists. When someone warned him that it was addictive, he said that, since he took fifty a day, he could confirm that they were not. Gordon was the living refutation of the notion, common in our philosophy, that one cannot feel the pain of another. You had only to look at those stumpy brown teeth to see and feel its refutation.

I neared the end of my first year at Cambridge without having made the brilliant friends whose company I might hope to enjoy for the rest of my life. I avoided loneliness with Tony Becher and John Sullivan, who entertained us with his terse Liverpudlian adventures (when his mother asked him where he was going, he would reply 'Out') and with his repertoire of bawdy lyrics. Working with a parody of scholiastic solemnity, he produced a manuscript edition of 'Eskimo Nell', complete with variant readings and pseudo-pedantic footnotes. He also knew the full text of 'The Good Ship Venus', on which the cabin boy 'stuffed his arse / with broken glass / and circumcised the skipper'.

His resourcefulness *in malis partibus* was crowned, later in a distinguished academic career, by Professor J. P. Sullivan's upward reappraisal of the work of Martial, *The Unexpected Classic*. John was an expert on sexual perversities of a rare order. His bedside reading was a fat volume of Magnus Hirschfeld's sexual aberrations. John devised an Aristophanic Greek term, *homartallelophagia*, for the pleasure, detailed in Joyce's *Ulysses*, to be derived from a man and a woman masticating the same piece of cake and passing it, in their kisses, from one mouth to the other. In trimmer style, Tony Becher devised the acronym 'Snip', to stand for 'smart new perversion'.

Tony seemed not to need to be as diligent as John. First-year mathematics required accurate concentration, not sustained library work. I do not remember seeing him reading a novel or any kind of history. He was not curious about the sexual habits of the Trobriand Islanders and took no interest in Christopher Caudwell's *Studies in a Dying Culture*, which, Sullivan advised me, tolled the end of bourgeois art. Tony expressed no political views and had no obvious devil to drive him. Had we not been billeted as neighbours, would we ever have spoken to each other? It was, however, thanks to him and Sullivan that I met Renford Bambrough who, like my friends, had rowed for LMBC. As an undergraduate, he had bumped so successfully that a Second Eight oar was hanging in his rooms.

We first encountered Renford during a pub crawl, at The Baron of Beef. In his late twenties, he was both a supervisor in Classics and an evangelical philosophical disciple of the late, but recent, Ludwig Wittgenstein. As teasing as he was earnest, he initiated us, softly, almost playfully, in the esoteric vocabulary that lifted Moral Sciences into a higher form of free-masonry. Commonplace phrases (such as 'We can never know the mind of another') acquired an arcane sense. Stiff hand gestures, derived from the Master, distinguished philosophical sheep from homespun goats. Raised eyebrows incited a man to think again, possibly, or at least to rephrase some callow truism. Renford's delivery made what he said, or did not, seem to sit in inverted commas; he rode an intellectual tandem, on which he was at once himself and a parody of what he wished to be.

Renford set an example of academic advancement that John Sullivan was determined to follow, although – unlike Tony Becher and me – John was not to be diverted from the subject that had secured his exeat from the working class. Renford was keen to make a junction between analytic philosophy and the second part of the Classical Tripos. He advocated a light-blue form of Greats, in which ancient history and philosophy, both ancient and modern, had always played a solemn part. This modest pro-posal ran up against entrenched positions, and vanities, in both faculties. Its promoter's insistent diffidence prevailed in time for me to be among the first to embark on the new course.

After a few glasses, Renford would giggle at good jokes, but he did not relish bawdy. At once young and elderly, as the precocious often are, he was already married and had two small children. His first name was John, but to be called by his middle name graced him with distinction. I never heard him answer to any other. He gave us the impression that philosophy was the kind of game that any bright person might learn to play. The first pupil from Sunderland Grammar School to win a Cambridge scholarship, Ren-ford had, like Baron Moss, been a Bevin boy during his National Service.

Working in the mines was far more dangerous than occupying Germany, but it lacked the hairy khaki glamour enjoyed by both John Sullivan and John Erickson, a small, dark historian, with a strong Hibernian accent, who told tall stories with the promise of their accuracy. Erickson had been a sergeant in whatever branch of the army was delegated to supervise transport. In the course of routine duties, he had signed a page that he hardly scanned, which was needed, along with other bumph, to authorise the departure of a train to Berlin. A few days later, he was summoned to his CO's office and told that the train he had signed for had been sold, presumably by its driver, to the East Germans and had disappeared behind the iron curtain. How did he propose to compensate the loss? Erickson blanched calmly and asked to see the copy of what bore his signature. When it was swivelled to him, scholarly attention led him to point out that he had signed only for the maintenance of 'discipline' on the train. Had there been any complaint in that regard? There had not. He saluted, turned and walked away without a dent in his wages or a bad mark on his record. Erickson promised that rolling stock often rolled, downhill as it were, into the German Democratic Republic. Post-war National Service seemed to be a matter more of keeping one's wits than of patriotic gallantry. The Korean War was too far away, and too American, to carry any practical threat.

Like Sullivan, Erickson was bent on academic escape from his native haunts. He had learned Russian while doing National Service and appeared already to be the ponderous authority who would write thorough volumes on Soviet military history. His researches led him, on one occasion, to a symposium in a camp, somewhere near Cambridge, full of Ukrainians whose nationalism he was unguarded enough to call 'Russian'. He was abruptly aware of the rage that then united his audience. He made a scampering exit, but was pursued, so he said, all the way to the gate by an angry mob, not a few of whom were likely to have been recycled SS men. John's amorous adventures were less sophisticated than his studies. His hearth-rug attempt to seduce a girl seemed to be 'almost there' when he felt a 'searing pain' in his left thigh. Convinced that his target female had stabbed him to the bone, he looked down and saw that the coffee-pot on the gas-ring was boiling over into his left-hand trouser pocket.

St John's was a large, rich college without snobbish or intellectual élites. King's and Trinity remained bastions of antique privilege, with places traditionally reserved for those with elegant connections or attractive qualities. Johnians had few common characteristics. Even the Fellows came from all over the social map and gave themselves no cabalistic airs. The astrophysicist Fred Hoyle was the only one of whom anyone in the wider world might have heard. 'Imagine the world as a cricket ball', uttered in an uncompromised Yorkshire accent, was his signature phrase. I should not have recognised him if I passed him. Professor Jopson, a ranking etymologist, was more noticeable: he always wore a beret, wheeled a bicycle and was never seen in public not wearing bicycle clips.

Our undergraduate *arbiter elegantiae* was Joe Bain, a modern linguist whose fine red hair, pinkish complexion and normative diction bestowed an air of decisive refinement. A Marlburian who had done his National Service in the RAF, Joe was an unassuming dandy who carried a posy of recondite literary references. He favoured a green corduroy jacket over a bone-buttoned yellow waistcoat. He despised my literary patron Donald Rudd, for reasons that seemed more sinister for being undisclosed. It was a small promotion to be beckoned to Joe's table in the Whim Café on a Saturday morning and to share his genial scorn for the passing trade. Although he did sport bow-ties, he abstained from Dunhill lighters, overlong, filtered cigarette holders, and the pipes of various calibres with which apes of the acting fraternity embellished themselves.

Since most people smoked in those days, an old woman found it profitable to stand all day at the top of Senate House Passage, with a tray of matches suspended from her neck. It was charitable to buy one's red-tipped Swan Vestas (deemed smarter than Bryant and May's 'safety matches') from 'Mother Matches'. Bints who smoked were taken to be more accessible than others. A girl who asked for a light was supposedly as good as yours. Hence the quip: 'Do you smoke after sex?' 'I don't know, I've never looked.'

Joe Bain advertised no sexual activity; but he was not above repeating his line about asking a girl round for a 'whisky and sofa' or offering her a 'suggestive biscuit'. An admirer of A. H. Clough's *Amours de Voyage*, he was much given to the lines 'Am I prepared to lay down my life for the British female? … Somehow, Eustace, alas, I have not felt the vocation.' *Double entendres*, such as 'a silent titter ran through the room' were very much his style. It was, however, a surprise when, eating curry at the Taj Mahal one evening after we had had a few beers at the Blue Boar, Joe's whimsy became gross. Regarded with what he took to be disapproval by a single diner, he came out with 'That old fool in the corner, *fart!*' He soon returned to decorousness, but he did indulge an abiding *faible* for disconcerting what no one yet called 'square' members of the college, by some mordant thrust, whereupon he would say, 'Sent 'er up!'

I was never sure of Joe's precise provenance, but he seemed to have some affinity with Wales. He relished the line, delivered in a Welsh accent, 'You fuck off, he said, quick as a flash, and witty too.' Joe made a whimsical class distinction between Johnians who wore bicycle clips (many did) and those who did not. Although a member of the ADC, he had no time for Peter Hall's quasi-professional company. He preferred to direct a modest Lady Margaret Players production of Alfred de Musset's *On Ne Badine Pas Avec l'Amour*. It featured a line that might have been composed in his honour: 'I should sooner be the first man in the village than the second in Rome.'

Joe liked to entertain and to be the centre of attention, but he resembled Oscar Wilde in never withholding his laughter when he found others amusing or – not quite the same thing – comic. He told me that he relished my uniquely scathing way of saying things.

'Really, Joe? What sort of things are those?'

Joe said, 'Oh … things like … hullo … and goodbye.'

He had come up a year before me and had a prefectorial air. I liked to play to his gallery. When someone said that something had 'crossed his mind', I remarked, 'Scarcely an overnight trip.' Among Joe's coterie I was slightly dismayed to find a Welsh medical student who, when we were both in Lockites, admired G. B. Shaw. He also told our dormitory the story of the man who fell asleep on the synagogue steps and woke up covered by a heavy djew. Jim, who later became my sergeant-major, remembered his Carthusian life with mortification, if only because he had been 'de-monitored' after he and a friend had decorated the pinnacle of the marquee erected for OC day with an upturned chamber pot. No doubt, he had been 'shown up' by someone eager to replace him in the house seniority. I had no memory of the events that so distressed him, nor did he ever make allusion to my tearful schoolboy request that he explain the reasons (as if there had to be any) why, all of a sudden, he and his friends had singled me out as the target of what one of them, a direct descendant of William Ewart Gladstone, called a 'Jew-bait'.

One Sunday morning, in the summer term of 1951, when I was sleeping off several rounds of mild-and-bitter philosophising with Renford Bambrough and others, there was a knock on my 'oak'. My 'sorry to bother you' visitor was Simon Raven, whom I had never seen before, yet seemed to recognise. Having been expelled from Charterhouse without being disgraced, he was now the secretary of the Cambridge OC society and had come to solicit my membership. I told him that I wanted nothing further to do with Charterhouse or Carthusians, quite as if he were the embodiment of all the proprieties that he had flouted. He said, 'I expect you're quite right' and went on his way.

I was told that the headmaster, 'Bags' Birley, who was also his housemaster, almost wept when he realised that he had no choice but to 'sack' the most delightful and comely member of Saunderites. Birley himself departed not long afterwards. Before becoming Provost of Eton, he was deputed to go to Germany in order to put the future education of that country in good hands. Since he spoke little or no German, he relied on the good offices of teachers and professors who spoke English. With their help, Birley is said to have confirmed any number of plausible ex-Nazis in their posts.

By the summer of 1951, I was all but a third of the way through my expectation of Cambridge life without having made any impression. I played too much bridge and, even there, I lacked the single-mindedness to study the higher skills of the game, even though Swinnerton-Dyer (later the Master of Trinity) circulated terse post mortems on our matches, identifying missed opportunities for squeeze play or 'master bids'. I seemed all the time to be adjacent to my contemporaries. I used the Union as a library, but rarely went to debates, where politically ambitious undergraduates, such as Hugh Thomas, delivered deutero-Churchillian orations. When in the Sixth at Charterhouse, I flinched even from reading the lesson in chapel, less because of pious reluctance than on account of the stage fright that had struck me, at my prep school, when I had had to read a passage from the Bible after running up from the beach. I seemed to be drowning in the air, like a gasping fish. The long consequence was that, while I had no reluctance to impersonate someone else on stage, or even in life, I shied from having to stand up in public and be myself.

V I

BEETLE AND I made plans to go to France during the summer. John Sullivan, who was staying up for the 'long vac term', agreed to be my beard: I was welcome to tell my parents that he and I were heading for the Continent together. My dread was that they might find out that Beetle and I meant to spend several weeks on the Riviera and, even though our trip was to be funded almost entirely from her earnings as a secretary, forbid me to go. Did they have any idea that we were lovers? I suspect that they preferred not to think about it. Even when clear of Balliol House, with my suitcase, I feared that our liaison might be reported before I had time to grow the beard that would certify Lawrencian emancipation from suburban morality.

Beetle was there, smiling, on the platform at Victoria. I looked around anxiously before embracing her. A blonde classicist called Veronica Crisp happened to be getting into the boat-train with us. I was less proud of my beautiful companion than nervous of gossip. Only when the train started was I purged of apprehension. To leave England was like escaping from one more forbidding school.

In 1944, Jean-Paul Sartre had remarked that everything that Britain had lived in pride, France had lived in shame. For a while, Frenchmen left and right deferred to '*les Anglo-Saxons*' with something like reverence. They soon got over it. By the time we landed at Dieppe, six years after the end of the war, France again stood above all for art and existentialism, *croissants*, *café au lait* and sexual liberty not easily available between British landladies' sheets. Laurence Sterne had promised, in *A Sentimental Journey*, that they 'order these things differently in France'. I was relying on it. We took the brown train from Dieppe to the Gare St Lazare close together on the slatted wooden seats in third class. It was mid-June and we were free as long as the money lasted.

The first Parisian hotel we tried refused us; so did the second; and the third. I took it personally; Beetle, who had been abroad before, did not. Toting our heavy bags, we found a room, more expensive than we could well afford, near the Madeleine. We made love there as we never had before, and many more times. I loved and I was loved, just as the Latin grammar promised; and I was happy, as I had never been before, and so, she promised me, was Beetle. Cambridge ceased to matter, but I did have my portable typewriter with me.

The next morning, we removed to the narrow Hôtel des Deux Continents in the rue Jacob in the sixth arrondissement. Across the street, a dive called L'Echelle de Jacob advertised that Léo Ferré was performing. Having no idea who he was, we failed to pay a few francs to hear a legend who ranked with Georges Brassens. We went for coffee to the Café des Deux Magots, which, the bill promised, was the '*rendezvous des intellectuels*' (many of them tourists, even in 1951). I hoped that we might fall into conversation with Jean-Paul Sartre and discover whether existentialism was a humanism and why it mattered one way or the other. The best cheap restaurant in the Latin Quarter was Raffi on the other side of the Boulevard St Germain, where thick, rare *Chateaubriands* cost us three shillings. It was worth ordering them just to hear the waitress call down the hatch, '*Deux chateaux, je commande!*'

Eliot Paul's *A Narrow Street*, about his pre-war Left Bank life, had taught me more about pre-war bohemian life in Paris than anything by Sartre, Hemingway or Scott Fitzgerald. The street in question was the rue St André des Arts. We discovered that it threaded through the Latin Quarter to the Boul' Mich, via the market where we bought the cardboard box of *choucroute garnie* that we took back to our ten shillings-a-night bedroom in the Deux Continents. We had £35 between us and we hoped to spend at least six weeks in France. Before we went to catch our charabanc to the south, I bought paints, brushes and canvases in the rue Bonaparte, where Picasso was said to have a studio.

In *Hay Fever*, Noël Coward's Jane Sefton 'in her scarlet Hispano swept out of the Place de la Concorde into the rue Boissy d'Anglas'. We left Paris, in a Phocéen Car, *en route* via Lyon to the Riviera, where Scott Fitzgerald, D. H. Lawrence, Aldous Huxley and Somerset Maugham had done their boldest work; so too Matisse, Cézanne, Dufy, Bonnard and Picasso. Our charabanc lumbered out of the Place St Sulpice at 7 a.m. It would take two days to reach Nice, first along the Route Nationale Six and then over the foothills of the Alps along the Route Napoléon. We scarcely noticed our fellow passengers as we literally shook off Paris. The bus bounced and bumped along the *pavé*, which lasted all the way to Melun. In open country, the road grew smoother but it was never more than a single lane in each direction. The plane trees that once shaded Napoleon's army on the march now served as hard buffers for French drivers whose impatience regularly hurtled them in the ditch.

Every now and again, the driver pulled up at a *relais* and called out '*Dix minutes, m'sieudames*' to offer relief to those with weak bladders. The lunchtime stop was at Saulieu, where the Hotel du Lion d'Or had a restaurant with three stars in the Michelin. Some of our fellow passengers may have eaten there; we did not. '*Un de ces jours,*' someone said; we doubted it. The bus arrived at Lyon at nightfall. We were deposited at a tall, gaunt hotel not far from the station. Our room might have served as a set for Jean Anouilh's *Point of Departure* (which we had seen, with Mai Zetterling wearing nothing but a silk slip), but the bed was a bed. The *cabinet* was a hole in the ribbed enamel floor in a cupboard on the half-landing. Squares of old newsprint were spiked on a nail, the only recourse after a necessary squat.

The ride over the knees of the Alps was accompanied by the long blare of our driver's klaxon. We never wondered about the state of the bus's brakes or what would happen if an equally large vehicle was coming down the hill we were climbing or up the narrow mountain road as we hurtled down, a low wall between us and the ravine below. Nothing bad could happen to us. France was spread out for our pleasure. '*LIBÉREZ HENRI MARTIN*' was whitewashed on several bridges that crossed our route, but what did his incarceration have to do with us? The vanity of victory excused us from concern with the fate of a Communist jailed for campaigning against attempts to keep Indochina French.

We arrived at the bus terminal in Nice late in the evening. Touts offered us their hotels. A grey-haired woman was offering a room and breakfast for five hundred (old) francs; less than ten shillings. She led us to a horse-drawn *calèche* and we rode, in nervous style – how much was the journey going to cost us? – to her house in the suburbs. The fare was fair enough. The room proved airy and clean. It was easy, and cheap, to be happy.

We took an early-morning bus from near the flower market in Nice to St Tropez. In mid-June, it was still an uncrowded fishing village. We found a room in a little *pension* called Au Bout du Monde. It had a red-tiled floor and two single beds, of which we used one. We bought a picnic (bread, ham, one banana, a packet of *Petit beurre* biscuits) and went to the beach. I told Beetle that I had the kind of skin that never burned. She claimed that she did too. So we lay under the Mediterranean sun for several bright hours. By evening we were cooked raw. Somehow we still made love.

One of Beetle's friends in the London University history faculty, a German refugee who later committed suicide, had recommended a nearby hill village called Ramatuelle. After a couple of days, we set off, in the *midi* sun, toting our luggage, to walk eleven hot kilometres to Ramatuelle. We were not far out of St Trop, where the cork forest began, before our unbending sandals had blistering consequences. We marched on until our blisters seemed to have blisters. A French army jeep passed, stopped and backed up. Two camouflaged soldiers gestured to us to put our things in the back and drove us past the olive trees and the vineyards to Ramatuelle. '*Merci, merci!*' '*De rien! Bonnes vacances!*'

Ramatuelle carried a turban of white ramparts on the top of a small hill. The one café had a vine trellised over its wide, deep terrace. Across the polygonal *place* was the Alimentation Générale. Women were taking water in tall metal jugs from two spigots in a round fountain under the shadowed lee of the church. Behind it, the walls of the town were pierced by a dark arch. We asked in the café where we might find a room. '*Allez chez la mère Isnard; sait-on jamais.*' We walked through the arch and along the narrow, cool, curve of the alley to where Madame Isnard had her several houses. All she could offer was an attic bedroom and the kitchen below it at five thousand francs a week, just over four of our precious pounds. The bed was big and low. The toilet was in the next house, not far away. The kitchen had no running water. Madame Isnard's daughter Marcelle lent us two tall tin jugs in which to bring water from the fountain. We never discovered what had happened to Monsieur Isnard.

At the Alimentation Générale, the one-toothed lady smiled on us and mounted four fresh eggs in a cone of newspaper. Tomatoes, olives, tinned sardines, potatoes, bread, milk, tea, *Vache Qui Rit* cheese furnished our larder. Our extravagances were *Ambre Solaire* and mineral water. Everyone knew what Continental water did to people. The *consigne* on the glass bottles was worth a few *sous* when we took them back. We kept the butter fresh by floating it in a foil dinghy on the zinc water tank in the cupboard over the kitchen basin. I topped it up daily from the fountain.

In the mornings I sat at the kitchen table and typed what was intended to be my first novel on my Olivetti portable. The hero's name, like that in *Of Human Bondage*, was Philip. I cannot remember what his last name was; it must have been vaguely Jewish, but not foreign. I wrote without flourish. Maugham and Fleet Street led me to keep things simple. Philip was and was not me. He went to a public school that I think I called Greyfriars and he was, like Maugham's club-footed alter ego, lonely and misunderstood. My Philip's lameness was that he was a Jew. I cannot recall precisely what happened to him or whether I got sufficiently far for him to be liberated from his solitude by love.

What did Beetle do while I clicked at my flimsy pages? A writer relies on the tact and patience of the woman he lives with. She promised me, when I handed her the morning's work, that it was going well. At lunchtime, we had fried eggs, beans and sauté potatoes, and then we went to bed. We made love and we slept and then we walked to one of the two nearby beaches. The more convenient was Escalet, where there were rocks and other people. A blond Swede sunned himself naked on a tall rock under the burned-out villa that we dreamed of being rich enough to buy. We were too timid to take off our swimsuits at Escalet, but one day the Swede called down to us, quite as if we were naked, 'Adam and Eve, Adam and Eve!'

We had to walk an extra three or four kilometres to reach the long, empty, sun-blanched beach at Pampelonne, where – seven years before – the Americans had landed in strength on their way to Berlin. There we could swim naked in an empty sea and lie on the deserted sand, under a gleam of *Ambre Solaire*, and read our Penguin *Anna Karenina* and *The Charterhouse of Parma*. Oh, to be a modern Fabrizio del Dongo! One afternoon, a party of French people came onto the beach several hundred metres from us. I was British enough immediately to pull on my swimming trunks. '*Bougez pas!*' one of them called. '*Nous sommes aussi des naturistes!*' A decade later, Pampelonne became the first nudist beach on the Côte d'Azur. Sex-starved Anglo-Saxons came to get their first *plein air* sight of brazen breasts.

On the road back to Ramatuelle, we knew we were halfway when we passed the shuttered pink house that I called 'Eyeless in Gaza', thinking more of Aldous Huxley than of John Milton. My thickening beard was partly in homage to Mr Gumbril in *Antic Hay*. The days passed, and the nights. We could not afford to go out to a meal, although the village artist recommended the Auberge de l'Ancre, a kilometre along the road through the olive orchards. It was worth a visit if we wanted something '*un tout petit peu différent*'. The implication seemed to be that the company was louche, perhaps orgiastic. We did walk out to have a look at the place one evening. I stopped and pissed by the roadside, like a Frenchman. Beetle had never seen anyone do that before.

I even bought a beret. I had no idea that such headgear had been a distinguishing mark of the Vichy *Milice*. Our conviviality was limited to an occasional coffee under the wide vine of the café in the square. One evening, a party of English smarties, who had parked their open Ford Consul by the communal fountain, asked us where we were staying. I said, 'Here.' One of them said, 'What do you find to do?'

We hardly spoke to anyone else during our weeks in Ramatuelle. The exception was a *soignée* Swiss woman, in her later twenties, who was also staying *chez* Madame Isnard. Isabelle had unblemished red fingernails and dressed to go nowhere as if it were a very chic destination. She was pleased to tell us that she was a *speakerine* on *Télévision Suisse Romande*. She had come to Ramatuelle to get away from publicity. She was in retreat in order to decide whether or not to marry a rich older man. Nothing seemed more grotesque than making a decision about, as we presumed, whether you loved someone or not.

Jean-Baptiste, the village Cézanne, who invited us to see his nice paintings of fruit and flowers, called our Swiss neighbour 'Isabeau'. Knowing little French history, I took this to be his own sarcastic invention. *La Suissesse* left after a few days without disclosing her decision. Two years later, I wrote a short story entitled 'The Lacquer Set' featuring Isabeau and her immaculate fingernails. It was accepted for publication by Peter Green, who had been appointed editor of a compendium which was to be called *The Book of the Year*. The publisher went broke before my story could appear. Peter and I have remained close, if often literally distant, friends ever since.

Beetle and I decided to do the romantic thing and have a midnight swim under the new moon. We walked the silvered road to Pampelonne and turned down through the vineyards, unseen dogs barking, to the long beach. We hesitated and then plunged in, and out, and ran towards our towels and then preferred each other and made love on the shining shingle. When we had finished, our wet skins were badged with the ocean's small change. I may have quoted Ezra Pound's line about 'fish-scale roofs'. The excursion was unforgettable; but we did not feel the vocation to repeat it. On the Quatorze Juillet, we danced in the village square and Beetle cried and when I asked her why she said, 'Because I'm so happy.' As our tally of days dwindled into single figures, I realised that I would never complete the sad complement of Philip's schooldays nor achieve his Lawrencian liberation from woeful chastity. With less than a week left, I had accumulated a hundred and some pages, but I was too conscious of their gaucheries to believe that I should ever return to them.

Then I remembered that Noël Coward claimed to have written *Hay Fever* in three days. If he could do it, so could I. My play was called *With This Ring* and the main character was called Tynan, a tribute, no doubt, to the precocious Ken, who was already the tyrant of Shaftesbury Avenue. Mr Maugham was right; if you had a facility for dialogue, you needed only to take dictation from the voices in your head. When we boarded the sad train back to Paris, I had the eighty and some pages of a finished play in my luggage.

We stayed our last sad, happy nights together at the Hôtel des Etats Unis on the Boulevard Montparnasse. I hunted adjacent shops for a present nice enough to sweeten the lies I was going to tell my parents about the weeks I had spent, somewhere or other, conning Virgil with John Patrick Sullivan. On our last evening, I persuaded Beetle to come to Le Jockey, a nightclub where there were girls with naked breasts. She did not seem to enjoy it all that much.

To arrive back in England was a return to childhood. I was spineless enough to be less distressed by separation from Beetle than nervous of being discovered to have been happy. I meant my black beard to be the bristling announcement to Manor Fields that I was now a grown-up writer. I gave my parents a nice glazed dish with a green bird in the middle that I told them came from the Boulevard Montparnasse where John and I had stayed. They asked few questions about where else we had been. It would be nice to suppose that it pleased them to think of me having a good time.

Before my beard was removed, as my parents insisted, Jack Piesse wanted to come and see it. Bronzed from the English summer sun, he asked me to open my shirt so that we could compare the depth of our tans. He laughed and, more with a gesture than any actual physical contact, seemed to embrace me. The scene remains in my mind like the prelude to something that never, in fact, happened. I had a sense, nothing more, that he would not have been as effusive, in a manly way, if Margaret had been there. Since my beard grew in thick curls under my jaw and was quite prickly, I was not very sorry to be shorn. A petty Samson, not eyeless, in Putney not Gaza, I was deprived of my badge of virile independence. At the same time, I was glad enough of my success in avoiding detection to resume life in Balliol House with furtive relief.

VII

THERE WAS TIME, before the autumn term, to take my new play to a meeting of the Alumni Dramatic Society. Thanks to the enthusiasm of Jackie Weiss, the company agreed to stage *With This Ring* before I went back up to Cambridge in early October. I was confident enough, among Jews, both to direct the play and to take the leading role. I also supplied the paintings (one of the pink house we had called *Eyeless in Gaza*, others of Ramatuelle) with which we decked the set. It was easier, and more enjoyable, to be the first man in St John's Wood than the umpteenth in Cambridge. Synagogue members and friends came to the play in generous numbers and laughed at my jokes. The plot of the piece escapes the lucky dip of memory. I do recall one line, in which someone said, 'He chased her all through the Olympic games and she fell at the last hurdle' and another, concerning a divorce case, in which the plaintiff was proud to announce, 'The judge said he'd never been so shocked.'

I never imagined that any critic would trek to Westbourne Grove for an amateur production, but *With This Ring* received a half-column review in *The Stage*. It congratulated the author on his wit and on his energetic direction, but remarked that he had '*walked backwards*' on stage. How was I to know that there was anything anomalous in such a move? When the play's brief run was over, I packed my trunk to go back to Cambridge. Beetle found a job as secretary to a freelance journalist, Leonard Rule, who lived near Abbey Road and was sure that the future of mankind depended on nuclear energy. He paid her £8 a week. Her duties included walking his dog in Abbey Road.

My scholar's privileges no longer secured me rooms in college. I was allotted 'licensed digs', complete with chapel-going landlords, not far away, behind the Round Church and the Union, in Park Street. The Amateur Dramatic Club had its exclusive premises further down the same street. Tony Becher and John Sullivan had also been evicted from college, but Tony was immediately at odds with the landlord of the digs to which he had been assigned. His report of their altercation concluded:

Landlord: 'I'll tell yer chutor.'

Tony: 'I'm going to see him myself.'

Landlord: 'I'll be there before ya.'

The matter was resolved by Tony being offered a double set of spare rooms in college. Asked with whom he would like to share, he chose Sullivan. That evening, I went into Hall and sat deliberately alone, several places from where Joe Bain and Pat Hutton (a handsome, always smiling Old Wykehamist) and other 'arties' were grouped. Sensing that they were talking about me, I assumed that they were rejoicing in my ostracism by Becher and Sullivan. Carthusian experience has always disposed me to believe that I may at any moment be deemed a pariah. Suddenly, with a concert of cutlery, the company shifted down the long table towards me.

Chris Stephens said, 'You've written a play, do we gather?'

I said, 'How the hell do you know that?'

My despicable fear was that someone had discovered, and would spread the word, that *With This Ring* had been staged by a group from the Liberal Jewish synagogue.

'It was reviewed, wasn't it? In *The Stage*. Not bad. At all.'

I found myself all at once an accredited member of what its members called 'the Gaiety'. There was no overt homosexual implication. The Gaiety's camp style distinguished it from the Hearties, who regarded theatricals as effete, if not necessarily 'like that'. A founder member, who had gone down by the time I took my place in the company, had been notoriously and unashamedly queer. Joe Bain told of how Mike H. had picked up a paratrooper in The Baron of Beef one evening and came to collect his porridge the following morning twirling a crimson beret on one upraised finger.

In our day, H's outrageousness was echoed only by John Hargreaves, a tall, blanched, Yorkshireman. His long, square-shouldered black overcoat might have been seconded from some undertaker's wardrobe. It gave him the funereal allure of a corvine priest. His terse loquaciousness presaged the reproduction Yorkshire of Alan Bennett. In our first year, Hargreaves's air of mordant difference made him the target of derision from the louder members of the Lady Margaret Boat Club. Some of them, in a translated Oxonian spirit, threatened to debag him and dump him in the Cam.

At the outset of our second year, Hargreaves pinned a pronunciamento on the Junior Combination Room noticeboard. Headed 'To Whom It May Concern', it declared that, having been menaced with physical assault by a posse of the less savoury members of the college, Mr John Hargreaves had taken the precaution of arming himself with a swordstick. Should anyone lay so much as one finger on him, he would not hesitate to run him through. Hargreaves was a performance artist who never appeared on any Cambridge stage. Wherever he happened to be was his theatre. His catchphrase, uttered with exaggerated tykishness, was 'very beautiful and very sad'. Whether he was practically gay, who knows? Another of his favourite sayings was, 'The jewels I lavished on that boy!' I never saw him after he had left St John's. One rumour has it that he later became the deputy chief constable of Yorkshire; another that he contracted leprosy and literally fell to pieces.

Joe Bain, who was now sporting a gold-topped stick, needed no sword to enforce his modest superiority. Having come up for a fourth year, he was studying for a 'Dip. Ed.' (Diploma of Education) before embarking on a teaching career, first at Stowe, then as sixth-form master at Winchester. Unlike Tony Becher, Joe preferred arcane obscenities. The most memorable was of the Frenchwoman (it might have been Colette's Léah) who said to her young lover '*Doucement, doucement*' and then – with a tolerant sigh – '*Trop tard!*' The little phrase proved useful many years later: it supplied a succinct summary of the action in Ian McEwan's *On Chesil Beach* when I came to write an essay about a novelette on which Karl Miller, among other pundits, had lavished contestable superlatives.

In 1950s Cambridge, love and marriage were said, by both Frank Sinatra and Frank Leavis, in their different ways, to go together like a horse and carriage. There was fierce competition (from which I was happily exempt) for female favours, however rationed. The Lady Margaret Players held occasional readings to which females were invited. The most welcome was the beautiful Joan Rowlands, who was soon linked, somewhat permanently, with Michael Bakewell. On one occasion, organised by Harold Cannon, there was a shortage of texts of whatever Ben Jonson piece had been selected. Some resourceful performer equipped himself with a folio edition from the college library. Cued to enunciate a line that, in his antique text with its tall 's' was easy to misread, he pronounced it 'wind-fucker'. Harold Cannon, a solid person, glanced in shame at Joan and said, 'SUCK 'er, you fool.'

Soon after my enrolment as an accredited member of the Gaiety, Donald Rudd, who had printed my poem in the Young Writers' Group magazine, asked me to enter my play for the competition its new editor, Peter Firth, was running. The prize was a week's run on the ADC stage. Rudd told me, in an excess of candour, that Peter would be grateful if I submitted *With This Ring*, because there had been so few entries. I had no doubt that a comedy about a suburban romance, in which a girl not wholly unlike Hilary

Phillips was the put-upon bride, would never win prizes in the Cambridge theatre commanded, not to say commandeered, by Peter Wood and Peter Hall. If genius is certified by taking infinite pains, Hall showed early signs of it. When directing *As You Like It*, he took care to insist that any male actor costumed in tight breeches should wear a jockstrap. Folklore promises that a voice from the back called out, 'Does that include those with small parts?'

After Donald Rudd reported my reluctance to be an also-ran, Peter Firth sought me out to say that, if I delivered my play to what he conceded might well be a gentle execution, he would make sure that something appreciative was said about it in *Varsity*. I am surprised, looking back, that I had a copy of *With This Ring* in my narrow Park Street digs, but I gave it to Firth, with no hope of preferment. As a result, those three days in Ramatuelle during which I wrote my first play turned out to be cardinal in my life.

When the winner was announced, it was Hugh Thomas. His play, *Some Talk of Angels*, was precociously calculated to procure the prize. A fantasy in the style of Christopher Fry's *The Lady's Not For Burning*, it was set in a modern, still independent Venice, quite as if Ludovico Manin had never thrown his ring into the Adriatic and surrendered his city to Napoleon. Since *Some Talk of Angels* took place soon before the Second World War, there was opportunity for farcical portrayals of strutting Fascists and supercilious Nazis without any need for references to their later, less laughable activities. In the first years of the 1950s, Cambridge was a *repêchage* of the *bon vieux temps* in which foreigners were comic and Britain retained dominion over palm and pine (the University Appointments Board was still on the look-out for likely district officers).

We continued to live in the era of ration books, utility furniture and national indebtedness. The return of Winston Churchill to 10 Downing Street, in 1951, primed the illusion that the old gentleman (whom the left denounced as a 'war-monger') could restore Britain to what it was when Evelyn Waugh first visited Brideshead. Hugh Thomas's Waugh-like penchant for grandiloquence was symptomatic of the nostalgia that seldom dared to speak its full name. In the bipartisan spirit known as Butskellism, the ascendant Hugh Thomas reconciled patrician tones with socialist affiliation. As President of the Union, he became acquainted with Hugh Gaitskell, the new leader of the Labour Party.

In 1956, after resigning from the Foreign Office in protest at Eden's Suez adventure, Hugh was given an inside track to stand as the unsuccessful Labour Party candidate for Ruislip. He was then alerted, by James MacGibbon, to the fact that a reliable history of the Spanish Civil War had yet to be written. His pioneering, nicely balanced account was published in 1961 and has been revised several times since. In recent years, while remaining a Hispanic pundit, he has swung as far to the right as an ermined pendulum well can.

Peter Firth suggested that I audition for the part of the American ambassador to the Serene Republic. In Yankee guise, I was not in the least nervous. My Carthusian accent might as well have been an affectation and American my natural style. I wrung enough laughs from the selectors, feet up in the stalls, to imagine that my New York self was a shoo-in for the part. They thanked me and promised that they would 'let me know'.

A few days later, I was approached in Park Street, as I left my pinched digs, by the tall Toby Robertson, one of the auditioning panel. It was a sunny afternoon in early November. He said, 'Oh, Raphael ... I was, um, meaning to get in touch with you.'

'Really?' I said. 'And why would that be?'

Robertson said, 'You did by far the best audition for the Yank, by far. We all thought so.'

I said nothing; quite eloquently, I thought.

'Don't take it personally, will you? But we finally concluded that, good as you were, the part needed an experienced actor. So ... we've plumped for Peter Firth.'

I said nothing, again.

Robertson said, 'I hope you'll come and see the play.' I looked at him, as I had at George Turner when he denied me Oxford, and did not trust myself to speak without anger or tears, or both. I sniffed at the tall, fair, prefectorial prig and then I walked to Jordan's Yard, hoping there might be a bridge game that night. Over thirty years later, when Toby had become a shiny, bald character actor, he had a smallish part in a radio piece of mine, *The Daedalus Dimension*, which took place in ancient and modern Crete. I was pitilessly considerate in my brief comments on his performance.

Hugh Thomas's triumph occasioned the epiphany of Mark Boxer, freshest of freshmen. Mark designed a primary-colourful, unrealistic set. His Venice *à la mode* was a three-dimensional Mondrian. Boxer's transatlantically sourced, unEnglish chic announced the end of the austere spirit that had accompanied rationing and National Service. No one was sure where Master Boxer had come from; but there was no doubt that he had arrived, or that he was going places. He announced himself, in the Whim café and the Copper Kettle and wherever else the *gratin* queued for coffee and doughnuts, by the shrill reach of his greetings. Everyone wondered where he acquired those slim, dark, over-long jackets, single slit at the back, extra bone button on the cuff. With his blanched, narrow face and springing dark hair, he looked like a pen-and-ink caricature of an Edwardian masher. Poised between cad and dandy, he impersonated what Stephen Potter typified as a master of 'One-Upmanship'. Mark soon epitomised Cambridge smartness. He did as little as possible as well as it could possibly be done.

I presumed, from his freshness, that Boxer had spent the war in the US. He was, in fact, at Berkhamsted, a mundane, but co-educational, English boarding school. His knowledge of American magazine layout and Madison Avenue advertising techniques indicated a prescient sense of the style that would soon dominate London. Ken Tynan had been similarly quick to spot the imminent Americanisation of the post-war world. Ken's punctual, puncturing theatrical reviews, in the *Evening Standard* and then in *The Observer*, were spiced with quips that smacked of George S. Kaufman, Alexander Woollcott and George Jean Nathan. Ken was at no marked pains to credit their readily convertible coinage. His early book *He Who Plays the King* embraced a reference to the brief stage career in which he was cast as the Player King to Alec Guinness's Prince, to no loud acclaim. Was he aware of John Mason Brown's line in which it was said of some unhappy actor, 'He played the king as if someone had just played the ace'? John Mason Brown was a New York drama critic regularly featured on the BBC radio's *Transatlantic Quiz*, which was broadcast seemingly live, with the realistic waxing and waning of voices (brilliantly imitated, in due season, by Kingsley Amis) as they sighed back and forth on the transatlantic cable. Lionel Hale was quizmaster in London, Alistair (*ci-devant* Alfred) Cooke in New York.

Mark Boxer hid his origins in the open; the unique, he seemed to suggest, needed no precise provenance. He appeared to have the key to some atavistic box of tricks, dodgy and delicious and not without a false bottom. The shrill laugh suggested bisexuality, but made no promises. Mark was never boring because he made no effort to entertain; other people were there to entertain him. The shriek of his greeting, or its lack, told them whether they were in or out. We were never friends, but Mark did look at me, and I at him, as if we had some unspoken affinity: it suggested that we were both getting away with (and from) something, and I was pretty sure what it was. The last time I saw him, shortly before he died, of a brain tumour in 1988, it was at the wheel of his car in the Cromwell Road. In a characteristic show of brave egotism, he got out of his car, left the door open, and came to embrace me, unhurriedly, while the traffic complained.

Typical of Boxer's minimalism was the early resection of his first name, by a single letter. After Cambridge, he soon become Marc the *Tatler* cartoonist, later the first editor of the *Sunday Times* colour magazine, and – second time around the marital merry-go-round – the husband of elegant

Anna Ford, the ladylike newscaster. His advent as editor of Cambridge's literary magazine *Granta*, which Leavisites such as Karl Miller had made serious to the point of tractarian, converted that publication into something more like Oxford's *Isis*, in which Ken Tynan had figured as an 'Isis idol'.

Karl had established himself, very soon after he arrived at Downing, as the ruling literary pundit. Solemn and laconic, he was wise enough to offer no evidence of being either a poet or a candidate for prosaic publication. Brevity was all his wit. He avoided being judged by sitting in prompt, often negative, judgement on others. Once instated as editor of *Granta*, he was Cambridge's literary centurion: he bid some come; others he waved away to cheap prints such as *Varsity*. Those whom he selected were liege men who did not fail to endorse the accuracy of his taste. Nor did he lack female acolytes such as the 'giggling armful' Claire Delavenay, who later chose Nick Tomalin as a likelier, perhaps comelier, candidate for clever matrimony.

Nick became President of the Union and was soon a boy wonder on Fleet Street. He was one of the first English journalists to report on the Vietnam War. His article 'Zapping Charlie Cong' made such an impact that, a few years later, in 1973, Harry Evans, then editor of the *Sunday Times*, persuaded him to cover the war that had just broken out between Israel and the Arabs. Nick was killed on the Golan Heights by a Syrian heat-seeking missile, which struck the vehicle in which he was sitting while others took a road-side leak. Harry then appointed Claire literary editor of the *Sunday Times*.

Dressing self-importance as an austere, lifelong duty, the mature Karl Miller assumed the sighing supremacy of the man who cut and distrib-uted laurels. He gave the rudiments of a pulpit to the various editorial chairs that he occupied as the *pontifex maximus* of British letters. He saved and he damned and there was, as the Aberdonian preacher said to Byron, 'No hope for them as laughs.' Karl's capacity for sitting in judgement was unlimited. When, in due time, he reviewed *The Double Helix*, James Wat-son's account of his and Crick's Nobel Prize-winning discovery, with a little unacknowledged help from Rosalind Franklin, of the structure of DNA, Miller confessed that he was unqualified to evaluate the description of their activities in the laboratory. He was, however, able to confirm the accuracy of the account of the scientists' lunches in the courtyard of the Eagle (a Cambridge pub adjacent to the Cavendish), since he had eaten Scotch eggs there himself during the same period.

Karl's public sponsor was Noel Annan, the tall, bald young Provost of King's who had secured his own early elevation to high places by joining himself, closely, to experienced climbers. Annan did little significant academic work, but he was the pundit to consult, and impress, when it came to the North Face of English academic ascendancy. He advised a friend of mine, whose father was a well-known publisher, to abandon the study of Geography – of all things! – before it damaged her prospects beyond repair. After Dear Noel introduced her to Edmund Leach, she went on to achieve the smart distinction of a First in Anthropology.

As Annan's protégé at King's, Boxer gave off a licensed whiff of sulphur. His dark, unblinking glance promised access to diabolical improprieties. Had some latter-day Lord Queensbury accused him of 'posing as a sodomite', his shrillest laugh might well have welcomed the soft impeachment; secret straightness was more to be concealed than his aptitude for outrage. Narcissism was a convenient posture; it required the pursuit of nothing deeper than a polished surface in which to verify his allure. His cartoons enhanced the fame of those whom they lampooned. The leading Cambridge actress, who had a clever voice, very short legs and a plain, bloodless face, was caricatured as a sex symbol captioned 'Dudy Foulds, the well-known animal lover'. While there were several more attractive females in the register (Margaret Baron in particular), Dudy's primacy was crowned, her illusions of stardom sustained, by Marc's barbed generosity. There was no more desirable promotion than to figure in his pillory. I was not yet among those who did so, but when he became editor of *Granta* in the following year, I made bold to submit a short story about a Chelsea novelist who blamed his infidelities on the obstinate fidelity of his wife. Mark said he loved it and promised to publish (and illustrate) it.

In the issue previous to the one in which my story was to appear he printed a poem in which God was portrayed by one Stephen de Houghton as a tired old man, incapable of managing his unruly creation. The poem, no more than a naughty exercise, was deemed blasphemous by the university authorities. Despite a plea in mitigation by Morgan Forster, who was permanently encased in King's and whose reputation as our greatest living novelist became more and more unassailable as the decades passed during which he published few books and no fiction at all, the Vice-Chancellor ordained that Mark be sent down. Not since Shelley was dismissed from Oxford, for publishing a provocative squib entitled *The Necessity of Atheism*, had either of the great universities acted with such draconian piety.

Theatrical and literary Cambridge staged a show of indignation. Boxer became the smartest martyr ever to be sentenced to catch the London train. Blasphemy was established as a staging post on the way to fame, for the poem's publisher, if not for the poet. Thanks to Noel Annan's emollient diplomacy, Mark's sentence was reduced, at the last moment, to precisely one week's rustication during May Week. This was intended to ensure that he could play no pseudo-messianic part in the college's May Ball.

Despite the negotiated brevity of his imposed absence, Boxer's departure was accompanied by a procession of his supporters, complete with pipes and drums, down King's Parade all the way to Cambridge station. It was as close to a political demonstration as Cambridge ever came during my time there. I watched, from the window of the Copper Kettle in King's Parade. The mock funeral was organised by David Stone, a square-jawed boxing blue, whose devotion was as superfluous to Mark's redemption as it was ruinous to his own prospects. Having dived in to save someone in no danger of drowning, Stone neglected to turn up several of his Tripos papers, failed his exams and was sent down without exciting any show of reciprocal solidarity. He became the manager of a group of south London local newspapers. Soon after I had come down, I met him outside Stamford Bridge. He offered me a job writing up Chelsea FC's home matches. He died soon afterwards.

In their officious determination to make an example of Mark, the university authorities forgot that May Balls went on into the early hours. Since his period of exclusion ended on the stroke of midnight, the resurgent exile was within his swiftly claimed rights to make a spritzy entrance while revellers and their girls were still doing the valeta and whatever other dances Acker Bilk or Nat Temple and his orchestra were there to purvey. The small, lasting consequence of Mark's brief, not very bruising fall from grace was that he was barred from resuming the editorial chair of *Granta*, to which Karl Miller was promptly restored. Shortly afterwards, he informed me that my short story was not suitable for publication.

VIII

TONY BECHER AND I went to the last public lectures given by 'Bertie' Russell in Mill Lane. In all eyes but his own, he had been superseded, as the emblematic great philosopher, by his quondam pupil Wittgenstein. The biggest lecture room was thronged beyond its large capacity. Microphones had been rigged to carry the great man's words to the frustrated crowd outside. Not flattered to be viewed as the paragon of intellectual antiques, Russell regarded us with baleful hauteur. After delivering his lecture, with Whiggish precision, he said, 'I suspect that some people have come here for the wrong reasons. Accordingly, next week's lecture will be twice as difficult.' I have never again heard the word 'accordingly' used in colloquial speech. Tony and I returned, early, for the more difficult second lecture. As Russell may have calculated, it attracted a greater audience than the first.

My appetite for the new philosophy was excited by the notion that, by demystifying language, it would puncture prophetic pretentiousness and render void the confident Christian promise that He would come again. Religion and ideology would cease to sanction the forces of reaction. The existence of God could not be disproved, but His dominion could be shown to be superfluous to any useful explanation of the world (as 'phlogiston' was to combustion). The Jews, I liked to presume, would lose their millennial miasma.

In due time, Ayer's 'Verification Principle' was shown to be an unreliable measure of the truth of a proposition, not least because it could not itself be verified; but I was quick to assimilate it into my idea of fiction. I have never quite relinquished the idea that whatever was said in a novel should, in principle, be available to the senses: dialogue and accurate description, even of imaginary events, allow the reader to impersonate experience and to assess the honesty, if not the truth, of a story. Nouns and verbs are good, adverbs and adjectives suspect; speech is audible and plausible, or not; the stream of consciousness carries too much mud and too much confectionery.

Renford Bambrough's recommendation of Karl Popper's *The Open Society and Its Enemies* chimed sweetly with my appetite for iconoclasm. During a wartime professorship in New Zealand, Popper had learned ancient Greek in order to be sure that he fully understood what Plato meant to say, the better to dismantle his political thought. His diligence did not inoculate him against accusations, by prim classicists, of having misconstrued the original text. It was overenthusiastic to blame antique sources for unfortunate events in the present century. Master Popper could be forgiven for denouncing modern ideologues, but to arraign Plato, as the *fons et origo* of totalitarianism, was tantamount to blasphemy. Popper's polemic opened a second front against both Friedrich Hegel and his nemesis Karl Marx. Schopenhauer was cited to back the case against the prolific Hegel, one German against another. It was a relief to be told that Hegel, the voluminous trimmer, was not worth reading. As for Heidegger, did he merit so much as a mention among philosophy's guilty men?

Popper, like Wittgenstein, made no direct reference to what was later labelled 'the Holocaust'. Philosophical 'systems' in general were ripe for disparagement; but in the 1950s, no proper noun had yet been allotted to the systematic extermination of six million Jews, on a warrant primed by the Catholic Church and seconded by Martin Luther and, by implication, Karl Marx, in his reference to the Jews as a race of 'hucksters'. Of Jewish origin, Popper had been raised as a Protestant. Agnosticism allowed him, as if in accordance with a universal scientific rule, to discount all religious doctrines and vanities. The only respectable alternative to 'holistic' ideologies of all kinds was 'piecemeal social engineering'. Open societies should rectify their flaws in a case-by-case, consensual manner. The greatest treason of the clerks was to seek to cook humanity's books in line with *a priori* recipes.

After the war Popper was translated to a professorship at the London School of Economics. He became *persona non grata* in Wittgensteinian circles, as a consequence of a notorious fracas at the Moral Sciences Club in Richard Braithwaite's rooms in King's in 1946. In heated dissent from Popper's paper, which had announced that, while discounting old-style metaphysics, he did believe that there were such things as universal moral laws, Wittgenstein snatched and brandished the poker from the fireplace. Popper observed that one instance of such a law was that people should not threaten visiting lecturers with pokers. Wittgenstein then stormed out of the room. Popper was never invited to the Moral Sciences Club again. Cambridge myth had it that Wittgenstein had had the better of the exchange. The fortune that he had renounced still served to gild his halo. The unadmitted comedy was that both philosophers had donned *ersatz* personalities – the sublime, eccentric Cambridge genius and London University's leading Doctor of Science – but their antagonism could be read as an instance of 'the return of the repressed'. The spat was decidedly unEnglish, but hardly unprecedented in conflicts between ex-Viennese and (though no one said as much out loud) ex-Jewish vanities.

The neo-Wittgensteinian form of argument that Renford Bambrough advocated was known as 'therapeutic positivism'. Wittgenstein had come to consider metaphysical convictions as essentially neurotic: they could not be refuted, but they might be *cured*. The recommended treatment was to refrain from aggressive confrontation (however tempting recourse to the poker might be). Like Freud's neurotic, the metaphysician was to be encouraged, by sympathetic attention, into disclosing more, and more, of the 'reasoning' that lay behind his ideas. He might then come to see for himself that they were at odds with practical experience and that some absurd private logic had beguiled him into conjuring up self-contradictory and/ or irrational chimeras. Because there were lions, it did not follow that there had to be unicorns. As any number of egotists have argued, reason is the sovereign cure for egotism.

Renford told us how, on one occasion, Wittgenstein had met his disciple John Wisdom one day and asked him how his meeting had gone with a certain philosopher. Wisdom confessed that it had been an exasperating encounter. Wittgenstein said, 'Perhaps you made the mistake of disagreeing with something Casimir said.' Casimir Lewy, another refugee (although I never cared to guess it), was a Trinity philosopher who set himself such high standards that, not unlike Wittgenstein, he was rarely disposed to publish his work. Rigour made him an implacable opponent. Wisdom, who succeeded, with at least a show of reluctance, to Wittgenstein's professorial chair, brought Anglo-Saxon humour to a dour discipline. His skittishness did not always find favour among the *purs et durs* of the Moral Sciences faculty. Under his quirky aegis, philosophy offered a combination of recherché comedy, salutary high-mindedness and coterie conceit.

My private wish was that anti-Semitism could be shown, if not proved, to be nonsensical and, in a revised public language, might be rendered literally unspeakable. I did not disclose this ambition to Tony Becher. He regarded philosophy as an extension of mathematics, in which rhetoric had no place, except in arming scorn for the illogical. I wanted it to supply the muscular intelligence that would confound the barbarians, especially those already within the gates. My curiosity was both purposeful and limited. I never thought of attending the lectures of the thick-legged, brown-stockinged, allegedly knickerless Mrs Braithwaite, whose subject was 'the logic of a picture language'. She was no picture herself.

We were warned that to become a Moral Scientist entailed, almost certainly, that one would not get a first-class degree. Philosophers were the poor friars of the humanities. Unworldliness did not inhibit unnamed colleagues from ironising on the fact that John Wisdom had not got a first-class degree. 'But then,' they would say, 'he did go and get himself psychoanalysed!' Wisdom propounded his version of meta-Freudian therapy in a series of nine o'clock lectures entitled 'The psychology of philosophy'. They had no specific content and he never referred to traditional texts. He brought no books to the podium and rarely resumed the topic he had been dealing with last time, even if he could remember what it was.

A long, domed cranium, flanked by backswept wings of grey hair, like his quizzical eyebrows and hollow whisper, gave Wisdom an air of caricatural sagacity. Each morning, he seemed amazed that there we all were again. Initiates sat in the front row and were primed to offer topics apt for dissection. Wisdom could appear startled by even a planted query. Like a wise comedian, he would gaze at the speaker (often Mr McKnelly, later a parish priest, sometimes Mr Gomme, later a Leavisite professor, occasionally Mrs Gomme, later divorced) and pause, aghast, before responding in a voice at once hollow and carrying, dubious and assured. His words seemed urgent, even pained. They were also calculated to amuse.

Newcomers were not immune to gentle ridicule. When he first attended one of Wisdom's lectures, Piers Paul Read (a Roman Catholic writer, at Cambridge a decade after me) responded, perhaps too promptly to a request for a 'metaphysical question', by proposing 'Does God exist?' On Read's account, Wisdom looked at him with practised dismay and said, in a tone calculated to amuse the *cognoscenti* in the front row, 'Oh! I was thinking of something more along the lines of...' He tapped the desk on his dais. 'Is this a table?'

Wisdom reacted with affectations of dismay to naïve tourists, who demanded that he define his terms. 'It depends what you mean by X' was a sophism made popular by C. E. M. Joad on *The Brains Trust*. Joad, a professor at Birkbeck, was not held in high esteem in Cambridge. Asked to review one of his books, Russell had responded, 'Modesty forbids'. Joad fell from radio grace after being convicted of travelling on the London–Exeter railway without a ticket, a boasted habit of his. The publicised fine of £2 in effect ruined him. His name endures if only because his conduct on the tennis court figures in Stephen Potter's *Gamesmanship*. He is depicted as demanding a clear call of 'in' or 'out', even when his return of service had hit the back netting without touching the court. 'Cyril' was a Hampstead neighbour of Guy and Celia Ramsey and an unsubtle *coureur de femmes*. He thought nothing of female intelligence and proclaimed the sex to be good for only one thing.

Russell matched and outlasted him in that regard, but he was wise enough to refrain from loud disdain for women. Russell's amorous ambitions were not abandoned with age. Legend promises that on one Saturday night, when there was a large party at 5 Jordan's Yard, an old gentleman knocked on the door, announced to the foreign girl who had opened it that he was Bertrand Russell and asked whether he might come in. Monik or Ilse is said to have advised him to try the old people's home. This story is either true or untrue and so, in theory at least, it belonged to the realm of the empirical, even though, in practice, there is no way of verifying it. There were, as A. C. Ewing used to say, from the philosophical wilderness in which he grazed (his voice was famously sheepish), more things in heaven and earth than positivists could ever be positive about.

Definitions, Wisdom suggested, were a matter more of decision than of predetermined rigidity. 'How would I define a good book? *Must* I?' There was an anguished pause, then: '*Good!*' He tasted the word cautiously, as if it were stem ginger. 'Um, would it help to say, as a definition, that something was good if it added up to an even number?' One day, again pressed for a definition by some neophyte, he asked if any of us had read David Garnett's novel *Lady into Fox*. If not, no matter: the title encapsulated the plot, which was that one day, the wife of a fox-hunting man was transformed into a fox. Wisdom asked us to imagine the transformation, the lengthening of the muzzle, the rust of fur which then appeared on it, the levitation of the ears and the bushing of the tail, possibly. At what point, he wanted to know, would we be forced to say, 'By George, she's now definitely a fox!'? Wisdom made Garnett's story seem more subtle, or macabre, than it actually is. In the novella, the lady turns into a fox with instantaneous abruptness.

Wisdom's charisma secured the allegiance of his entourage, but it did not travel well. Lacking an impressive bibliography, he had no eminent standing outside Cambridge. In the 1970s, he would be struck off the register of philosophical worthies by Bryan Magee and Bernard Williams, the scrutineers of merit in the television age. If Wisdom's raising of the eyebrows suggested amazement at human credulity, there was also secret anguish in him. He would not go into a church even for the funeral of his painter wife, Pamela. His hobby was riding horses, though not to hounds. He quit the Moral Sciences faculty before reaching retirement age and accepted a chair in the University of Oregon, where he was reported to be happier than in pedestrian Cambridge. He kept a horse on campus and could leap almost directly from his chair to the saddle.

I discovered Cambridge philosophy to be a talking game which had something in common with amateur dramatics. There was, however, no cynicism in my zeal for therapeutic positivism. I shared what I took to be its aversion to religious beliefs. Wittgenstein's executors, Peter Geach (who never wore socks) and Miss Anscombe, were proselytising Roman Catholics. After he had died in Dr Bevan's house in Cambridge, they made sure that the Master, who had indeed been baptised as a child, was given a Roman Catholic funeral.

Although no one was coarse enough to say so out loud, post-war Cambridge philosophy (including the franchised version preached in Oxford) seemed *Judenrein*. There was nervous symmetry between the admitted wish, common to some extent to both Popper and Wittgenstein, to purge the world of the demons that had bedevilled Europe and an unadmitted desire to be done, in the most refined sense, with the Jews. As Wisdom said of invisible snakes in the lecture room: 'You can't see them, but they're *there*.' He meant, of course, that they were not; but then again, there they were. Jewishness was inherent in Wittgenstein's personal magic. Late in his life, he claimed, or confessed, that his thinking was '100 per cent Hebraic'. His attempt to purge the world of false gods was a kind of piety.

I heard the word 'Jew' during my first two years at Cambridge only once, when I was taking part in a Mummers' production of a play called *Musical Chairs*. Who knows why the committee selected, out of the whole European repertoire, a doleful, dated play that took place in the Romanian oil-fields in the 1920s? Perhaps there was virtue in denouncing the capitalist exploitation of a country whose present plight, under a Stalinist puppet, provoked small indignation from those in happier places. I was cast as an American businessman. Joe Bain played a Mitteleuropan oil-man. At the end of Act One, it fell to him to come in and say, 'We've struck a gusher!' The phrase was to come in useful when someone in the Whim Café became exaggeratedly effusive.

Musical Chairs was slated both in *Varsity* and by the usually indulgent critic in the *Cambridge Evening News*. After the first night, audiences came only to scoff. The disintegration of the production encouraged me to play for laughs by parodying Jimmy Stewart's slow delivery. After an applauded exit, I walked around behind the braced flats to get to the green room, while the rest of the cast continued to do their straight stuff. Adjacent to the buckets In Case Of Fire, I was confronted by a small man, known to me, like Horace's button-holing friend, *nomine tantum*, only by name, Harry. 'Brilliant,

brilliant! Best impersonation of a Jew I've ever seen!' God help me, I smiled and walked on. Nor did I say anything when, at a party in a Grantchester mansion, I heard my shrill host, a certain Kim Tickell, say loudly, but not in my direction, 'I will *not* have my mother's house turned into a synagogue.' Accurate memory can be a substitute for action; might that be why so many Jews have written reminiscential books?

I never asked, or wondered, why Tony Becher decided to abandon mathematics, in which he was certain to get a First. If he had demons to purge, he never spoke of them, even when, since his parents were still in India, he came to stay at 12 Balliol House at Christmastime. How could a Gentile have good grounds for being unhappy? Tony revealed himself, in a way, by sudden spasms of grotesquerie. On Boxing Day evening, he, Beetle and I walked down to deserted Putney High Street. At a zebra crossing, Tony elected to imitate Quasimodo, the capering hunchback of Nôtre Dame, and lurched backwards into the only stranger in the street, who happened to be a policeman. I also remember a sherry party in Queens' College in which one of the guests had left a silver-topped cane leaning against the chimney-piece. When its owner came to reclaim it, Tony called out, 'Well, aren't we an affected old thing, then?' The man said, 'Not really,' and tapped the stick against his wooden leg. One day, walking up King's Parade from a lecture, Tony and I met Karl Miller's very pretty attachment, Jane Collet. She was wearing a rather bold pair of leopardskin-patterned tights. Tony shrieked at her in a way that seemed at once randy and cruel. I was embarrassed, but I did not say anything.

Sexual desire and frustration went together in 1950s England. When Leslie Halliwell came back to Cambridge to manage the Rex cinema, he had the connoisseur's taste and the tradesman's acumen to screen Continental films that could be advertised as enticingly erotic. After his publicity announced an unimpaired view of Hildegarde Neff's breasts, long queues stretched down towards the Chesterton Road. Lust got what it deserved when the promised nakedness was visible only in a framed *portrait* of the unremarkable lady. Halliwell graduated once again to become the founder and decisive editor of the *Film Guide*. Cinematic omniscience warranted him to combine the roles of encyclopaediast and public executioner. He came to react with distaste to all the movies I had anything to do with.

At most times, Tony Becher seemed the very model of an eager-to-please middle-class Englishman. Yet his regular handwriting seemed to be impressed on the page with controlled fury. His Footlights lyrics were more ingenious in their internal rhymes than anyone else's. He composed them as he might some abstruse mathematical equation. Tony's heartlessness was declared, without deliberate malice, when Lord Montagu of Beaulieu was convicted of homosexual acts, with a social inferior, and sent to prison. Tony wrote and performed, at the next Footlights Smoker, a timely number entitled 'Lord Mount-a-Few of Beaulieu'. No one rejoiced in Montagu's very brief 'disgrace', from which he recovered in a sporting, finally triumphant manner; but it offered a cue that Tony's adroit intelligence could not resist, just as it gave Ken Tynan an opportunity for ostentatious courage in standing bail for Lord Montagu's journalist friend, Peter Wildeblood. The seeming virulence of Tony's lyrics had nothing to do with moral outrage. It may have done something to exorcise demons that Tony himself could never quite identify. He later wrote a witty parody of a Lorenz Hart 1920s lyric in a Footlights skit that began 'In a Graham Greenery / Where god paints the scenery'. It entailed no indignant distaste for popery. In most respects, Tony was a loyal and amusing friend. One of his ancestors had given his name to Becher's Brook, where he came a cropper.

According to Renford, there was no way I could be ready for Finals after only a single year of full-time attention to Moral Sciences. Conscious of how little I had achieved in my first two years, I was given a virtuous reason to ask my father to extend my Cambridge lease. It would be an unexpected tax on him, even though – thanks to Renford's solicitations and Howland's geniality – St John's offered to extend my scholarship. In one of our man-to-man chats, my father agreed without hesitation. Perhaps he was influenced by the fact that it had been mandatory, in his day, for Greats to require four years of study. I was grateful and surprised. I was given both a chance to further the redemption of the world from metaphysics and a lease of extra time in which to make a mark on Cambridge, though I had no clear idea what it might be.

At the end of my second year, I played Truewit in Ben Jonson's *Epicene* in an open-air production, directed by Joe Bain, in the St John's College Backs. I recall only a line directed at me after I have delivered one of Jonson's best quips: 'I do say as good things every day, were they but taken down and recorded.' I must have controlled my tendency to overact, except in the spirit of the piece, since I was elected President of the Lady Margaret Players, in Joe's place, for the coming year.

Had I been properly diligent, I should have proposed, as Sullivan always did, to return to Cambridge for the 'long vac term'. There were no lectures in those mid-summer weeks, but the college and the libraries were open. It was an ideal time for serious study. I had no wish, however, to consign myself to cellular chastity nor did I ever encounter a *maître-à-penser* sufficiently charismatic to exercise a demanding ascendancy over me. Renford was amusing and amused, informative and diligent, but the current never truly passed between us.

Beetle had been given the name of a landlady in Florence, where we could spend ten cultural days before repairing to the cottage she had discovered to rent on a high hill overlooking Menton, the Riviera town where D. H. Lawrence and Katharine Mansfield had stayed, although not together (he was repelled by her manifestation of the symptoms of tuberculosis, which they had in common).

Florence in August was burnt sienna. Signora Naldi labelled me '*dormiglione*' on account of my tendency to oversleep. We did the Uffizi and the

Accademia and the Ponte Vecchio and the Boboli Gardens and we took the bus to Fiesole to inspect the Roman theatre and remember Boccaccio, but our thoroughness generated no abiding affection for the city. We had lunch one day in a basement *buca* on the city side of the Ponte Vecchio. When the waiter said, '*Da bere?*', I said, '*Acqua minerale, per favore.*' A minute later, a man on the far side of the restaurant whispered something to the waiter, who came to us with a bottle of *prosecco* beaded with cold. We raised our glasses to the benevolent stranger, but never spoke to him. We had just one ice cream at the famous gelateria *Perché No!* before taking the train to Ventimiglia and on into France.

The cottage overlooking Menton cost £2 a week. It was at the top of a prolonged zigzag of steps, wide in the early stages, narrower and steeper as we climbed to the high shelf on which the little cottage stood. We made love; we cooked; we read; and, now and again, we played careful cricket on the tight concrete terrace, as if in a net, but without a net, using a slat of wood and a bald tennis ball. There was an outdoor privy and a phallic pump which, after prolonged leverage, drew what we took to be drinking water. The vine over the terrace was thick with ripening grapes. The locals called them '*framboises*': when they burst, plumply, in the mouth, they tasted of vinous raspberries. Beetle called them 'sex grapes'. We shopped at the *Alimentation* down on the main road and toted our supplies up those many steps. One day we met a neighbour coming down who married us with '*M'sieudame!*'

The Communist owner of the cottage had a Penguin library in which we discovered the novels of Rex Warner, an Anglo-Saxon Kafka, more comic than angst-ridden in his allegorical flourishes. The callow hero of *The Aerodrome* was informed, at one stage, 'Something rather rotten has happened. Someone's potted your old man.' Under Warner's influence, I began a novel in which I abandoned Maughamian realism and adolescent woes. The protagonist of *Mr Fraser's Ducats* was named Sandheim, after a character with whom my father and I had played bridge, several years before, at Mrs Mac's. Eye-deceivingly swift at shuffling and dealing, the real-life Sandheim was enough of an expert to be a regular collector of the other players' sixpences. We wondered why so good a player chose to play in such modest company. It turned out that he was a card-sharp. Blackballed in classy circles, he was reduced to swimming with minnows.

In my novel, Sandheim was translated into a businessman under the threat of violence from some rivals whom he has outsmarted by selling them tainted merchandise. He recruits protection in the form of three men who fortify his house and take turns in keeping him under armed surveillance. Their vigilance is so thorough that he never has an unobserved moment with his wife. She becomes more and more ostentatious, delectable, and impatient in her frustration. Sandheim's protectors grow increasingly over-bearing. Quite soon, he is their prisoner, his bullet-proof vest a straitjacket. His wife, who takes to crawling around the living room naked, becomes their common plaything. Sandheim is allowed to watch his protectors enjoy Sandra's gladly granted favours.

The trio of oppressive hirelings receive calls which, Sandheim is told, promise that his enemies are only waiting for him to take one step out of his house. Required to avoid showing himself at the window, lest someone take a pot at him, he is dressed in his wife's old clothes and made to bring refreshments when Sandra is being serviced by his loutish friends, who were recruited by my imagination from those snaps on the barbed wire on Wimbledon Common and named after certain Lockites. The last scene in the book, which I planned but never wrote, had Sandheim playing bridge with his parasitic captors. They are all wearing Hitler masks and address him as 'Sandyjew'.

Beetle and I resumed living as we had in Ramatuelle, with the unspoken assumption, *de part et d'autre*, that we were together for good. One night, we went to a poetry reading that we had seen advertised in the café where we sometimes bought an ice cream. The poet was a tall, very white American. One of his poems was entitled 'Nude by the Side of the Sea'. I knew, from the first line he declaimed, that he had no hope of fame, and little of publication. There was something gallant in his starchy elocution.

I could not imagine being any happier than we were in the cottage, until the drinking water from the pump had dysenteric consequences. When I reverted to infantile helplessness, Beetle dosed me with chapters from *Winnie the Pooh*, which happened to be on our red landlord's shelves. By the time we had to leave, I was still so weak that Beetle toted the much heavier of our suitcases down the hill. She did it again after we had taken the bus to Toulon and had to walk down the hot platform to the train that would take us north.

FOR MY THIRD academic year, which began in October 1952, John Sullivan had prevailed on me to share rooms in 'the Wedding Cake' (New Court) with another classicist, Bryan Moore, who had just gained a First in the first part of the Classical Tripos. He was tall, brushed his teeth with thoroughness, kept his brilliantined hair short back and sides, snored quietly on the far side of our quite large common bedroom, wore a tie slide, well-pressed grey flannels and a blue blazer. He had no visible girlfriend and no conversation. His smiling propriety, his meticulous scholarship and his clean collars rendered him beyond reproach. I could not stand the sight of him.

Beetle had found a new job as one of Victor Gollancz's secretaries. V. G. was probably the most famous, certainly the most flamboyant London publisher. His yellow-jacketed volumes were badged with puffs extracted from his friends, many of them more or less reformed veterans of the Left Book Club. His handwritten advertisements for the Sunday press knew no reticence: 'Reprinting before publication' was a common, underlined rubric. He gave Beetle a new nickname, 'Sheba', in honour of her black hair, bright dark eyes and, perhaps, her regal refusal to be intimidated. When enraged, V. G. was known to sit at his desk and drum his feet on the floor and yell at his underlings. His version of Judaeo-Christian socialism did not pacify his spleen, nor inhibit him from long lunches at Rules, in Maiden Lane, or at the Savoy Grill; but it did impel him, soon after the foundation of the state of Israel, to launch an appeal on behalf of 'the Arab brethren', an early, far-sighted and no doubt futile attempt to close the breach between Israel and her neighbours.

V. G. never shouted at Sheba. He found her so attractive that he disclosed to her that he had a secret alter ego – unless it was an *alterum id* – called Moses. Moses stood for the return of the repressed and shameless Jew. His caricatural form was an animated version of V. G.'s nose. When out of England, Victor required his secretaries to write him letters about what was happening during his absence. Beetle turned duty into insolent pleasure by making Moses the co-author of her letters. She did it with enough Gogolesque flair for V. G. to tell her that she should be a writer. If 'darling Daphne' – Daphne du Maurier, author of *Rebecca* and *Jamaica Inn* – could write bestsellers, why not Sheba?

Now accredited Moral Scientists, Tony Becher and I went regularly both to John Wisdom's lectures and to those of Charlie Broad, whose chair was in Moral Philosophy. Broad was bald, short, pear-shaped and unwrinkled. In his venerable sixties, his shining head and uncreased face gave him the appearance of a brilliant baby. Like the much younger Hugh Trevor-Roper, and unlike most writers, Broad regarded the index as part of the text of a book and composed (or supervised) his own. For both the historian and the philosopher, that last rift too had to be loaded with ore, or irony. In the index of Broad's most famous, early book, *Five Types of Ethical Theory*, one entry reads 'Church of England, the author's respect for'. Broad also divulged sympathy with the racial preferences of the late Adolf Hitler. What this amounted to, in harmless holiday practice, was an appetite for young Nordic men, a taste that he indulged, so far as anyone knew, only on discreet Scandinavian excursions. Wittgenstein had had similar blond inclinations.

In contrast with Wisdom, Broad lectured with prepared precision. He repeated everything he said, in a way which suggested that we take careful note. I still have manuscript pages of transcriptions of his account of Berkeley's theory of perception. Only when the bishop's own arguments had been rehearsed, twice, did Broad say, 'I shall now list seventeen objections to this theory, I shall now list seventeen objections to this theory.' I wrote them all down. I am sure that they were cogent and coherent. I cannot remember one of them.

Broad entered and left Mill Lane, with Kantian promptness, but he did not socialise with his audience. It was a surprise when, one day later in the year, he crossed Tony Becher and me in Trinity Street and said, 'Hullo, *boys*!' It did not occur to me to wonder whether he had been waiting for us or, more particularly, for Tony, whose appearance honoured the Aryan prescription. A week or two later, Broad again intercepted us as we returned to St John's, and invited us to dine with him one evening in Trinity. We were served, by a college servant, with a modest meal and a decanter of wine, followed by port. Our conversation had no heavy philosophical ballast. If there was even the mildest amorous motive for his invitation, his interest must have been in Tony; but he treated me with undifferentiated courtesy and I did my best to amuse him. Can he have held serious Hitlerian views? It seemed evident that he could not recognise a Jew when he saw one.

Broad had the unassertive pride of the solitary. His prose was ironic but without flourish. He was both opinionated and broad-minded. He deplored Bertrand Russell's pacifism in 1914; he also campaigned against Bertie's eviction from his Trinity fellowship. Broad's logic allowed room for a certain amusement at the consequences of rigour: rational in his professional stance, he also held the presidency of the Psychical Research Society. This was less because he believed in ghosts than because he took it that, if a case of psychokinesis could be verified, it would offer evidence that the mind could affect the physical world at a distance. Such an occurrence, of which no example was recorded during his tenure, would justify the notion of a mind–body duality.

Was Charlie Dunbar Broad at all fazed by the publication, in 1949, of Gilbert Ryle's *The Concept of Mind*, in which the author established, to his own satisfaction at least, that there was no 'ghost' in the human machine? He gave no sign of it. Yet in Ryle's seemingly solemn opinion, everything attributed by philosophers of mind to premeditation could be accounted for, fully, by taking note of our practical conduct. A man's intention to go out was established by his putting on his coat, not in the light of some shadowy mental motivation. Ryle was the demon barber of Oxford philosophy; Ockham's Razor was plied with stringent dexterity. In his hands, it cut down a veteran regiment of misconceived obfuscations. Quick to adopt Ryle's jargon, we began to spot 'Category Mistakes' in all kinds of philosophical (and social) contexts.

How many readers suspected Ryle of being engaged in straight-faced provocation? Wittgenstein's biographer Ray Monk, now professor of philosophy at Southampton, maintains that he has never understood how to recognise a Category Mistake. At the time, Ryle's arguments appeared as elegant as their conclusions were counter to common sense. In the 1950s, a printed text, from a reputable publisher, carried scriptural authority. Accordingly, we subscribed to Ryle's view that to have an idea 'just was' to pick up a pencil and write down a series of words. Yet who genuinely doubted the possibility of a mental rehearsal of the merits and consequences of an action before public enactment showed that we had made a decision to do something, or not? J. L. Austin, the supreme Oxford philosophical instance of commonsensical sophistication, would say that he had never met a determinist who, in his day-to-day life, showed any genuine sign of believing that there was no such thing as free will. Would Ryle have denied that he ever put his mind to a problem?

When he came to give a lecture in Cambridge, his notoriety ensured a full house, though it did not procure an overflow. He preached with the solemn air of an unfrocked cardinal. At one point, he adverted to a logical instance, in which p was suspected of being the cause of q, or perhaps *vice versa*. He developed his argument about the similarities of these two putative entities by referring to the 'q-ness of p and, if you will, the p-ness of q'. No low smirk disturbed the gravity of the occasion. We assumed Ryle to be too unworldly even to be aware of the base pun he had uttered. In fact, he was a witty Oxonian paronomasiast; Ryled, as it were, by his Christ Church friend Hugh Trevor-Roper's penchant for riding to hounds, he observed that his colleague suffered from 'chronic tally-hosis.'

Ryle must have known precisely how to twit puritanical Fenlanders with base allusions. It may well be, however, that he was a sexual virgin, as A. J. Ayer reported him in his autobiography. Ayer, who carried his sexual reputation on his fly-leaf, so to say, claims to have asked Ryle – while on a railway journey – whether, if obliged to declare his preference, he would sooner go to bed with a male or female. Ryle is said to have opted, after thought, for the former. Was *The Concept of Mind* a premeditated joke at the expense of Russell's classic *Analysis of Mind*? If so, Russell had his revenge on Ryle when, in 1959, Ernest Gellner's *Words and Things* was not deemed suitable for review in *Mind*, which Ryle edited. Russell made a loud fuss about the Oxonian's censorious refusal even to acknowledge the existence of a critic of the analytic school. I was slightly shocked when Tony Becher, then within the loop of philosophical insiders, blamed the hoo-ha on 'that old trouble-maker Russell'.

In Cambridge, I went less often to the theatre than to the movies, especially at the Arts Cinema, where they showed Cocteau's *Orphée* and *Le Sang d'un Poète* and Jacques Becker's unforgettable *Edouard et Caroline*. Daniel Gélin's winning last line, to his unhappy wife, '*J'ai envie de toi*', has not been lost on me. I did go to the ADC to see an original play by John Barton. Peter Hall must have recognised how easily rather grand persons

(Barton was a minor aristocratic Old Etonian) could be enrolled into eminent lieutenancy. Barton's play was a neo-romantic whimsy in the style of a prosaic Christopher Fry, whose versatile plays were fashionable on Shaftesbury Avenue until Ken Tynan put a match to their preciosity in order to foster the new 'socialist' drama, which rarely had Fry's linguistic resource. I remember only one of Barton's high-flown lines: 'With a wild cry the last March earl flung himself into the watery weir.' Or does that confuse Barton's play with Henry James's last, absurd attempt to find fame and fortune in the theatre? Asked why he thought his play had not been a success, sincerity disposed H. J. to be unusually monosyllabic: 'I don't know,' he said. 'I tried so hard to be *base*.' Barton's subsequent play-making was limited to scissors-and-pasting Shakespeare's historical dramas.

Early in our third year, Tony Becher went to audition for the Cambridge University Footlights. The all-male club was notorious for its members-only, dinner-jacketed 'Smokers'. Two or three times a term, initiates pitched camp in the large upstairs room of the Dorothy Café, where they solicited each other's laughter and applause with spoofs, songs and drag acts. The best, polished and thoroughly rehearsed, were eligible for inclusion in the annual May Week revue, which took place, of course, in early June. It was a certificate of sophistication to imitate the clipped delivery and internally rhymed ingenuity of Noël Coward.

Fearful of being asked to sing, I funked accompanying Tony. A few days later, he came to the rooms I shared with the impeccable Bryan Moore, bringing with him a nicely dressed, smooth-faced, pale-eyed, light brown-haired young man who, he said, wanted to meet me. In only his second year at Caius, Leslie Bricusse was already secretary of the Footlights, of which Peter Firth was now president. Bricusse had overtaken me without even knowing I was there. I noticed that his spectacles were not of Bryan Moore's National Health, horn-rimmed variety. They had been selected, not wished upon him. Becomingly dressed, in no specific style, he spoke in no specific accent.

Leslie's announced ambition was to compose musical comedies, in the style of the shows by Rodgers and Hammerstein, Cole Porter and Irving Berlin, which were dominating Broadway and London's West End. Since there was no CU Musical Comedy Club, Leslie proposed to found one. For its first production, probably in a year's time, he intended to write the lyrics and most of the music; the Footlights' director of music, Robin Beaumont, would do the rest.

In search of a collaborator to write 'the book', Bricusse had asked Peter Firth who wrote the best dialogue in the play competition that Hugh Thomas had won the previous year. So what did I say to writing a musical comedy with him? And, by the way, why was I not yet a member of the Footlights? When I told him that I was averse to auditions, Leslie said, 'For goodness sake! Consider yourself a member! It's no big deal. This musical comedy idea, are you interested?'

'What is the idea exactly?'

'That's what I'm here to find out.' It came with a nice Kolynos smile. 'Your play, what was that about?'

'Suburbia,' I said. 'What we're all trying to get away from.'

Leslie said, 'What do you say we go and see Hugh Thomas, see if he has any ideas?'

'You don't need my permission to go and see Hugh Thomas.'

'I want you on board, you and your dialogue, of course!'

We went to Queens' to call on Hugh. Even in private, he had a public way of talking. Already highly placed in the Union, he was a major scholar in History on his way to further distinction. He listened, curly-haired head appraisingly tilted, as Leslie explained that we were open to any ideas he might have about a plot. Hugh wondered whether it might not be droll to place the whole thing somewhere in the Balkans. Leslie wiped his glasses, looked at me and then at Hugh and said, 'The Balkans. That's a thought. Why?'

'Doesn't it furnish grounds for … satirical fantasy? In view of the present situation.'

Leslie said, 'For instance?'

'Conflict between folkloric specificity and Communist indoctrination.'

'How would that … fit into a musical comedy exactly?'

Hugh said, 'You could have half the chorus consisting of youth leaders and a contrapuntal set of … fairies.'

'Fairies?'

'Balkan fairies, local spirits, they have a whole range of them in those parts. Think of Dracula.'

'Dracula,' Leslie said.

'For instance.'

Had the success of his Venetian extravaganza convinced Hugh of the merits of theatrical whimsy or was he, in his measured fashion, 'sending us up'? I listened with unamazed bemusement to his far-fetched fancy. Leslie temporised with the politeness that, I would discover, enveloped all his responses.

After we had recrossed Queens' mathematical bridge to Silver Street, Leslie said, 'Youth leaders and fairies? Perhaps he was joking.'

I said, 'How can we ever know the mind of another?' It amused me to watch my remark pass over Leslie's head.

I had no wish to write a musical comedy and little sense that Bricusse and I had much in common. Pitched into one more exam, however, I felt the Pavlovian impulse to come up with winning answers. Leslie impersonated Opportunity. He had a practical worldliness not to be found in my Johnian contemporaries. With no doubt about what he wanted to do, he was confident that it could, and would, be done. There was enticing proof of his useful nerve in the casual way in which he had nodded me into the Footlights. Intellectual condescension and vulgar ambition set me to join him on the low road with a brisk step, while never quite losing sight of the high road.

The Footlights proved to be composed of wits whose repartee was not always unanswerable. New members were treated to a seminar in lyric writing by Peter Tranchell, a queer (as we used to say) music don from Trinity, famous for his outrageousness: 'It's springtime and we're feeling ourselves again' was his kind of quip. He had his skittish aspect, but he was also capable of serious musical compositions. His advice about lyrics was very practical. It was always, but always, better, he told us, to put the unlikelier part of a rhyming couplet first: 'The vice squad wrangle / In the nice quadrangle' rather than the other way about. What sounded effortful one way sported a neat and fitting cap the other.

The Trinity chaplain, Simon Phipps, had been responsible for a number of instantly classic Footlights numbers, in particular 'Can anyone think of an Original Sin? / Can someone please tell me where to begin?' He too played the part of the old pro in assessing the merits of callow lyricists. He was known to be one of Princess Margaret's favourite, or at least regular, escorts. When she visited his rooms to meet some of his friends, HRH received the call of nature. The enchanting sound of the princess and her pee came clearly to the privileged auditors from the adjacent jakes. Phipps may also have been the author of a particularly brilliant solo number in which a camp odalisque was discovered on stage and sang a lament that began, 'There is not a man / On my Ottoman and there hasn't been one for weeks'. She looked back wistfully on the days when 'They came across the Bosphorus / And didn't even toss for us'.

Tony Becher and I were soon writing and performing numbers for 'Smokers'. Two or three of our pieces seemed likely to make the cut to be included in the May Week revue at the end of the year. Leslie sometimes chose to add finishing touches, and his persuasive name, to our efforts. Thanks to the little play that I had tapped out in those last three days in Ramatuelle, I had been beckoned into the company of a character who could elevate my Cambridge fortunes and transform, if not determine, my future.

Leslie was reading French at Caius, where he had a nice ground-floor set of rooms. I never noticed any French books on his shelves nor did I ever catch him in the process of writing an essay or preparing for a supervision. He gave himself no clever airs; he knew where he was going and, he told me, he wanted me (and my dialogue) to go with him. It was up to me whether or not to share the luminous staircase to paradise which, like Louis Jourdan in Vincent Minnelli's *An American in Paris*, he was all set to climb, with a new step every day. He had, I was sure, never heard of Wittgenstein (though he could, no doubt, have contrived a rhyme for him). Whatever kind of a Francophone he was, he carried no trace of Gallic *sérieux*. As for Sartre's idea of art, I doubted whether Leslie had ever read *La Nausée*, or even heard of it.

Clean-shaven, in a freshly laundered check shirt, hacking jacket with double vents, often with a patterned silk waistcoat, sometimes with a bow-tie, Leslie was a spruce advertisement for himself. His name was both exotic (of Belgian provenance, he told us) and easy to pronounce. His desk carried his silver-framed photograph in subaltern's uniform, but I never heard him use barrack-room language. He knew many jokes, almost all of them of transatlantic provenance, none risqué. Luck, which doubled for good management, had led to his evacuation to North America. He had not only survived the war, like the rest of us; he had given it a miss. By the time he returned from Hamilton, Ontario, to Pinner, Middlesex, he had already learned to drive, a rare accomplishment among insular contemporaries. He brought to Cambridge a precocious transatlantic desire for fame and fortune. Cole Porter, Ira Gershwin and Lorenz Hart were his models; his lyrics were the fruit of diligent mimesis. All were distinguished by an indispensable something called 'a Middle Eight'.

I cannot recover from memory's sediment why we elected to set *Lady at the Wheel* in the south of France; perhaps because it lent itself to Leslie's neat rhymes: 'Here we get sand in our sandals / Here we get scanned

in our scandals' and witty puns: 'They were never incompatible / He had
… income / And she was pattable'. The Monte Carlo Rally, then a much
publicised annual event, furnished opportunities for a comically guttural
German, a silly-ass English gentleman (Leslie came up with the name Sir
Roland Butter) and a couple of Americans, one a handsome driver, the other
a lugubrious, finally golden-hearted tycoon. The only character drawn from
life was called Britannia, a comic, middle-aged Cassandra who wandered
around making predictions that no one cared to hear. My parents had told
me of such a female who haunted the beach at Juan-les-Pins where they
spent two weeks every summer at a little hotel called Mon Repos.

My role as book-writer was to accommodate Leslie's and Robin Beaumont's musical numbers between as many laughs as I could contrive to put
in the mouths of our confected characters. The hero had to be Pete, because
Leslie had already composed a song entitled 'Pete, y'know' (he was 'kinda
sweet, y'know'). For some similarly lyrical reason, the female lead, who
drove the ramshackle English entry, which won the rally, came to be called
Jinx Dando. How could a classical scholar lend himself to such a lowbrow
project? With the greatest of imitative ease, since Leslie laughed gladly at
my jokes and had none of Toby Robertson's condescension. His ambitions lay beyond Cambridge: the places he was going had much brighter
lights and he had every intention of seeing his name in them. It was up to
me whether I came along.

Bricusse *père* was said to be 'in charge of distribution' for Kemsley Newspapers (he supervised the loading of printed copies into the vans that carried
them to the far corners of London). Leslie's contacts in Fleet Street were
good enough, his salesmanship and samples plausible enough, for him to
be commissioned by Kemsley's *Sunday Graphic* to supply a weekly 'box'
of funny verses, an English travesty of the *New Yorker*-ish style of Ogden
Nash, one of whose imitable couplets ran 'When you shake the ketchup
bottle / None'll come and then a lot'll'. Like the famous American gagster

Goodman Ace, who wrote for Bob Hope and other seemingly spontaneous comics, Leslie did not hesitate to ape his betters, whether they knew it
or not. On his shelves were two fat anthologies of jokes collated by Bennett
Cerf, from which he extracted regular plums, as well as the Noël Coward
and Cole Porter songbooks.

Tony Becher's contributions to our Footlights number were quick proof
of his rhyming facility. He was also recruited by Leslie, as his uncredited
journalistic collaborator (a double byline would have compromised Leslie's standing with the editor). Tony never told me what his share of the take
was, but he was glad of it. Leslie was a piper who promised such cheerful
rewards that it would have been churlish, if not self-defeating, not to follow
his lead. Between teatime sessions in his rooms (Leslie always had a ready
supply of milk chocolate P-P-P-Penguins), I did not at all abate my enthusiasm for the therapeutic treatment of humanity's metaphysical delusions.

Tony and I went together, in our gowns, to Renford Bambrough's supervisions. We read and then discussed our essays in a serious, sociable way
and at untimed length. Renford seemed not to find either of us more able
than the other, but there was an unadmitted competition to impress him.
Tony showed knowledge; I preferred wit. Well-read as Renford might be in
modern philosophy, there was something of the truant classicist about his
involvement in it. While he need have had no motive other than intellectual
honesty for embracing the universalism that our programme of subservi-
ence to science implied, it may be that, just as I hoped to apply an incidental
purge to old ideas (anti-Semitism the oldest), Renford wanted to put pro-
vincialism behind him. He never spoke of his parents nor of the north. He
was a version of what C. P. Snow, in his sequence of then current novels,
Strangers and Brothers, had called 'a New Man'. Renford combined academic and collegiate ambitions with a touch of levity. As things turned out,
he had more than we knew in common with the character of Jago, in Snow's
best novel, *The Masters*. When first proposed as Master of St John's, he was

deemed too young; some two decades, later, his candidature failed because he was considered too old. After all that time, he had to settle, unhappily, for *proxime accessit*.

An American graduate student called Norwood Russell Hanson sometimes sat in on our discussions. His presence introduced a measure of solemnity. Hanson challenged glibness with unsmiling severity. A philosopher with a mission, he wore a flying jacket and had the air of someone just in from one dangerous flight and apt for another. He had been a Golden Gloves boxer and a marine fighter pilot during the war in the Pacific. He shot down pat or pert answers with a sure aim. He had also played trumpet to professional standards. He went on to do innovative work in the philosophy of science and had several books in gestation when he was killed, in 1967, while piloting his own plane. The heartless rumour was that the advocate of careful scientific planning had failed to check how much fuel he had before taking off.

In an essay on C. L. Stevenson's pioneering notion of 'Persuasive Definitions', I dropped the conventional, neutral style and quoted Macaulay's 1833 speech on the Emancipation of the Jews. He had the nerve to declare that 'the Jews' had been unjustly typified by their degradation. What contingency had forced upon them had then been taken to be their essential, immutable character. I alluded not only to Jean-Paul Sartre's unlikely recommendation to Jews that they embrace the identity that others wished upon them (they alone were debarred, however well-meaningly, from the self-determination that Sartre regarded as the morally imperative prelude to human emancipation from Bad Faith), but also to T. S. Eliot's dismissive description of Macaulay as a stylist contaminated by 'journalism'. What seemed an aesthetic judgement carried persuasive baggage: to define Macaulay as journalistic enabled the sainted Tom to disparage liberal arguments in general without meeting any of them in particular. Macaulay's 1833 speech was, I claimed, a proleptic counterblast to Eliot's 1933 lecture *After Strange Gods*.

I refrained from saying that Eliot's speech, which his many defenders continue to pass off as an aberration due to personal stress, had coincided with Hitler's accession to power and was of a piece with the contemporary anti-Semitism preached by Charles Lindbergh, Father Coughlin and Henry Ford. How many of Eliot's admirers have chosen to notice that the speech delivered at the University of Virginia was also congruent with the restrictive admission policy of Harvard University during the presidency of A. Lawrence Lowell at the time that Eliot was a student under his waspish aegis? Eliot's standing in Cambridge critical circles was still paramount, despite the falling away that Frank Leavis and his censorious 'Connection' had detected in his recent work. If it disturbed my companions that I even alluded to so vexed and embarrassing a topic as 'the Jews', they were decent enough not to show it.

I was as easily seduced into seriousness by therapeutic positivism as into frivolity by Leslie Bricusse. I discovered that 'Lezzers' had a knack for finding female company, if for no salacious purpose. He talked of 'dating' girls and was very aware of their statistical details, but he was unlikely to commit the *faux pas* of one of his Caius friends, Stanley P., who pulled out his handkerchief during a social occasion and exploded a packet of Durex into his tutor's wife's lap. L. C. B. set out to enrol a company of pretty girls, preferably of 36–19–36 dimensions, who could sing and dance (or at least 'move').

Hardly any Cambridge theatrical females had, or needed, such attributes. Dudy Foulds's literary intelligence earned her the lifelong envy of her peers and her articulate personality made her Peter Hall's leading lady for all seasons; but she was no Cyd Charisse. When she happened to come to a Jordan's Yard Sunday lunch, I approached her to play the Cassandran part of Britannia; but she declined. More than thirty years later, when Claire Tomalin was the literary editor of the *Sunday Times* and Dorothy Nimmo had been hailed as a poetic genius by Craig Raine, I suggested that Claire offer 'Dudy', as we still called her, a book to review. I knew her to be alone and destitute. Claire chose to remember that when they were involved in Dr Leavis's 'common pursuit' (of first-class degrees), Dudy refused to share her trenchant, clever essays with other Newnhamites.

Leslie's plans were so confidently laid that it was a form of election to be invited to share them. His lyrics and their sentiments might have what John Sullivan called 'the inevitability of a popular song'; but that was precisely what they were designed to be, the more popular the better, in conformity with very good models. What Ovid had been to me, 'Cole' was to Leslie (the two versifiers had 'Let's Do It' as their common theme). Leslie had no urge to be well regarded in smart undergraduate circles. I doubt if he ever spoke to Peter Hall or recognised Karl Miller if he saw him. The Footlights and the Musical Comedy Club, of which he assumed the presidency, took most of Leslie's efficient time. He never pretended that they were anything but rungs on the ladder to an extra-mural, post-Cambridge paradise. How different, in moral terms, was Sullivan's determination to be a scholar from Leslie's to become the king of Shaftesbury Avenue and, if possible, the president of Old Broadway?

I first met Brian Marber, who came up to St John's in my third year, when he was sitting in Leslie's rooms, seeking entry into the Footlights. Brian was short, light brown-haired, thick-chested and wore high-sided (handmade) black boots. He made no secret of being a Jew and had no reticence when he detected another. He was unimpressed by my notion that philosophy would be a cure for anti-Semitism and, at the same time, dissolve the peculiarity that set Jews apart. He had been in the Jewish house at Clifton, lived in Abbey Lodge, adjacent to Regent's Park, owned a great many suits and knew how to drive. An unlikely athlete, he was a very able fencer and was soon in the university squad, later its president. It was traditional for presidents of half-blue sports to be admitted on the nod to the Hawks' Club. Although he was clean in his habits, the committee chose not to nod at Brian.

He had in common with another Johnian of his year, Jonathan Miller, the supposedly typical Jewish talent for solo mimicry and clowning. Even as a freshman medical student, Jonathan contrived to have a full waiting room. I saw him first in his first-floor 'set' in the Wedding Cake. I was in a deputation of the Gaiety that sought to enrol him in the cast for a 'college revue' which, when it happened, included prolonged imitations of *The Goon Show*'s 'Bluebottle', as played by Peter Sellers. He was sitting on the floor, aflame with ruddy curls, barefoot, in blue jeans and a circle of admirers.

Already vested with a reputation for precocious polyvalence, Jonathan was known to have appeared on comic radio broadcasts for which he wrote and performed monologues in a variety of accents, most memorably those of the poetic cricket commentator John Arlott and the naturalist Brian Vesey Fitzgerald. His father, Emanuel Miller, was a psychoanalyst; his mother, Betty, an authority on Keats. Jonathan seemed not to need friends, but was readily accessible to admirers. His hermetic habits never inhibited him from retreating into any available limelight.

Marber was a north London Jew of a thicker stripe. His father was a wholesale clothier, of Belgian provenance. He devised a routine in which an anglepoise lamp, bent and held in a variety of postures, was his only, versatile prop. There was something unnerving in his acceptance of and pleasure in being a Jew. That he was reading economics seemed to announce mercenary interests with unnecessary loudness. His friend Trevor Chinn had been with Brian in the Jewish house at Clifton. They lacked the wariness, hardly distinct from cowardice, with which Charterhouse had saddled me. They had no apprehension of being thought crude, even when they told low jokes. One of Brian's was about the mouse whose obsessive ambition was to make love to an elephant. When, at last, he succeeds in mounting her, the elephant twitches at some vexatious bird. The mouse says, 'Not hurting you, am I, darling?' I winced at the Cliftonians' brashness, and envied it. Chinn's father owned Lex Garages. Trevor was so eager to be done with academic life that he abandoned King's without taking a degree in order to hasten his entry into the real, lucrative world. Trevor was at the helm of Lex Garages when, in the financial crisis of 1974, the shares fell to 17p. If I had had the mercantile wit that is supposedly the badge of all our race, I should have ventured a modest sum on them and been able to, as Guy Ramsey used to say, 'clip coupons' for the rest of my life.

My final bow in college theatricals was in December 1952, when I was persuaded by Joe Bain to play Samson in *Samson Agonistes* in St John's college chapel. Vanity was the spur that prompted me to learn the hundreds of magniloquent lines in which Milton dressed his heroic alter ego. I learned them during one weekend in Jordan's Yard, with Beetle 'hearing' me, over and over again. Giles Gilbert Scott's chapel was a tall and heavy example of Victorian Gothic revival architecture. The college's celebrated choir had to contend with the worst acoustics in Cambridge. When I started to rehearse, Milton's words recoiled to muffle the next lines I had to say. To increase the volume served only to augment the echo.

Joe Bain supplied the solution: spoken softly, but with distinct clarity, the consonants winged the words. The key was to give each syllable distinct weight, bite and emphasis. Emotion and credibility depended less on how the actor felt inside than on getting the stresses right. Make the consonants as punctual and pointed as possible: get the words right, enunciate them cleanly, and keep the voice *up* at the end of the line and you could dispense with Stanislavskyan 'preparation'. Charlie Chaplin always insisted that precision and economy of gesture conveyed emotion without any need for an actor actually to be emotional. Art follows accuracy.

We performed *Samson Agonistes* only three times, but the production attracted large audiences. I was flatteringly reviewed, in a pretentious flysheet, by a visiting pundit from the ranks of Tuscany. Thanks to Bain, Milton's words did the work of conveying tragic pathos. At one performance I had an experience not uncommon, I have discovered, even among experienced professionals. Running smoothly along Samson's sonorous lines,

I became conscious that much further up ahead, but coming closer, was a black hole into which a set of verses had fallen, as if in the Tay Bridge disaster. I continued fluently, and with no loss of pace or confidence, towards the abyss, hoping that as I got closer to it, I might retrieve the lost passage. I did not. When, however, I reached the lapsed segment, I managed, with scant hesitation, to accelerate, leap across the rupture and resume the words that lay on the far side.

The only other person with me on the altar steps was Harold Cannon, a stolid Philistine, who had to interject a line or two, leaning on his spear, in the section that had slided into Avernus. When I gave him his next cue, he came up with the few words that he would have spoken in the middle of the section that I had elided. I had to retreat, and repeat myself, with furious emphasis. With a Punic frown, he gave me the subsequent cue and on we went to the end, which coincided with the conclusion of my career in the straight theatre.

I wrote the 'book' of *Lady at the Wheel* in the Easter vacation. It was a relief from communing with great minds to create trivial characters whose principal purpose was to ease the way from one of Leslie's numbers to the next. The plan was to stage the musical near the beginning of the following academic year. Meanwhile, in his role as secretary of the Footlights, Leslie's business was to select a cast and material for the 1953 May Week revue. As his adviser, I found myself by chance promoted, as I had been in the corps at Charterhouse. Like the House Platoon, the Footlights had its 'O Group' and I was a member. It so happened, though we never cared enough to guess it, that Peter Firth, the president, was undergoing a spiritual crisis and did not regard the selection of material for the revue as a *summum bonum*. My abiding ambition was to be a published novelist. I might have chosen a more subtle model than Mr Maugham, hardly a more instructive one. The writer's business, he said, was to build up an *oeuvre*: you spied on the world and compiled your reports without embroidery.

In my notebooks, I concentrated on noticing what was done and said by those around me rather than indulge in introspection. Why people did things was better discovered by close observation of language and gesture than by seeking to detect the ghost in their machinery. Writing things down induced clarity. Fingers had their own way of thinking. Inspiration did not prime but follow practice: *solvitur sedendo*.

As austerity lost its hold on post-war Britain, Leslie Bricusse knew just the kind of things he wanted to have when success could procure them: three white telephones on his desk and a white convertible at the door. He personified charm without egotism, salesmanship without vanity. His spruce appearance recruited a cast of good-looking females, locally and in London, on whom he made no seigneurial demands. One of our imminent chorus was Julie Hamilton, the shapely blonde daughter of Jill Craigie, a prominent Pinewood screenwriter, the wife of Michael Foot MP. Leslie told me that 'Michael' used to make sure that his red tie was *not* on straight when he left for what he called 'the boys' club', otherwise known as the House of Commons. All the world was a stage.

During my third year, the ADC had a tributary influx of American graduate students, sponsored by beneficent foundations. Bob Gottlieb moved smartly into a directorial role by claiming to be an experienced exponent of the Method. Whether or not he ever attended Lee Strasberg's Actors' Studio, he had certainly acquired its jargon. His assumption of maturity was certified by his already being married. At Cambridge, Gottlieb and his then wife both wore spectacles of the same circular, horn-rimmed style. Joe Bain put it about that the reason that they were rarely seen in public together was that they shared one pair of eyes, affixed to the back of their sole pair of horn-rimmed glasses. When one Gottlieb was out and about, the other had to sit in the dark. Joe was, I am sure, motivated neither by anti-Semitic nor by anti-American malice; it amused him to compose flights of fancy. Gottlieb's access to the ADC was eased by another American, Gordon Gould, who was already its president. Gordon too seemed older than his English colleagues, and certainly more mature. As an actor, he had a delivery slow enough to appear modishly Methodical. If he is the same Gordon Gould who appeared in Woody Allen's *Zelig*, he was born in Chicago only a year before I was.

I found myself in the cast for the summer Footlights revue, thanks largely to Leslie, but also to a sketch that I wrote satirising the weekly *Free Speech* television programme, in which Bob Boothby, W. J. Brown, A. J. P. Taylor and someone else (never a woman, often Michael Foot) discussed politics in a heated, yet mutually enhancing, manner. After supporting Churchill during the latter's wilderness years, Boothby was dumped by Winston for alleged financial irregularities. As an Old Etonian Scottish MP, he became a maverick toff with a taste for louche company, such as that of the East End's gangster twins the Kray Brothers and, on a pre-war occasion, Adolf Hitler. Never short of chutzpah, he had the nerve to respond to the latter's greeting, 'Heil Hitler!' with 'Heil Boothby!'

Impersonating Michael Foot's man-of-the-people braggadocio, I allowed the desire to get a laugh to trump my solemn conviction that socialism was indeed the medicine for all social maladies. On the first night, when I delivered my line 'We in the Labour Party will do everything in our power [pause, frown] to get everything in its power', I was amazed, if not shocked, by the volume of laughter, then applause, that greeted my on-the-nose crack. As we sat there, probably for no longer than ten seconds, the realisation broke, two years after Winston Churchill had been returned to Downing Street, that the resurgent bourgeoisie was now in a triumphant majority, at least in Cambridge.

Cabbages and Kings was an unlikely success. Its solitary star was Peter Townsend, a short, very fair, large-nosed harlequin whose bloodless complexion needed no blanching. He played no part in anyone else's sketches and said scarcely a word in his own; it involved only one prop, a brown paper parcel on which he somehow conferred a life of its own. If success gave him any pleasure, he scarcely showed it. He walked by himself. He got a First in English; had a brief, joyless excursion in show business; then vanished into J. Walter Thompson as a copywriter. He wanted to be a novelist, but never published a book; perhaps undue cultivation in Frank Leavis's nursery had dried his sap. I saw him thirty years later when I gave a paper (*Some Philosophers I Have Not Known*) at a colloquium in London University. He still wore that bleak, boyish air of deferential superiority. He had had a brief marriage with the musical comedy star Elizabeth Seal.

After the last night of *Cabbages and Kings* and before the cast disassembled, the outgoing committee was due to elect the 'officers' who would lead the club in the following academic year. Leslie proposed that I should be in charge of 'press relations', either because I had told him of my father's role in Shell or because I knew Guy Ramsey. Leslie himself was a shoo-in to rise from secretary to the presidency. Since I was on his 'ticket', my selection was, he promised, a formality. Tony Becher went on back to college while I waited, literally in the wings, for Leslie to come out of the long meeting. He did so tight-lipped. Some people on the committee – Dermot Hoare and Peter Stephens and Kennedy Thom, the vice-president – were of the opinion that a Jew should never be an officer of the club. These three, a freckled Hibernian rugger player, a moustachioed clerk and a cadaverous apprentice divine, held the accursed shears over the thread on which my silly future depended. As outgoing president, Peter Firth did not have a vote nor did he interject any elder statesmanlike objection to my ostracism. Years later, after he had become head of religious broadcasting at the BBC, he sought to persuade me to do a radio 'feature' about the Wandering Jew. He went so far in his solicitations as to accompany me in my taxi to London Airport on my way to California. I did not feel the vocation.

Standing in the wings of the Arts Theatre, I hope I laughed or at least shrugged. There was, I assumed, nothing further to be said or done. Leslie was not of that view; he was my friend and he would not allow the outgoing committee's decision to stand. Peter Stephens had been elected secretary for the coming year, but Leslie, as the new president, intended to find a way to unseat him. Meanwhile, he had a few ideas about how I might 'tickle up the book' of *Lady at the Wheel* during the long vac. He could not, if he had planned it, have devised a better way of securing my loyalty.

I stayed in Cambridge only for the few days needed to see the Tripos results framed on the Senate House railings. Both Tony Becher and I were given 2.2s in 'prelims' to Part Two. There was a very small number of candidates in that category; none had done any better. To no one's surprise, including his own, John Sullivan was given a starred First in the second part of the Classical Tripos. Brian Moore, to whom I cannot remember saying goodbye, had got also a First in Classics, starless, I think. He became a long-serving schoolmaster in Bristol.

Renford told me that the examiners had been amused by my essay on the relationship between religion and ethics. I had dared to say that the two things seemed as closely bonded as Brahms and Simon. The Brahms I had in mind was, of course, Caryl, who collaborated with S. J. 'Skid' Simon in writing *Don't Mr Disraeli* and *Bullet in the Ballet*. I was surprised to discover that Richard Braithwaite, the chairman of the examiners, had even heard of such frivolous compositions. I liked to think of philosophy as a very solemn business.

In the early summer, Hilary Phillips telephoned my mother. She was married and living in Hendon and had recently had a baby, with some difficulty. She would like to see me sometime, if I had nothing better to do. I called and arranged to go to tea. I took the Underground to Hendon Central and walked past a long parade of suburban shops and up to the side street of similar 1930s houses in which Hilary and Gerald lived. She was alone in the house. She had had a hard time with convalescence but she was still a very pretty woman. I told her that I was happily in love with someone else. She said, 'Then why have you come to see me?'

'Because you asked me to tea.'

She said, 'I'd better make some then, hadn't I?'

When she came back with the appropriate tray and, after a due delay, poured out the contents of the teapot, my cup was filled with hot water. Hilary laughed and threw her hands in the air and then lay back full length on the wide sofa. 'I only forgot to put the tea in. What do you make of that?' She lay there looking up at me. Frank Harris would have seized his opportunity to, as he said with enviable frequency, 'improve the occasion'. I lacked the desire or the recklessness. I took the teapot into the kitchen and she came and put some tea in it. I suppose I had gone to see her to prove how happy I was without her; and she without me, perhaps.

I walked back past all those hedged and gated houses, distinguished from each other only by their gardens or their paintwork, and along the Hendon Way past the row of shops, a hairdresser, a laundry, a United Dairy and the paper shop with a two-sided billboard pitched on the pavement. By the time I was waiting for the train to take me back to civilisation, I was somewhat pregnant with my second novel, *The Earsldon Way*, although I had not yet written my first.

X

SINCE SHE WAS still working for Victor Gollancz, Beetle could take only a month's holiday, during August. Nicolai Rubinstein, a great authority on medieval Tuscany, recommended the ancient walled city of Lucca. I knew of it only because Julius Caesar, Pompey and Marcus Licinius Crassus had met there, in 60 BC, to compose the three-headed tyranny later known as the First Triumvirate. We travelled third class by train from Paris to Pisa and by bus to Lucca. There we found a *pensione* where we could have two meals a day for the equivalent of eight shillings each. The only available room was on the top floor of an annexe run by two old ladies. They were unlikely to disturb us on account of the number of steps it would require them to climb. There was a big bed and a desk overlooking the mossed and lichened roofs of the old city.

I had promised Leslie that I would come back to Cambridge with a revised script in which his songs could be heeled in time for us to begin rehearsals. I put more jokes and routines in the text, which Leslie had agreed that I should direct, while he concentrated on staging the musical numbers. I also wrote some sketches for the first Footlights Smoker of the new academic year. One was a two-handed send-up of Evelyn Waugh and Graham Greene, in which they preened themselves on their command of the English literary scene and on the eagerness with which publishers pursued them ('We were nearly subjected to rape / By the man from Jonathan Cape / 'Victor Gollancz?' / 'No thanks!' etcetera.) Tony Becher later supplied me with the perfect capper: 'I'm the Greene to end all Greenes / And I'm the Waugh to end all Waughs!'

Beetle and I took the bus to Viareggio and swam or lay on the busy beach. A man toting a wide basket trudged in the soft sand, calling out, '*Bombolini, gelati, aranciata*…' Basted with sun oil, our bodies were badged with evidence of the mosquitoes that plagued our nights in shrill shoals. The white walls of our high room became covered with the bloody dottle of crushed insects. The generous food at the *pensione* compensated for our scratchy sleep. The cook was a squat, smiling woman who, when you thought you had seen it all, came out with a dish of *cipolline* glazed in the oven. A resident set of Italian army officers occupied a central round table. Their colonel was a stamp collector who asked us to send him any used covers we might have. There was, it seemed, a kind of innocence even in military men.

We often spent a hot hour playing our soft version of cricket in a malodorous culvert under the thick city walls. Now and again, we bought the tissue-paper airmail edition of the *Daily Telegraph*. I saw one day that Peter May had scored an unsurprising century in his first Test match against the Australians. I watched him score centuries at Charterhouse in the course of almost all home matches on Big Ground. I met him only when I was drawn to play against him in the school tennis singles. He arrived on court punctually and explained that he had never played before. He would be glad if I would run through the rules. We knocked up for a short while and then he said we might as well play. He won 6–0, 6–0, without taking his first XI hasher off. He was so good at all sports that, while aged by his own precociousness, he displayed no vanity. The ex-Leicester and England bowler George Geary coached Peter until he was fifteen years old, after which he said that he had nothing left to teach him.

In 1961, ill health accentuated by his lack of success against Richie Benaud's Australians, forced May's retirement from the England captaincy. My literary agent, George Greenfield, suggested that I ghost a book of his memoirs. He arranged a lunch at which I tried to discover what kind of secrets Peter might have in his locker. He had none whatever. He had had his problems, but he remembered no quarrels and had no dirt to dish. In an effort to show knowledge, I asked him how, when facing (and destroying) the legendary West Indian slow bowler Sonny Ramadhin, he could distinguish between a googly and an orthodox off-break. 'I couldn't,' he said. 'No one can.'

'So how did you…?'

Peter said, 'The only thing to do is to hit the ball before it has time to turn one way or the other.'

The memory of Charterhouse recalled the weekly 'art lectures' given, with black and white slides on the epidiascope, by A. L. 'The Uncle' Irvine, a recently retired, already legendary sixth-form master. The Uncle had inspired both Hugh Trevor-Roper and Peter Green to excel in Greek and Latin. Trevor-Roper acknowledged the quality of Irvine's scholarship but considered that he had been coercive in imposing his views on ancient literature and life. Trevor-Roper absconded to history. Peter Green has displayed no difficulty in challenging or discarding *idées reçues*, whether from The Uncle or from anyone else. If Peter ever made a prosaic mistake, it was in diplomacy: at Cambridge, he gave abrasive notice of his heterodoxy before he had secured himself an academic pulpit. Simon Raven claimed that Peter's first and great mistake was to have refused to apply for a commission in the RAF. This allowed his iconoclastic scholarship to be attributed to a bolshie character rather than to the freshness of his ideas.

Simon was given a research fellowship at King's, of which he was deprived after he breached the ethos of the college by a heterosexual adventure leading to the pregnancy of the nice Susan, who was later my patron at the

Sunday Times. Peter, the outstanding scholar of his year, was suffered to teach undergraduates but never to become a member of the Trinity establishment. He found a rewarding world elsewhere, especially during the years he lived, wrote and taught in Greece. Unlike Trevor-Roper, Peter had dared to dissent from The Uncle's opinions even as a schoolboy. When he won the Craven scholarship at Cambridge, The Uncle said, 'I understood that you are to be congratulated. In which case, congratulations.'

The Uncle had been a keen traveller in pre-war Italy. He summed up at the end of one sequence of art lectures by saying, 'Of all the plaishes I have ever vishited the one I should mosht like to shee again is Shan Gimignano.' Beetle and I went to the Lucca bus terminal to inquire whether there was a bus to such a place. Her Italian was better than mine but she left me to do the talking. There was a daily departure to the place I had named every morning at ten. We bought rolls and ham and cheese and a bottle of water and boarded the antique bus along with a few old peasants and their baskets. The driver headed inland, through Bagni di Lucca, past the 'Ponte del Diavolo', a pedestrian bridge steeply canted towards its off-centre crest and paved with cobbles untenable for cloven feet, and into the hills. We climbed through many bends in the narrow road until we stopped and the conductor called out '*San Gemignano*'. No one else got off.

We were at the foot of a hillside olive grove at the entrance to a small village of not more than a dozen and a half houses. I willed myself to echo The Uncle's rapture. Strings of corn husks hung, dark yellow, alongside wattled red peppers, from the tiled eaves; chickens ran and clucked as a cock strutted in to make his choice; grapes depended from wire trellises. It was a small Tuscan village. We walked down the rough street without seeing anyone at all. The low-built church had an unyielding door. We gazed at the olive trees and I wondered what The Uncle had treasured so keenly. Perhaps, more romantic than I had supposed, he had imagined the bucolic Virgil and Sabine Horace in the huddled cottages and the stone-walled allotments (Arnold Toynbee had recently claimed to have had a box seat at the Battle of Marathon). There was no café, no *trattoria*, no *brava gente*. The bus was not due to return until three o'clock in the afternoon. We sat in a field under an olive tree and ate our picnic.

I am not sure when it occurred to me that my mispronunciation – '*San Gemignano*' for '*San Gimignano*' – had carried us to the wrong place, but we discovered my error and, a few days later, took a smoother bus to the city renowned for its *campanilismo*. We could now see what The Uncle had admired, the competing towers conspicuous among them, and try to share his admiration. The baked beige streets seemed airless and without magic. Only Barna da Siena's murals had a spice of enlivening irony. As I remarked solemnly in my notebook, his sequence of panels in the Collegiata seemed like an obituary of the dying Middle Ages. The characters of Jesus's time were revised in the eye-narrowing light of suspicion and self-interest.

In the panel depicting the crucifixion, the figure on the cross, being humanely speared by a mounted squaddie, attracted little reverence from the attendant crowd of frescoed extras. While, in a corner, grieving women huddled around Christ's mother, Barna's central image at the foot of the cross (destroyed by Allied gunfire) was of Roman soldiers throwing knuckle-bones for the Saviour's raiment. Their scavenging presaged the vulturous advent of men such as the pitiless English *condottiere* Sir John Hawkwood, who came to pick up the pieces of what was left after the plague had done its worst. Barna included the only clear image of a grown-man's penis that I have seen in ecclesiastical surroundings. The drunken Noah was displayed, without a loop of tactful drapery, while his manifest manhood is mocked – or envied? – by his sons. *Campanilismo* of a kind? Or was the artist suggesting that, when floods come, the likeliest survivors are those who know no shame?

We sat on a beige stone wall and shared a small pot of chocolate-freckled ice cream and determined to find a way of not being separated when I went back up to Cambridge. For our fourth year, Tony Becher and I were free to live in 'unlicensed digs', without being irked by the rules of prompt homecoming at night and chastity thereafter. Tony found a furnished terrace house to rent in Montagu Road, well out of town along the Chesterton Road. There were four bedrooms, the largest of which, on the first floor, Beetle and I could share.

Once back in England, she spotted an advertisement for a job at the University Appointments Board. This employment exchange for graduates was housed in a four-square Georgian building off Chaucer Road, at the far end from the city to Montagu Road. Beetle was interviewed (and obliged to take an intelligence test) by J. G. W. Davies, whose fame derived from his having bowled Don Bradman, at the height of his powers, for a duck when the touring Australians played Cambridge University at Fenner's. He did wonder why Miss Glatt should seek a job for which she was manifestly over-qualified, but she did not indulge his curiosity. She left V. G. with more regret on his part than on hers.

When my mother heard of Beetle's plan to live in Cambridge, she was displeased, although no mention had been made of our sharing the same digs. By this time, Irene had surely guessed that we were lovers. Even her daily help, Mrs Garrod, asked me what it was like making love with that beautiful dark-haired girl. Irene called Beetle's mother to inform her of her daughter's imminent delinquency. Ray was neither shocked nor intimidated. She had winced when first informed of Beetle's decision but she knew better than to hope to change it. Ray told Irene that Beetle was a grown woman; she had no wish, or ability, to interfere with her life.

We filled the other rooms in 28 Montagu Road without difficulty. One was rented by a Siamese student whose surname was Punyanita. 'Poony' spoke pidgin English with a fluent paucity of vocabulary. Her response to any jest (and there were many) that she failed to understand was 'You clazy!' Her father was said to own all the prisons in Thailand as well as a zoo. 'Poony' was soon attached to Paddy Dickson, an always smiling medical student who also played piano for the Footlights. Paddy had an equally cheery double, a Johnian called Robert Busvine, who hung on the fringes of the Gaiety. So alike were they that I was never sure which one I was talking to until the course of the conversation veered towards some identifying marker. David Gore-Lloyd, who was also reading Moral Sciences, although he never came to supervisions with me and Tony, rented the top room in Montagu Road.

David made no marked contributions to our philosophical causeries, but he did once suggest that a machine for sorting bad eggs from good could be said to be 'biased' against the bad ones. This seemed to imply that a machine could have mental attitudes. The prospect of sophisticated computers programmed to disqualify certain people, or types of people, from benefits or even from medical attention, makes the notion of a biased machine less comic now than it seemed in the 1950s. David formed a romantic attachment to Poony's sister 'Pussy', who lived in the dormitory for foreign students run by 'Pop' Prior at an address that Poony called 'Nigh Ada Lo' (otherwise 9 Adam's Road). One day, David discovered that he had a lump in one of his testicles. His mother insisted that he go to London to be seen by a specialist.

Since our house was so distant from the centre of Cambridge, I spent a good deal of time in Leslie Bricusse's new rooms in a Caius annexe on the other side of Trinity Street. He approved of the work I had done on the 'book' and set himself to getting costumes, sets and cast for a December production. Although he showed no interest in the ADC, he was eager that their new president, Gordon Gould, play the part of our (in fact Canadian) heroine's American millionaire father. I had written a scene to open the second half in which Jinx, as I called our heroine, in memory of Mary Jane Lehman, whom I had loved briefly, but keenly, in New York, was at breakfast, at a very long polished table, with her badly hungover papa. It called for clever playing, in very slow motion, as the two of them slid various elements in the breakfast diet, with exhausted effort, from one end of the table to the other. I have no idea why we thought that this would be funny, but Leslie endorsed it, so long as we could get Gordon to take the part. No one in literary or theatrical Cambridge thought well of Leslie or of his artless ambitions. Not without a prolonged show of important doubt, Gordon Gould did, however, eventually agree to be of our company.

I rehearsed the actors with a facsimile of the confidence with which I had drilled my Lockite platoon. My jokes amused the cast enough to convince them that they would get laughs from the audience. Armed with the licence of authorship, I did not hesitate to coach Gordon Gould. If he came to scoff, he remained to play. Brian Marber was recruited to play a Dago racing driver based on Juan Fangio; Joe Bain (who had stayed in Cambridge to do a 'Diploma of Education') was Sir Roland Butter, the father of the tenor Dai Jenkins, a handsome Welshman who was engaged, in reality, to a very pretty, if short-stemmed, English rose called Norma. Tony Becher had not been slow to coin the phrase 'See Norma and Dai'.

Leslie had written all of the lyrics and composed several of the tunes. The rest of the musical work, and the orchestration, fell on Robin Beaumont, a handsome, versatile musician. Leslie took it for granted (neither Robin nor I chose to dissent) that he himself deserved a shared credit in both the writing and the music. The three of us were a triumvirate in which there was no doubt who played Julius Caesar. When the programmes for *Lady at the Wheel* arrived, a couple of days before we were due to open, the front cover announced the credits that we had all agreed, but there was a supplementary line, at the bottom of the page, in bold capital letters: 'The entire show devised and produced by Leslie Bricusse'. I was not pleased. When I indicated as much to Leslie, he said, 'Bloody printers!'

Success swept away petty resentment; in truth, Leslie could fairly claim that it could never have happened without his organisational thrust. The first-night house was full; laughs came immediately and loudly. Judging from the applause, the songs, however jejune ('Somewhere, somehow, some day…'), might have been by Jerome Kern. Leslie and I sat on the top steps of the circle swamped by a delectable torrent of laughter and cheers. I was anxious lest the second-act breakfast scene would be too slow, but Gordon Gould's drollery proved even funnier than in rehearsal. Another American recruit to the show, Mike Kitay, did a virtuoso meta-Charleston dance routine that capped the final scene, in which, of course, Jinx's car won the rally, the German driver was disqualified and everything ended as happily as contrivance could manage. Even the ranks of Tuscany could scarcely deny that we had had a triumph. Gordon Gould had the grace to seek me out and apologise for his lofty reluctance to give himself into our hands.

Yet another American graduate student, James Ferman, had been in our audience and declared himself willing to be involved in a future production by the Musical Comedy Club. He had had experience of the musical stage while at Cornell. Like Norwood Russell Hanson, he had been in the US air force, although never in combat. With a keen smile and a drop-head second-hand MG, he soon took up with Monica Beament, who was, in Groucho Marxist terms, something like the 'college widow'. A divorcée famed for her lack of inhibitions, she rode round Cambridge, in red slacks with obvious fly-buttons, on a hand-painted bicycle with an unfeminine crossbar. I had acted with her in a production by Miles Malleson of Turgenev's *A Month in the Country*.

Malleson was recognisable in British films because of his lack of a chin. He had played the obsequious hangman with the silken cord in Robert Hamer's *Kind Hearts and Coronets*. His beautiful wife Constance made him the best-known, and most complaisant, cuckold in the theatre: she was Bertrand Russell's mistress. I played the part of Turgenev's sulky artist. Malleson instructed me in tactful direction by asking whether I 'felt like sitting down' on a certain line.

After the last night of *A Month in the Country*, there was a party in a big house somewhere off Jesus Lane. I left my coat in a deep closet and had

to go in, and out of sight, to find it. While I was in there, I heard two people, one our business manager, a north Londoner called Derek Taylor, the
other John Tanfield, our leading man, who was a star teacher at the Perse
School, talking quietly about someone who 'could be charming when he
wants to' but tended to be 'a bit too clever for his own good'. I wondered for
a minute or so who this vexing person might be. Then Derek said, 'What
can you do? That's Freddie for you!' I stayed in the closet until, as movie
people say, they cleared.

Lady at the Wheel was denounced as flash, vulgar and much too American for the taste of Cambridge critics dedicated to the common pursuit of
self-importance. Leslie's rooms became a mecca for chancers of one kind
and another. An aspirant literary publisher, Peter Marchant, came for advice
on raising funds for a new magazine, in which he promised to feature my
work. Peter de Brandt, a handsome, well-funded playboy, appeared in the
hope of making contact with some of the pneumatic girls who had rallied
so willingly to Leslie's call. He had been introduced to a beautiful French
call girl in the summer vac. Uncertain how to begin, he tried talking about
Balzac. The girl looked at her watch, took off some of her clothes and then,
'as if she were going to pray to me', made a wanton frontal attack on her client. 'Well worth the ten pounds.' I never saw de Brandt again, but I attached
his name, slightly modified, to Julie Christie's demon lover, Miles Brand,
played by Laurence Harvey, in *Darling*.

At the beginning of the following term, I returned to the offices of *Varsity* and proposed myself as a contributor to the new editor. Like Trevor
Chinn, Michael Winner was a curly-haired London Jew of a brasher style
than I ever dared or cared to flash. He sported an unreformed accent that
owed nothing to Oxbridge phonetics and a slouchy black leather *blouson*.
Before coming up, he had bluffed his way into the job of movie critic for a
clutch of suburban newspapers. I never guessed from his impersonation
of an upwardly mobile barrow-boy that his father was a very rich man.

I played the old Fleet Street hand and was offered a column in the paper. It was no great chore to compose 800 words on weekly topics that might yield a laugh or provoke brief outrage.

Nicholas Tomalin was president-elect of the Union, as well as a joint editor of *Granta*, in which he had sniped at *Lady at the Wheel* for selling out to what is now known as 'product placement': in a café scene, Colin Cantlie (a general's son) had asked, in a Teutonic way, for 'drinking chocolate'. In return, Cadbury's agreed to buy a full page of advertising in the programme. It seemed an innocuous iniquity, but Nick denounced it as the insidious thin end of venal commercialisation. Envy and moral presumption are the twin propellers of journalism.

Not long afterwards, Tomalin sensationalised his presidency of the Union by inviting Oswald Mosley to come and speak. Mosley's Fascist past had not disposed him to post-war self-effacement. He advocated his cleansed version of 'Europeanism' with the rhetorical adroitness and virile posturing that had won him admirers literally left and right. In a *Varsity* interview, Nick announced that our soft generation had been intimidated by what amounted to 'a row of asterisks' into reacting with incoherent indignation at ideas that we could not articulate. For our political education, Mosley merited a hearing. The Holocaust was never mentioned either in the debate or in print.

The column in which I denounced Master Tomalin appeared after Mosley had paraded the civilised version of himself at the Union. There had been no ugly scenes, although the police were out in some force and the CU Socialist (i.e. Communist) Party had deployed a phalanx of its five or six cadres to cry down the Fascist. I remarked that, while Mosley 'behaved quite well', it had been Nick's crude pleasure to put the cat among the goldfish and the plutonium into the reactor. Ignoring what Mosley's Fascist friends had done, he depicted as hooligans only those who opposed him. Tomalin's self-promotion made me quite eager for a cup of honest drinking chocolate. If I had a desire to give Nick a double dose of his own medicine,

I had no solemn grudge. My sarcasm owed more to the rhetorical vanities of Cicero and Juvenal than to personal animus. One display of undergraduate grub-street opportunism deserved another. Michael Winner was pleased to report that Nick was consulting his solicitor. I was sure that he was conducting an exercise in intimidation; and I was right: no suit was brought.

A few years later, I had lunch at Overton's fish restaurant, in Victoria, at a table next to Mosley and his friends. Dressed in a whitish tweedy suit, like a bookie in his Epsom best, he was liver-spotted, thick-bodied and hump-shouldered. His most noticeable feature was the large, jutting nose. He called out in a cultured voice, 'Two more brandies, waiter,' and smiled without showing too many uneven, varicoloured teeth. He spoke of 'Hugh' (Dalton) and 'Nye' (Bevan) and 'Anthony' (Eden) with equal familiarity.

My *Varsity* column's term of eight issues impelled me to obey the dictum of Byron's pugilistic coach and 'mill away right and left'. Under deadline pressure, I found occasion to repeat in print Joe Bain's allegation that Bob Gottlieb and his wife, like the three Greek mythological crones who shared a single eye, disposed of only one pair of spectacles between them. What fellow citizen of Dorothy Parker and Alexander Woollcott would resent a little knockabout? In fact, my squib made Gottlieb my lifelong and, in due time, powerful enemy. Did my willingness to make him my butt have anything to do with the fact that he was, as I was under the skin, an American Jew?

Gottlieb's sights were set on a career beyond Cambridge and outside England. He accelerated to literary, rather than theatrical, importance. He joined, and later presided over, the New York publishers Simon & Schuster. In 1987, he was appointed editor of the *New Yorker*, only to disappoint its owners. They replaced him with Tina Brown, whose cosmetic extravagance goosed the magazine into the Age of Celebrity. Once in an influential position, Gottlieb took remorseless revenge on me for my juvenile squibs by scorning my novels in the US, for which he could be forgiven, though not by me. He had by that time disposed of his first, bespectacled wife.

When I heard that Jim Ferman, whom I scarcely knew, had passed scathing comment on the witlessness of *Lady at the Wheel*, I used journalistic licence to refer to him as 'Grim Jim'. As my deadline approached, even the beautiful Joan Rowlands, with whom I played tennis on the Newnham grass court, was labelled 'the Bakewell Tart' with Grub Street lack of scruple. The celebrated future Baroness Bakewell took it well, and I was glad; but I learned how easily journalism becomes a solvent of loyalties.

I took my cue from Bernard Levin's pseudonymous column in *The Spectator*. His 'Taper' was the scourge of the resurgent Tories. The attorney general, Sir Reginald Manningham-Buller, had been promptly, not all that subtly, dubbed 'Sir Reginald Bullying-Manner'; Sir Hartley Shawcross was re-sectioned into 'Sir Shortly Floor-Cross', which was indeed apt: the suave 'socialist' lawyer who had said, in 1945, 'We are the masters now' was soon to rally to the capitalist cause and became the chief legal pundit for Shell Oil. My mother went shopping with his wife in Putney High Street.

David Gore-Lloyd was absent from Montagu Road during most of the summer term of 1954. Diagnosed with testicular cancer, he had to go into hospital for the treatment then current for what is now one of the more easily cured forms of carcinoma. The bedroom above mine and Beetle's was taken over, at least some of the time, by little Dudy Foulds and her very tall lover John Nimmo. He walked her around Cambridge with his hand resting on the top of her head. At night, they made protracted love directly above our heads. 'Our gal Rosemary Clooney' singing on the American Forces Network was not enough to drown the sound of their accelerating bed. When David Gore-Lloyd returned, briefly, it was at the wheel of a grey Ford Popular, a present from his parents. It had a vertically striated metal radiator and a crank for emergency starts. Believing that he was cured, David drove us to Royston for celebratory tea in a nice hotel.

Beetle's job at the Appointments Board was not unduly testing. Jack Davies took her to Lord's and showed her the mementos in the Long Room.

He wore his handkerchief up his sleeve and referred to his son as 'the boy'. The other secretaries treated 'Miss Glatt' politely, but she became aware, as she consulted the cabinets in which were filed the confidential details of undergraduate job-seekers and their possible employers, that Davies's colleagues took candid appraisal to anti-Semitic lengths. One of our acquaintances was ticketed as 'looks Jewy and wears Jewy-cut clothes'. Nor were prospective employers spared: 'Looks like a Jewish Mr Truman.' Jack Davies was innocent of these routine reflexes; but Beetle was sufficiently indignant to take discreet copies.

During the vacations, I returned like any creeping Turk to Manor Fields. I purloined the phrase 'creeping Turk' from a poem in the works of T. E. Hulme, a pugnacious Johnian of proto-fascistic tendencies acquired mainly from French sources. Hulme was killed at the age of thirty-three in the Great War. His *Speculations* were lodged in a trenchant, abrasive volume of philosophical *pensées*, inspired by Georges Sorel. His 'Complete Poems', consisting of a dozen or so pieces in a bony symbolist style, supplied the appendix. At once anarchist, playboy and stylist, Hulme was a coiner of tellingly far-fetched phrases: one poem begins, 'In finesse of fiddles found I ecstasy'. It supplies an apt rubric for modern financiers and politicians. One apocryphal story tells of Hulme pissing through the railings of Berkeley Square in the early hours. Approached by a constable in corrective mode, Hulme said, 'I would have you know that you are addressing a member of the Middle Class.' It is claimed that the constable said, 'Beg pardon, sir,' and folded away his notebook.

During my absences, Beetle continued to work in Cambridge. She did not lack handsome company, but I never doubted her fidelity, even when she was, unsurprisingly, found attractive by 'Tadge' Leadley, Olympic oarsman and president of the CU Boat Club; and not only by him. Her presence in Cambridge was sufficiently remarkable for her to be noticed, black hair streaming, as she pedalled, long-legged, past St John's on her way to Chaucer

Road. I was told that Guy Lee, who had taught me Latin verse composition in my first year, met my tutor, R. L. Howland, and said to him, 'Do you know about Freddie Raphael living with this beautiful dark-haired girl out in Montagu Road?'

'No,' Howland said.

Guy said, 'Neither do I.'

XI

MY FOURTH YEAR went quickly towards the mundane moment when I should have to decide, as my father said, frequently, how I proposed to make a living. I never considered going to the Appointments Board. While determined to be a novelist, I had no idea of where to find a suitable garret or how I should pay the rent. My idea of being a writer had nothing to do with money or even with success; to be published would be heaven enough. Leslie had plans for us to 'write together': he foresaw a future with an office with a big two-faced desk, a secretary and a convertible 'wagon'. Meanwhile, I had my *Varsity* column to write, new numbers to devise for the May Week revue, and my approaching Finals. Compared with Tony Becher, I was inadequately prepared. I relied on lacing a pastiche of analytic jargon with clever instances. David Gore-Lloyd, whose medical treatment had procured him another year, which his parents could afford, before he had to take his Finals, was sure that if any of us was to get a First it would be me.

Early in the autumn term, Leslie contrived the resignation of Peter Stephens from the secretaryship of the Footlights and of Dermot Hoare from the committee. Without any manifestation of resentment on their part, I was co-opted as press secretary and Leslie's grateful lieutenant. He and

I and Tony Becher wrote several funny sketches. David Conyers, the vice-president, joined me at one of the Smokers in doing the Evelyn Waugh and Graham Greene number that I had composed among the mosquitoes in that Luccan *pensione*.

Leslie was determined that the 1954 revue would not resemble the haphazard *Cabbages and Kings*. The selection of material and of the cast for *Out of the Blue* would have nothing to do with fair shares. Only the best material and the best performers were to be involved. Although his renown as a sophisticated mimic – Bertrand Russell a speciality – was well established, Jonathan Miller rarely attended any of our Smokers. Even after he became a member of Princess Margaret's set, he claimed not to own a dinner jacket. Jonathan let it be known that he was reluctant to be distracted from his medical studies. Nevertheless, his light shone very brightly from under its bushel.

Jonathan's aloofness contributed to his *réclame*. He agreed only very slowly to be of our company, and on his own terms: his solo spots were not to be subject to the clock and he must not be required to take part in choruses or play a subsidiary role in any of the sketches. He had better things to do than to rehearse with the rest of the company. Although I did not even know of the Cambridge *conversazione* society's existence, Jonathan had been convoked as a member of 'the Apostles'; so too his homonym Karl Miller, who was no sort of a relation, although they later became brothers-in-law. Self-selecting intellectual grandees (John Maynard Keynes and Lytton Strachey had set the mark), the Apostles, past and present, constituted a lifelong freemasonry that disdained publicity but had no aversion to intellectual and social preferment. The two Millers could be sure of friends in high, and hiring, places.

Cabbages and Kings had had a large cast, not least because Peter Firth had neither aptitude nor appetite for imposing himself. He had gone on a monastic retreat immediately afterwards and was now training to become a clergyman. Knowing that Firth had been approached by a London management company with a view to transferring the show to a West End theatre, but had turned them down, Leslie had invited the same impresarios to come to see *Lady at the Wheel*, which he told me they had greatly enjoyed and wanted 'to talk to us about'. Of course, he remained in touch with them. Not for nothing did he already have that fat address book with alphabetic sections for London, Paris and New York.

At the beginning of the summer term, Leslie asked me to come for a walk with him. If he, like the Beaver in the old Fleet Street story, was now Napoleon, I was Marshal Yea. He had drafted a list of the proposed cast for the revue. Tony Becher was not on it. Did I think that he would mind? I was pretty sure he would. Leslie made the point that, being a non-singer, Tony added no volume to the choruses and now figured in only one or two of the sketches on the shortlist. Could I not put it to him, as his friend, that he would do better to concentrate on his Finals? Leslie would have done it himself, but it would be more convincing coming from me. Of course Tony's name would still be in the programme, as author of the things we had all written together.

Tony appeared less mortified than I feared. His ground-floor back room in Montagu Road was a hermetic cell in which he applied himself to canonical texts with such diligence that he rarely changed his socks. The pungency of the atmosphere secured uninterrupted privacy. He came to the communal lunches that I always prepared and for which Beetle often cycled home from Chaucer Road, but his housekeeping was limited to helping with the washing up and returning burlap sacks of the small glass Express Dairy yoghurt bottles ('yogs' in Becher-speak) that had accumulated during the week. For the rest, he kept his nose in his books.

28 Montagu Road was too inaccessible to rival 5 Jordan's Yard as a social fulcrum, but Joe Bain and John Sullivan, who had stayed in Cambridge to do research in some Silver Age mine of underrated texts, were regular visitors.

When Michael Jurgens arrived with a tomcat kitten for Beetle, Tony Becher took a cruel dislike to it. John Sullivan's erotic life had been in abeyance during previous term-times, but he was now emancipated enough to invite his Liverpudlian lady, to whom, to our surprise, he announced himself to be engaged, to come and stay for a few days.

Mary turned out to be a person of a certain age, at least thirty it looked, and of little pronounced charm. Could this be the woman who, with delectable shamelessness, had reached between his legs, and hers, to bring him off? She came to a meal at Montagu Road at the same time as Joe Bain, who was never unwilling to entertain the company. We laughed; Mary did not. Sullivan reported that she had concluded that there was nothing wrong with Joe that a bit of hanging wouldn't put right. Why had John chosen to marry her? It was as if, now that he was able to cut free and sail away from Liverpool, he had decided to haul up the anchor and lug it with him.

Renford Bambrough listened impartially to our essays, but had an easier harmony with Tony Becher than with me. I shall, however, forever be in his debt. Towards the end of my last term, Renford alerted me that the college administered a bequest, by a clergyman called Harper Wood, which funded an annual studentship of £350 to allow a prospective 'creative writer' to go on his travels and widen his horizons. The award was wholly outside the usual run of academic prizes: no one studied 'creative writing' in 1950s English universities. People had to go to Iowa for that sort of thing.

In the previous year, Harper Wood's bounty had been bestowed on Thom Gunn. I once sat opposite him on an 85 bus going up Putney Hill, but we did not speak. Pock-marked, unsmiling and zippily leather-jacketed, he looked as if he would be happier astride a Harley Davidson. He dedicated an early volume of his poems to his lover Mike Kitay, the pale, freckled, curly-haired American whose solo dance had been a *tour de force* in *Lady at the Wheel*. Thom Gunn followed Kitay to the US, where he came out as a butch, biker-style homosexual. His precocious first volume of verse, published in 1954, was entitled *Fighting Terms*. He was aggressively committed to the lifestyle that he found in the Haight-Ashbury neighbourhood in San Francisco, where he died of substance abuse without apology or, I imagine, regret. Mike Kitay was with him to the end.

The only hurdle between me and the almost literally heaven-sent opportunity to enjoy the Reverend Harper Wood's legacy was an interview with Hugh Sykes-Davies, a portly, bibulous don who taught English literature and had rooms in Chapel Court. An ex-Communist Apostle of the same generation as Guy Burgess and Anthony Blunt, Sykes-Davies would emerge briefly from cloistered obscurity, in 1964, when Blunt was revealed as a Soviet spy. In accordance with Morgan Forster's ethos, he disdained to turn his back on the unfrocked knight and announced that, if Anthony called, he would welcome him with a friendly glass. Such conduct was in character with the author of Sykes-Davies's surrealist novel in which, after a period as a rat-catcher, the hero, one Andrew Melmoth, elects to go down into the sewers and join the vermin who will take over the world and manage it more equably than human beings. Sykes-Davies himself would be appointed 'college rat-catcher' in 1967.

Joe Bain told me that Hugh, who had instructed him in the genius of William Wordsworth (another old Johnian), had been in the habit of leaving his claret-coloured curtains drawn during sunny afternoons, as a result of which, according to the college housekeeper, the material was fading and threatened to perish. He was formally requested by the formidable lady to open his curtains during daylight hours. He did as he was asked, but took to walking around his rooms, with the curtains wide open, in a state of ostentatious and rubicund nakedness. The interdiction on drawn curtains was rescinded.

H. S.-D. was fully dressed, if rumpled, when I went to see him. I had prepared an impressive catalogue of novels that I had read and admired and a list of socially responsible reasons why novelists, no less than Shelley's poet, should and could be the unacknowledged legislators of mankind. Sykes-Davies did not invite me to sit down. Did I really want this Harper Wood thing? Indeed I did. If he asked a few supplementary questions, he took small note of the answers. The brisk upshot was that the thing was mine if I really wanted it. With no marked sense of election, I walked back into Chapel Court after being promised enough money to keep me on the move for at least six months.

Thanks to Renford, Sykes-Davies and the Reverend Harper Wood, my immediate future was immune to mundane considerations, except for the matter of nationality. Since both Great Britain and the US still maintained conscription, I could not retain my dual citizenship. During the four years in which I had led, in the Empsonian sense, a pastoral life, secluded from brute realities in the bell jar of undergraduate playfulness, the war in Korea had been concluded, if not quite won, by Douglas MacArthur's master-stroke in landing a large force behind the North Koreans' front line. According to the liberal press, MacArthur had wanted to eliminate the menace of Red China by using nuclear weapons. He was recalled, in glorious disgrace, by Harry Truman. Dwight D. Eisenhower had been elected President in 1952 not least because he promised a quick, negotiated end to the war (as Charles de Gaulle proved, a decade later, once-victorious generals can best bring off such quiet retreats). The US no longer had need of a large army; although conscription remained on the statute book, recruitment had been suspended.

Great Britain was engaged in no overt war, but unrest in various parts of the Empire, as well as tension in the Suez Canal Zone, kept conscription in practical operation. I dreaded two years of khaki sequestration in some dull English posting, with or without pips on my shoulders. I wanted to live with Beetle and be a writer. If I told myself that I should be wise to keep the option of easy entry into the US, it was not because I ever expected to live there permanently. I opted for US citizenship and was rewarded with a card from President Eisenhower which thanked me for my loyalty and confirmed that there was no likelihood of my being required to report for duty.

Out of the Blue opened a week or so after Tony Becher and I had completed our last Tripos papers. Jonathan Miller was the undoubted star, but David Conyers and I received an ovation at the end of our impersonations of Evelyn Waugh and Graham Greene. The applause went on and on. There were cries of 'more'. We took one step towards a reprise, but the stage manager, Peter Scroggs, waved us away. Thanks to Leslie's energetic diplomacy, the offer that Peter Firth had rejected, for the revue to transfer to London for two weeks, was renewed; this time, it was promptly accepted. We were to go first to Oxford and then to the Phoenix Theatre, off the Charing Cross Road, opposite Foyle's (and the Damarrhoid dispensary).

During the last days of our run at the Arts Theatre, Cambridge, which had been endowed by Maynard Keynes, Leslie took me for one of our walks in the secluded first court of Caius. The show would be strengthened, he thought, if two or three of the best numbers from the 1952 Footlights revue were added, and the weaker of the present ones deleted. One of the latter featured me and David Conyers as a couple of bitching dogs. Leslie proposed that 'Not a Man on My Ottoman' and a number called 'Joe and the Boys' as well as the final chorus with the refrain 'It will always be the same' and a succulently sucrose tune, should be resuscitated from the archives.

When I made a sour face at the reduction of my appearances, Leslie suggested that I audition for the part of the Joe Loss lookalike band leader in 'Joe and the Boys' from the 1952 revue. He had to admit that he had already mentioned the part to Brian Marber. Brian was a genuine droll and, as he had shown in the tango-type song he sang in *Lady at the Wheel*, he could sing in tune. I was sure that Leslie was going through the motions of offering me a chance to do something that he did not think I was up to; I also suspected he was right.

A few mornings later, Brian and I turned up for our *mano-a-mano* in

the empty Arts Theatre. There was no band of extras to back our performances. Everything seemed to depend on how one presented oneself on
stage and made the opening announcement:

> Good evening, ladies and gentlemen, and welcome to Joe and the Boys. I'm
> Joe and these are my boys. We'd like to do a little number written by one
> of the boys in the band: 'Who's got the key, got the key to the cupboard?'
> With a one and a two and a three and a four…

Brian and I tossed a coin and I was sent in to bat first. I went into the wings,
while Leslie lolled in the front stalls and Brian stood to one side. Something possessed me to enter with my knees bent almost double. I seemed to
ride across the boards on a low trolley of air. In a voice of suitable Tin Pan
Alley vulgarity, I made Joe's little declaration, smirking in a way that would
have earned applause from the Harry person who met me backstage after
I had mugged so blatantly in the Mummers. My improvised funny walk
had gained the day before I said a word. Assuming that I would fail had
made me shameless and, it proved, unbeatable. Brian did his best to follow
and trump me, but he conceded, very sportingly, that there was no contest.

Leslie took the view that the material retrieved from earlier years was
the property not of individual authors, but of the club. As president, he
exercised seigneurial rights. We rehearsed the new numbers during the
next few days and were all set to try out the invigorated show at the Oxford
Playhouse. The day before we left, the results of Part Two of the Moral Sciences Tripos were hung on the Senate House railings. I went with Tony
Becher to see how we had done. Against precedent, two Firsts had been
awarded: Andor Gomme had one, Tony the other. I was among the three
or four who received a 2:1. I looked and looked again and shook Tony's
hand. 'Well done, Tone, you deserved it.'

I walked away and into King's and across the bridge onto the Backs.

I walked around for a while, digesting my deserved disappointment. I had been properly found out: I had lacked the resource to dress clever phrases with due scholarly allusion. Had I got a First, the tame horses of vanity might have pulled me towards an academic career. As it was, I had a wallet primed with specie and a warrant to be a writer. I went to meet Beetle for Scotch eggs and salads at the Arts Theatre Bar, which our cast had turned into their clubroom. An old West End chorus boy turned chef, Hedley Briggs, gave us extra-large portions from his glass-fronted buffet.

Beetle acted as dresser and, as Leslie put it, 'Mum' during the Cambridge run of *Out of the Blue*. Everyone liked her, including Peter Stephens and Dermot Hoare, who now landed the delectable part of the odalisque in the Ottoman number, and performed it with rouged and mascaraed aplomb. Beetle had resigned from her job at the Appointments Board, to Jack Davies's disappointment. She was working out her notice during the week we went to Oxford. Our hosts there were the president of the Experimental Theatre Company, Gareth Wigan, and Ned Sherrin, an officer in the OU Dramatic Society. After joining the BBC, Sherrin would become the impresario of *That Was the Week That Was* and achieve lifelong fame within the establishment that he and his crew huffed and puffed and pretended to blow down.

As I walked around Oxford, I was conscious that, had I never written that ill-advised letter to the Provost of Guildford, I might have gone to Christ Church and read Greats, just as I might well have chosen to be British. My old head monitor and tennis partner from Charterhouse Jeremy Atkinson was still in residence. He must have done his National Service and then returned for some post-graduate studies. I was surprised at the warmth of his welcome. There were several old Lockites among his Oxford friends. I was in no hurry to renew our acquaintance.

When Jeremy introduced me to his girlfriend Janet, a fair-haired, comely young woman, she offered to show me Christ Church meadows and the Isis boathouses. One of them had served as a diving platform from which Max

Beerbohm's *femme fatale*, Zuleika Dobson, made her meta-Sapphic plunge into immortality. Before we left Cambridge, Jim Ferman had told Leslie that he was planning to make a musical comedy out of *Zuleika*. Peter Tranchell was going to write the music. It threatened to be a very good idea. Leslie rather wished that we had had it ourselves. As we set out on our stroll, Janet indicated that I had been a not infrequent subject of conversation among Oxford's old Carthusians. She had gained the impression that I was a person of rare intuition. That was why she wanted to ask me something.

'What might that be?'

'Do you think I'd be a good thing for Jeremy? As his wife.'

'A good thing? I honestly have no idea. I don't know you and, if the truth be told, I scarcely know him.'

'He thinks you'd be able to tell.'

'You grace me with rarer qualities than I possess.' I was never more elaborate than when embarrassed. 'You both know much better than I do. You know…'

'Yes? What were you going to say?'

'Wittgenstein said, "The person who asks the question is in the best position to answer it."'

She said, 'I daresay he's quite right, whoever he is.'

XII

*O*UT OF THE *Blue* was greeted in London by an effusive
press. Even Ken Tynan and Milton Shulman were of the same
mind: iconoclastic intelligence had alighted at the Phoenix
Theatre. We played to sell-out houses. The run was extended
to three weeks. We were each paid £15 a week. Danny Kaye, who was filling the Palladium at the time, endorsed Jonathan Miller as Britain's answer
to Danny Kaye. My performance, with pencil-thin moustache and brilliantined hair, as Joe in 'Joe and the Boys' was not clever, but it had an unsubtle
triumph. One hot afternoon, Leslie and I played several sets of tennis on an
asphalt court off Haverstock Hill. I wore gym shoes that did little to protect my feet as I turned and ran and turned and ran again. When I took off
my sock, the bottom of my left foot came away with it, in one long white
fillet. I did my usual stuff that night on a raw sole and danced off in a shoe
tacky with blood.

Thirty years later, I was invited to a dinner party because the guest of
honour, the Nobel Prize-winning biologist Peter Medawar, was eager to meet
me. Since he had recently debunked the pseudo-scientific casuistry of Pierre
Teilhard de Chardin, I looked forward to a philosophical soirée. He had
perhaps seen some of my recent critical essays. A quadruple paraplegic of

philosophical good humour, Medawar wanted only to have me know that my performance in 'Joe and the Boys' was the funniest thing he had ever seen.

Free of the Appointments Board, Beetle resumed her popular place backstage, where Judy Birdwood, the very, very large and always smiling daughter of a field marshal, acted as wardrobe mistress and den mother. Judy was married to the stage designer Oliver Messel's cousin Rudolph, who had been at Oxford with Evelyn Waugh. Both were members of the legendary, because notorious, Hypocrites Club (a coven, it was said, of homosexuals). Encyclopaedic sources claim that Judy and Rudolph lived an idyllic life in their large country house. In truth, by the early 1950s she was pining cheerfully while he amused himself with young men in foreign parts. His fellow Hypocrite John Betjeman also married a field marshal's daughter; so did Hugh Trevor-Roper, although he was no sort of a known hypocrite.

The success of *Out of the Blue* opened doors; Leslie made sure that we went through them. Willie Maugham had said that he was unsurprised by fame; once achieved it seemed no great achievement. We were invited to a Ken Tynan party, in some borrowed mansion north of the park. Annie Ross, who was born in Scotland but whom I took to be American, was cool before her time and sang in a syncopated fashion that sounded dangerous and subversive. Ken took me to meet Frankie Howerd, who was an outrageous, but never outed, BBC television star. Ken said, 'This is F-Freddie Raphael. One of the most b-brilliant young men in the F-Footlights show at the Phoenix.' Howerd looked without appetite at my outstretched hand. 'I hate talent,' he said.

One evening towards the end of our run at the Phoenix, Leslie called out to me to come into his dressing room. A man wearing a grey, wide-brimmed fedora was sitting in the low armchair. Jock Jacobsen was an agent with MCA, in those days the most powerful transatlantic talent agency. He had come to see the show because of Jonathan Miller, but he had been more impressed by Leslie, both in the monologues that we had written together and in a number in which he and Brian Marber did a nifty song-and-dance routine that began, 'We have the Time of our Life in America / Good old USA'.

Jacobsen was an ex-drummer who, with one of the boys in his band, saxophonist Norman Payne, had started a variety agency. It had recently been absorbed, to their enrichment, by the American conglomerate (at that time MCA's president, the legendary, quasi-omnipotent Lew Wasserman, also controlled Universal Studios). They had big offices at 145 Piccadilly. Leslie told Jock Jacobsen that, thanks all the same, he had no wish to be a performer; but he did want to write musicals and things, with me as his partner. Jock Jacobsen agreed to sign me as well as Leslie as a client of MCA. It had a literary department run by Elaine Greene, the sister of the novelist whom I flattered by my lampoonery every night ('Religion is my pigeon') and twice on Saturdays.

Having got word of my little number about Evelyn Waugh and Graham Greene, which ended with 'Victor Gollancz?' 'No thanks', V. G. asked Beetle to get him tickets. He invited us to dine with him and his wife Ruth after the show. In the taxi on the way to a dining club in Hill St, Mayfair, he asked what I was going to do. I said that I wanted to be a writer. He thought that a very bad idea; it was no way to make a living. It turned out that it was his and Ruth's wedding anniversary. If she was not pleased to be celebrating it in our company, she showed no sign of it. V. G. was sixty-one years old but, like my British grandfather Ellis, he seemed a venerable old gentleman.

The Footlights' success brought us to the attention of the BBC. Leslie, Jonathan, Brian Marber and I took part in the popular TV programme *What's My Line?*, which was presented by Peter West, a nice, rather nervous ex-soldier who blinked a lot. Whether or not we were put up to it by the producer, we demonstrated Cantab insolence by lifting West's chair from behind its desk and carrying him off the stage on it. Such was iconoclasm in the summer of 1954.

Brian Marber had use of his father's large black Austin Princess. One very early morning, after the show, he drove me and Frankie Francis (our drummer and son of the millionaire owner of a Caribbean island or two) and others of the company down to Charterhouse. We rolled in over Bridge, under the arch of Brook Hall, around the perimeter of the main school and up to the headmaster's house. My double-act partner David Conyers wound down his window and called, 'Bring out your lovely headmaster!' No light went on. No face appeared. We drove back to London. Before *Out of the Blue* closed, in late July, the committee met to decide on Leslie's successor as president. Brian Marber was the obvious candidate. Leslie was doubtful whether Brian was good-looking enough, but he was elected without prolonged discussion or any mention of the Jewish question.

A senior radio producer called Roy Speer invited Leslie (and me) to put together a satirical half-hour broadcast. We adapted some of the old numbers and wrote some new ones. However callow our comedy, it must have gone down quite well. Roy was sure that he could find us work at Broadcasting House. He introduced us to the radio talent agency run by Kevin Kavanagh, the son of the unfairly forgotten genius who wrote all the *ITMA* scripts and paved the way for *The Goon Show*. We were welcomed onto their patch by other BBC scribes with a generosity that we were smug enough to take as our due. Frank Muir told us that he and Denis Norden had recently received a letter from Broadcasting House accounts department saying that they had been overpaid for repeats of *Take It From Here* by £12.10s. Their cheque for that sum would be appreciated. 'We wrote back,' Frank told us, 'saying that we regretted that we had no machinery for repaying money.'

'And never heard another word,' Denis said.

If Beetle dreaded my departure on my Harper Wood travels, she had the style to insist that I should go alone. Dreading it myself, I clung to the romantic notion that solitude fostered genius. On my own, my responses to the Europe I had never seen would be keener and more authentic. Leslie may have wished that I was going to be there to tickle up the *Lady at the Wheel* book yet again, but he had been approached by the Tennant organisation, which then dominated the West End theatre, to take part in *An Evening with Beatrice Lillie*. Suitably revised, the two monologues that we had composed for him to deliver in *Out of the Blue* were very much what was needed to give Bea Lillie a breather between her numbers, most of which she had done on pre-war Broadway.

The most famous was the one in which, in the course of drinking copious drafts of gin, she telephoned an order for 'two dozen double damask dinner napkins'. The comedy derived entirely from the garbling effect of the alcohol as she repeated the order for what turned into 'danner nipkins'. Another old favourite had Bea telling how she sat with her friend Maud in the lobby of a louche hotel, where she announced, 'I've come here to be insulted and I'm not going home until I am.' The number ended with, 'We're rotten to the core, Maud / And Maud agreed'. The show was due to open in early December. Jock Jacobsen had me sign a contract stipulating that I should receive a £6.10s royalty for every week in which Leslie performed our material in London. Showbiz appeared to be a very easy touch.

In early October, on the eve of my departure, Beetle and I had supper chez Victor in Soho. Perhaps we went to a film. I so hated the thought of leaving her that I wished the evening to end. We walked down to Hyde Park Corner, where she could catch a 52 bus to Willesden and I a 74 or a 30, to Putney. As we stood there, someone came up to me and said, 'Fred? Hullo.' It was Robin Jordan, with whom I had been at Lockites and who was given the scholarship to Christ Church that I had craved. As the witness of my humiliations at Charterhouse, Robin exercised a watchful, if not morbid, neutrality. Now he smiled at Beetle and seemed unaware, and yet somehow entertained, that he had intruded on our last moments together.

Beetle's bus came and I kissed her, in front of Robin, and she got on and was driven away. I smiled and laughed with Robin, as if Beetle's departure had been a relief. I read the gleam in his eyes, a sort of admiration, as close to voyeurism; it flattered and displeased me. Trading on an intimacy that was never cordial, he played on knowing my schoolboy secret. He was planning to leave England soon and go to South America. I had the feeling that there was something that he wanted from me. I suspect that it was nothing personal: he practised his seductive competence with no intention other than to be sure that he still had it. Robin Jordan was never a star, but he had a stellar aptitude for turning on a certain provocative charm.

St John's College gave me a tranche of £75 of the Reverend Harper Wood's bursary. When I had got through it, I was free to apply for another slice. I bought a BEA ticket to Paris. One had to begin somewhere. I went, with too much luggage, to catch the Royal Sovereign flight. It was the first time, since my infancy, that I was ever in an aeroplane. When we were living in St Louis in 1934, Jimmy Doolittle – who in April 1942 led the first bombing raid over Tokyo – worked for Shell Oil. He took my parents and me for a baptismal spin around the city in his plane.

Sir Bernard and Lady Docker were at the bar in the lounge, drinking whisky. He was a tallish man in a grey suit; his chin receded into his collar, giving him an air of genial imbecility. Norah wore a little black dress, a beaver-lamb coat and a flat fur hat. An elderly secretary held a glistening hank of silver fox, fine as candy floss, in case madam's rich shoulders felt cold. Lady Docker had poise, if not breeding: she might have been one of Colette's courtesans. They were escorted to the plane ahead of the rest of us and were greeted with salutes by the crew.

I found a spare seat adjacent to where they sat, with their backs to the engines. Food came to them first, with a bottle of complimentary champagne. As we throbbed towards Paris, Sir Bernard said that he had heard that BEA had helicopters these days. His aide said, 'You could have one, Bernard,' rather as if he were selling picture postcards. 'Not safe enough yet, in my opinion.' They were met on the tarmac at Orly by a large Daimler, with an attendant van for their seventeen pieces of luggage.

I could have wished not to go to places that reminded me of Beetle, but silly homesickness took me back to the Hôtel des Deux Continents. I went to La Hune, the bookshop adjacent to the Café des Deux Magots and bought two volumes of the plays of Jean Anouilh and sat, wearing my black corduroy existentialist trousers, in the Rendezvous des Intellectuels in the hope of election. After a solitary while, I crossed the Boulevard St Germain, went to Raffi, in the rue du Dragon, and had a sorry *chateaubriand*.

I spent the late evening at Les Halles, the great central food market that Emile Zola called *Le Ventre de Paris*. *Putes* of various aromatic flavours thronged the *trottoirs*. The most attractive stood, hair piled in individual red lights, on high platform heels, in *décolleté* advertisement for *plaisirs tarifiés*. I watched, and lusted, but I did not approach any of them; none approached me. I was naïve enough to be surprised when a tall French army officer, in képi, with polished riding boots and leather-sleeved swagger stick stopped and spoke, at length, with a tempting tart. She listened to his requirements, which I was unable to hear, and must have named a price for their satisfaction that he found too high. He took a step away. She called out an offer. He followed her into a dark building, slapping his tall boot with his swagger stick.

A couple of days later, I used the last of my Métro *carnet* to go to the Porte d'Italie and started to hitch-hike southwards. Several short lifts took me to the far side of Melun, beyond the *pavé*. From there, a quite large grey corrugated iron Citroën van took me onto the N7, towards Saulieu. After a few kilometres, my driver pulled out to overtake a *poids lourd* just as, without warning, it began to turn left. We were driven across and off the road, slid between two plane trees, and bounced across the furrows of a ploughed field. We stopped and did not start again. The driver said, '*Faut trouver une autre voiture.*'

My last lift of many reached Lyon as the light was fading. He dropped me on the far side of the bridge across the Rhône. I walked, with my clumsy bag, into and through the city. I skirted the long wall of the railway station and trudged on towards the southern suburbs. I dreaded the loneliness I should meet when I stopped. At length, I went into a small hotel restaurant with a bright bar that was blue with what I took to be honest *travailleurs*. As I waited to hear if they had a room, I heard one of them say, '*Ce n'était pas une vraie défaite. La France était vendue en Quarante. C'était les juifs. Ils ont vendu la France. Que voulez-vous? Ces gens-là, chez eux, ce n'est que l'argent qui compte.*' The salt of the earth lost its savour.

The next morning, *de bonne heure*, I tramped back to Lyon station and caught a train to Nice. From there, I took the bus to Juan-les-Pins, where Scott Fitzgerald had had the inspiration that led to *Tender Is the Night*. I went first to my parents' favourite hotel, Mon Repos. Finding that it was about to close, I walked through the shuttered town to the Hôtel des Voyageurs. My thousand-francs-a-week back room offered a close-up view of the main-line railway. My dreams were torpedoed by shafts of juddering sound, but I had a place to work.

I bought an unlined quarto pad of white marbled paper and a biro and began to write a novel. I had no urgent subject in mind. Mr Maugham said that a writer had to write every day. When dry of material, he had had recourse to writing his own name over and over until he bored himself into invention. I recalled going with Guy Ramsey (he had two complimentary tickets from the *Daily Telegraph*) to see and hear Johnny Ray at the London Palladium. The star's signature number was 'Cry', which he contrived to do at its climax, twice nightly. His other hit, 'Oh what a night it was, it really was!', was clearly a gay anthem. It gloried in what was, at the time, a criminal offence.

Guy flinched at the American's lacrimose emotionalism, but there was something appealing in Johnny's sorrows. I sat at my marbled pad for a few minutes and then, quite as if I were taking dictation, I began to write about Frank Smith, a Putney greengrocer's boy who dreams of becoming a star and, with anguished spontaneity, composes the songs that turn him into one. The characters of Frank's parents in *Obbligato* owed more than a little to Frank Muir and Denis Norden's sketches in *Take It From Here* featuring Ron and Eth ('Oh Ron, here we are out in the country and alone at last! Just you, me and that couple on the verge'). Although I knew little about the greengrocery business, I remembered someone telling me that it was a trick of the trade to put the best of the fruit, which will retain its freshness longest, at the back and along the bottom of the box. Mr Maugham had said that, in order to describe the taste of roast lamb, it was not necessary to consume a whole sheep, but it was a good idea to have eaten a lamb chop.

The showbiz caricatures were based on my brief experience of West End life. Jock Jacobsen had proved that he was offering us the key of some kind of kingdom by sending Leslie and me to see George and Alfred Black, who put on shows at the London Palladium. George or Alfred (it was hard to be sure which was which) had just been to Paris, where he saw a sketch, perhaps in the Folies Bergère, so good that 'as soon as I saw it, I thought of it'. Perhaps we could do an English version just like the French one, but also, of course, unrecognisable as such. Jock, with his hat on, was depicted in *Obbligato* as Franco Franks, 'the agents' agent'. He had a rival called Oscar Hammertoe (his name inspired, I suspect, by a movie director called Orson Kaart in 'Flook', Wally Fawkes's sly strip cartoon in the *Daily Mail*). Another of Franco's colleagues was 'Mugs' Marber, who bought a showy American car and then found he lacked the means to fill the gas tank. Franco Franks said of Frank Smith, 'Go down Liverpool poss!' It was the last place in the UK that I could imagine being associated with pop singers.

My brush could hardly have been broader, but I accumulated wordage with daily regularity. I was alone, but not lonely, not when working. I had not written more than a dozen pages before I was certain that, when it was finished, my innocent little book would be published. It was a relief to find a topic other than woeful adolescence, the prejudices of the bourgeoisie and the misfortunes of the Jews. I laughed at my own jokes quite as if they had been delivered by someone else. Frank's improvised songs were those of an anglicised Johnny Ray, full of rhyming lamentation and then, as the plot developed, of the joy of true love with the girl of his dreams.

In the afternoon, I walked into Juan-les-Pins and bought *Le Figaro*. Mr Maugham had advised travellers who did not speak the local language to buy a newspaper and, in the privacy of their hotel bedroom, read it aloud. If you had any kind of an ear, you would recognise when you were beginning to sound like a native. The *Librairie* where I bought the paper had a rack of English-language books, among them *My Life and Loves* by Frank Harris, in four field-grey paperback volumes. It was a classic hot book still banned in England, but the Reverend Harper Wood funded its purchase. I was stimulated by the efficiency with which Harris threw women's skirts over their heads and addressed himself, to cries of outrage and then delight, to applying his head between their legs. From time to time, he emerged to say, 'Oh you little dear, you!' before finishing things in a more or less conventional pose.

On my second day in Juan-les-Pins, I summoned the nerve to write to Maugham and ask whether I might visit him up at the Villa Mauresque. His response, in his own handwriting, came almost by return: since my letter was undated, he was not sure whether I was still in the region. He named a possible day for me to visit him, but warned me that his house was somewhat remote. He was not certain how I should get there unless I had a 'motor bicycle'. Alternatively, I might get to St Jean Cap Ferrat by bus, in which case he would have me met in the *Place St Jean*.

XIII

A MAN IN A pork-pie hat was already sitting on the single stone bench in the little square of St Jean Cap Ferrat. We remained side by side for several minutes and then he said, 'Mr Raphael?' His name was Alan Searle. He was Mr Maugham's secretary. He led me to a grey Citroën. The uniformed chauffeur opened the door and I got into the back. The grey-felted front seats had chromium bars across the top.

Maugham's signature Moorish talisman was branded on the white gatepost of the long, white villa. The front hall had black and white tiles and a twist of staircase, with an *art nouveau* metal balustrade. Alan Searle took me past an unmistakable Picasso, of a grey dying harlequin, and another big canvas, of a crouching figure, into the bright sun-lit drawing room. Two triple sofas, in blue upholstery, faced each other across a low, lacquered table.

Like the narrator in Maugham's 'The Voice of the Turtle', I waited for my first sight of a legendary man of letters. In the story, the distinguished, bearded man who comes downstairs to meet his deferential caller appears 'every inch a poet' (Maugham never feared a cliché), but turns out to be a retired brush salesman. The narrator has called at the wrong house. When a small, brisk man in dark grey flannels and blazer, a Paisley scarf at his throat, strode into the living room of the Villa Mauresque, Alan Searle said, 'Here is Mr Maugham.'

I shook the offered brown hand and he sat down next to me on the sofa. I had no sense of being coldly appraised. 'Now,' he said, 'we must see about getting you some tea. Or perhaps he'd prefer a cocktail?'

It was four-thirty in the afternoon. I said, 'Tea, please.'

A white-jacketed manservant brought tea and *petits fours* badged with candied cherries. After the stale bread in my *pension*, they tasted like manna. For some uneasy reason, I asked for my tea with lemon; Mr Maugham took it the same way. He asked me what I was writing. I said that it might seem a strange thing to do on the Riviera, but I had started a novel about people who lived in Putney. 'Not at all,' he said. 'Old Kipling, whom everyone despises these days, was quite right when he said, "What know they of England, who only England know?" It's only when you get away from somewhere that you can describe it. You recall the s-salient features and all the irrelevant d-details f-f-fall away.'

When I told him that it seemed that *Lady at the Wheel* might be on in London, he said that he had had to wait ten years to get anything of his on the stage. The last time he had been in London, he had seen *The Boy Friend*, Sandy Wilson's skittish pastiche of a 1920s musical. 'I didn't enjoy the joke as much as I should, because I stopped going to musical c-comedies in the '90s of the last century.'

After tea, he told me that I should get a job. That way, I should have some experience of the 'rough and tumble' of ordinary life. He started to light a cigarette. The match jumped from between his skinny fingers and fell into a crevice between the blue brocade cushions on the sofa. He was suddenly an old man, flapping at the fugitive ember in elderly panic. I felt pity and affection for him as he recovered his dignity.

He asked me how old I was. I said, 'Twenty-three.'

Maugham said, 'You've got plenty of time, plenty of time. You won't go

into the BBC, will you? There was a man called Carn who won the Maugham
Travel Award some years back. He went into the BBC and nothing's been
heard of him since.'

He recalled another young writer – was his name Dahl? – a dozen of whose
stories he had read recently. The first two were promising, but only three
or four of the rest were up to standard. 'And that's not enough, you know.'

Not long before, he had called on Max Beerbohm in Rapallo. 'I was
shocked at the change in him. He looked a very old man. He must be eighty-
nine, of course, but he looked about a hundred and fifty. We were all young
together, you know, in those far-off days. Do people still read Max?'

I told him that I had read the essays and parodies and that *Zuleika Dobson*
was being made into a musical comedy by a Cambridge friend of mine. He
nodded. Perhaps he was more concerned about whether we read *him*. He
feared that the Edwardians (which he pronounced to rhyme with 'guardians') were dying out. Who knew how the fossils would be filed by the new
curators of the literary world? Or, he might have added, how the curators
would themselves be screened in time future. I did not tell Maugham that his
only mention in *Scrutiny* was in a brief, dismissive review of *Don Fernando*,
his memoir of youthful travels in Spain (including a visit to a brothel, where
the girl was revealed to be so young that he could not continue). Who now
regards Frank Leavis and his 'connection' as decisive in literary matters?

Maugham was soon to go to London to see his doctor. The ones in the
south of France were altogether too casual. 'They advise me to let nature
take its course. At my age, that's the last thing one wants.' His journey was
necessary because he had fallen over while extinguishing a fire in his garden.
His ribs were still strapped up, which did not inhibit him from laughing
heartily when I confessed that I was carrying an Old Carthusian tie in case
I needed to establish my respectability if I had to call on help from some
British embassy.

I told him how much I envied the range of his reading. 'I've had a long

life in which to acquire it. But there are still gaps. Books in Swedish and
Portuguese must be rejected at once.' He received, on average, five manu-
scripts and some four hundred letters a week. They came mainly from young
men and old ladies. 'They frequently enclose photographs of themselves,
but rarely any stamps.' It seemed an odd grumble when you were sitting
in a room hung with paintings by Monet, Pisarro, Manet, Renoir and, if
I was right, Boudin.

I mentioned bridge. His appraisal of the top players seemed accurate
enough: he particularly liked Kenneth Konstam and declared another famous
player, no doubt Boris Schapiro, 'very rude and unpleasant'. Konnie's son,
Michael (later attorney general of Kenya) played in the St John's College
bridge team under my captaincy. Also an amiable man, he did not have his
father's skills at the table. In 1960, soon after I had published a novel called
The Limits of Love, Kenneth Konstam's bridge column in the *Sunday Times*
featured a hand in which I and my partner, in one room, 'sacrificed' against
a certain slam by bidding six hearts, which went a few tricks 'light'. When
we compared scores, our other pair, Michael and his partner, in 'the other
room', had also – after a bidding mix-up – played in six hearts, unfortunately
with only two hearts in each hand, although they held all the remaining aces
and kings. Such contracts have been made, but not in this instance. 'Konnie'
remarked that his son's performance must have 'strained the limits of love'.

I told Maugham that I intended to hitch-hike from Juan-les-Pins into
Spain. Alan Searle asked how I proposed to get about inside the country.
Maugham said, 'He'll take the omnibus. You'll find the people in Spain
wonderfully polite and charming. Alan, we must give him some maps and
that list of Paradors.'

They had been in Spain recently and 'stayed at the most expensive places
we could find. You see, I have some quite large royalties tied up there and
I wanted to spend them while I could. At the end of the trip, I asked for the
account. They refused to bring it.'

Alan Searle said, 'They were so privileged to have Don Guillermo with them that they couldn't possibly accept any money.'

Maugham asked Searle to be sure to give me a letter to a man who would, he said, 'open all the doors in Madrid'.

After I had been there an hour, I thought it tactful to take my leave. Maugham said, 'Would you like to look at the pictures on the way out?'

He led me past an ormolu console, its slab of marble supported on the spread wings of a Napoleonic eagle. I suspected that it was the one that he had invited his brother, Frederick, to admire. The then Lord Chancellor looked at it for a moment and then said, 'A bit florid, isn't it?'

In the chequered hallway, Maugham stopped in front of that large canvas of a crouching man. Could I guess who painted it? The name Toulouse-Lautrec came immediately to mind: something about the modelling of the head betrayed his hand. For fear of seeming foolish, or a smart alec, I shrugged.

'Toulouse-Lautrec,' my host said, 'Sir Kenneth Clark is the only man ever to have identified it.'

Sensing that my host might have been disappointed if I had guessed right, I felt a little like the pushy, almost certainly Jewish, Max Kelada, in Maugham's short story 'Mr Know-All', who had a moment of untypical tactfulness when he consented to look a fool in order not to compromise a young woman whose pearls he knew to be the valuable gift of an admirer rather than the cheap souvenir string that she desperately wanted her husband to believe that it was. The story ended, 'At that moment, I did not entirely dislike Max Kelada.'

The chauffeur took me in the grey Citroën to the village square, where I waited for the bus back to Juan-les-Pins.

I had written no more than a third of *Obbligato* when the manager of the Hôtel des Voyageurs told me that it was about to close for its *fermeture annuelle*. I caught a train to Portbou, on the Spanish border, where the track changed gauge. The wooden carriages of the Spanish train shone with brown varnish, like those in the newsreels of recruits waving with required cheerfulness as they were hauled away to the Civil War, less than twenty years earlier.

I walked from Barcelona station down to the Ramblas. With small appetite for roughing it, I checked into a staid bourgeois hotel with a rotating door onto the street. After a lunch of dry diced fish doused in old oil, I bought the *Green Guide* to Spain and a primer of the Spanish language and walked towards the centre of the city. It was a sunless afternoon in October. The Plaça Catalunya looked beige. The gantry of an unlit electric advertisement stood on the roof of a high, light-brown building, like a huge spider on black stilts.

Most of the customers on the terrace of the Café Catalan, in the southwest corner of the square, were men. They sat on collapsible brown wooden chairs with hand-holes in their backs. To command the attention of waiters, the customers clapped hollowed palms – once, twice – in peremptory summons. Bossy rings glinted on little fingers. Those soonest served wore sharp shoes and brown chalk-stripe suits, pouting white shirts, narrow, dark, knitted silk ties with gold tie slides, officious moustaches.

A shoeshine boy stopped and pointed at the shoes of a man reading a copy of *ABC*, the monarchist newspaper published in Madrid. Without looking directly at the boy, its reader applied one thick-heeled shoe to the ramp on the sloping lid of his box of equipment. The boy slid a leather shield on each side of the man's ankle to protect his silk sock from being soiled. The box, with an open compartment for polish and rags, appeared to be made of ebony. The black surface was dotted with many rows of brass nails. I sat down and clapped my hands and ordered *un café*.

A dead tank stood like a beige sentinel in the far corner of the square. Orwell's Catalonia was an occupied country. I took a little square Renault taxi to Gaudí's *Sagrada Familia*. I looked and I was amazed, and unmoved, and then I walked back through the city and back to my dull and proper hotel and studied my Spanish grammar. In the evening, I walked down to the *Barrio Chino*, the district of bars and brothels adjacent to the harbour. Joe Lyde, an Irish jazz pianist who was one of the louche habitués of 5 Jordan's Yard, had told me that you could have a woman in Barcelona for one and ten pence.

I went into a loud casino, canted barrels in three rows above the zinc bar, and told myself to listen to the conversation of the working men. I understood even less than I might since they were talking Catalan. I drank *una caña cerveza* and wondered where the women were. I knew that I should be too squeamish to go with one, but I was not above wanting to have, as they used to say, a squint at the menu.

The next morning I took several sheets of my hotel's finely woven, pale yellow stationery and went back to the Café Catalan, clapped my hollowed hands and ordered a *café con leche*. I wrote and wrote to Beetle, a very long letter, edge to edge four sides of the nice paper. I loved her and I could not wait to see her again and would she marry me? I was looking forward almost more than I could say to seeing her at Christmastime. I hated being without her and I would not let it happen again if I could help it. I told her about the women in their tall black lace *mantillas* as they paraded in the *Ramblas* for the early-evening *paseo* on the arms of their unsmiling husbands and then I told her again how I wished she was with me. Did I say that, woeful as I was, I was learning things that made solitude worthwhile? I doubt it; but I was: for instance, that I did not like myself all that much; I provided myself with a lacklustre companion.

I posted my letter and set out to abate my loneliness by making the rounds of the Gaudí apartment houses, asymmetrical scribbles of ironwork on their bulging balconies. Then I took a dated little Renault cab to the zoo where he had designed the outdoor furniture, stairways and polychrome mosaic balustrades. I cannot recall speaking to anyone during my three days in Barcelona. I heard the sound of my own voice only when I was sitting in my hotel bedroom reading aloud, as Maugham had prescribed, from the pages of *ABC*. The paper was grey, the headlines rusty red, the reactionary content irrelevant to my slow conquest of the *idioma Español*.

After three days, I took the train to Madrid. The *Green Guide* recommended the *pensión* Argentina, on an upper floor of a tall building in the Calle Alfonso XII. I never discovered which doors Maugham's letter of introduction might have opened to me because I lost it before I got off the train at Atocha station. The only person who opened any doors for me during my four days in Madrid was the *serreno* who patrolled the street after nightfall with a jangle of keys on his thick leather belt. When you arrived home late, you clapped your hands and he came running. In return for a peseta, he opened the grille across the entrance to the building and shut it behind you.

Some Argentinian visitors in the *pensión* assured me that the purest Spanish was spoken in Buenos Aires. Lacking *porteños* to imitate, I worked at my grammar and eavesdropped wherever I could. Something inhibited me from trying to make conversation with strangers, male or female, whether in bars or in the Prado, where I tried to conjure some original response to Velazquez and Bosch and Murillo and El Greco. Goya's Black Paintings were in the basement, quite as if they had been relegated to the chamber of horrors. What other court painter was ever so subversive? He had gone from nugatory pastoral to the savage heart of the matter.

I went out for a breather into the forecourt of the Prado. A young American couple, the tall slim man in a seersucker suit, his wife in loafers, sweater and skirt, were giving their small daughter an ice cream. I heard the man call out, 'You all by yourself?' He could say that again. 'Had lunch? Care to join us?' His name was Herb Oppenheim and this was Judy. Herb was thirty years old, with a fair complexion, short greyish hair and blue eyes. Judy had a pleasant smile, but she was no beauty. And this was Linda. She was three years old.

Herb had just graduated from Columbia's school of architecture. Garlanded with a Guggenheim, they were driving through Europe with studious zeal. Loneliness made me talkative; my accent entertained them. Herb was impressed by my academic record (I did not mention that I had failed to get a First). They were planning on leaving for Toledo next afternoon and then driving on down into Andalucia. There was room for me if I cared to join them. I did not wonder why a strange couple should so generously take a stranger on board. I liked myself better when I had an audience.

We arrived in Illescas, just short of Toledo, in late afternoon. Herb was driving a small blue Simca car with a bench seat in the back and red international number plates. He had discovered from his guidebook that there were several El Grecos in the Santuario de Nuestra Señora de la Caridad, in the main square. The big wooden doors were padlocked. Herb was a rich man's son. Persistence (and perhaps a suitable donation) procured the arrival of a very small, very old nun. She brought not only the key to the Sanctuary, but also an oil lamp by which we were able to inspect paintings in a suitably sepulchral light. Since she was so short, the light spilled upwards and darkened, in dramatic fashion, into jagged shadow.

As we drove on up to Toledo, the purple sky, fractured by lurid patches of brilliance, towered over the jagged city. I had not spent time with Americans since I left New York as a small boy. It was a deliverance to be in unsuspicious company. Herb was a Jew; Judy was not, nor did she come from a prosperous family. She told me that she had liked Herb, because he was gentle, before she realised, from the drawings in his thesis, how brilliant he was. She came from a Midwestern state where the word 'measure' was pronounced 'mayzher'. It was easy to present them with an agreeable version of myself. Herb taught me to look up at old buildings in modernised streets in order to appreciate what they had looked like before the ground floor had been improved. He was quick to believe that I was going to be the writer I wanted to be. Beetle soon came into what I told him about myself.

We went to the Alcázar and read the words of the Franquist commander, El Coronel Moscardó, who allowed his own son to be shot by the Reds rather than surrender the citadel. He told the boy, over the field telephone, to recommend himself to God and cry *Viva España*. There was an old motor-bicycle which, when jacked up by the besieged cadets, generated the only available electricity. It was difficult not to side with the beleaguered bad guys.

Herb led the way to the great church of Santa Maria, which had been the central synagogue before the *Reconquista*. When we visited El Greco's house, I recalled Willie Maugham's suggestion, in *Don Fernando*, that the Greek's flamboyant superficiality was typical of, as they used to say, 'queers' (Herb's term was 'fruit'). I had no idea that Maugham was painting an incidental portrait of himself. Herb said he had never met anyone of my age so well read. Judy seemed happy that Herb had talkative company. She occupied herself with Linda, who had derived small pleasure ('playzher') from spending weeks in the little Simca, as they honoured Herb's virtuous, demanding itinerary. He wore his father's money modestly, but it dressed him with the presumption that he was entitled to the best. He had a three-dimensional camera, which he wielded assiduously. We broke our pot-holed ride south, through Aranjuez and along the wide, monotonous plain of La Mancha, by stopping overnight in Ubeda. The four-square, thick-walled Parador was an early Renaissance castle of unadorned brown stone.

The following morning, as Herb and I were loading the car while Judy was busy with Linda, we were approached by the son of the last private owner of the property. He had a round, heavy head, like a polished bean, and a front tooth missing. His suave English had the rueful cadences of those who had known cosmopolitan days. When Judy arrived, with the fractious Linda, he asked why they didn't hire a *muchacha* to look after her. A local girl would work fifteen hours a day for between 150 and 300 pesetas (£2–£3) a month.

We had to stop at a level crossing on the Ubeda–Linares narrow-gauge railway while a train shunted back and forth several times. A throng assembled around the alien Simca. They smiled at Linda and offered us cigarettes (*Celtas* were only a few pesetas for twenty). The ragged children were often misshapen: skin eruptions, oozing ears, gummy or already divergent eyes. Others might have been Murillo angels. Dark eyes stared, enviously but without malice, at the plump American kid.

Judy Birdwood had recommended the *Hotel de Cuatro Naciones* at Córdoba. Herb rated it 'minimal' but its blue tiled floors and white walls seemed quite elegant to me. The city was an impacted monument to the centuries of the *Convivencia* when, under a tolerant caliph, the dominant Muslims lived on easy terms, some of the time at least, with both Christians and Jews, who occupied powerful positions in the city. Monotheistic Judaism made better sense to the Muslims than the Christian Trinity. The magnificent *Mezquíta* and its fate stood in unique witness to the city's history.

I wrote in my notebook:

> … there is a great Moorish gateway of tawny stone. Through it, a court of orange trees (*naranjos*) and a black-and-white pebbled path to the entrance of the *Mezquíta* … Inside, the ceiling and shell of the building are suddenly exalted. The double Moorish arches seem not to need their pillars. They fly up and support the roof with no effect of effort; like formal foliage, they rise apparently independent of the marble trunks below them. Arches stride away in all directions. The desecrated, roped-off Mihrab evokes more awe than any crucifix or statue. (In Toledo we saw an exhibition of Virgins; the only one of merit came from the Congo.)
>
> The cathedral pillars – pink, white, mottled with black, quartz-like and marble – had been cannibalised, probably from a temple of Janus. In the centre, the ornate and gilded chapel of the Christian cathedral is a wilfully tactless intrusion. The reticence of the ruptured mosque comments, with stylish sarcasm, on the presumptuous rhetoric of Christianity.

You are always aware of the arrogance of the Church. I never met a polite priest. At Ubeda we were told that 'the Reds' destroyed many Christian ornaments. They were woefully unthorough. Of all that I have seen, only one ghastly piece of work achieved its effect: in Toledo Cathedral some Baroque artist plastered the pillars supporting the lantern and frescoed them with figures that thicken into three dimensions. Statues step up through the domed opening and climb into the pink heavens until they seem to stand on naked air. Concealed light from the lantern gives an impression of lurid infinity. It is perfectly appalling. Who could dream up anything in worse taste? But what showmanship!

Whatever the Reverend Harper Wood might have thought of my insolent sentiments, thanks to him I was seeing things in a way I never had before. Alone in my hotel bedroom, pen in hand, I was no one in particular, sure only that he was a writer.

In the starched streets of the ghetto, Maimonides's house had been turned into a museum of tauromachy. The little synagogue where the great Rambam had prayed was clean and void of memories, a square, blanched, lifeless room; no black elders; no bewigged women looking down from the balcony; no light, no ark in the niche. The old guardian, who had but a single tooth, announced that it was a '*Monumento Nacional. Antigua sinagoga Ebraica.*' He indicated where the Torah had been kept and how it was wrapped and I nodded as if to imply that what he was saying was familiar to me. Delusions of Sephardic origin prompted furtive aggression. I wrote in my notebook: 'The Jews, we are still told, must learn to behave. Must they? How many people have *we* driven from their homes; burned, murdered, crucified? Before the walls of Jerusalem, Titus crucified seven thousand men who had defended their city. *Eso no es lo peor*, far from it.' I cadged the phrase from the title of one of Goya's *Desastres de la Guerra*.

Herb was a New York Democrat. He believed that the Rosenbergs were innocent. Certainly they had not deserved the death penalty. Greenglass, the chief witness against them, had everything to gain by saying whatever the FBI wanted. Even so, he said only that he had heard of a man called Julius who was some kind of a 'leader'; the name Rosenberg was not mentioned. Did I know that Klaus Fuchs's middle name was Julius? Surely he was the 'Julius' who was alleged to have memorised and passed on information about the mathematical formulae necessary for making an atomic bomb. Rosenberg had failed every mathematical grade in school.

Einstein and another physicist, Harold Urey of the University of Chicago, had said that it was inconceivable that such a man could remember abstruse information. The Supreme Court said that if the defence had been properly conducted, the case could, at one stage, have been thrown out; had it not been, they would have had grounds for allowing the appeal, but only if appropriate objections had been voiced during the trial. Even so, three Supreme Court justices dissented from the judgment, all Liberals. Herb maintained that the Rosenbergs would never have been convicted, on the evidence, by an impartial jury. America was on the way to Fascism: you had only to compare Judge Medina's attitude to the trial of Communists to his conduct in the federal anti-trust case over which he presided at the same time.

Herb was neither loud nor heated. He had no intention of living anywhere except in the US. He was a keen advocate of the international style, all glass, steel and concrete of the kind celebrated in Siegfried Giedion's *Space, Time and Architecture*, which I made a note to read; and in due time I did, all four volumes. The name of Alvar Aalto sticks adhesively in the mind, the man to be if you wanted to come top in any index. I also remember Baron Horta, whom Giedion accused of betraying the modern movement by deciding that there can be too much steel, glass and concrete.

I asked Herb what he thought about the Willie McGee case. McGee was a Mississippi black man, sentenced to death for rape in 1945 and eventually electrocuted, after a series of appeals, in 1951. A number of famous people from William Faulkner to Albert Einstein pleaded with Harry Truman to reprieve or pardon him. Herb thought it likely that McGee was having an affair with the white woman, who accused him of rape, to avoid being called a nigger-lover, when rumours started to spread about them.

Linda cried and cried. We stopped for coffee on the way to Granada and ate the cakes we had bought in Sevilla. Herb crumpled the *pasteleria*'s cardboard box and left it on the table. As we were going, the waiter punched the box back into shape and took it into the café. By the time we reached the gardens of the Alhambra, all the rooms in the Parador San Francisco had been taken. A young American, in slick clothes, called Russell, advised that 'the neatest of you' go into the Alhambra Palace Hotel and have them recommend somewhere within our means. Russell told us that Granada was 'wonderful', quite as if we might not have heard. He was figuring to stay till at least – I expected him to say the following year – '*Monday*'. He wrote travel pieces for *Holiday* magazine. Herb said, later, that he was a 'snide Ivy League snob'.

We found rooms at the Pensión America, a hundred yards up from the entrance to the Alhambra. My bedroom window looked across the deep, steep valley to the Sacro Monte, where the gypsies lived. Since I was down to my last few £5 traveller's cheques, I went to the *Correos* and sent a telegram to St John's College asking for another tranche of money to be sent to the Banco Central. The following evening, the son of the *padron* took us, in a party of tourists, to see and hear some flamenco. The '*Zambra*' took place, under unshaded electric bulbs, in a large cave lined with wicker-seated chairs. We sat down, awkward, and looked at the few gypsies already there. Two guitarists strummed listlessly. Our lame guide whispered that the dancing would probably be bad. At the back of the deep, whitewashed cave, you could see an old iron bedstead with a red cover. A tired tiered dress hung on a wardrobe.

A fat-armed gypsy with an elusive brassiere came and sat down, yellow flowers absurd in her towered hair. Others, older, wrinkled, with rounded noses and thin reddened lips, wore similar flowers. Six elderly gypsies, in washed-out costumes, began to dance. The routine might have been the sad opening chorus of 'Why go to Granada?' You felt like a visitor to a brothel; wishing you weren't with people you knew, insufficiently excited to forget your embarrassment.

A young gypsy girl sat beside me, mouth heavily rouged, and clapped with petulant servility as a solo dancer replaced the sad sextet. The newcomer whirled, and nearly fell, and clicked her castanets, brows contracted. More gypsies arrived and more chairs were brought, and more. A new young girl, fourteen or fifteen, very slim, no bosom, darker than most, luminous black, accusing eyes, pride in her shaken, lustreless hair, thin fingers with crescents of whitened nail, stared unblinkingly over our heads, serving a different god. She snapped her fingers and the clapping resumed.

Perhaps her technique was bad, but there was no separating the dancer from the dance. Her young repertoire was instinct with proud resentment. Her heels spurned the red tiles as she jumped forward, skirt raised, rapping the rhythm with her heels, claps, cries. Suddenly she would stop; hands writhing in the silence, eyes frowning at them, dark and love-ready, flicking across the audience now, available for a moment and then, oh no; then secret, guarding the flame within. She bent back over the floor, red lips, white teeth, face knit yet reposed; beauty.

Then she was moving her hands again, arms so slowly moving, as she watched and watched them. Up again, shaking her shoulders, eyes narrowed and suspicious; more clapping, sharper, demanding. The cries of the onlookers more earnest now, the dancer's hair tumbled over her nose, dark eyes, knit brows, red lips, heels rapping and rapping; head flung back, virgin eyes dark with knowing innocence; then the hair flung forward again: climax, stillness, applause. The god spent, all that was left was a shy girl who nodded to the company and went to sit down.

A girl of twelve, with broad flat feet and the wide-apart hazel eyes of a Velázquez princess, came in and danced, brows drawn in concentration, breastless chest arched, hair long and lank and brushed back. A young boy danced with her, almost a dwarf. The angular, haughty postures of his puny body, the slanting contempt in his little eyes left you uncomfortable at how perfectly he mimicked the big man he would never be. He beckoned to Linda and the little American girl seemed possessed; she writhed like a Bacchante, her eyes caught fire, legs twitched, hands straining to clap in a kind of sexual paroxysm.

An old man with a long nose, sad small eyes in a pale face, quavered some flamenco; he was said to be the most inspired of the singers, but his voice was past its best; when the singers are young, their voices are suitable, but they lack the wisdom. You can never hear a perfect flamenco singer.

I ended the account in my notebook with: 'When the girl danced again, briefly, it was more calculated. You wanted to give her your heart, but she wanted only pesetas.'

XIV

A FTER A FEW days, the Oppenheims were ready to drive on to the next architectural landmark. They urged me to come with them, but each time I went down the hill to the Banco Central, I was greeted by a head-shaking clerk: there was still no sign of my money. I was not entirely sorry to be alone again. Herb and Judy had made things easy, for which I was grateful, but I had been drawn out of the anonymity with which I now resumed spying on the world. What I overheard seemed truer than anything said to me directly. A Welshman staying at the *pensión* with his teenage son snatched at the *moscas* that blackened the buffet tablecloth at breakfast. 'Nothing like Spanish flies, boy,' he said. I noted the leer. Why would a man say that, like that, to his son?

I went back to the Alhambra and, on the advice of Russell (he seemed more cogent because I did not like him), bought a five-day ticket that included the bonus of a visit to the gardens by moonlight. I took my Oxford Complete Shakespeare. The fountains were all dead. It was shadowy and cold. I read a few sonnets by what I could cadge of the moon's own borrowed light and then went back to my narrow bed.

In the morning, I went again to the Banco Central and gave them my name 'Raphael, Frederic'. There was still nothing. I went to the Capilla Real and tried to enjoy the unSpanish precision of the Dutch paintings that happened to hang there. I bought and pretended to enjoy Washington Irving's *Tales of the Alhambra*. In the Court of the Lions, I overheard a guide explain that the Moorish recipe for covering the ceilings with that pendent plasterwork included white of egg, which rendered it proof against the weather. When the Christian conquerors tried to repeat it, in order to efface the original mouldings, with their Koranic citations, the added plaster fell off.

Among the tourists, I saw the couple who owned the hotel Mon Repos in Juan-les-Pins, where my parents stayed. I smiled and said, '*Bonjour.*' They were not responsive. One afternoon, an Englishman whom Herb had befriended came in search of a fourth for bridge. His name was Murdoch; he was staying at the Hotel Washington Irving. When I told him that Linda and her parents had left, he said that they would have been wise to give her 'a good hiding'. He had been at Cambridge and had served as a supply officer in the Far East. The Chindits kept asking for things he couldn't provide. When the next war broke out he knew exactly what he was going to do: 'I shall polish up my Morse and become a wireless officer on a small ship.' The bridge game was not of a high standard. We did not play for money, but I happened to win every rubber. Murdoch and his friends looked at me as if my name might be Sandheim.

I trekked again to the Banco Central and was greeted again by a shake of the head. '*Nada.*' I could not believe that St John's College had let me down. It occurred to me to say, '*Por favor, mire sobre effe. Frederic.*' The money was there. They had, unsurprisingly, taken Raphael to be my first name. After two weeks, unlike the last Moorish sultan, I left Granada without a sigh.

I took the bus to Algeciras and caught the morning ferry to Tangier. The enclave was still governed by an international consortium. Bourgeois timidity led me, past a red British pillar box by the harbour gate, to the Hotel Bristol in the European quarter. After lunch, I walked up to the casbah. A Moroccan boy, perhaps twelve years old, in a faded brown shirt and dirty trousers led me up a cobbled alley faced with blank walls to a cruciform café. Dark-stained doors opened onto three tiled rooms with black tables, few chairs. A man lay unconscious on a stone bench against the wall. Another Arab sat beside him, in a fez and brown *djellaba* (collar and tie underneath), a small violin upright on his knee. He sawed at it with no effort at tunefulness.

In a corner, by the unglassed window, a boy was smoking a long bamboo pipe with a tiny clay bowl. In the room across from us, unshaded electric light shone on Arabs sitting or reclining as they smoked pipes similar to the boy's. On the sawdusty ground in front of the bar, several glasses lay on their sides. The elderly landlord, in a soiled suit and yellow apron across pyjama-like trousers, brought me a tall glass of black coffee, another of tea for my companion, who told me that he did not work; he smoked *kif* all day to dispel the blues.

The boy informed me that marijuana in its dried state was pale green. You had to pull away the diamond-shaped leaves and remove the tiny yellow seeds. The stalks and seeds were too strong to smoke. The leaves had to be chopped finely, like parsley, and left to dry. The boy filled a new pipe and handed it to me. The bluish smoke tasted mild, not at all like Player's No 3. When I had finished my bowlful, the boy indicated that I should blow down the cob. The dottle popped out onto the floor. The violinist looked alarmed when I was offered a second instalment: I should be careful, he said. The other Arab and the boy laughed. They smoked all day and look at them. The unconscious Arab rolled off his narrow bench and thumped on the floor, without waking.

The boy walked me back to the Hotel Bristol. He promised to come back at eight o'clock that night and take me on a tour of the brothels. He knew all the best places where the girls were clean and would do whatever I liked. Or did I prefer boys, like so many of the Europeans in Tangier? I suppose that I gave him some money, but I was already too sleepy to remember. I went upstairs in a leaden haze and fell on the bed. I woke at eight o'clock the following morning, after a dreamless fifteen-hour sleep. I never did go to the brothels. I arranged to leave my big suitcase at the Bristol before I caught the train to Fez.

Two manifest Jews shared my compartment, alongside a heavily built European, in horn-rimmed glasses, reading André Maurois' *Ariel* in Spanish. The older Jew was tall and wore a brown suit, baggy but expensive, with broad lapels, and a floppy brown hat. When it was removed, there was a black skull cap underneath. He had a full black beard, pale skin, harsh hair brushed back from his shiny forehead. His nose was rounded and fleshy, lips full and soft, the lower one drooping, a dip in the centre. His mouth was always ajar. Perhaps he was adenoidal. He spoke in a very British accent, with the odd middle-European consonant. He wore brown shoes with black socks. His hands were broad and white, like Dover soles.

His companion was a francophone Moroccan, olive-faced, smallish eyes, nose curved to a dark upper lip, profile almost semi-circular. He too wore a *yarmulke* and scanned a Hebrew book from time to time. The brown-suited man quizzed him, with explicit loudness, about the conduct of Zionist affairs in north Africa. He seemed to be a sort of Lawrence of Morocco. His only commendatory remark, not infrequently uttered, was, 'He's a very *clever* boy.' Something possessed me to ask him whether, by any chance, he knew the Test match score. He seemed quite shocked. He had something of the obsessive humourlessness of the character played by Joseph Wiseman (in a similar hat) in *Viva Zapata!* When he opened his very big brown suitcase, with reinforced corners, to get some apples, I saw that the contents had all been compressed into tight cylinders. He might have been toting a range of pork-free sausage rolls.

My guide in Fez was an Arab who had been a sergeant pilot in the RAF. I could call him Ahmed. He wore a plum-coloured fez with a tassel and a fawn linen robe. The Hôtel de la Paix was in the modern European quarter. Between it and the old city was the Sultan's summer palace; it had been turned into a barracks for French native forces. Mohammed V had been sent into exile for demanding independence for his kingdom. The riots that followed, and their repression, had ruined the tourist trade. We passed a Bren-carrier that had tipped into a ditch. A French officer was supervising its removal under the eyes of a carefully expressionless crowd of Berbers and local Arabs.

The Berber camp was under the battlements of the old city: dark tents, a brown and white dog, women carrying children tucked under their bosoms; seated men, in white robes, made a large double circle around a story-teller. Ahmed promised that the stories came from the *Thousand and One Nights*, but a good raconteur, like a Homeric rhapsode, added his own flourishes. The ancient world was coming to life in front of me, too late.

The French supervised the *souks* where workshops and stores were combined in tiny alcoves. There were pools of dirty water and a yellow reek of urine. Beggars squatted in the dust; rich men straddled their mules on turreted saddles. The side streets were so narrow that we had to sidle between the bulge of the white walls, as if the houses had overeaten. Tight cedar doors gave off a faintly scorched odour. The lintels were no more than five feet above the dusty ground. They had slim brass hands for knockers, pendent fingers, for luck.

One of the metalworkers took a disc of brass, like a cymbal, and laid it across a vice and took up a small chisel and a light hammer. Looking about him as he did so, he tapped the wedge and tooled the surface of the metal with a pattern of leaves in an intricate flow of curving lines. One false stroke and it would be ruined. He subdued his material with a kind of humble contempt for the admiring stranger who watched him.

The salesmen all told me how lucky I was: things were going cheap; they needed money badly. Ahmed did not quite convince me that he was arguing my case when we were bargaining. He leaned up and kissed a seller's forehead rather too quickly. I bought a silver bracelet for Beetle, but backed away from thin teapots, coffee pots, coasters, gongs, chandeliers and incense burners gaudy with green and white and blue and red enamel.

Behind the old Arab market, with its blackened cedar arcades, now a police station, a single fat gendarme leaned, in blue shirtsleeves, over the first-floor balcony. Below him, ironworkers made grilles for windows. The forges were black as funerals. Squashed against the back wall squatted a boy clutching and pumping the double bellows with both hands so that, like alternate lungs, they breathed first one, then the other, on the hidden fire. The tip of its tongue darted, like the pulse of an insatiable passion, quick and thrusting at the bolts of iron pressed up to it by the smith's tongs. When the arm of iron was red, he drew it out and beat on it before its heat could run away. He hammered it into curlicues, flexing it with no more than the hint of effort you might apply to bend a sheaf of spaghetti in boiling water. Behind him, the dark child, feet packed away in a curve of dark toes and pink soles, pumped and pumped as though priming his own heart.

After the bridal dresses, with their cinctures of gold twine braided on linen and the grooms' white-belted costumes, we came to the dyers' quarter. Pots of colour lay like fractured rainbows on the roadway. Vats of natural dye bubbled under corrugated iron hoods, cadging colour from boiling flowers and leaves. Women drowned fresh bolts of white in the vats and prodded them to stay down, like memories dumped into oblivion. Between the old and the new town – literally middle men – came the Jews in their black cowls. Their houses resembled those in Toledo: open wooden balconies on the first floor; tall windows below, where the Arab houses were closed and secret. The Jews were detached, aloof and vulnerable.

The sunset, when it came, blushed quickly, a tissue filter pinking the distracted clouds. At five-thirty the light was lit on the principal minaret of the main mosque. Crowds hurried to pray in one of the 134 mosques in the city, some grand and elegant, others like the dark box near where ironworkers filled the brazen air with their hammering. Donkey carts with lanterns bobbing fore and aft clopped along; an Arab sideways on a donkey, kicking its neck with his heel in rhythm with its agreeable movement. The muezzins' cries rose as the sun crumbled into ash. The sky glowed hollowly in its husky wake. Night had fallen.

I went by train across the desert to Meknès. In the new town, where I found a clean hotel, the *colons* behaved as if they were in France: they sat in the sidewalk cafés and shook hands with each other on meeting and parting. The buildings were white and sheer and impersonal. The road curved up into the old town and dwindled into pot-holes and cracked concrete channels. I came to an Arab café, flies and more flies, blackness inside; soiled wooden benches and old card tables; the Arabs' clothes were crusted with sweat. There were donkeys' hoofprints in the crusted dung below the high triple gateway to the medina. Inside, there was a broad rectangular square, domed like a shallow breast, where the native buses left for Moulay Idriss, the sacred town that Europeans had to leave by nightfall.

In the modern, French quarter, I found my way to La Comédie Humaine, a *librairie* run by a Russian émigrée who told me that her name was Princess Kubowsky. She wrote novels and memoirs, published by Plon, under the pseudonym Jacques Croiset. She had won the *Prix de Paris* for her 1949 novel *Europe et Valérius*. She said she was delighted to meet an Englishman. She had escaped to London in 1941 and had a wonderful time as a journalist. She met Cyril Connolly. A short, thick woman in a black suit, she looked like leftover puff pastry in a black pie dish. She had a flat thick nose, pudgy cheeks, a large, loose mouth, blue eyes, chin depending from a big jaw. Her husband, a Pole, was in Brussels, trying for a job with some international agency. He always told her that she talked too much and was too inquisitive for the British taste. She did not ask me why I was in Morocco nor what I had done or planned to do. She did, however, warn me, urgently, against making a joke about a French *légionnaire*'s képi. I could not easily imagine feeling the temptation.

She had put her life's savings, 4 million francs (roughly £4,000), into buying the shop, four years earlier. Now, in the midst of a war without a shot, since there were no tourists, she was broke. Local French residents used La Comédie Humaine as a social centre (always shaking hands with everyone present, both on arriving and on leaving), but they bought few books, it seemed. One of the women had a twelve- or thirteen-year-old daughter of whom a *colon* remarked, with a shaping gesture, '*Elle a déjà sa petite poitrine.*'

There was, Jacques Croiset told me, 'no such thing as justice; divine justice perhaps, human never'. She seemed to think that because the Germans were beasts they could not be blamed for the concentration camps. She told me about a Russian woman, a writer, not Jewish, who was in one of the camps. A girl of fifteen was included in a list of those who were to die. When she began to cry, the woman said, 'Don't take it so hard. Death is not such a terrible thing. If it will help you, I will come with you.' The woman took the girl's hand and they went into the gas chamber together. I had not heard any such stories before.

Jacques Croiset secured me an invitation to dinner at the house of a Moroccan prince, Moulay Ta'ib, to whom she had rendered some service *chez les Français*. A friend of his, a slim Arab in European dress, with an inch-long beard along and under his jaw, met us at the gate of the medina. The low cedarwood door to the house was in an unlit street. The hall was angled sharply to the left, like the city gate. Pairs of open-mouthed, shucked shoes lined the tiled wall inside the door.

The central room was bare of furniture. There was a basin of washing by the wide fireplace. An open doorway led to the kitchen and the women's quarters. The high beamed ceiling was continuous with that in the small, oblong room into which we were shown. A pale blue cotton curtain hung in the square archway. There was a radio on an inlaid table; a cheap alarm clock (bell on the top), mirror on the wall above it. We sat on the lowest of three couches. Backed by a row of plump pink cushions, it was covered with floral, blue-green linen.

When Moulay Ta'ib joined us, Jacques Croiset exchanged courtesies and then withdrew. Both the prince and his friend had sworn not to cut their beards until Mohammed V was reinstated. They were suffering financially for their loyalty. Moulay Ta'ib was short and dapper; he had a dark leathery face, the colour of roast turkey, fine-featured, with black, amused eyes, neat brown hands. He curled his small feet, in grey socks, under him as he sat between us on the highest couch. His nephew, a thin boy of twelve or thirteen, in a grey suit and dark tie, brought a silver basin and a kettle from which warm water was poured over our hands, then towelled away.

My guide cut flat loaves into six. Pieces of lamb came on long spits on which they had been grilled over a wood fire. You tore out the centre of your bread, gloved the meat and drew it off the spit. Only the right hand was to be used; the left never. As soon as one spit was empty, another came. I assumed that this was all we would get, but the kebabs were followed by a huge bowl with lumps of meat and spiced cabbage leaves, swimming in gravy. You heaped a mixture on your bread and put it in your mouth in one quick movement. It was bad manners to have your fingers touch your lips. I dropped a piece onto my lap and retrieved it hurriedly, too hurriedly, with my left hand.

Moulay Ta'ib and his friend ate with clean dexterity. We talked easily, unfazed by the clash of plates and cutlery. After the big dish was removed, the boy brought a heaped bowl of grapes. Then came the basin and warm water, now with a piece of soap, to purge the grease. We reclined on the pink cushions and smoked Gauloises while tea was prepared. Only the master of the house and his closest friends had the right and the art to make it. Various kinds of mint came in gilt coffers. There was a gilt teapot of chased metal, sugar crystals like nuggets of salt. The mint was put in the pot, with lumps of sugar, and boiling water poured in from a tall, thin-necked kettle.

Then it was passed to the visitors. We drank many glasses. The pot was refreshed with more mint, before being replenished.

Moulay Ta'ib had read Spinoza, Descartes and Plato. He was both intelligent and, it seemed to me, naïve: he wanted the French to stay as the administrative servants of the restored Sultan, who would have supreme jurisdiction. Having thus advocated a civilised compromise, he said that he hoped that the French would kill them all. Salvation lay in dying as a martyr. I do not remember that the Jews were ever mentioned. At that time there were still several hundred thousand in the country. Moulay Ta'ib's friend went home quite early, but I stayed talking with him till one-fifteen in the morning.

When I went out into the mazy streets of the medina it was very dark. I had only a vague notion of where the European quarter was. There was a curfew and no one about. I was stopped by a suspicious and (at first) hostile Foreign Legion patrol. I was not at all disposed to make a joke about their képis. My passport excited no immediate solidarity. I was at once alarmed and aloof: what did Morocco and its animosities have to do with me? My French was improved by apprehension. When I asked the sergeant to indicate the way to the hotel, he and his men escorted me to the door. I marched along with them, invisible swagger stick under my arm.

It was now late November. I had written several letters to Beetle, but I had not, of course, received any of hers; they had had to be addressed care of American Express, Rome. It was time to go back to Gibraltar and catch the USS *Constitution*, on which I had had the foresight to book passage to Italy. I had bought Beetle presents in the souks and loaded them, with some of my stuff, in a new blue sack before going to the station to catch the afternoon train to Tangier. I waited on a stone bench, reading Henry de Montherlant's *Carnets*, which I had bought at the Comédie Humaine, as a thank you to Jacques Croiset. When the train steamed in, I got up and hurried, with my backpack, to get a corner seat. We had been on our way for half an hour when I realised that I had left the blue sack on the station bench.

A woman in the compartment said, '*Ah oui! Je l'ai vu, un sac bleu, n'est-ce pas? Sur le banc, et je me suis dit...*' I smiled and shrugged. I could have killed her. At the next stop, the ticket collector called Meknès station and asked for a taxi to bring the sack to Petitjean, the oil refinery town where we had a forty-five minute halt. '*Ne vous inquiétez pas, monsieur. Tout va s'arranger.*' When we reached Petitjean, the conductor was told that my sack was still at the station in Meknès. The taxi, *numéro trente-neuf*, was leaving right away. It would take an hour to get to Petitjean. With no one to blame but myself, I decided to let the train go and wait. The conductor said that the taxi could take me to the border with Spanish Morocco, but no further.

The station yard was rough, bare and muddy. The refinery was across from me as I waited and told myself to be observant: tubes and canisters, dials and gauges, towers scaled by ladders, topped with curling pipes, metal platforms with heron-necked lamps. Flags of flame flew from the vents where waste gas scorched the sky. Sentries stood with rifles in boxes along the road; guards at the gate. The service road was flat and deserted. A sentry forbade me to walk along it.

There was a Berber camp beyond the refinery, surrounded by a plaited grass fence about five feet high. The shanties, of corrugated iron, tins hammered flat, broken packing cases, sticks and dried mud, were pitched on a slope for the sake of drainage. Some were thatched with bamboo fronds, others roofed with tin sheets or sacking. Children rolled in the dust. Mortified by my own ineptitude, I sat facing the vacant station yard and the refinery. The banners of flame flew in a darkening sky, black at the edges. By 5.45 it was evident that I could never catch up with the train. Even alone, I could not take a joke. I walked to the crossroads where taxi 39 had to come, if it ever did. The sign on the Shell station was turned on. In the darkness, Arabs and Europeans cycled out of the refinery gates, laughing together. An old Morris came round the *rond-point* and I thought it was just my luck if it turned out to be my taxi. My luck was not that good: it contained a large contingent of Arabs and plodded past like a metal donkey. I flung myself on a concrete pier by the refinery gate and cursed and cursed. I wanted to cry. An Arab woman with a baby watched me curiously as she passed.

At 6.30, taxi 39 arrived, a big Ford. The driver showed me my sack in the *coffre*. Nothing had been taken. There was a bus from Arbaona, at the frontier, at *vingt heures*. The driver wanted 8,000 francs to get me there. I sat by him, the sack on my knee, knapsack on the seat behind me. He asked me what was in the sack that made it worth all this trouble. It occurred to me, rather late in the day, that he might dump me in the desert and make off with the treasure. '*Que des cadeaux. Pour mes parents et ma fiancée.*' I had never called Beetle that before.

We drove along the highway for a while and then he turned off down a dirt track. We came to a small, dark village. He stopped the car and got out. '*J'ai de quoi faire.*' He whistled and a light came on in a doorway. If they were going to rob me, then they were. It was the Reverend Harper Wood's money. I should put it down to experience; unless they killed me. The driver and two men came out and went to the back of the Ford. They took some boxes out of the boot. The driver came back to my window. '*Excusez-moi, monsieur, ce sont mes cousins. J'ai de quoi leur livrer. Ne vous inquiétez pas.*'

Inquiet? Moi? We drove on after I had refused tea. The headlights hit on plodding native carts with red lanterns as we neared Arbaona. There was no bus that could take me on to Tangier. We arrived at the *Douanes*; strip lights and policemen. My driver went over to a long black limousine, a chauffeur in the front, an old gentleman in the back. I sat and fumed. The driver came back and said, '*Vous avez de la chance, monsieur.*' The dignified old Arab was willing to give me a lift into Tangier.

The radio played as the great car's headlights split the purple of the night. The old man hummed and burbled, shrivelled away in his cushioned

225 of them at top

corner. He wore a turban with a little yellow soft hat settled in its folds. On his orders, the chauffeur stopped to pick up a couple of women with their bundles. They called him '*effendi*'. On reaching the Tangier frontier, he had the chauffeur take care of all the passport formalities. When he left me outside the Hotel Bristol, I thanked him becomingly. He waved me away.

XV

ON THE FERRY to Gibraltar I fell into conversation with Mr True, a furniture salesman from Hamptons of Knightsbridge. He was broad, round-shouldered, of medium height; small light eyes. He wore an unbelted mackintosh and a floppy brown hat, brim down all round. There were several initials on his briefcase. He had been on a six-week tour of north Africa: Addis, Aden, Oran, Tunis, Cairo. 'I'd like to have gone to the Varsity,' he said, 'not to study, to play games and all that. I'm a rugger man. My school switched in '26, just as I arrived. Know why? You have to have ball sense to play soccer. And ball sense, either you have it or you don't. But rugger! You can take a boy without an ounce of ball sense, bung him in the scrum, all he has to do is stick with the ball basically. Chances are, a keen boy'll be quite useful at rugger where he'd be hopeless at soccer. That's why they switched.'

I told him I had played soccer but preferred cricket. 'Surrey man myself,' he said. 'But that's not why I'd like to see Lock in Australia. Wardle, he's a defensive bowler, but Tony Lock! There's a match-winner for you. I know Bill Edrich. Met him in business. Reckon he lost £10,000 by turning amateur. Only did it because he thought he'd get to captain England. I reckon he'd've got as good a benefit as Compton if he hadn't jumped the gun. My guess he doesn't make above ten thousand a year in his job. I would've coughed up for his benefit; can't help liking old Edrich.'

'Drinks, doesn't he?'

'Not only drinks, old boy. That's why they daren't take him on tours. Every time they did, his wife divorced him afterwards. Some people have all the luck. Only joking. I like to combine business with pleasure myself. These Arabs, you know, they're incredible. Reckon they're impotent if they can't function sexually about five times a day. In Addis I saw this local doctor giving these natives a shot in the behind. Smack!' He crashed his fist into his palm. '"Drop your pants," this doctor'd say, and then, smack! In went the needle and off they went.'

'What did he give them?'

'Oh, it's quite harmless. Vitamin B, something like that.'

'What was wrong with them, then?'

'Wrong? Nothing. They can only come twice a day so they think they're impotent. One of our chaps was out in Saudi Arabia for three months, without the wife, you know, planning the furniture for one of the big nobs' palaces. They think nothing of spending £400,000 on a single palace. They kept putting things off but he stayed and stayed. The Arabs were amazed at him.'

'His persistence?'

'No, no, no. They couldn't understand how anyone could go more than three days without his wife. I think they kept him hanging about to see how long he *could* go. You know, if I had my life over again, I'd like to go up to the Varsity and then become a journalist. I often think of things I'd like to write up. Never do. I suppose you have to get born with the gift.'

'Not at all,' I said. 'Only sub-editors have to be born with the gift.'

'Anyway, that's what I'd like to be if I had my life again. Sports journalist. What a life! I'm keen on sports, you know, and I think I could make a sporting journalist, get on with people and so on.'

When we docked at Gibraltar, he gave me his card. If my ship was delayed,

I should come and look him up at the Rock. He could lend me some cash if I needed it. I had time before boarding the ferry to Algeciras to walk up the main street. Player's cigarettes were one and fivepence for twenty. I bought the *Sunday Times* and *The Observer* in a dark brown teashop full of army wives and squalling children. It was good to have an English cup of tea again. I saw that Ken Tynan had called Leslie Bricusse 'a flaccid comedian from Cambridge … Ruthlessly cut, he might escape obloquy.' The great iconoclast of the 1960s wrote, in 1954, in the tones of a sententious sixth-form master.

I had been on holiday from myself, in a state of weightlessness that rendered me all eyes and ears, free of sentiment, alert only to the present. Now, reading the London press, I was heavy again, not wholly dismayed by what Tynan said, yet conscious of England as a place of sly and eager knives. I was reminded of Leslie's adhesive wish to be my partner in writing all the kinds of things that I had no wish to write. I hated the songs his Sirens sang, but feared that I lacked the will to escape their allure. It gave me good reason to stay away from England.

Once aboard the USS *Constitution*, I had to share a cabin with an American of about thirty called Dick Knights. He slept in his vest and pants and had a rancid odour. I avoided him during the day. The crossing to Naples, via Genoa, took two days. Most of the passengers had embarked in New York. On the last night out, they were given a farewell dinner: paper hats, garlands, rattles and bells. 'Americans', I noted, 'think they are giving you a treat if they let you behave like children. Such occasions license their latent infantilism.' I was neither American nor British, it seemed, and neither Jew nor Gentile.

After dinner, an accordionist played Neapolitan tunes and sang them with an accompaniment of the children's rattles and squeakers. The Purser, tall, Germanic, with a balding egg-shaped head and a nose like an ant-eater, played double bass. The ship's photographer, short and thick, with wavy brown hair and a handsome, apish face, was Master of Ceremonies. He crooned and got the words wrong and did a tap routine. His hair flopped about; he waved his arms and flopped on the floor an unhinged gollywog, oh, and he smiled, he smiled and smiled. He came back to the microphone, panting. It squeaked – naughty! – as he adjusted it in order to gasp: 'After doing that, anyone else would be out of breath!'

When the band had packed up, the children pulled the balloons from the walls and collected the empty hats. The purser reappeared with a fat German. They had lighted cigars behind their backs. They would go up to a child with an armful of captured balloons and, as one talked nicely, the other popped the balloons. The room was soon full of crying children. I wanted to go and hit the bullies. I walked over and looked at them. They seemed to realise that they had gone too far. The purser unstuck more balloons from the walls and tried to force them on the children. They redoubled their cries. He became tough and mature: they must shut up or go to bed. They stood, open-mouthed, still tears on their cheeks, holding balloons they did not want. The purser walked around the saloon responsibly, tearing down the decorations and peeling sellotape from the walls. He whistled as he did so and upped children, tenderly, from his path.

I was on deck, reading Nietzsche's *Le Gai Savoir* (a present from Jacques Croiset), as the *Constitution* steamed into Genoa. A woman in a red suit came by and started to talk to me in Italian. She was shiny-faced with hairy legs, a pointed nose, wide contorted lips. She must suddenly have caught sight of the person waiting for her on the dock. She shrieked and ran about in arrested spurts, as if snagged on a leash. She cried in gasping convulsions and plunged her head in her arms as if the sight of her friend was too exciting to bear. She resurrected her head and resumed the panting sobs. Her fur fell to one side and she dropped her umbrella.

The man on the quay raised his arms above his head (it had a soft hat on it) and waved, more friendly than passionate. The woman panted and groaned as if delirious. When the gangway was lowered, she ran down it, scampering, half-falling, towards the dumpy man. An American woman told me that the woman had tried earlier to talk to a young Lebanese. When he said he spoke no Italian, she dealt him a sharp kick on the shin, which inflicted 'a terrible wound'. Might it be that the man in the soft hat was not the lover she imagined but some relative delegated to escort her to an institution?

As I walked down the gangway at Naples, I felt a clap on my shoulder. It was Dick Knights. 'Where are you going to stay?' He stuck with me. 'We could maybe share a room.' I found it impossible to deny him. We went to a big hotel on the Via San Felice. A single room would cost me more than sharing a double. I had three more rancid nights ahead of me. In the morning, I escaped Dick's company and went to Pompeii on the narrow-gauge railway. I had no camera and did not at all wish I had one. My notebook was enough.

Men cluster round the entrance to the *scavi*, trying to sell postcards, some obscene. You go up a steep street and under a damp arch. The road is of round muffins of grey volcanic rock, like elephants' feet, veined with mud. The city looks bombed, scythed off at a height of about eight feet, except for some temples, the theatre and a few houses. The place brings home to me the faint-heartedness of the classical education. What good are appraisals of literature and historical characters without reference to the architecture, art and social habits of the ancient world? It is idle to chide Catullus or Juvenal for their obscenity or Ovid and Martial for their lasciviousness without appreciating how accurately they reflected the habits and attitudes of their contemporaries.

The House of the Vettii has a wooden box at the front door. You give the guide a few lire and he reveals a painting of Priapus weighing his elongated prick on the scales. The guide then took the male tourists to the locked door of what he called 'the fuck room'. The wall paintings depicted a menu of sexual positions, an animated illustration of what grammarians call conjugations. There were more of the same in the *lupanar* near the Stabian baths; the men all red-brown and muscular, the women inclined to fat and very white. The pictures seemed more instructive than titillating, as if the women did not want to have their time wasted by incompetence; many showed women in the dominant position. There were five *cubicula*, each with a stone bunk and bolster, in a space no larger than the living room at 12 Balliol House. The partitions between them were about seven feet high, like those between the 'cubes' in the Lock-ite dormitories. The cash desk at the door had a slotted urn for coins, a seat for the madame. Upstairs there were private rooms for the rich or those with more complicated appetites. The guide made sure we understood the merits of the various postures and was given cigarettes for their names.

I ate pizza for the first time in Naples. I was reminded that Aeneas was told by an oracle that he should land his men when he came to a place where the natives 'ate their tables' when they dined. Antiquity was suddenly all around me. I walked up to the Naples museum and paid a few more lire to go through a gated arch into a room with more obscene paintings, lifted from Pompeii. I took keener note of a round canvas by Brueghel the Elder. A venerable figure in a blue-black cloak, face almost hidden by its fall, was walking with the aid of a stick; behind him, hunched in villainy, a boy of fourteen or fifteen, fat and deformed by a goitre or some glandular deficiency, expression brutish and sly. With a wide-bladed butcher's knife, the boy was cutting the old man's red purse-strings, which hung from the lower folds of the old man's gown. The purse dangled like a heart; you had the feeling that the cutting of the string would also cut the old man's lifeline. The monstrous child was encased in a pair of hoops that intersected at right angles. The circular motif of the canvas was repeated in the bizarre cage in which the malign boy was framed. It had a cross on the top. Behind, there was a windmill, grazing sheep, an untroubled shepherd.

My last night in Naples, 8 December 1954, coincided with the end of the 'Marian year'. I took notes as I watched from the iron balcony outside our hotel window:

A blaring band moved up the Via San Felice and turned left into the Via Medina. It was followed by a parade of ordinary people, wearing brown or dark-blue suits and modest dresses, led by a marshal with a flag. A thin fence of citizens watched the contingents go by; so many people were on the move that it seemed that only a few were left to admire their piety. Platoons of schoolgirls in black smocks and white Eton collars were kept in order by nuns, their habits inflated by the wind like black balloons. Then came older girls, under a blue-green banner with a forked yellow tongue on it. Four outriders held streamers attached to the four corners of the flag to keep it at full stretch.

Next, a section of starched nuns with unlit candles; followed by girls in virginal dresses that shone in the gloaming; fresh, solemn faces, budding lips and white hands. As the evening thickened, people brought lamps and easy chairs onto their balconies. Down the road, towards the Corso Victor Emmanuele, the Christian army changed its nature; file on file, in glittering coils, marchers came with lit tapers sheltered from the breeze with paper muzzles. The light brought the dark; people lost definition; all you could see was the show of black robes, velvet settings for the spangles of candlelight. 'Ave Maria!' they all sang, the deep voices of the priests, the innocent notes of nuns and virgins. Broken-stepped but unstoppable, they were borne past us up the hill until the whole slope was filled with the dazzle of tapers. Through half-closed eyes, I saw twin snakes of golden light, chains of stars, pressing upwards under the urgency of the chant. A loudspeaker van surged up the open centre of the road. Bystanders should come to the Piazza del Plebiscito to be addressed by the archbishop.

When the leading lights had disappeared, a row of priests in white vestments, others in black cloaks, scampered along; some had doused their tapers, one or two slipped away down side streets. The remaining ranks broke up. Earlier contingents had the serenity of martyrs; the stragglers lacked coherent conviction. Then a whole new army appeared, with tapers lit. Like an orchestra that falters and then recovers its unison, the parade resumed its grandeur; but the hurrying all-too-human tail-enders breached the magic.

At last the dignitaries appeared, fat old men stumbling slower and slower as the duration of the upward march sapped their energy. Finally, up strutted a posse of swordsmen in blue cloaks, policemen alongside, and the image of the Virgin in an illuminated truck of the kind that usually carried bricks but was now upholstered in greenery, floodlights flaring through it. More swordsmen followed and a wide crowd chanting 'Ave Maria!' Behind the culminating concourse, the lights of automobiles and buses. Laggards were hooted aside by drivers with schedules to honour. The secular usurped the clerical with no pretence of respect. Soon the street was full of the usual loud, unmannerly rush of nocturnal traffic.

I was relieved to be done with the company of Dick Knights. I neither liked nor disliked him. I asked him no questions and he asked me none. What was strange, and has happened many times since, is that I was unable to break a casual relationship that I found unappetising. It has been the same with agents, producers, collaborators and neighbours. I fear those whom I cannot disarm with genialities; I take polite pleasure in deceiving them with smiles. Dread of unpopularity keeps me amiable to people I should prefer to lose. More times than I can count, I have accepted commissions for things I do not want to do, for fear that I might never be asked again by people whom I have small wish to know and whose patronage diverted me from more worthwhile work.

It was a comfort to be on the train to Rome. Hill towns clustered on the razor edges of sharp hills, pinks underlined with green and umber, whites clouded by weathering water, buildings blended with landscape. Where was that woman walking, basket under her arm, along a mud-caked lane, head high, as if with the discipline of a vessel upon it? Black cattle shifted over the thick green, turned their heads to the train like stately buffoons. Acre on acre, mile on mile, the common world of the Mediterranean peasant; gates, fences, herds and flocks and their solitary guardians, soon to be their killers. I had seen them in the cracked mud of the Moroccan desert,

among the dunes where the sea works the shore; in creaking carts on the
bald stoniness of Spain, real people in dungarees, *djellabas*, denim. It was
easier to be ignorant of the city than to leave it. Horace, even in those artful
verses, meant what he said about his Sabine farm; Virgil, in *Eclogues* and
Georgics, contrived genuine sentiments into urbane hypocrisy (he gloried
in his town house on the Palatine). Then I remembered a number that Gordon Pask had written back in Jordan's Yard: 'The country's the place for
vice / The country is not quite nice'.

   In Rome, I found a third-floor *pensione* on the Via Cola de Rienzo in Prati.
You had to put ten lire in the *ascensore* before it would take you up. As soon
as I had dumped my luggage, I boarded a bus to the Piazza di Spagna. In
those days, the blue-faced American Express offices were next to the little
house where Keats died. Yes, there were letters from Beetle. I sat in the sun
on the Spanish Steps, between the flower sellers, and discovered that she had
never received the long, urgent letter I wrote to her in Barcelona, although I
had referred to it, and repeated my desire to be married to her, in a later one.
Of course she wanted to marry me. She would come to Paris on Boxing Day.
I should be able to recognise her because she would be wearing her new dark-
green coat; it had a little fur collar and she loved it. I blinked and looked up.
Men were unloading Christmas trees from trucks parked against the boat-
shaped fountain in the square. A boy darted through the traffic, drank hard
cold water from one of the spouts, shook his head, ran off.

   I went into Babington's tea rooms, on the other side of the Spanish Steps,
and ordered a waffle. The green cups with white interiors had linen napkins
folded into them. There were copies of *Tatler*, the *Illustrated London News*
and the *New Yorker*. Foil-wrapped Christmas puddings stood in a row on
the chimneypiece. Silent, elderly waitresses wore caps and aprons, like my
grandmother's Winifred Stanley, with a bow at the back. Two women were
talking about bridge; there was a club near the English cinema, on the Via
Venti Settembre. I wished I could go there and play without cease until it

was time to go to Paris and meet Beetle. The women told me that in London they played at the Ladies' Carlton Club. They were impressed by my membership of Crockford's. I was back in the world of one-upmanship.

The women were staying at the Grand Hotel, where Marlon Brando stayed, they told me. Meals cost 3,000 lire. They claimed not to be rich, but they roughed it only in the best places, confident that anywhere lower down the scale they would encounter bedbugs, larceny and indecent assault. One of them (small, black-suited, dark-haired) had to ask me where I went to school. When I told her, she said that she had thought I was a Carthusian; Carthusians had a singular way of enunciating. I was marked, I thought but did not say, by a kind of vocal circumcision. When I mentioned how beautiful Fez was, the other, tallish, blonde, woman said that thirty years earlier her brother had been dying in a sanatorium in Switzerland. Of course, he didn't *know* he was dying, poor lamb, but an hour before he did, on New Year's Day 1924, he said, 'When I'm better I'm going to take you to Fez.' She had still never been. Perhaps they would fly there next week.

I walked up the Spanish Steps, looking again at Beetle's long letters. Boys were throwing ivy berries at each other on the half-landing. One child, fat in tweed shorts, blue jerkin, thick-rimmed glasses, pretended that the game was over in order to approach close enough to be sure of hitting his unguarded target. He then threw his pellet with vindictive force. A smaller boy, whose energy made me suspect that he was a disguised adult dwarf, threw his berries with the same savage intensity as the fat one. I could have been at school with either of them.

I stayed in Rome for two weeks. I cannot remember that I had any conversations any deeper than with the two ladies at Babington's. I did not go to the bridge club. I went to the Forum and the Colosseum and walked in the rain to the Pantheon. I took silly pleasure in noticing that Raphael's tomb was permanently illuminated, unlike the adjacent tombs of the kings of Italy. There was a puddle of water under the round hole in the coffered roof, pimpled by the steady rain. I was dutiful enough to visit any number of Roman baths, galleries, circuses, tombs and museums. Perhaps in homage to D. H. Lawrence's celebration of the Etruscans and their enigmatic virility, I particularly liked (and still like) the Etruscan relics at the Villa Giulia.

I trekked to the Vatican museum and the Sistine Chapel, though I missed the less advertised adjacent chamber where Vasari's murals honoured a papal commission to gloat piously over the massacre of the Huguenots. I walked back to the Piazza San Pietro and paid a call on Michelangelo's then unscreened Pietà and noted the worn big toe, which I had no inclination to kiss. St Peter's was the Grand Central Station of Catholicism. Young men and boys were playing soccer in the dry moat of the Castel San Angelo. Unlike English schoolboys, they all played very showily, juggling the ball from foot to foot, flipping it over their heads when it seemed to have escaped them. The wall of the fortress gave them opportunities for fancy footwork: if nimble, you could pick up a ricochet pass to yourself. None of the players chose to be a defender.

For all my diligence in conning the ancient sights and sites, I took more pleasure in the *commedia continua* of modern Rome. In those days, there was always a policeman on a podium in the Piazza Venezia. He did not direct the traffic; he *conducted* it, lean flexible fingers in white muslin gloves, each finger with independent jurisdiction. Under his dark-blue topee, his eyes flashed approval or disappointment, pain when motorists failed to respond with the alacrity and elegance he bent upon them. He faced down the Via del Corso and never looked in any other direction. He *sensed* the traffic as it amassed behind him; just as you were sure that he had forgotten it, his arms were raised and, with a gesture at once restrained and compelling, he let it go. As the cars passed him, he fluttered white fingers, promising the significance to him personally of even the smallest ingredient of their concert. It would not have been surprising to see him reviewed in the arts pages of the *Corriere della Sera*.

indefatigable melody-making the Putney Palais' clientèle disported themselves. A microphone into which the clarinettist had lately been singing the richly respectful lyrics of the 'Sermon on the Mount Waltz' stood beside Bill Steadish, who clutched at it now and then as if to steady himself. He was a broad-shouldered man with a tapering waist, so that he reminded you at first sight of one of Frank Lloyd Wright's mushroom pillars. This worthy spent most of his time doodling his baton before the glazed eyes of his boys, who, you felt, would have gone on playing, like an automatic piano, whether Bill Steadish, their leader and paymaster, doodled his baton or not. Actually Bill had little notion of the rhythm of any of the numbers which his band executed. He often took several minutes to get the hang of what was being played, after which he was able roughly to keep the time the boys were setting. But it was a struggle. The only times at which he flourished were during the performances of his novelty numbers when he could don a funny hat and play a penny whistle. People had congratulated him on his virtuosity with the penny whistle.

Frank sidled up to the dais and stood behind and beside it, against the back wall. He had a candid view of the profusion of personal belongings which the band concealed behind the Bantu shields. To begin with, each had four or five bottles of beer, and in addition there were copies of the *Beano* and, pasted on the stands themselves, agreeable portraits of near-naked ladies arrayed in paper-thin garments which clung so tightly to their forms that you knew that they would emerge from them only to the accompaniment of that exotic sucking sound which surgeons make when they extrude themselves from their rubber gloves. Since this was a suburban band there was no hashish, but the drummer, a frenzied blond youth with teeth which rattled like dice as he drummed, had a

56

XVI

ON 23 DECEMBER, I took the night train to Paris, where I took a room with a big bed at the Hôtel des Deux Continents. Jackie Weiss, who had been our godmother when we staged *With This Ring*, was staying in the same hotel. Her family had come from Strasbourg. On Christmas Day, I took her to dinner – turkey and chestnut stuffing – at the *Pré St Germain*. She was about to move into rooms in a flat in Crimée which belonged to relatives of the owners of our hotel.

On Boxing Day, I went to the terminal at Les Invalides to wait for Beetle's bus from Orly. She came towards me, head slightly on one side, same smile, same eyes, in the new green coat with the little fur collar. I cannot remember how we got back to the hotel. Probably we walked. When we got there, she took off her coat and lay back on the wide bed in her little black dress and we were happy again.

Enough remained of the Reverend Harper Wood's bursary to keep us in Paris for at least two months, while I finished *Obbligato*. In mid-January, we flew back to London for the few days we needed to get married. To please Beetle's parents, we paid a call on the orthodox rabbi Shapira, who was to officiate. He lived not far from 84 Mount Pleasant Road. I feared that he would quiz me on my Judaic knowledge and perhaps disqualify me, but his only technical question was what my Hebrew name was. Frederic would not serve, but Michael did. He asked what I meant to do in life. When I told him that I was going to be a writer, he turned to Beetle. 'A scholar! You'll have to go out to work to support him.' Many copper coins were distributed on the carpet next to the rabbi's desk.

I stood under the *huppe* in the synagogue and waited for Beetle to come to my side, quite as if I had never seen her before. I had to wear a dark suit and a homburg hat, bought specially for the occasion and never worn again. She wore a pretty light-brown lace dress and a little hat. She whispered, 'Hullo, it's me' and then the antique, incomprehensible ceremony began. It ended with the ritual of my stamping on a wine glass, under a white napkin. There was no going back, except to Paris, which we did that same evening, after a wedding feast at the Berkeley Hotel. Apart from members of our families, the only guests included Guy and Celia Ramsey and Leslie Bricusse and his girlfriend Julie Hamilton, Jack and Margaret Piesse and my father's prep school friend from before the Great War, the anaesthetist David Aserman and his wife, Estelle. I cannot remember who served as my best man. I think it was Beetle's sister's husband, Arthur Stone, the dentist. Nor do I know how Leslie Bricusse came to be there. His wedding present was a paperknife, of the kind I had seen on sale in glinting numbers in the *souks* of Morocco. It was, he said, a small token of something bigger to come. Beetle deterred him from ever sending anything more lavish.

I had to make a speech in reply to someone. I recall only that I could not resist saying that the difference between a wedding and a funeral was that in the latter case it was less likely that a mistake was being made. It was as if someone else was standing in for the writer who had done the little grand tour and had met the woman he loved, wearing that green coat with the little fur collar, and taken her back to that big, low bed in the Hôtel des Deux Continents.

When we told Jackie Weiss that we meant to live for however long we could in a hotel bedroom, she had the instant generosity to propose that we take over the rooms she had booked in the Crimée apartment of M. and Mme Lambel in the *onzième arrondissement*. We had two secluded rooms at the end of a corridor. M. Lambel was blind. From time to time he would shuffle, in tartan slippers, past our door to the store room, where there was a brown-paper sack of coal nuggets. We had a small stove, our only heating, in the sitting room, which had a slightly domed parquet floor.

I rented a hefty Royal Sovereign typewriter with an English keyboard and we settled into a routine that has rarely been broken: I worked all morning; Beetle shopped and cooked lunch on a pair of gas-rings in a pantry down the hall; in the afternoon, we explored Paris, especially the Left Bank; in the evening we went to the opera, or to the *Opéra Comique*, where upper circle seats cost only a few old francs; more often to the cinema, often one just off the rue St André des Arts that screened classic movies.

Afterwards, we shared a pot of *chocolat chaud* at the Café Flore. When it was very cold I imitated Inspector Maigret and ordered *grog*, which came in a glass inside a metal cage with a handle. I loitered in La Hune, the adjacent bookshop, where you were free to stand and read Camus and Sartre and who all else, so long as the pages had been cut. On one of these sorties, we fell into casual conversation with an American photographer, Jack Nisberg, who said he was a friend of Ken Tynan's. He asked whom we knew in Paris.

I said, 'Tell you the truth, we don't know anybody.'

'How long have you been here?'

'Six, seven weeks. We don't especially need to know people.'

'You don't even have a fun group? You have to have a fun group.'

Obbligato fattened day by day. I was often surprised into laughing at my own jokes ('Our bankers are Coutts, sir.' 'That's not my problem, is it?'). I never doubted that the book would be published exactly as I wrote it. It might be a small work, but I was an artist and I lived in Paris with a beautiful woman.

Crimée was a working-class district. Our rooms were in a three-sided tenement block set around an interior courtyard, often snowy that winter. The cinder paths were lined with upended bottles. A tall metal tree had acute-angled branches on which the tenants spiked their empties. There was no television; we never listened to the radio. I knew that the French were losing Vietnam, from which Pierre Mendès-France was promising to extract them with honour and I was, of course, on his side. His many enemies called him '*Ce monsieur curieusement surnommé France*'; like me, he accepted the denomination but was indifferent to religion. Socialism, seconded by linguistic philosophy, would put an end to those obsolete distinctions.

I regularly bought *L'Exprèss*, the Mendèsistes' house magazine, edited by Jean-Jacques Servan-Schreiber and his lover Françoise Giroud. Mendès was a frequent contributor; so were François Mauriac (his very grown up *Bloc-Notes* reminded me of Harold Nicolson's column in *The Spectator*, which I had hurried to read in the Charterhouse library) and Jean-Paul Sartre, when he took time out from his own house magazine, *Les Temps Modernes*, named after Charlie Chaplin's 1936 movie. There was something enviably assured about French intellectuals and their pedestalled *prises de position*.

When we did not go out in the evening, we sat close to the black iron stove in our little living room. If I crossed the creaking parquet floor, even in stockinged feet, to stoke the fire with nuggets from the bag at the end of the corridor, the petty noise provoked the fury of our downstairs neighbour. He was a *poids lourds* driver whose articulated lorry was often parked, half on the pavement, tilted close to the wall of our building, ready for an early start. Any movement from us after we had eaten our evening eggs and bacon provoked a shout of '*Il faut dormir!*' I was all for workers' rights, but I was not persuaded that they included sending us to bed at eight-thirty. One night, when I had fed the stove like T. E. Hulme's creeping Turk, my stockinged tread was still enough to evoke the usual yell. I knelt down and, with my face a few inches from the shining floor, I barked, at length. I stopped and then I did it again, a last menacing growl, like the MGM lion's. Our neighbour never uttered another complaint.

By early March, Pierre Mendès-France had been ousted from power, I had finished *Obbligato*, and the Reverend Harper Wood's money was running out. Our blind landlord had never seen the grease marks on the pantry wall. His wife had never ventured in our direction. Now, however, she took sudden loud exception to the spattered grease on the back wall of the pantry where we did our regular frying. We were to pay for the damage and leave at once. Beetle and I both had flu and still had temperatures.

I went through the curtained sliding glass doors of the Lambels' sitting room and saw that Madame had summoned her large downstairs neighbour to lend muscle to her demands. I denounced him with feverish fluency (and a zest of British disdain for the duplicitous French) as '*Monsieur l'agent du Gestapo*'. The large blue man made no response. We never paid for the damage but we did have to pack our bags and walk out into the snow. Since the Lambels and the owners of the Hôtel des Deux Continents were kin, we went to the Hôtel de la Sorbonne.

On our return to England, we took a furnished room in Vicarage Gate, off Kensington Church Street. I felt as if the years Beetle and I had been lovers had been amputated from our lives. To be married and in London was to be reduced to the commonplace. My parents were in no hurry to read my first novel, but my father suggested that I show it to his friend George Greenfield, a literary agent. Beetle had made several neat carbon copies, one of which I delivered to Greenfield's office in Red Lion Square. He was not there, because his five-year-old son, Georgie, was ill.

Our first visitor in Vicarage Gate was Leslie Bricusse, who was still appearing in *An Evening with Beatrice Lillie*. He had survived the bad notices without noticeable bruises. Despite the hostility of Bea's large and jealous manager, John Phillips, Leslie had been able to enter many new smart names and telephone numbers in his plump address book. He was glad I was back because he had work for me to do on a film for Jock Jacobsen's top client, Max Bygraves. Leslie had already made a deal for the script of *Charley Moon*, which was to contain several original songs. I did not have to worry about those. What I was good at was dialogue. Since he had the lyrics and music to do, did I agree that £250 was a fair share? I was never informed what it was a share of. It seemed a lot of money.

I resumed our collaboration with relief and revulsion. Leslie was sorry to say that I would not be able to have a credit, because the contract was already signed and sealed. On my travels, I had become a writer; more myself by being less so. In Paris, I was a working novelist. Beetle and I had answered only to ourselves. In London, Leslie was blithe and benevolent and I was powerless to reject his favours. How else were we to live?

Thanks to Beetle's parents and to the money she had saved (and the £6.10s a week royalty that came to my bank from *An Evening with Beatrice Lillie*), we could afford to pay the 'key money' for a two-room basement flat at Turner's Reach House, 9, Chelsea Embankment. It cost £800, but that included the furniture. It was a rich address (George Weidenfeld had the first-floor flat, which had a fountain in the foyer), but we had to have the light on in our flatlet all day. We did, however, enjoy having a telephone with a FLAxman number. Our one tall window was onto a shaded yard at the back where Mrs Richards and Mrs Lewis exchanged loud matutinal opinions.

Dorothy Tutin was living in a barge anchored a few hundred yards upstream of us. After we had had lunch at a nearby pub, Leslie was keen that we should visit her. Dotty seemed pleased to see him, and me. He always had a way of seeming to have favours to dispense. He had told me that, as a matter of fact, people always liked him and seldom liked me. I should stick to doing the work and leave it to him to make the contacts that would advance our fortunes.

Dorothy Tutin was having an affair with Laurence Olivier, but no one was supposed to know. If Vivien Leigh found out, there would be a terrible scandal. Fear of her vengeful fury left Dotty unable to eat. When Vivien did indeed storm aboard, there were shrill scenes. Olivier took fright. Dorothy made small effort to retain him. There was something predatory, or so it seemed in those days, in the way the great actor had exercised *droit de seigneur*. Dotty went on to have a long and often successful stage career and a durable marriage, but she never recovered her youthful insouciance.

Impatient to hear what someone thought of *Obbligato*, I took a copy to the MCA office and left it for Elaine Greene to read. A few days later, I called George Greenfield's office and was told that he had yet to read my manuscript. His little boy was dying. I turned my thoughts to writing screenplays. Graham Greene had compared it to slavery. The noticeable difference was that it paid very well. Before starting work on *Charley Moon*, I asked to see a film script. Its scheme seemed less demanding than Greek iambics. Our director, Guy Hamilton, was past thirty and had already done a couple of films. He dismissed several of our bright new ideas as 'page one in the book', but the script eventually passed his examination. Max loved Leslie's songs. The film was made. I was not wholly sorry not to figure on the credits.

George Greenfield did not read *Obbligato* until a week or so after his five-year-old son, Georgie, died. Meanwhile, Elaine Greene did read it, enjoyed it, and wanted to talk to me about it. Then George called to say that he was confident that he could find me a publisher. Elaine Greene did not take my good news well. It was, she told me, a breach of protocol to have sent the manuscript to two people at the same time. Thirty years later, a publisher friend, the late Stanley Baron, wrote to say that he and a companion were planning a trip to south-western France. Might they call in, perhaps for a night, at our house? I replied that it would, of course, be a pleasure. It turned out that his companion was to be Elaine Greene. When he mentioned their putative hosts' name, she declined to come anywhere near us. She had neither forgotten nor forgiven how unethically I behaved in 1955.

Since Beetle had worked for V. G. and I could claim to have dined with him, George went first to Gollancz, where V. G.'s nephew, Hilary Rubinstein, was the heir apparent. V. G. had recently had a great success with a first novel by an Oxford friend of Hilary's, Kingsley Amis. I listened to a Third Programme excerpt on our battery-powered portable radio. It was a section in which Jim Dixon burns the sheets in the guest room of his smart girlfriend's house and cuts out the scorch marks with a razor. It seemed an unlikely, scarcely side-splitting episode to be broadcast on a station normally so solemn. I was unsurprised to read a dismissive review of *Lucky Jim* by Julian MacLaren-Ross at the end of a column headed by unmitigated praise for Alfred Hayes's *In Love*, a novella that Guy Ramsey also applauded in the *Daily Telegraph*. Nearly sixty years later, Peter Owen asked me to write an introduction to a reprint of *In Love*. It read as well as ever.

I was told, through George Greenfield, that Hilary Rubinstein was not entertained by *Obbligato*; whether V. G. himself ever read it, who knows? George sent the manuscript to Macmillan's, where it evoked enthusiasm from, among others, Jack Squire, a literary sportsman left over from the 1930s. 'This man has twenty more funny books in him,' he said. 'Grapple him to you!' Another Macmillan reader queried my assertion that a 'wing three-quarter' would have a rare turn of speed. Squire endorsed my simile: I was evidently someone who knew his rugger. The only time I had played the game, or something like it, was at Charterhouse, when we used a soccer ball and goalposts.

My editor at Macmillan was Alan Maclean. His brother Donald had decamped to Moscow in 1951. Although never suspected of treason, Alan had to leave the Foreign Office. He was relegated to easy internal exile in the panelled offices of Macmillan's in Sparrow Street, behind the Haymarket. His nervous chortle may have been a consequence of his brother's misconduct, but Donald's name was never mentioned. Alan had a flat in Oakley Street and two season tickets for Chelsea. When I went to games with him, he always carried a silver flask of whisky. The plan was to publish

Obbligato in May 1956. I had my photograph taken by Mark Gerson. I wore my Adamson's suit and smoked a sophisticated cigarette. The smoke made me narrow my eyes.

Whenever Leslie and I went to the MCA offices, Jock Jacobsen would say 'Hullo there, Leslie, and … heh heh heh.' I seemed powerless to evade Leslie's company. Dreading the places that he promised we were going, I was unable to resist going with him. He took me to Binkie Beaumount's office above the Globe Theatre. We went up, slowly, squeezed together in a tiny lift that resembled the one of which Robert Benchley said, 'One more person in there and it would've been adultery.' We were joined by Billy Chappell, whom Leslie had recruited to direct the professional production of *Lady at the Wheel*. Billy was dressed like a juvenile lead in an Edwardian musical: check tweed suit, waistcoat with little lapels, its buttons covered, like those on the jacket, in the same tweed. His clipped, nasal voice empha-sised the drollery of *absolutely every word* he said.

Binkie was fleshy and sleek, with whitening abundant hair, cool, damp hands. Through the window behind his desk, I could see the backside of the letters EILLIL ECIRTAEB on a rack around the front of the theatre. He smiled with seasoned charm, forcing bonhomie into grey-brown eyes. The mask never slipped; that was how you knew it to be a mask. No one could have looked more imperiously impartial; thumbs up or thumbs down, the expression would never change. Little Billy sat in a green wing chair, high-backed and so deep that he had to perch on the edge for his feet almost to reach the ground. His exchanges with Binkie had a coded innocence, like the pre-arranged passwords of seasoned spies. Leslie had told me that if he were ever invited to Binkie's place in the country, known to insiders as 'Pinching Bums', and anyone tried anything, he would immediately get married to Julie Hamilton.

One afternoon, on some futile, show business-like mission, Bea Lillie and Leslie and I drove out in a taxi to Borehamwood Studios, where Leslie had some appointment to which I was not privy. He left me in the ticking cab to look after Bea. Bundled like a fleshless bird in a fur coat, she said, suddenly and sadly, 'Is there an afterlife, do you know?'

Aware that she had lost her husband and her only son in the war, I said, 'Oh Bea, I wish I could say that I thought so. I truly don't know.'

She said, 'Well, if you don't know, does Hannen Swaffer know?'

Hannen Swaffer was a *News Chronicle* journalist with a frequently pronounced belief in spiritualism. Bea's perky change of register implied that she had little faith in the advocate of what she so much wanted to believe. I recalled that it was said a pigeon had once flown into her room in a New York hotel. She looked up and said, 'Any messages?' I was sorry not to play the happy pigeon for her. I also wished I was not wasting my day.

Thanks to Leslie, who was celebrating his last night at the Globe Theatre, Beetle and I were invited to another of Ken Tynan's late-night parties. A master in the art of taking while seeming to give, Ken had borrowed Larry Adler's house in Norfolk Street, St John's Wood. A maid let us into a hallway where there was an electric xylophone. Flattened geraniums figured in the wallpaper; there was red paintwork on the stairs and on the frames of the glass doors to the kitchen. Tall and languorous, Ken saluted us and dangled a white hand. It was as if you were being dared to reach and touch something fishy in a penny arcade. He had a pale, pendulous face, loose lips, half-closed eyes. In his grey suit with a white shirt, his torero's string tie throttled in a leather toggle, he might have been a dissolute scoutmaster.

Hermione Gingold, a *grande dame* in a tattered, flowery blue garment offering glimpses of grey underwear, was at the receipt of custom on a prolonged brown sofa. 'Is there room at your feet?' the young men asked. 'There is *always* room at my feet.' Among the company was Diana Dors, whose ready-when-you-are bearing announced her to be the bargain basement Jayne Mansfield; and so, it was said, was Jayne Mansfield. The last job of Miss Dors's pneumatic career would be to play the middle-aged,

overweight Helen of Troy in *Of Mycenae and Men*, a satirical substitute
I wrote for Aeschylus's lost Satyr play, as an appendage to the television
production of my and Kenneth McLeish's 1978 translation of the *Oresteia*.
Dors seemed to be more difficult, and much later to rehearsal, than her tal-
ents justified. In fact, she was dying, bravely, of cancer.

The brightest star at Ken's party was Pamela Brown. Her air of dangerous
scorn had brought her great success in Christopher Fry's *The Lady's Not
for Burning*. The eyes were brilliant and unseeing, like a drug addict's; she
moved with smoothly concealed lameness. When Ken's diaries were published, with their almost touching mixture of vanity and self-incrimination,
sentiment and heartlessness, wit and puerility, it was disclosed that one of
his many fugitive affairs had been with the delicious 'cripple' who proved
complicit with his spanking desires. His whole life, from Oxford onwards,
was dedicated to making and breaking, in one way and another: fan and
assassin, self-advancing and self-destructive, soloist and dramaturge, Ken
was the theatre's chief whip.

As we left Larry Adler's house, Hermione was pecking at the xylophone
in the hall, singing 'Strangers in Paradise' in a garlicked French accent. I saw
her again not long afterwards, for professional reasons. Roy Speer had produced the radio version of *Out of the Blue* and was now preparing *Grande
Gingold*, a radio series for which he recruited me to supply material. Would
I go and discuss ideas with her? Hermione was living in Capener's Close,
an enclave off Lowndes Square.

I climbed a long, straight internal staircase into the black-walled drawing
room where Lady Eulick Brown, Hermione's adjutant, greeted me expan-
sively. Hermione arrived and said, 'Hello!' I noted later that she was 'like
emery paper trying to pass for chiffon'. She was wearing a blue dress with
a pink rose at the throat and long pink gloves. It was as if *Fallen Angels* was
still running.

Her counsellor, Lord Eulick Brown, was tall and disjointed, in a brown suit; dirty brown hair; yellowy, lean face; prominent nose; long white hands, fingers held apart from each other as if they were drying. His wife wore bi-focals, the smaller lens set like a bull's-eye within the larger; at the centre, the black pin-head of her iris, as if an expert marksman had just plugged her. It was scandalous, she told me, how much publicity that dreadful Hermione Baddeley got from working with Gingold.

The latter's slim, fair-haired boy, Miles-y, turned up as we were sipping Nescafé from Rosenthal china cups decorated with stripes and little lozenges, like cough sweets on the ends of fishing lines. He had just fetched her poodle from the vet's; one good poodle deserved another. Hermione's four-legged darling had had a swelling in a place he simply couldn't mention. Because madam had never bothered to house-train it (it lifted its leg everywhere, but *everywhere*!), it was moored downstairs in the yard, where it could flirt beyond its means with the Browns' tall terrier bitch. I left with a brief to supply a ten-minute monologue in which Hermione would deliver advice to her female listeners in something like the tones of Evelyn Home, the agony aunt who featured weekly in *Women's Own*.

Thanks to Leslie's zeal for networking, we had a meeting with Eric Maschwitz, who had been Hermione's pre-war lover. Now head of light entertainment at BBC television, he wore a dark suit and had a shrivelled face, a bank manager's flat, grizzled moustache, clubby tie and caution with funds. It was difficult to visualise him as the composer of *These Foolish Things*, which he had written in Hermione's honour. 'A cigarette that bears a lipstick's traces / An airline ticket to romantic places / And still my heart has wings / These foolish things ... A telephone that rings but who's to answer / The winds of March that made my heart a dancer ... / A fairground's painted swings / These foolish things remind me of you.' The potency of cheap music, and sophisticated lyrics, supplied the very stuff of romance *à deux*; oh, how the ghost of them clings! Now the once delectable Gingold and her rhymester lover were prosaic and raddled antiques. I was reminded of two facing photographs in an old edition of *Lilliput*. On one page was the frozen beauty of Rodin's *The Kiss*; facing it was the image of a creased old lady who, in her youth, had been his model.

While Leslie was on tour with Bea, Tony Becher and I got together, in Chelsea Embankment, every weekend to compose Hermione's monologue for *Grande Gingold*. Tony's first-class degree had secured him a prestigious job at the Cambridge University Press. He now called Wisdom 'John' and was able to report the latest philosophical gossip from Oxford, where the caustic J. L. Austin was the current arbiter of sagacity. Best known for the term 'performatives' (utterances – such as 'I apologise' – which are also, allegedly, actions), Austin had a destructive dryness that withered his challengers, even the tart Freddie Ayer. His prose style was singularly desiccated: unlike almost any other writer I have known, he made a fetish of putting a comma after 'a', allowing for the insertion of some punctilious qualification of his main point. There seemed not to be a lot of fun in meta-Wittgensteinian philosophy; its wine was so dry that there might as well have been nothing in the glass.

Tony and I shared the £25 fee for our Gingold monologues, but not the happy chore of going to rehearsals, where I did last-minute cutting and stitching. My £12.10s covered the rent and our household bills. It had to: the weekly payment of £6.10s, for the numbers in *An Evening with Beatrice Little* I had written with Leslie, had stopped abruptly. When I called Tennant's offices to ask why, I was advised to look at the contract. Close inspection would show that it stipulated that I was to be paid only so long as *An Evening with Beatrice Lillie* was running in the West End. Now that it was on tour, therefore, my stipend ceased; his payments did not. D. H. Lawrence said 'business is no good'. I have never been good at it.

When Tony had gone to catch his train, I typed the final draft of our weekend's work, delivered it to Capener's Close and then waited in Chelsea Embankment for Hermione's reaction. On the first occasion on which she phoned, she said, 'I've read the script, darling, and it's *all wrong*. Will you come round first thing in the morning?'

'When's that exactly, Hermione? Eight-thirty? Nine?'

'Eleven o'clock, darling. No later.'

Hermione was leading me towards a cushioned alcove when a man's voice called out, 'Let's have a dekko at your latest then, Hermene.' A British film director with a hyphenated name, more or less in pyjamas, and in need of a wash, was somewhat under a single grey sheet on the sofa in the drawing room. I stood there and he looked at me for a second or two. Then he said, 'Never mind.'

As Hermione dissected the script, I thought her tactless and peremptory. In truth, she was patient and educative. The following week there were fewer ineptitudes. *Grande Gingold* was broadcast live, from the Playhouse Theatre on the Embankment. Miles Rudge wrote a segment in which subsidiary parts were played by Ken Connor and a genial, obese actor called Alexander Gauge, who had been Friar Tuck in a BBC TV series, starring Richard Todd as Robin Hood. In a *Take It From Here* sketch, Frank Muir and Denis Norden did a parody of *Destry Rides Again*, set in Sherwood Forest, in which the Marlene Dietrich *chanteuse* dared to sing, 'See what the Boys in the Buckram will have, and tell them I died of the same!' For our purposes, Gauge was now christened Gregory. Hermione had a regular line: 'Tea, Gregor*ee*?' Pause. 'Millock?' Who else could have got laughs from such tepid material?

I had the silly satisfaction of corpsing her, once, on mike. Our household hints included a recipe for whale meat, which had, until quite recently, been part of the nation's austere diet. The script required Hermione to say, 'When you ask your fishmonger for it, he may well respond, "Whale meat again, don't know where, don't know when."' She had sighed when first she read it, but declaiming it live, *à la* Vera Lynn, she was suddenly convulsed. She averted herself from the microphone, turned back, tried again and then had to turn away again. The audience caught the contagion and covered the hiatus with laughter; there was no unprofessional breach of continuity.

David Gore-Lloyd was having radiation treatment for his testicular cancer. My father always visited sick friends when they were in hospital. I went several times to the Westminster Hospital and tried to amuse David. White as the sheet on which it had been written, he gave me his short philosophical paper, in Rylean style, on Intention. It seemed like proof of his determination to recover. He was confident that the treatment was making him feel rotten, not the disease, which was 'under control'. I feared that he was dying and pretended I did not, which made my visit a performance; and easier to sustain. He never complained about the cruelty of his affliction. He was the only person I ever met who called a teaspoon a 'winder' (as if for winding things up). He insisted on withdrawing cash from the bank in pristine red-brown ten-shilling notes. He was forever supping on his fingernails, one after the other, as if mouthing some silent flute.

In the street outside the Westminster Hospital, a barrow-boy was selling second-hand books. One of them was *Henry Sows the Wind* by Brian Glanville, with whom I had once shared the task of writing the football reports in *The Carthusian*. When he proved the *miglior fabbro* in that field, I switched to reviewing films. In that role, I made a point of not joining the chorus that sang the praises of the British documentary style as manifest in the 1936 *Night Train*, with its fellow travelling commentary by W. H. Auden. Glanville was now not only already in print, he was published by Secker & Warburg and this was his *second* book. I gave sixpence for it. It was better than I wished.

We rehearsed *Grande Gingold* at the Playhouse all day, in a serious, light-hearted manner. Radio comedy was not arduous for performers; no one had to learn lines; but clarity of diction was paramount. The main technical concern was to avoid pages rustling as they were turned over. Our rehearsal on 15 July 1955 was without the weekly smiles. Ruth Ellis had been hanged that morning, for murdering her faithless lover, a racing driver called David Blakely. Despite distinguished appeals, from V. G., Arthur Koestler and others, the Home Secretary, Major Gwilym Lloyd-George, refused a reprieve. She was twenty-nine years old.

The public response, of shame and outrage, ensured that Ruth Ellis was the last female to be executed in Great Britain. The horror was in the detail: apologetic jailers obliged her to put on a pair of rubber knickers, for sanitary reasons, before they led her out for Mr Pierrepoint to break her neck. Did our audience laugh as usual that night? And did we want them to? We did; and they did. The judge in the Ruth Ellis trial, Mr Justice Havers, had entered a strong private plea for mercy. He was the grandfather of Nigel Havers who, some twenty years later, appeared (in the part of a character based somewhat on John Hargreaves), in my BBC Two series *The Glittering Prizes*.

One weekday, at 11.15 in the morning, never a time at which I welcome visitors, our doorbell rang. It was David Gore-Lloyd. 'Hullo, it's me.' He looked quite well until he sat down and relaxed. Then you saw how pink his cheeks were, how grim the flesh. He was brisk, almost gay, as he felt for his cigarettes. He had been out of hospital for several days. He had not been discharged; he had absconded. His parents did not know where he was. He had become engaged, he said, to Pussy, the sister of the Siamese girl who had shared 28 Montagu Road with us, in Cambridge.

When Poony began to sleep with Paddy Dickson, she feared that her sister would write and inform their father. In the event, Pussy preferred to emulate her sister's liberties, with several men; David, it seemed, was one of them. When he learned, perhaps from Pussy herself, more likely from the kind of friend whom few people lack in such circumstances, that she was sleeping with someone else, David climbed out of his bed in the Westminster hospital and went to her flat in Fulham. She told him that she loved him and belonged to him. That night, she went and slept with another Siamese.

The following day, while David was at Pussy's place, her Siamese lover came round to see her. He disclaimed any knowledge of David's existence.

David told us that he intended never to see Pussy again. He was carrying a bottle of heavy pain-killers suspended in pink fluid. Jonathan Miller told us that such concoctions were known, in the medical profession, as 'terminal cocktails'. David had nothing to do other than to walk the streets. I took him to lunch at Crockford's. Then we went to the Oxford and Cambridge Club, where we played snooker. He won easily. Towards evening, I settled him into a hotel in Bloomsbury where, he said, he had once stayed with Pussy. Beetle and I presumed that his 'love affair' with Pussy was a fantasy and that she did not, in truth, care for him at all. Many years later, we visited her sister and Paddy Dickson in Bangkok. Poony told us that David had been the love of Pussy's life. She had never got over his death.

As we parted, I shook David's hand warmly and told him to telephone us any time, but that I was busy for the next two days: I had a bridge marathon planned with a freckled, balding, gingery-haired person called Donald Simmonds, who had also played bridge for Cambridge. Our occasional sessions, in a basement in Earl's Court, lasted till the small hours of the next day. Don introduced me to Tom Maschler, a young publisher at MacGibbon & Kee with whom he had been at Leighton Park, the Quaker school. Simmonds had no advertised job or ambition. I never sought his company, but I was reluctant to shake him off. He made doing nothing into a form of superiority above the dutiful and the industrious. We lunched now and again at the *Ox on the Roof* in the King's Road. I attached Donald's ominous nihilism to an unsmiling bridge-playing character, whom I called Gladstone, in my 1963 novel *Lindmann*. The surnames of minor characters in my fiction, when I dislike them, are almost always those of my English schoolfellows.

By the time Leslie Bricusse's provincial tour came to an end, *Charley Moon* was being shot. Jock Jacobsen's watchword, 'There's such a thing as timing, fellers', came to fruition: the Rank Organisation, which had its panelled home at Pinewood Studios, offered Leslie and me a contract to write two films in the coming year. There was no distinction between our remuneration: we were each to be paid £1,150. Jock began to call me by my first name.

Leslie had found an accountant whose services he recommended. Eric Barnacle was a pockmarked, slab-faced clerk with the usual spectacles, the usual grey flannels and sports jacket, the usual cubbyhole office (on the north side of Oxford Street). He told me that he hated being an accountant. When he woke up in the morning, he was sorry to discover that he was still the same boring person. He bored himself even in his dreams. After the paperwork was done and signed, he proposed that I pay him and the Revenue simultaneously. 'It'll save trouble if you just add the two together and make the cheque out to me. I'll pass the tax on to HMG.' I had a strong feeling that I was doing the wrong thing, but I did as he asked.

A year later, the Revenue demanded payment for what Barnacle had promised he was going to pay. I found that he had absconded with what was always described in those days as 'a chorus girl'. The law eventually caught up with him. When he went to jail, I was not sorry; neither was he perhaps: he had succeeded in being somebody else for a little while. He now had some furniture for his dreams. Since he was not a chartered accountant, no professional insurance covered his delinquency. I am still credulous, but not so easily conned.

After Beetle had nursed me through a long, debilitating, very sweaty bout of glandular fever, Leslie invited us to stay in his parents' house in Shirley, near Manchester, in order, once again, to 'tickle up' the book of *Lady at the Wheel*. While ill, I had had a very high temperature and agonising headaches. The janitor's wife and her friend Joan were in the habit of having loud conversations in the yard outside the bedroom's dark window. One morning, Beetle's mother arrived, with a bag of necessities: smoked salmon, cold chicken, a cake from Maison Sagne in Marylebone High Street. We told her how persistent and percussive the noise was. Ray had a simple solution: she would give the talkative ladies ten shillings and explain that I was unwell.

Socialist principles led me to insist that we not demean the working class by offering them money; the right thing to do was to reason with them. Ray promised to take care of things in a way that would not be offensive. I heard her explain my condition, and winced at the silence in which I knew she was giving them the money. The ladies never disturbed me again. I consoled myself that overtipping was one thing Marcel Proust and Jean-Paul Sartre had in common; prolixity was the other.

While we were staying with his parents in cold suburban Shirley, Leslie gave me driving lessons in his new white Ford Consul convertible. Since I was nervous of pressing too heavily on the accelerator, the L-plated car did many kangaroo leaps. Leslie sat, imperturbable, beside me until I achieved some kind of competence. He promised that one day I should be able to change gear and go round a corner at the same time. It seemed unlikely.

On our return to London, Beetle and I took BSM driving lessons. We both passed the test first time. I cannot remember ever again having to perform the tricky exercise of 'backing around a corner'. We went to Lex Garages in Soho, hoping for a bargain from Trevor Chinn. He took us up the steep ramp to the first floor and pointed to a second-hand green Ford Anglia, PLD 75. 'This is your car,' he said. It had no heater and was not in gleaming condition but we had his promise that, for £250, we would never do better. He was probably right: with a transfer depicting all the roadsigns likely to be encountered on the Continent stuck on the inside of the windscreen, we were to drive many, many miles in it on all kinds of rough roads, even if I did have to turn round and back up a one-in-ten gradient in Andalucia. When, several years later, I came to trade in PLD 75 for something better, Beetle's cousin Geoffrey had no doubt that it was composed of the welded halves of two cars that had been in shunts.

Herb and Judy Oppenheim came to England in the autumn of 1955. They had been touring Europe ever since they left me in Granada. At dinner in Chelsea Embankment, they were pleased to tell Beetle that I had talked about her 'all the time' when we were travelling together. As she cooked pineapple lamb in the tiny kitchen, the Oppenheims were quick to whisper that they were not surprised that I had married such a bright, beautiful girl. They were proposing to go to Sicily, their last excursion before they returned to the States. What did we say to joining them?

They were still driving the little Simca with an unsprung bench seat at the back. Comfortable enough for three of us and the smaller Linda, it was tight for five. I was different now that I was with Beetle. Our intimacy soon made Herb and Judy uneasy. The warmth that I had turned on them when we were in Spain was now directed almost exclusively at Beetle. We were less tolerant of Linda and her understandable misery than I had been when I was grateful for the lift and the company.

We went south along the Route Napoléon into the foothills of the Alps and then Herb branched off to take the frozen and seasonably 'déconseillé' Mont St Cenis pass into Lombardy. He negotiated the deserted, alarmingly icy corduroy road with purposeful skill. The high road was the most direct route to the stadium, designed by Luigi Nervi, near Torino, with the largest unsupported roof in Europe. Herb's three-dimensional camera put it on record.

We still had a long way to go. On the level road from Turin to Pisa, Judy took the wheel, to give him a break. Not used to low-powered, stick-shift European cars, requiring synchronous skill with the clutch, she drove only in top gear. After she had had to slow down to pass through a village with a fair, the Simca regained speed with clunking reluctance. Out on the narrow, tree-lined Lombardy road, Judy decided to overtake a large, fast-moving lorry. Having pulled out into the only other lane, she failed to accelerate with sufficient firmness to get on past the throbbing lorry. It did not diminish its speed. We willed her to change down to third gear and accelerate on past. The moaning Simca yawed back and forth. We rolled on in the tight space between the high wheels of the truck and the thick, frequent plane trees. Huge hubs and black tree trunks came and receded, came and receded. Had anything come in the opposite direction, we should certainly have been killed or badly injured. Eventually, we were past the lorry and Judy regained control of our course. The silence was sustained and divisive.

In Pisa, Herb pulled up outside a hotel adjacent to the Campo dei Miracoli. We could stay in the car while he went in to make a deal. I advised against bargaining with undue insistence. 'Listen,' he said, 'it's pretty well November, right? Believe me, they'll be only too glad to cut a deal.' He came back out to say that the place was 'strictly minimal', but they had offered an enticing rate.

After dinner, which ended with a floral bowl of *zuppa inglese*, Beetle and I walked out into the cool darkness to look at the Leaning Tower. Judy was putting Linda to bed. Herb emerged alone and walked on the wide grass. We did veer over and talk to him, but the rupture proved irreparable; not least because he seemed to blame Beetle for it.

Judy never drove us again. We reached Naples in good time to catch the night ferry for Palermo. Before going on board, we dined at one of the row of restaurants on the quay. Each had an orchestra, in full fig, playing in front of it. The grander ones had three-tiered platforms on which instrumentalists in black ties were conducted by some inglorious, tail-coated maestro. We had fish soup with squid and giant prawns in it and split the bill with precision.

A row of open carriages with beribboned, blinkered, nose-bagged horses was waiting on the quay at Palermo. To reach the hotel that Herb had selected, in the centre of the city, we clopped past Baroque villas behind ornate gates. Not long before, an Alfa Romeo had exploded in the driveway of one of the villas, the mafia's routine way of killing a recalcitrant politico and encouraging the others. The razing of the antique dockside quarter, and its replacement with yellow, gimcrack tower blocks, would not start for another decade. 1950s Palermo had sinister shadows, even on a fine autumn morning, but it was still grandiose with the mouldering *palazzi* of the decadent nobility who would find their stylish sarcophagus in Giuseppe Tomaso di Lampedusa's *Il Gattopardo*.

Herb's guidebook knew just where to go and what to admire. We drove up to Monreale to see the Byzantine mosaics in the cross-bred cathedral (part Catholic, part Greek Orthodox). In Cefalù, we lunched in a waterfront trattoria. Herb invited a solitary diner to join us. He was an ex-GI who had been in Sicily ever since the war. I imagined that he had been seduced by the myth of Aleister Crowley, the pear-shaped Great Beast 666, who had lorded it, during the 1920s, in the adjacent Abbey of Thelema, where he proclaimed that the only law was 'Do As Thou Wilt'. Somerset Maugham's skimpy novel *The Magician* paid scathing homage to the intimidating charlatan. In the late 1960s, I played soccer in Brian Glanville's twice-weekly pick-up game in Hyde Park. Among the casual company was a wilted individual who had been an acolyte in Crowley's Abbey. D. H. Lawrence too had passed that way; he blessed the unsmiling Sicilian males with primal phallic virility.

Herb asked whether our temporary friend had a disability pension to sustain him in Sicily. 'No, I can stay here because, OK, I do occasional jobs for people locally, which keeps me eating at least.'

'It's certainly a beautiful spot to be stuck in,' I said.

'Think so? Hate it; hate the people too.'

'Why stay?'

'How about I'm wanted by Uncle Sam for desertion? Pays to keep my head down, only not a whole lot.'

We drove on to Taormina. The transparent November sea off Giardini Naxos was just warm enough to swim in. In the evening, we played bridge, in a scintillating storm, in on–off–on light in the glassed terrace of a little hotel up on the hill, next to the Roman theatre. Herb's schedule kept us looking and leaping with timely vigilance. In the Greek theatre outside Syracuse, where boozy Aeschylus previewed one of his plays, I slowed things down with an abbreviated lecture on the Athenians' disastrous Sicilian expedition in the grand harbour, which we could see in front of us.

Then it was time for Agrigento. The old town, high above the famous row of sixth- and fifth-century Doric temples, had been damaged in the war; but it retained the tight heat of ancient Akragas, where the pre-Socratic philosopher Empedocles was born. Today's eviscerated city is an agglomeration of concrete, on which the mafia has the monopoly. While the Oppenheims had breakfast, Beetle and I walked to the ruins. I heard myself lecture her on the temples' gods as if we were strangers. The expedition had divided us from my friends and, to a degree, from each other. We lacked the wit or the will to put things right. Nothing unpleasant was said by any of us. Everything I said was very polite, in the British style.

We did the full round of the island, where the ancient sites, from Selinunte to Segesta, were still unfenced. The villages reeked sweetly of straw and donkey dung. In the sudden twilight, peasants rode past in their carts, rakes and scythes silhouetted in a stiff frieze against the last of the low, lurid light. The carved tailboards of their carts bore polychrome hand-carved reliefs of folkloric figures. There were few cars. Just short of a box-bridge, on a wet evening, we were overtaken by an Alfa Romeo with flaring lights and a loud klaxon. As he took the narrow-shouldered bridge, the alpha male driver lost control. The car spun round, once, twice, within the stiff bracket of the girders, halted for a split second, then plunged on as fast as before. Beetle and I, on the bench at the back, looked at each other. Herb glanced at his mirror and saw the look. He smiled a blue smile.

Outside Castelvetrano, where the outlaw Salvatore Giuliano had died five years before, after lording it over the region in a short season of international fame, we bought unglazed terracotta dishes and a bell-shaped jar from a wayside vendor. A year later, Gavin Maxwell would embellish the

Giuliano myth in *God Protect Me From My Friends*. Half in love with a ruthless and virile bandit, Maxwell's elegy dignified him into a modern Robin Hood. Leslie Bricusse and I visited the movie producer Raymond Stross, a short, fleshy man of small charm, hoping that he might want to make a movie out of Giuliano's story.

We were served with tea by his luminously beautiful young blonde wife. Clare endeared herself to me by murmuring, in a convent-educated undertone, how wonderful I had been in 'Joe and the Boys'. Stross was not seduced by our enthusiasm. Eventually the film *Salvatore Giuliano* was directed by Francesco Rosi from a script by Suso Cecchi d'Amico, the senior of Lucchino Visconti's trusted scenarists, whom we would meet in Rome in 1964. Suso sustained the Giuliano myth by portraying him almost entirely as a distant figure. In brave relief, he could stand for a sullied, gun-toting saviour in a white mackintosh.

Riding north in the Simca, Beetle and I held our Sicilian pots in our laps, like obstinate trophies of the worthwhileness of the trip. After disembarking from the ferry at Naples, Judy decided that Linda was fretful only because the car was so full. The two of them would catch the train and meet us again at Ventimiglia, on the French border. Alone with me and Beetle, Herb was as nice, and informative, as he could be. He even let me drive. There was a level crossing at the top of an embankment somewhere along the Appian Way. I had to stop, on the tilt, at the top. I tried, as Leslie Bricusse had taught me, to hold the car by idling the engine and staying in gear. I must have depressed the clutch too far. The car rolled backwards down the long slope. Luckily, there was nothing behind us. I waited at the bottom, until the barrier was raised, and then drove up the gradient and over the railway line. After a few more tactful miles, Herb resumed the wheel. Judy's absence sat with us.

Herb determined on one last detour, via Marseille, in order to see Le Corbusier's suburban *Unité d'Habitation*. It exemplified the modernism that

Siegfried Giedion claimed would make people better, more sociable and well-adjusted by encasing their lives in a common, clean-lined framework. Glass and concrete were expected to furnish a world purged of baroque exaggeration. Architecture was the moral brassiere of the future: its uplift would make mankind positive and outward-looking, preferably through picture windows. The tenants of the *Unité d'Habitation* certainly enjoyed a brighter life than we did in our SW3 basement; but Le Corbusier's regimental uniformity echoed the brave new classlessness we were supposed to admire in Sovcolor documentaries in which untiring Ukrainians sowed, reaped and sometimes sang their way to the socialism at the end of Comrade Stalin's rainbow.

Herb seemed unaware of Europe's demons or how the hydra could always grow new heads. Perhaps because he did not look like a Jew, he appeared not to feel like one. He considered anti-Semitism a social disease. Architecture, he thought, could redesign nature and make life's rough places smooth and easy to keep clean. Like the photographer who called on everyone to say 'cheese' at the same time, the master-builder would fix a regular smile on humanity's face.

As we returned north along the Route Nationale 6, in discrete silence, Herb spotted in the *Guide Michelin* that there was a three-star restaurant at Saulieu, the *Lion d'Or*. Beetle and I recalled not eating there when on the way to Ramatuelle. Herb reckoned that if he stepped on it, we could make it by half past one. Wouldn't it be nice to seal, and heal, our trip with a great meal? We did not arrive till nearly a quarter to two. Herb played the rich American, but neither charm nor his pocketbook could recall a chef who had quit his kitchen once the last *plats de résistance* had been scanned on their way to table. All that anyone could offer was some *pâté* and salad and a dessert, from a limited list. What was meant to be a celebration was cold comfort.

In Paris, we parted from the Oppenheims, with a show of gratitude and a last contribution to the cost of the gas. The rectitude of my goodbye reminded me of my tight-lipped father. I was sad and relieved, Beetle merely relieved. She never saw them again; I did, when I was in New York in 1967, for the première of *Two for the Road*. Herb's career had peaked with his designs for the Playboy Club in New York City. He was now on the board of a liberal synagogue. Linda was fifteen, a pretty young girl who remembered, with more good humour than I deserved, what a pain she had been on our travels. If they ever saw it, the Oppenheims just may have seen themselves in the characters of the Maxwell Manchesters in Stanley Donen's movie. Linda was never as obnoxious as the fictional Ruthiebelle.

Beetle and I caught the train to Calais with the terracotta pots and jug and returned to Chelsea Embankment. When we turned on the light in the living room, it revealed a congress of cockroaches, the size and colour of prunes. I stamped my foot and they took cover, without haste. The next morning, I resumed work on *The Earlsdon Way*. Every evening, Beetle scanned the day's output of pages. If she guessed that my heroine, Karen, was based on Hilary Phillips she did not remark it aloud. As a reader, Beetle was tactful, but not passive. At one point Karen's valetudinarian mother Lesley complains of her bad shoulder. Later, her husband Edward asks how her shoulder feels. My typescript had her reply 'What shoulder?' Beetle suggested that I delete the 'what'. Less was more accurate: '*Shoulder?*' was exactly what Lesley would have said. A decade later, Beetle became one of Jonathan Cape's best readers. Even Edna O'Brien was grateful for her always specific attentions.

Tony Becher had become co-editor of the *Cambridge Review*, a prim 10-point print publication, its long paragraphs aimed at senior members of the university. He asked me to review David Garnett's *Aspects of Love*. I found it to be of no intimidating brilliance. Reviewing resembled the composition of prosaic Latin verses: you had to be elegant and sparky within a limited space and, if possible, end with a twist. It was a quick means of getting your name in print and you could keep the book. Garnett's novella combined Bloombury sophistication with winsome sentimentality. In the 1990s, Andrew Lloyd-Webber asked John Schlesinger and me to turn his and Don Black's musical version of Garnett's novella into a film. The operetta version had stuck, tight, to the plot and dialogue, which struck me, once again, as falsely simple. When John and I proposed bold changes, the project was shelved.

Not long after Beetle and I had returned from Sicily, Tony Becher called. He had met a woman whom he wanted to marry; her name was Anne and she had been a pupil of Helen Gardner's at St Hilda's. Might he come and introduce her to us? And by the way, did I know David Gore-Lloyd had died while we were away? I wrote to his parents, of course, and we exchanged Christmas cards for many years. After the publication of *The Glittering Prizes*, which I dedicated to David's memory, Mrs Gore-Lloyd took offence. I never heard from her again. It may be that she was less upset by my requiem for David than by my depiction of his mother.

'Here we are,' he said, leaping out of the car and coming round to help Karen out. 'This isn't too bad.' He led the way up to the bamboo door and pushed it open for her. Originally El Torero had been a junk-shop, and it still retained vestiges of its earlier role. There were tubs of assorted rubbish in the window and a moose head hung, open mouthed, over the door. On the walls were crossed *banderillos* and posters advertising *corridas* in Cordoba, Jerez, and Ciudad Real. The chairs and tables were of unseasoned pine, and Andalusian copper pots adorned the tops of the alcoves in which they were placed. Youths with mossy beards and young girls with dirty feet sat round the tables. A gramophone was playing *flamencos*.

'Oh, this is heaven!' Karen cried as they sat down at one of the tables. The waitress, in faded gipsy rig, offered them the menu. At the top was written: '*café negro* 9*d.*, *café con leche* 11*d.*, *naranjada* 1/–, *el chocolate* 1/–' Underneath were the main dishes.

'What do you fancy?' Alan asked. '*Tortilla?*'

'What's that?'

'Omelette,' the girl answered in a bored nasal voice.

'Perhaps you'd prefer *paella*?'

'What's —'

'Risotto,' the waitress said.

'Is it good?'

'If you like that sort of thing.'

'Do you like that sort of thing?' Alan asked Karen.

'I don't know.'

'Let's give it a try.'

It was ten minutes before the boiled rice with potted shrimps and curry powder arrived.

'So this is *paella*, is it?'

'That's right. *Paella*,' the waitress said.

'Well, there it is,' Alan said.

'What's the time?' Karen asked again.

'Now what is this? It's early yet. Only just ten. Do relax! You haven't got to catch the night boat to Dublin, have you?'

'Practically.'

'I said I'd buzz you home. Now then. Where is home, incidentally?'

78

The Earlsdon Way

XVII

L IKE THE VICAR of Oliver Goldsmith's deserted village on his £40 a year, we were passing rich. A monthly cheque came to Chelsea Embankment, via MCA, from the Rank Organisation. Neither Olive Harding nor any Rank producer suggested a movie that Leslie and I should write; nor did they look to us to volunteer any ideas. It was an ideal arrangement. I worked at *The Earlsdon Way* every weekday morning; in the afternoon I went up to town to play bridge; sometimes in the two-shilling room at Crockford's, more often at the Oxford and Cambridge Club, where I could read *The Spectator* and the *New Statesman* before continuing to work on my manuscript until it was time to go upstairs to the bridge room. The stakes were only sixpence a hundred, but the chances of winning were enhanced by the amateurishness of the players. Tea and a toasted teacake cost one and sixpence. It was a club rule not to tip the staff.

The company was composed mostly of members of the Bar and the county or High Court bench. There was also a brace of magistrates, one called Pereira, who sometimes figured in the *Evening News* feature 'The Courts Day by Day'. While Pereira carried traces of Sephardic caution, the beak known as 'Master Humphrey' was disposed to booming Anglo-Saxon candour. He announced one evening that he had had a frustrating day; the case before him had concerned two sets of blacks and, 'of course, it was impossible to tell which were the bigger liars'.

The most distinguished judge was Cyril Salmon, a scion of the Salmon and Gluckstein fraternity. One afternoon, while we waited for a four, he proposed a game of backgammon, at which my mother had been my tutor. At one point, Salmon threw an awkward pair of dice and said, 'I shall have to open my legs!' After the race riots of 1958, the first violent response to the influx of Caribbeans during the 1950s, several 'Teddy boys' were accused of inflicting grievous bodily harm on black people. Mr Justice Salmon presided over the trial. In due time, he delivered a four-hour summing up, without notes. He told the jury that, in a free society, men were free to think whatever they wish, however repugnant their opinions; if, however, they translated them into violent action they could expect severe punishment. When convicted, Salmon sentenced the guilty men to four years' imprisonment. No similar outrages took place in England for several years.

I asked Cyril whether he ever feared being attacked by people whom he had sent to prison. '*Sans* wig and robes, they rarely know who you are,' he said. 'One good reason for keeping the fancy dress.' If the odd criminal did recognise the man who had sent him down, in the 1950s, home-grown felons adhered to social niceties: none expressed resentment. Perhaps they took their cue from the rarely vicious villains portrayed by Alec Guinness and Peter Sellers in Ealing comedies.

Among those who came up to the O&C bridge room was the same Mr Murdoch who had enrolled me to make up a four at the Washington Irving Hotel in Granada. One day, Judge Sir Shirley Worthington-Evans told us that Murdoch had been charged with assaulting a black man on the train. He was acquitted, but then took to drink with even more application than previously. Not long afterwards, word came that he had been killed in an incident on the promenade at Eastbourne. Norman Richards QC, to whom

I sometimes gave a lift in what he called my 'barouche', murmured conventional sentiments.

Humphrey Tyldesley-Jones, a wartime colonel, now a commanding officer in the Territorial Army, offered a merciless obituary comment on 'Master Murdoch': 'I don't know which I disliked more – the sight or the smell of him.' Tiddly's smile was part of his unassuming civilian kit. I have no idea if he knew, or cared, that I was a Jew. He told me one day that, very late in the war, the RAF had bombed two ships that were at anchor in a Baltic bay. They were, in fact, prison ships with 'Displaced Persons' on board. After the ships sank, the SS shot any prisoners who managed to swim ashore. Soon afterwards, British commandos captured Schleswig-Holstein, where they found dozens of bodies washed up or left on the shore.

The German Field Marshal Milch had surrendered to Tiddly (then an acting brigadier) in order to avoid capture by the Russians. Arrogant and bombastic, he insisted that the British and the Germans should have united to destroy the 'Bolshevik savages'.

'Savages? What about your concentration camps?'

'For Slavs and such creatures,' Milch said.

'I want you to come for a walk with me.' The Brigadier led the Field Marshal to the shore, where the bodies had been heaped by the tide.

'Well?'

'Look closely,' Tyldesley-Jones said. 'Each of these men was murdered.'

Milch sniffed and bent to inspect the bodies. Each had a bullet wound in the temple. After he had looked at three or four, he burst into tears and sat on the wet beach.

My awareness of the horror that Tiddly encountered at first hand was entirely by proxy. Simon Raven claimed that his generation felt guilty because it had escaped the test of battle. I felt more indignation than guilt, although I did not yet have any idea of the scale of the indifference with which the Allies had regarded the extermination of Europe's Jews. I was lucky to have spent the war on the right side of the Channel, but I was not grateful; I might be an Anglo-American Hebrew hybrid, but I was not a refugee; Chicago Semite maybe, but never Viennese.

I had no conscious model when I was writing *The Earlsdon Way*, but the novel exemplified my cultural doubleness: presuming that suburban Tories were the sole repository of insular prejudices, I used the many-voiced method of Sinclair Lewis and John O'Hara (whose methods are more frequently imitated than acknowledged) to satirise the bourgeoisie, even as I solicited their applause and their pennies.

The war was already subject to sentimental rehearsal in the cinema. When Leslie and I went to Pinewood in his new pink Citroën Metropolitan to have lunch with a producer, the panelled dining room was filled with actors on a lunch break from sinking the *Bismarck* or defending Tobruk. Officers (often Johnny Mills and Jack Hawkins) and men (such as Brian Forbes, Dickie Attenborough and Mickey Medwin) sat at different tables. Few stars played other ranks. Curd Jürgens played the regular, unsmiling German commander; but the name of the ice-eyed actor regularly employed to play a ruthless SS man has slipped memory's net. Although I never knew it at the time, John Schlesinger was occasionally among his *Jawohl*-ing subordinates. Virginia McKenna was the loyal British wife for whom good soldiers and steady-as-you-go sailors yearned. The war had been a close-run thing; victory determined whose scripts would prevail.

George Greenfield, who had won the MC at El Alamein and, as a literary agent, made a speciality of sporting and war memoirs, asked me whether I cared to ghost the memoirs of a secret agent who had been dropped into occupied Europe during the war. I arranged to meet Jacques Doneux in the front hall of the Oxford and Cambridge Club. Arriving early, I made myself as conspicuous as would be polite. No one who came in looked like a spy. Ten minutes after the fixed time, I sighed and glanced again around the crepuscular foyer. A bespectacled person seemed to have materialised, without ever making a noticeable entrance, next to the grandfather clock. I went over and said, 'Are you by any chance Mister Doneux?' He was. He had been there for some time, he said. Punctuality was something he had learned during the war; so too, it seemed, virtual invisibility: like Agatha Christie's milkman in *Why Didn't They Ask Evans*, he was as close to negligible as a man could well contrive.

The artless manuscript of *They Arrived by Moonlight* explained why, unlike so many, Jacques survived without capture: he had obeyed the simple rules inculcated in him during training. Once in occupied Europe, he did not take public transport, except when it was unavoidable, never loitered at a rendezvous, did not spend money or time on women and drank nothing more intoxicating than communion wine (in private life, he was a Roman Catholic church-furnisher). At wise, irregular intervals, he moved himself and his wireless set to different addresses and was discreet in its use.

After several quietly dangerous months in Brussels, it was decided in London that Doneux should return to England. He was given the address of a 'safe house' in Paris, where he could hole up before joining the escape route to the Pyrenees. He arrived in Paris on a glacial day and went to a flat, near Châtelet, where the concierge let him in. While he waited for money for a rail ticket to the next rendezvous, he stripped off his soiled clothes, washed them and hung them to dry while he took a chilly bath. He was roused from it by a telephone call. A voice told him that he must leave at once. The Gestapo was on its way. Jacques had to put on all his wet clothes and go out into the cold. He walked along the *quai*, past the *Jardin des Plantes*, to the Gare d'Austerlitz where he hoped to catch a train to Lyon. Short of money, he feared that his false name might now have been passed to the Germans. His manuscript continued: 'I managed to get onto the platform and, when no one was looking, I slipped under the train and inserted myself on top of the metal struts and hung, face down, a foot or so from the permanent way.' The next chapter began, 'When I got off the train at Lyon...'

In due time, Jacques and an RAF escapee passing down the same escape route reached the town of Pau, just short of the Pyrenees. The Germans and their dogs were on snarling patrol. The RAF man fell sick but, after a little while, 'he pronounced himself as fit as a fiddle and as strong as an ox'. Jacques's shoes were worn out. The only available new footgear was a pair of cotton and rope *espadrilles*. A *passeur* led Jacques and his companion to safety by taking such a steep path up into the mountains that the Germans did not bother to patrol it. When he reached the snow line, Jacques had to kick foot-holds in the ice with his cotton toes. By the time he had crossed into Spain, he had severe frostbite. The nuns in a convent took long care of him.

Once able to travel on to Madrid, Jacques made his way to the British embassy. He hobbled into the presence of the ambassador, Lord Templewood, who looked at his visitor with no marked warmth. 'I sometimes wonder', he said, 'whether you people aren't more trouble than you're worth.' As a Chamberlainite appeaser, the quondam Sir Samuel Hoare had been despatched in eminent disgrace to Franco's Spain by Winston Churchill. His Lordship did not, it seems, appreciate Iberian rustication.

When my revisions of his text were approved for publication, Beetle and I were invited by Jacques and his wife to visit them in their house near Sevenoaks. All of the furniture had the odour of sanctity. The runner on our bedroom dresser was an altar cloth in reduced circumstances. Jacques had scarcely noticed how I had deleted his clichés and with what terse invention I had stocked his lacunae. One or two of his stories were not suffered to figure in the text, for 'security reasons'. For instance, somewhat later in the war, a member of his *réseau* came to his colleagues and reported that he had been sitting in a café in Brussels when a man in plain clothes and a black hat sat adjacent to him and called him by his code name, Max. Max informed his friends that he had, of course, claimed not to know what the man in the black hat was talking about. The man then named all the other members of the network. The latter was, he said, a ranking official in the Gestapo; he could have them all arrested whenever he wanted. However, it was now clear that Germany could not win the war. He had to make his own arrangements to survive. If he was given 100,000 sovereigns, which he knew they had recently had parachuted to them, he would keep quiet. Max was to bring them the next day and had better come alone.

The group decided that it had no choice but to pay up. Max took the money and set off for the rendezvous. He was never seen again. A recent Belgian TV series made use of a very similar plot. On the day of Jacques Doneux's publication party, Beetle's mother had a stroke and was taken into St Mary's hospital. I was sure that he would understand but we had to be at her bedside. He took offence and, as he might have said, disappeared as silently as he had come.

I saw on the Oxford and Cambridge Club noticeboard that a candidate with a Ghanaian name – similar to that of Johnny Quashie-Idun, who had been in the Footlights with us – had been turned down for membership, even though he was an Oxford graduate and a judge in his own country. The chairman of the election committee, Guy Coleridge, was a partner in Knight, Frank and Rutley. He had a lame leg, from a war injury. He had advised me that when I wanted to buy my wife a mink coat, I should tell him; it was much cheaper to get these things at auction, especially if one knew the auctioneer. When I told Guy that the evidence of a colour bar meant that I was going to have to resign from the club, he said, 'Freddie, you don't understand. It's not a question of what colour the chap is, he's just not the kind of *judge* we want in the club.'

Alan Maclean was eager to have my second novel 'in the works' before *Obbligato* was published. When *The Earlsdon Way* was finished, he asked to see it immediately. Reluctant to let go of the literally only copy (taking carbon copies blighted spontaneity), I was flattered by his impatience and handed it over. A few days later, I left Beetle and went to have lunch with Leslie and some of his many showbiz friends at the Mayfair Club, in Berkeley Square. Fuelled with the sparkling hock that the generous Leslie always ordered (one of his guests described it, quietly, as 'sparkling *ad hoc*'), I walked back to Chelsea Embankment to find Beetle looking grim. She had had a telephone call from Alan Maclean. I had better try to keep calm. He had left his briefcase, with my manuscript in it, in his unlocked office when he went out to lunch. On his return, it was gone. He was very sorry. Would Beetle ask me whether perhaps I didn't have another copy somewhere possibly?

He knew very well that I did not. I raged and I daresay I tried to weep. I threw a few things around. Beetle said soothing words and I was not soothed. We got in the car and drove along the Great West Road. It was palliative to be behind the wheel, the master of my silly fate. We got as far as Bath, had a six o'clock cup of tea, and then we drove back to Chelsea Embankment. When I next spoke to Alan, he offered £50 for me to rewrite the book. I scowled and sulked and rehearsed being dead for a day or two. Then I went and typed up the few handwritten chapters still in my notebook. Copying and improving them gave me the thrust to go on into the long section of which I had no trace whatever. I reproduced it pretty well word for word, even after taking care to put two carbons in the machine.

When John Sullivan abandoned Oxford, and his first wife, to seek his academic fortune in America, he was prompt to acquire a new worldly vocabulary. One of his favourite transatlantic phrases was 'When the going gets tough, the tough get going'. I have never been tough, but I have always been determined to keep going. After six weeks of sour, laborious days, I was able to deliver the top copy of the rewritten version of *The Earlsdon Way* to Alan Maclean. Might it possibly be that his briefcase was abstracted by someone from MI5 who spent futile weeks trying to decode my enigmatic text?

I took the second carbon copy of the rewritten novel to Manor Fields on the next evening when we went to see my parents. I imagined that my mother would feel at home with my recension of Sinclair Lewis. On our next visit, she handed the manuscript back to me and said, 'You'll do better.' She must have taken the uncomely Lesley Keggin to be a portrait of herself. It cannot be denied that the problem that Mrs Keggin had with her shoulder duplicated one of Irene's regular complaints; but in fact my grey and proper character was based on a nice Mrs Broke with whom I sometimes played bridge in the Crockford's two-shilling room. Years later, I discovered her to be the not entirely conventional mother of Richard Broke, the script editor who was assigned to *The Glittering Prizes*. My father's only pronounced reaction to *The Earlsdon Way* was to report that Dan Keggin, at Wimbledon Park gold club, was amused by my purloining his name for my hero.

Alan Maclean took his time in reading the rewritten manuscript. Then his secretary rang to ask me to have lunch with him and his colleague 'Auntie Marge'. I left Chelsea Embankment, in my second-best Adamson's suit, brightened black shoes, St John's College tie and with warranted misgivings. Simpson's in the Strand was garrulous with suited businessmen having what was then habitually called 'a spot of lunch'. Trolleyed joints of roast lamb and beef rolled among them as they inhaled the fumed mahogany atmosphere.

After Alan had crossed the carver's palm with silver, he told me that they admired much of the writing, but *The Earlsdon Way* was 'not a Macmillan book'. Social realism, in which the local Conservative Party was held up to ridicule, was not the species of light-heartedness that Jack Squire had promised that I was good for. Auntie Marge hoped I didn't mind them saying so, but I should never make any friends if I went on writing in this fashion. I told them that I had not become a writer to make friends, but to tell the truth, however much it might hurt people. I could imagine the shade of George Turner shaking his head: some people never learn.

I stayed for profiteroles and then I went and phoned George Greenfield (careful not to press button A before someone answered). He had already spoken to David Farrer at Secker & Warburg, where his client Brian

Glanville was an established author. When they came through, Secker's readers' reports were so enthusiastic that George could hardly understand why Farrer elected not to take the book. He sent it across Red Lion Square to Desmond Flower at Cassell's, who soon offered a £100 advance. I had a new publisher.

Over one of our irregular three-and-sixpenny lunches at Schmidt's in Charlotte Street, I told my new friend Tom Maschler how pleased I was. He looked unimpressed: no one who mattered was published by Cassell's. 'No? What about Robert Graves?' Tom said, 'What about him?' Maschler had had the alert wit to commission, and was about to publish, a collection of polemic essays entitled *Declaration*, to which he supplied a modest intro- duction. I had got to know him too late to be a candidate for inclusion. The collection was loudly bruited as the manifesto of the Angry Young Men. Doris Lessing was an honorary member of their fraternity. For politic pub- licity purposes, the contributors were taken to share some coherent sense of outrage and purpose. The watchword of their parade was 'By the left, quick march'. What they did undoubtedly have in common was militant self-righteousness. Legend insists that Kingsley Amis was a contributor; in fact, showy Oxonian self-deprecation disposed him to decline Maschler's solicitation to join the dance.

Ken Tynan, Lindsay Anderson, John Wain, Stuart Holroyd and Colin Wilson rallied to Tom's 5,000-word call. Lindsay Anderson's essay was enti- tled 'Get Out and Push'; but what he, and the others, pushed was mainly their own bandwagon. John Osborne's was already rolling, thanks largely to Ken Tynan. Osborne had given resentment emblematic form in Jimmy Porter, the anti-hero of *Look Back in Anger*. The play, starring Kenneth Haigh and Mary Ure, owed its delayed triumph and abiding mythological status to Ken's advocacy. As it was about to close, he announced that he could never love anybody who did not think it a masterpiece. Osborne's fame was established. By the 1970s, he and Tynan had become rancorous enemies. They exchanged regular, well-publicised paper punches in available publications.

While impersonating Jimmy Porter, Ken Haigh seemed bound for stardom; but he never achieved it. Failure to find sustained favour sat heavily on him. Some time later, Nigel Stock, a mild character actor, never out of work, had a small part in a film I wrote. He told me that he used to go to Lord's in the afternoon; the Large Mound stand was a nice quiet place to smoke his pipe and learn lines. One day, he was aware of Ken Haigh sitting behind him. Between overs, Ken leaned forward, heavy hands on the white slats of Nigel's seat. 'Tell me something, Nige, honestly: why is it people don't like me?' Stock put his script on his knee, took his pipe from his mouth, and said, 'Probably because you're such a cunt, Ken.'

Tom Maschler was now the non-playing captain of those who advocated a menu of new Jerusalems. Colin Wilson was the manifestly prodigious genius. He had come to public attention in corduroys and a roll-topped orange sweater, straight from sharing a sleeping bag with a woman called Valerie (many girls were in those days) on Hampstead Heath. Her father was widely reported to be looking for Colin with a horsewhip. *The Outsider* was acclaimed by both grand masters of the Sunday press, Philip Toynbee and Cyril Connolly.

Colin's autodidacticism was primed by the literary savvy of his namesake. Angus Wilson, then a librarian at the British Museum, armed the young unknown to amaze the pundits by his cull of Continental sources, from Herman Hesse, whose Steppenwolf was the archetypal outsider, to Nietzsche, Camus and Sartre. At the height of Colin's fame, I interviewed him, not without a trace of Cambridge philosophical condescension, for BBC radio. He was more bemused than besotted by the publicity. I envied him his orange cable-stitched, roll-top sweater more urgently than the feathers in his cap. Beetle knitted me a duplicate for my birthday. The author of *The Outsider* flamed briefly in the forehead of the morning sky and then, after the publication of his second, clumsier collage, was reduced to the ranks of has-beens.

Deserted by the smart critics whose want of cosmopolitan literacy he had exposed (they would not otherwise have saluted the originality of his notion of outsiderdom), Colin fell as summarily as he had risen. He accepted relegation from genius to crank with such good grace that it doubled for eminence. As if stalled almost at the peak of his Icarian ascendancy-cum-fall, he scarcely changed, in appearance or wardrobe, over the years. Living in Cornish seclusion, he wrote many more books, about violent crime, sexual aberration and the supernatural, some enjoyable, some scabrous, all art-lessly dotty. In the late 1980s, after I had congratulated him on something he had written, he took me to a meeting of the Savage Club where 'Brother Savages' sang salty songs.

The Royal Court Theatre in Sloane Square was the centre of Ken Tynan's smart hopes for a new kind of drama that involved socialism, sexual liber-ation and his own bandmasterly supervision. George Devine, an earnest, plain, middle-aged actor of small charisma, was the Royal Court's presiding dramaturge. He was seconded, in the back office, by Oscar Lowenstein, a small, anxious person whose knees literally knocked together when I went to see him about a play of mine for which he expressed impotent enthusi-asm: in the new, no longer oligarchic theatre, George made all the creative decisions.

Aspirant writers were encouraged to attend rehearsals at the Royal Court. I dropped in one day to see Tony Richardson directing George Devine, who was on his knees, in a canine position. Tony Richardson, the Oxonian equivalent of Peter Hall, though in a higher social register, was standing over the temporarily four-footed actor, chin in one hand. He considered the matter and then he said, 'You don't feel like growling at all, do you, George?' I walked out into Sloane Square and along the King's Road to Ward's Bookshop.

In the 1970s, we rented a house from Tony Richardson in King's Road, off Sunset Boulevard. It had a good many David Hockney paintings, of swimming pools, with and without boys. They hung high in the lee of the advertised 'cathedral ceiling'. Tony Richardson's last film job, in 1989, was to direct a version of Hemingway's *Hills Like White Elephants*, one of a trio of 'Tales of Seduction'. In the same triad, I directed Elizabeth McGovern and Beau Bridges in my adaptation of Mary McCarthy's *The Man in the Brooks Brothers Shirt*, which won the Ace Award for the Best Film on Cable TV. I never had occasion to speak to Tony Richardson, who was dying of Aids at the time. My award was lost in the mail.

Almost immediately after Leslie and I collected our last monthly stipend from the Rank Organisation, we were approached by a Pinewood producer, Vivian Cox, who proposed that we write a movie about Cambridge. His idea was that it should be like *The Guinea Pig*, in which the juvenile Dickie Attenborough had made his name as an oikish outsider given a place at a posh public school. Vivian had been a hockey Blue (and international), played rugger for Wasps, and drove a white Aston Martin. During the war he had gone into action, as Flag Lieutenant to Vice-Admiral Bruce Fraser on *HMS Duke of York*, during the sinking of the German battle-cruiser *Scharnhorst*. A connoisseur of good wines, Vivian was a hard-working *bon vivant* (he told me that '*bon viveur*' was not a genuine *locution française*) and an eager patron of Michelin-starred restaurants, especially his friend Raymond Thuillier's Baumanière at Les Baux-de-Provence. Thuillier had not become a chef until he was over fifty and now had three stars.

Since Leslie's and my two-picture contract had just lapsed, Jock Jacobsen had to negotiate a new deal, for another nice fee, for us to write *Bachelor of Hearts*. The cinema was, it appeared, an indulgent Maecenas. In due time, our original working-class 'guinea pig' was transformed to accommodate Hardy Kruger, the young German star of a recent hit, *The One That Got Away*. Sylvia Syms, the English cinema's principal *jeune première* after

Jean Simmons, had defected unpatriotically to Hollywood with Stewart Granger, was cast as a rather better-looking Girton girl than any I had seen pedalling along the Cambridge streets. When Vivian took us to meet her, Leslie kissed her hullo with West End ease. Lacking his smooth cheek, I held out my hand.

Some thirty years later, I wrote a play, *From the Greek*, a modern version of *Oedipus Rex*, set in New Mexico, which Jonathan Lynn commissioned and was to direct. He approached the mature Miss Syms to play the part of my Jocasta. She did not refuse him; but said that she would like to meet me, again. As I leaned towards her, I was greeted with an outstretched hand. 'I remember the last time we met,' she said, 'and you refused to kiss me.' I suspect that she took some pleasure in declining the part that went to Maxine Audley, who had also been a great beauty. She told me that, in her youth, if she saw a man she fancied, she would say to herself, 'I'll have a bit of that' and was rarely denied.

When, at length, *Bachelor of Hearts* was greenlighted, Vivian gave a dinner party for Leslie and me in his Curzon Street *garçonnière*. As he opened a celebratory bottle of 1945 Château Margaux, he told us how, during the Great War, an Englishman and a Frenchman shared a dug-out. They had one bottle of a rare and delicious vintage, which they swore that they would not open until victory came. On the eleventh hour of the eleventh day of the eleventh month of 1918, the Englishman reached for his corkscrew. The Frenchman took the bottle from him as he prepared to pour it. '*Non, non, mon cher ami! Pas si vite! D'abord on en parle un peu.*'

Hardy Kruger had been fourteen years old when the war ended. Like other young Germans of his age, he had already been recruited into the Hitler Youth. That he was cast in our movie excited little indignation. Tom Wiseman, the much feared *Evening Standard* showbiz columnist, was an exception. As a small boy, he had fled Vienna with his mother in 1938; his father remained behind. After living dangerously, and profitably for a while,

Wiseman senior was arrested and murdered. As our movie was about to come out, Tom went to interview Hardy in his hotel suite and grilled him on his service to the Nazis. Hardy defended himself on the plausible grounds that few young persons in his position could have resisted the patriotic call. Tom was not easily mollified, but had to concede that Hardy was no sort of impenitent ex-Nazi. As the meeting ended, quite amicably, Hardy's wife, who had overheard their long conversation, said to Tom, 'Mr Viseman, so far as ze Germans and ze Jews vere concerned, vy don't we ve just agree zat zere were mistakes on both sides?'

Our director was Wolf Rilla. His half-Jewish father, the actor Walter Rilla, had quit Germany in 1934, when Wolf was fourteen. He had no problem working with Hardy Kruger, but he was a rather solemn film-maker, not wholly suited to Leslie's and my larky screenplay (based, with all but slipshod looseness, on *As You Like It*). Wolf had been at school at Frensham Heights and then went up to Cambridge, but he remained irredeemably foreign in manner and dress (his scripts were holstered in a Mitteleuropan leather music-case).

During the making of *Bachelor of Hearts*, Wolf lived near Rutland Street with the actress Valerie Hanson. When they came to dinner, he told the first story about drugs that I ever heard: two potheads are walking down a long steep hill. A man comes running at full tilt from the top of the hill and with a yell of 'excuse me' passes clean between them and runs on down to the bottom. After a long moment, one pothead looks at the other and says, 'I thought he'd never go.' Wolf had high ambitions as an *auteur* but lacked the force or luck to fulfil them. A few years later, after the failure of his own solemn production *The World Ten Times Over*, which Beetle and I applauded as long and as loudly as we dared, Wolf's career folded. He married an English woman and went to run a hotel in Provence.

Vivian Cox had been an associate producer on *Trio* and *Quartet*, in which Somerset Maugham had introduced clutches of his own short stories transposed to the screen. The presence of the renowned Old Party, and his shyness, had intimidated the unit. During an afternoon break, one of the sparks broke the ice by going up to the great man and saying, '´ave a cuppa tea, Somerset'. Vivian gave us to understand that he and Willie had been on quite close terms. When I told him that Maugham was in town and that Alan Searle had asked me to arrange a bridge game for him at Crockford's, Vivian told me to be sure to give Willie his regards.

At dinner, with Guy Ramsey, Edward Meyer (the *Times* bridge correspondent) and Kenneth Konstam, the Old Party recalled that I had been on my way to Spain when he last saw me. I told him how much I enjoyed it, but not that I had lost his 'Open Sesame' letter. When I found occasion to deliver Vivian Cox's message, Maugham did not recall the name. 'Ah well,' he said, 'more people know Tom Fool than Tom Fool knows.' He was courteous enough to ask about my musical comedy. On learning that the production date seemed regularly to recede, he was not at all surprised. When we went upstairs to the two-shilling room, Maugham clenched his cigarette-holder in his prognathous jaw and addressed himself, with unnecessarily apologetic modesty, to the matter in hand.

Leslie and I were contacted about a musical that was already on tour and needed expert attention before it could be exposed to Ken Tynan and his unkind cuts. It had been written by two doctors, Al Kaplan and Robin Fordyce. Al was in his early thirties, a sleek, handsome, rich, bisexual Canadian, married to Susie Sieff, of the Marks & Spencer's dynasty. By the time our deal was confirmed, Leslie had already driven himself, in his new 'wagon', down to Plymouth where the show was being tried out in front of dwindling audiences. Al offered me a lift in his grey Rolls Bentley convertible. It had a diminutive, clitoridal gear lever empanelled between the seats. He had meant to use his other, sporty car, but its transmission made unhealthy noises. 'Take my advice, Frederic: never buy one of those tinny Lagondas.' When we were crossing Salisbury Plain, Al asked if I had ever driven a Rolls. I really should; it was so easy.

'One day,' I said.

Al said, 'And why not today?' He pulled in and invited me to take his place. It was true: the car was smooth and almost silent (David Ogilvy had recently advertised the Rolls-Royce to America by claiming that 'at 60 miles an hour the loudest sound is the ticking of the dashboard clock'). I drove with proper wariness. Al became impatient. 'Put your foot down, it'd be good to get there today.'

When I accelerated, the smoothness of the ride made it seem that we were not going very fast. The Great West Road was only one lane in each direction. I was enjoying the silent speed and Al's approval when, in the straight distance ahead of us, I saw one big lorry pull out to overtake another. They rolled towards us, side by side. The inside driver was reluctant to give way. In a strange conjunction of the slow and the sudden, I was aware that the overtaking lorry was heading straight at us. I pressed the brake pedal, but the Rolls was much, much heavier than anything I had ever driven and it did not have power-assisted brakes. I pressed down with panicky weight and the car slowed, slowly. So did the lorry on our side of the road. We stopped, almost bumper to bumper, while the other, unyielding, lorry driver thundered past Al's window. I was afraid that he would reproach me for our close-run thing. When I looked at him, he was smiling.

The star of *Jubilee Girl* was Lizbeth Webb. I had seen her in *Bless the Bride* when I was first going out with Hilary Phillips. Now a big star, Miss Webb was gallant enough not to desert a sinking enterprise. She wore 'me mink' as proof of her buoyant stardom. With blithe Cambridge ruthlessness, Leslie and I decided to change her leading man and also to dispense with the services of Irene Handl, who had been memorable, although uncredited, in *Brief Encounter*, in which she doubled as cinema organist and a Kardomah waitress. She accepted my Judas kiss on her abrasive cheek and probably considered herself well out of the show. She later wrote a singular novel entitled *The Sioux*. She was replaced, to no marked effect, by an actress whose claim to fame was that, for many years, she had been the musical comedy star Cicely Courtneidge's understudy.

I rewrote many of the scenes in *Jubilee Girl* and directed the actors in their new lines and moves in the mornings and afternoons. In the evening they had to go on and honour the script we were in the process of dismantling. The *doyenne* of the cast was Marie Lohr, the star, in 1930, of Maugham's *The Breadwinner*. In her mid-sixties, she was, in my eyes, a venerable old lady. I was touched by her punctuality – she was always the first to arrive, with her knitting, at rehearsal – and heartened by small nods at my directorial suggestions.

Marie had one wistful song in the show, 'Style, Form and Grace', which she impersonated perfectly. We stood with her on the foreshore at Southsea when Khrushchev and Bulganin sailed out of Portsmouth harbour on their way home to Russia after their double act had completed its brief British tour (leaving the secret service's frogman 'Buster' Crabbe dead in Portsmouth harbour after venturing too near the Russians' ship). Should we wave or should we not? Marie thought it would be polite, so we did. She had stood in the same place when the Grand Fleet passed in review before the king-emperor in the summer of 1914.

The choreographer John Cranko came down, at Al's invitation, to inspect how we were doing. He had just directed the innovatory revue *Cranks*, in which the young Anthony Newley was conspicuously brilliant. Cranko's verdict was that we had replaced bad direction with what was no better. Leslie allowed it to be thought that the direction had largely been my work. He may have had Cranko to thank for his introduction to Tony Newley, with whom he later had a successful collaboration, most notably in creating the hit musical *Stop the World – I Want to Get Off*. Getting on was much more Leslie's wish; and it was thoroughly fulfilled. He wrote some lyrics for Hank Mancini's theme music for *Two for the Road*. I was not eager that his words should feature on the soundtrack of what Stanley Donen told me was my film. They were heard elsewhere and still adhere to the movie's credits on the DVD.

Jubilee Girl had another director or two before it opened at the Victoria Palace, where it did not last long. In 1969, Al Kaplan telephoned me from Italy to say that he wanted to produce the script of Iris Murdoch's *A Severed Head*, which I had written originally for John Schlesinger. John refused to accept the casting of Larry Harvey (or Dirk Bogarde) as Martin Lynch-Gibbon and the project was dropped until Elliott Kastner acquired the rights. Al told me that he knew that I had a controlling interest. If I did not consign the rights to him he would have me killed. He then rang off. He died shortly afterwards, of an overdose of the drugs he was said to have supplied to the higher echelons of Italian showbiz. I sometimes wonder how nice Dr Jekyll really was.

I met Tony Newley only once. During the run of *Stop the World – I Want to Get Off*, he and Leslie dropped in when I was visiting Vivian Cox. On their way out of the *garçonnière*, Newley offered me his hand and said, 'Good luck in whatever you choose to do in life.' A few years later, when I had won the Oscar for writing *Darling*, Leslie was the first person to call from California to congratulate me; he was followed by Yvonne and, after that, by his chum Tony Newley and his then wife Joan Collins.

XVIII

I N MAY 1956, we gave a publication party for *Obbligato* at Chelsea Embankment. I decorated the blank hall wall with a large pastel mural that recalled the bucolic San Gemignano. Alan Maclean was not of the company. Nevertheless, we seemed to know a lot of people. Ken Tynan brought the gauntly beautiful, long-haired Elizabeth Jane Howard. She posed at the head of the short stairs into our basement as if she was likely to be photographed. She had already published a couple of elegant novels and had had a famous liaison with Arthur Koestler. She would put it to fictional use in *After Julius*. Ken embraced Dotty Tutin as the reassuring evidence that the company did not lack class.

Obbligato was reviewed amiably, if patronisingly, by a double-barrelled Marie in the *Sunday Times*. Her weekly batch, in which I came last, was headed by a fanfare for *Tunes of Glory* by James Kennaway, who had been at Oxford with Tony Becher's new wife, Anne. Guy Ramsey assured me that to be reviewed at all, and at decent length, was quite something. Vanity and a certain shame, at the levity of my first book, impelled me to feel that it was not enough. The Suez crisis was brewing. *Obbligato* was a nugatory squib published just as the illusion of Britain's hegemony was about to be fractured and the Angry Young Men taken to be the harbingers of a new society.

On a grey Sunday afternoon in late October, Beetle and I were in the loud crowd in Whitehall. Banners and voices were raised against Eden's war. Wedged among the synchronised yells of the committed, I was uneasy when people started rolling marbles under the hooves of the police horses ('Eden's cavalry'); it did not seem sporting. Although I thought the attack on Egypt was ill-conceived and worse managed, I remember thinking, as we surged towards Downing Street, that we were doing Britain's cause, whatever it was, no good by baying at the Prime Minister's door. Even cynics did not yet realise to what extent the whole operation was rigged, with Israel as the patsy, to lend virtuous allure to the Franco-British 'intervention'.

We met Poznan Mirosevic-Sorgo and another old Jordan's Yard *habitué*, Stefan Danieff, coming, solemn-faced, down Whitehall against the current. They had just heard Imre Nagy's desperate appeal to the West not to allow Khrushchev and his friends to crush the Hungarian revolt. Poznan feared, and perhaps slightly hoped, that the West was about to go to war with the Soviet Union. Eden's post-imperial paroxysm had created a rupture between Europe and the US at the worst possible moment. I was ashamed of the West's politic indifference to the repression of the Hungarian revolt and, later, the execution of Imre Nagy; but I was relieved that the crises were followed by peace with dishonour. If anyone else recalled Jean Cocteau's remark, after the French surrender in June 1940, '*Vive cette paix honteuse!*', no one was tactless enough to cite it.

Eden fell. After Randolph Churchill had gloated in the *Evening Standard*, 'Rab Butler has had it', Harold Macmillan, who had panicked when his displeased old colleague Eisenhower threatened to scupper the pound, entered 10 Downing Street. Rab's disappointment was the ultimate revenge of the Churchills on the most durable of pre-war appeasers. In the 1970s, as President of the Royal Society of Literature, Butler told an after-dinner story about two 'Jewboys'. I took it upon myself to write to him in reproachful terms. He responded with appeasing hauteur. My life has been littered with mutations of the Provost of Guildford. I rather wish I had once struck one of them, instead of writing reproachful letters. Sometimes, like the late Sir Ian Gilmour, when met in person, they turn out to have disappointing charm.

Beetle wanted daylight and she wanted a baby. I was reluctant both to leave Chelsea, where we could not afford anything above ground, and to bring another Jew into the world. Beetle was not about to have Mr Hitler determine our lives. It was not long before she was pregnant. We discovered that Celia Ramsey's friend Marion Slater wanted to sell the lease of her cottage in Rutland Street, not far from Harrods, where she may well have acquired her elegant accent. Her husband, from whom she was separated, was a handsome society portraitist. If the young Celia had not had an affair with him, she was not disposed to deny it.

Before the lease could be ceded, I had to be approved by the landlord, a Greek gentleman called Tachmindji. He had a City office with a hump-backed roll-top desk. I had never before met a Greek, of whatever confused Levantine lineage. I passed his exam without difficulty and we moved into 14 Rutland Street. The rent was £6 a week. In the usual way in those days, we had to buy most of Marion Slater's furniture. The double bed had a gammy leg; after it gave way, we splinted it with disused historical and philosophical volumes.

A day after our arrival, I drove up to find the space directly in front of our house taken by another vehicle. I parked in an adjacent void. That evening, a card came through our letter box, headed 'From Mr Justice Hinchcliffe'. It read: 'Please refrain from parking your car in front of number 12. It blocks the light and air from the basement room and causes great inconvenience to all.' We never had another neighbourly communication from his lordship. He later presided over the libel action brought by Brian Glanville against the actor David Kossoff, whose speciality it was to play endearing, folkloric Jews. Brian was accused of commercially motivated 'anti-Semitism' when writing his 1958 novel, *The Bankrupts*. In it, he anticipated Philip Roth's

Goodbye, Columbus in taking a scathing, 'disloyal' view of middle-class Jewish society; in Brian's case, the Golders Green community among whom his father had his dental practice. Mr Justice Hinchcliffe directed the jury decisively, and rightly, in favour of the plaintiff. Kossoff had to pay suitable damages and costs.

1950s London did not lack people of a certain age who made a habit of standing on their dignity. One afternoon, I happened to cut a retired, no doubt gallant, brigadier as a partner in the Crockford's two-shilling room. I made a rather bold opening bid, of 'one spade' with only three of that suit in my hand. As a result, the opposition was bluffed out of making a cold game. The brigadier considered himself to have been misled, albeit to his own side's advantage. As the cards were being reshuffled for the next hand, he said, 'Do you mind if I say something to you rather frankly?' 'Not at all, sir,' I said, 'as long as you don't mind my saying something equally frank in response.' The brigadier said, 'I've never been spoken to like that before in my entire life.'

Our life in Rutland Street was well-lit, constricted and genteel. The woman who lived across from us had a dog named Bertie, when she was pleased with him, Bert*ram* when she was not. I had worked well in our murky but romantic Chelsea basement; in Knightsbridge I did many things, but almost all were incidental, although sometimes lucrative. Thanks to the initiative of a young singer called Jim Dale, I composed a radio version of *Obbligato*, in which he starred as the improvising natural, Frank Smith ('It's all false and fake / Yes, every move I make'). Once the youngest professional comic on the variety stage, Jim Dale went on to have a long career as a versatile performer (he was in many of the *Carry On* movies) and lyricist: he wrote the hit song *Georgy Girl*. He was frequently nominated for Tony Awards for his performances on Broadway.

Toting a heavy army surplus wireless, I continued to do a number of BBC radio interviews. Several were with Caribbean writers who were establishing themselves in London: George Lamming, Samuel Selvon and others. There were few black people in Knightsbridge and none in our social life. Johnny Quashie-Idun had been in *Out of the Blue*, in which he sang to a guitar and took part in a number entitled 'No Room at the Inn'. Based on a news story that some visiting black celebrity had been denied a room at the Ritz, it scarcely raised the colour question in any pressing form; but we imagined ourselves taboo-breakingly bold.

Bernard Sheridan – an articled clerk during Beetle's time at the legal partnership Aukin, Courts – was now a qualified solicitor. He invited me to attend one of his *pro bono* surgeries at a legal aid centre off the Holloway Road, where I posed as an intern. A white couple sought Bernard's advice because their landlady was trying to chase them out of a flat they had occupied for fifteen years. She wanted to put 'Negroes' into it. Why would anyone want to do that? Simple: they could be racked for much higher rents.

I longed to be taken for a writer of the kind applauded by Cyril Connolly or Jack Davenport; but I was particularly pleased when George Greenfield sold one of my short stories to the down-market *Everybody's*, for £40. It was based on my adventures in Morocco and my encounter with Mr Tree on the ferry to Gibraltar. Big, floppy, vulgar *Everybody's* was not a magazine that any Leavisite would deign to read, but I could be sure that it had bought my story for no snobbish reason. I continued to review the odd book for the *Cambridge Review*, but I made no prudent contacts in London literary circles. Karl Miller had resigned from the Treasury as a protest against the Suez operation and became literary editor of *The Spectator*. I did not hear from him.

The irksome local effect of Suez was petrol rationing; its surtaxed price soared to six shillings a gallon. Leslie Bricusse bought a blister-shaped, three-wheeled bubble car, big enough for two. Its hatch opened upwards and outwards at the front and it did 100 miles to the gallon. I dreaded its puttering arrival in Rutland Street. It was, however, easy to park without vexing Mr Justice Hinchcliffe. Nothing that Leslie wanted to do answered any of my genuine ambitions, least of all his repeated request that I take yet another look at the book of *Lady at the Wheel*.

One day, I ran into Richard Bird, my old bridge partner. We began to have irregular lunches at L'Escargot in Greek Street. In decorous style, we chose to pay the bill alternately. Whoever's turn it was to pay next would call the other to fix a date. Richard had joined the Ministry of Transport and had amusing stories to tell about the vanity of little Ernest Marples, the man who drilled the often flooded tunnel under Hyde Park Corner. We played bridge again and seemed to have become the kind of grown-up friends one was supposed to make at Cambridge. One lunchtime, as he paid the bill, I remarked that it was a shame that he had not met Beetle. Would he come and dine with us sometime? An evening was fixed; Beetle took great care with the food and I with the bottle; Richard left with expressions of warm gratitude. I assumed that the dinner party was the equivalent of a lunch and left it to him to call me to fix our next date. I have never seen or heard from him since.

When commercial television started, Jock Jacobsen arranged for Leslie and me to go, with a Granada TV producer, Kenneth Hurren ('Call me Kenneth; or Ken, obviously'), to see (Sir) Douglas Fairbanks in his office overlooking Hyde Park. Our mission was to suggest a way for him to do his projected television show, which would be 'different' and colourful; someone had recently described the star, a legendary figure, not yet fifty, as 'grey all over'.

His door was badged with plaques declaring various Fairbanks enterprises. 'We have to have them for tax reasons,' one of his sidekicks told us.

Inside, we were greeted by the trademark smile, inherited from his daredevil and acrobatic Hollywood father. 'The sun is over the yard-arm, gentlemen. I'm afraid I haven't any gin. I can offer you whisky, vodka and tonic…' Below the winning eyes, the face was triangular; there was just room for a brief nose, a scimitar of moustache and the irresistible grin. He sat down behind the wide, vacant shelf of his desk. 'I'm unique,' he said, 'unique good or unique bad, depending on how you look at it.' He spoke of himself as he might about a very old and dear friend. 'If I do what everyone does, I might as well not be on the programme.'

'What did you feel about last week's show?' I asked him.

'Here's the consensus. This is of friends, you know. They thought I was nervous. That's ridiculous. I was not nervous. Then they thought I was condescending. Of course, I'm *not* condescending, but that's what they thought. And gushing…'

'That's ridiculous,' one of his aides said. 'You're not gushing at all.'

'How's the billing going to read?' Fairbanks said. 'Can we get a lead there? "Granada TV and Douglas Fairbanks present…"'

'Can't have that,' Kenneth said. 'Granada have to be the programme contractors. That's under the Act.'

The telephone rang. It was Selwyn Lloyd, the Foreign Secretary, to say that, yes, he could come for cocktails on Saturday. Mrs Fairbanks had to be informed right away. It seemed that Selwyn Lloyd was subbing for some brighter light who was not able to make it.

'Now, gentlemen, a refill?'

'What if we put you in an office?' Leslie said.

'Too formal.'

'Or with a —'

'No props.'

'Perhaps you should start by doing something funny. To put people —'

'I'm not a gag man.'

'What about a backstage approach?' Leslie said.

'A knock on the door, you mean, "You're on, Mr Fairbanks", that kind of thing?'

Kenneth said, 'How about the Garroway approach?'

Even Leslie could not pretend to know what that was.

'This guy did this show on TV in Chicago. Dave Garroway. It's the Chicago version I'm talking about here, not the New York one. He just sort of ambled on and announced the next act, very casual – he had this manner, it got to be so famous that they called it "the Garroway approach".'

'Casual?'

'Totally. Totally casual. The Chicago show, this was.' Kenneth looked at his watch, took his hat. 'I've got to go. That's just a suggestion. You people carry on.'

'Of course,' Dougie said. 'That's the way we do things here. We just bounce an idea off the wall and … see where we get.'

Two hours later, we accompanied Fairbanks and his entourage to the street, where he got into his Rolls Bentley and sat democratically next to the chauffeur.

I said to the chief sidekick, 'How does he really see himself doing the show?'

He said, 'I'll tell you. He sees himself doing it in the ambassador's room in the American embassy, in front of the crossed flags of Britain and America and wearing the uniform of an Admiral of the Fleet.'

One afternoon, when my parents were on holiday in Juan-les-Pins, Dr Cove-Smith telephoned to say, 'I'm afraid we've lost Mrs Raphael.' For a moment, I supposed that my grandmother had been mislaid and that I was being summoned to assist in the search. In fact, after many an autumn, Amelia Sophia had breathed her last. I went to Dorset House, where Winifred Stanley was dutifully determined to have me 'see her'. She lay in the same bed under the same covers, much the same in death as in old age except that her jaw was parcelled in a knotted kerchief that was tied in a firm bow on top of her head.

I met my parents with the news at London Airport and drove them to Manor Fields in PLD 75. My father was tight-lipped, ashamed of not having been with her at the end. The service took place in the chapel at the Willes-den cemetery. Amy had not relished Jewish society in life; in death she could not avoid it. My late grandfather's sister, my great-aunt Polly, was with us in the car as we passed through the cemetery gates. My mother sought to lighten the atmosphere by asking a standard, flattering question: 'Did any-one ever tell you that you looked like Marie Tempest, Poll?'

'Everyone did,' Polly said. 'She was an ugly old cat. But what a voice! I was going to be in the chorus of *The Geisha* with her. Had me photo taken in the costume.' My father's relatives, on each branch of the family tree, were nothing if not performers.

Cedric went in alone before they nailed down the coffin. The rabbi arrived in a baby Austin, a dark, fleshy man with plummy eyes. After an abbrevi-ated service, we followed a slow, long-handled, two-wheeled handcart to the graveside. As the coffin was lifted, the attendant linked his hand, for bal-ance, with one of the labourer's. Effort fattened them. After a few prayers, Cedric was handed a narrow shovel. 'Three times, please.' He dug three times into a pile of cinders heaped beside the heavy clay. I put my hand on his shoulder. He seemed so near the grave that I wanted to keep him this side of it. When we were back in the stiff shelter of the chapel, my father sat down for a while on a varnished bench. The rabbi shook hands with all of us and went.

I took Polly back to her rooms in Oxford and Cambridge Gardens and then we all went to Rutland Street. Cedric lay down on our orange-skirted divan, but he could not sleep. He went down the road to Harrods for a hair-cut. He told our regular barber, Number Three, about his troubles.

Number Three said, 'See that bloke over there? His son came back from Cyprus with cancer of the throat. He died after a nine months' illness. Nine-teen years old.'

XIX

I N 1958, HUSBANDS were not encouraged to be present when their wives gave birth. At two in the morning, when Beetle's contractions increased in frequency, we did the prescribed thing and called an ambulance to 14 Rutland Street. I followed it to the Middlesex Hospital and stayed with her for a while. She said I should go home and get some sleep. She would call me when she had some news. There was no point in coming back to the hospital earlier, because they would not let me see her. I suspect that I might have insisted with some success, but I was squeamish and docile. I went to have lunch with John and Dudy Nimmo in Upper Addison Gardens.

I had scarcely known Dudy when she was the most famous actress in Cambridge. While I was on my travels, she had been cast as a young girl in *The Duchess and the Smugs* by Pamela Frankau, directed by John van Druten, an American dramatist and director best known for his hit play *I Am a Camera*, adapted from Christopher Isherwood's Berlin stories about Sally Bowles. The *New Yorker* review had consisted of two words: 'No Leica.'

Beetle was driven by John to see the show in Brighton. Dudy was miscast and inept. She might be short, but she was no little girl. She was replaced before the play reached London. It put an end to her, and John's, expectations that she was going to be the next Peggy Ashcroft. Somewhat humbled, Dudy asked my advice. I was bold or callous enough to say that she should go to drama school, which she did, at the Webber Douglas, just off Gloucester Road. John had been a bookish *flâneur* since coming down from Cambridge, but now he needed a job. He found one at the Zinc Marketing Board, in Berkeley Square. He and Dudy seemed to be our best, certainly our most regular back-and-forth dining friends.

No longer dreaming of stardom, though still hoping for employment, Dudy was minded to have as many children as her mother, Elfrida Vipont Foulds, a dedicated Quaker and the author of any number of successful children's books. Dudy had three siblings, 'sister Anne, sister Bo and sister Co'. The last was the beautiful one. Her beauty, and its quietness, was due, in part, to her happy, passionate marriage. She and her husband lived in Kenya, where he worked for a large company. One day, they left their daughter with a local nanny and went on safari with a Kenyan driver. There was some kind of an accident, or a blow-out; the Jeep flew off the road and into a tree. Co (Carol) was not badly injured; Ricky was killed. The silly driver sat there. Co came back to England and took a flat somewhere in London which she shared with another woman. Such were the things that happened to other people.

Sister Co's tragedy inspired me to write a play about a woman, Caroline, who comes back with her young daughter Claudia from Africa, after the death of her husband in a similar absurd accident. Since she has to go out to work, she advertises for a mother's help. Claudia finds it easier to confide in Rachel than in her mother. Caroline is lonely and jealous and, in a way, falls in love with Rachel. The two women, for different reasons, find consolation in each other. Claudia guesses and cannot quite guess what is going on between the two women (I had been reading *What Maisie Knew*). In due time, Claudia claims that Rachel has been abusing her, which was, I hinted, what she wished had been true.

I sent *Come, Claudia, Running* to Dotty Tutin. She never acknowledged receipt. She was, my mother told me, seriously sick, the aftermath of Vivien Leigh's furious verbal assaults on her. Larry Olivier had taken fright, not least of the publicity that might result if Dotty's breakdown was linked with him. Thirty-five years later, I again made fictional use of Dudy's sister's experience in an episode of *After the War*. Directed on TV by John Madden, Claire Higgins played the part as truly and movingly as any author could ever wish.

Albert Finney and his then wife, Jane Wenham, were at lunch at the Nimmos' flat, with their baby, on the day Paul was due to be born. The telephone rang when we were finishing our baked apples and custard. John held the receiver out to me. I heard Beetle say, 'Well, we've done it.' Her use of the dual was characteristically generous. It was a boy; I could come as soon as I wanted. She sounded strong and proud. Dear God, I was a father. When we talked about names, I had suggested Peter-Paul, which had an artistic swagger. I even proposed 'Ludwig' at one point. Beetle thought the hyphen pretentious; we settled for Paul.

At first sight, he looked like a small, elderly, Semitic gentleman. He soon turned into a handsome, demanding infant with long dark eyelashes, large brown eyes and an unblinking stare. Beetle had waited patiently to have a child; more patience was needed in ministering to him. Paul suffered from colic and was reluctant to sleep. The sole effective narcotic was to put him in the car in his carry cot and drive around London until he fell asleep. Cyril Connolly had warned that the greatest enemy of promise was the pram in the hall. Beetle made sure that I need not endorse that glib sentiment. Paul was exhausting, but – in the mornings at least – he was not my concern. I worked.

One afternoon, I left Beetle with Paul and went to the cinema in the King's Road. I sat almost alone to watch a double-bill of *The Killing* and *Paths of Glory*, both in black and white, both directed by Stanley Kubrick. His name meant nothing to me. I emerged dazzled by what movies could do, if anyone had the grim wit to break the mould that determined the shape and contents of whatever was produced at Ealing and Pinewood. On Saturday afternoons I went occasionally to Craven Cottage to watch Fulham. Johnny Haynes distributed cleverer passes to his team-mates, 'Tosh' Chamberlain and 'Chinner' (later, when bearded, 'the Rabbi') Jimmy Hill, than they were capable of anticipating.

When *The Observer* announced a play competition, under the potent aegis of Ken Tynan, I had visions of escape from Leslie Bricusse's commercial clutch. I wrote *The Man on the Bridge* with inventive speed and anti-establishment calculation. It featured an Everyman with the characteristics of the pedlar who regularly came past our window, leading his donkey and cart, calling 'Och'n'beechy locha', which, being interpreted, meant 'Oak and beech logs'. The bridge in the play was between two antagonistic societies that turned out to be mirror-reversed images of each other.

Apart from my Little Man, I remember only an American businessman who came in with a golf bag in which were holstered a collection of hunting rifles. He put it down and said, 'I shot seventy-six this morning.' He may have been called Brad. I did what the terms of the competition required, enclosing a stamped addressed envelope (the badge of all my freelance tribe), and waited for the results, in the state of suspenseful apprehension from which few writers, of any age, are ever exempt.

The first round of judging was said to have been concluded and my play was not returned. It seemed that it had passed the initial *triage*. The longlist was due to be published in a few days' time. Then, like the character in *With This Ring*, I fell at the last hurdle: I heard the thud of a heavy envelope on the mat and saw my own writing on the front. So inescapable was Leslie's charm that I feared I should waste my life pedalling his silly tandem. One day, as we were crossing the King's Road, he asked me whether I would 'stand beside him'. I was not sure what he meant. 'I'm getting married to Bonbon, at St James's, Spanish Place. Will you be my best man?' Bonbon was the shapely young Yvonne Romaine. I was very sorry, I told him, but I could not take part in anything that took place in a Roman Catholic church.

According to Billy Chappell, the book of *Lady at the Wheel* was still not up to professional standards. Leslie was sure that I would not mind if 'big Lucienne' had a go at it. The regular translator of Jean Anouilh, Lucienne Hill was joined at the hip with a postulant impresario called Andrew Broughton, known by Leslie as 'Broughtipoo'. Leslie's personal slang included 'puddy-paws' for hands; 'scanties' for female underclothes; 'Brig-ton' for Brighton, where he had a flat; 'wagon' for car; when things went badly, he would say 'suddenly … boom!'; now and again, he used 'nignog' for a fool, a term which, in those days, carried no racist undertones. I never heard him utter any four-letter word. Culture was not his bag. However, when the manuscript of *The Earlsdon Way* was stolen, he had had the clever generosity to give me the Everyman edition of Carlyle's *The French Revolution*, the sole first draft of which had been used by a maid in Cheyne Walk to light the morning fire.

Leslie introduced me to Dr Jan van Loewen, said to be the most powerful theatrical agent in London: he represented Maugham and Noël and Christopher Fry. Van Loewen wore a pepper and salt suit and the rimless oval glasses I associated with secret police chiefs. His first-floor offices were adjacent to the Prince of Wales Theatre. As we sat below his dais, I could observe two appetising tarts who, in broad daylight, paraded for custom in front of the National Car Park, adjacent to the fire station, on the far side of Shaftesbury Avenue. The more shapely wore a low-cut, flare-skirted white dress with large red dots on it. Dr van Loewen told us that our thirties would be the time to make money. He had an assistant called Betty Judkins, who promised to read any new play I wrote. She was happy to tell me that *The Man on the Bridge* had found favour with Peter Phethean, who ran the local theatre in Brentwood, Essex. The woman with the red spots on her dress seldom spent more than ten minutes with each of the clients with whom, after a brief conversation, she crossed the street into Soho on the way to some quick bed.

One day, Leslie popped into Rutland Street wearing a businesslike face. He had prepared a contract that he wanted me to sign, renouncing my rights in return for a token fraction of the proceeds of *Lady at the Wheel*. He remembered me saying that I had better things to do and he quite understood. I sat on our new square, red-topped Heal's stool and looked at him. I said I had no objection to Miss Hill doing what she thought was best, or better, but I was not about to sign away my rights. I recalled how my royalties on the material in *An Evening with Beatrice Lillie* had stopped. Leslie said that was all because of Binkie's bloody lawyer. 'So, listen...' I sat there, until he said, 'You're holding a gun to my head.'

'It's the one you brought with you.'

'You know what this means, don't you?'

'I certainly hope so.'

'Because I've been very patient until now.'

I felt sick and elated. Beetle would be pleased to have me free. My fear was I should no longer have access to Leslie's expertise and contacts. Our association ended decisively when our new agent, Leslie Linder, told me that he could not understand why chalk wanted to work with cheese. The truth was, I told him, that I was not sure that I could make a living on my own. 'You can,' Linder said, 'and you must.'

When *The Earlsdon Way* was published, it received a flattering review by Peter Green in the *Daily Telegraph*: suburbia might have been anatomised before, but never, he said, with such precision. After I thanked Peter for his eulogy, he said, 'It's the least one can do for one's friends.' I have known many who did less. In *The Spectator*, even Simon Raven flew the old school tie, in his fashion: he wondered why I had started so well and then, in his view, abruptly 'stopped writing'. I had encircled the minatory fictional life of Edward Keggin and tied it up with the words 'Soon he was back on the Earlsdon Way'. It was, I thought, a becomingly understated indictment of the British habit of resuming a way of life that was limited, joyless and compromised.

Simon would adopt a more slashing style in *The Feathers of Death*, the first of many novels blending nostalgia with scandal. The ten-volume *Alms for Oblivion* sequence harped on his own proud, disgraceful history and relished the humbug of his contemporaries, above all William Rees-Mogg. Simon always suspected the Mogg of engineering his defenestration from Charterhouse in order to enhance his own prospects of advancement in school seniority. If the Mogg was indeed the agent of Simon's eviction, he acted in accordance with a very Carthusian notion of Christian morality.

A pale playwright called Michael Voysey, who doubled as a producer and script editor at BBC Television Centre, commissioned me to turn *The Earlsdon Way* into a play. Knowing nothing of the technicalities, I asked to see a TV script that Voysey admired. He showed me one of his own. It did not seem unbeatable. When I rendered my novel into the stipulated form, Voysey said he could not wait to show it to people on the sixth floor. Meanwhile, how did I feel about 'coming inside'? The BBC had a year-long course, for which he would be happy to recommend me. It involved learning the ins and outs of TV, and carried a modest salary. On gradua-tion, I should be qualified to join 'the strength'. I was, as always, tempted: security was not a displeasing prospect. The little house in Rutland Street had only a small, paved yard at the back. Beetle wanted Paul to be able to crawl in a garden, with trees and better air.

After longer than good news would have taken, Michael Voysey called to say that, despite the lively qualities that his superiors recognised, sev-eral of them, the consensus on the sixth floor held that *The Earlsdon*

Way was too radical, in certain respects (I could guess what those were) for the Corporation's style. I was chagrined, as usual, but as usual dolefully determined not to make concessions. I stepped free of another nice noose. I am not a great believer in the improvement of creative work by confabulation.

George Greenfield rang to say that Odham's were keen for me to do a second ghosting job about secret agents. They would pay £600 if I would take over the task of putting together Maurice Buckmaster's account of the French section of SOE (Special Operations Executive). A heap of papers and memoirs, by various agents who had been dropped into occupied France, had been collected by David Tutaev, but he felt he could not meet the deadline and had resigned.

Tutaev delivered four shoeboxes of raw material to Rutland Street. Small and dark-eyed, with artistically disposed long grey hair and an expression of haunted profundity, he had translated a number of Russian plays and might have passed for the glum artist I had impersonated in *A Month in the Country*. The assembled archives had excited sleepless suspicions of callousness and double-dealing. At their interviews, Tutaev had been unnerved by Colonel Buckmaster's blue-eyed insouciance. As he took his leave, Tutaev mentioned that, on the eve of his visit, he had seen a remarkable actress, Dudy Nimmo, in a television version of *The Cherry Orchard*. He had been impressed by her soulful performance. 'She might have been a Russian.' I was glad to tell Dudy as much the next time she and John came to dinner. Beetle told her that she was reading Anthony Trollope. 'Oh good!' Dudy said. 'Soon you'll be ready for Henry James.' Dudy never asked me what I was writing, nor did she admit to having read either of my novels. On the last occasion I ever saw her, however, at a literary festival in Lancaster in 1989, she said she had read all my books.

In 1958, Dudy was given a small part in Robert Bolt's first play,

Flowering Cherry, which starred Ralph Richardson. 'Ralphie', as David Lean and others called him, was a mannered classical actor whose want of good looks gave him an air of ageless integrity. He had a scene with young Robin Ray, whose offstage stammer asserted itself if he was hustled. Dudy told me that Richardson, with his back to the audience, would wait for one of Ray's pauses and then mouth, 'One, two, three, four,' and sometimes 'five, six, seven...' until the young actor managed to enunciate the next line.

Maurice Buckmaster lived in one of the big houses across the bottom end of Wellington Square SW3. He now worked for the Ford Motor Company in a PR role like my father's in Shell. Manifesting no symptoms of having been in a tragic bind, he conceded, rather than confessed, that a number of operations had gone wrong. It was not uncommon in military matters. Some things might indeed have been better managed; the fact remained that the casualties in the French section, however sad or – occasionally – avoidable, involved a lower percentage of its personnel in the field than any frontline infantry commander, for instance, was likely to match.

Having studied the dossiers, I came back to Wellington Square to tell him that there were breaches in the narrative that needed to be filled in. As David Tutaev had noted, some agents who had been 'turned' by the Germans continued to receive messages from Baker Street, where SOE had its offices, and further arrests were made as a result of what was gleaned from them. Why was that? Buck's honest blue look carried a glint of ice. It was sometimes necessary to protect another unit in a given region by giving the Germans the impression that the one they had penetrated was the only one operating. War was an ugly business, secret war especially so. I was lucky to have had nothing to do with it. I asked how he would like me to deal with events where key details were missing. He smiled and said, 'Oh, my dear Freddie, make anything up that looks plausible. It's likely to be as near the truth as not. I'm sure you're up to that.'

I met two or three of the surviving SOE operatives. None displayed rancour with regard to Buck. Dark rumours did, however, circulate about his failure to take tender care of female agents. One of Buck's Baker Street staff, a proto-feminist called Jean Overton Fuller, had a brace of reproach-laden books on the subject published by Victor Gollancz (who called her 'the egg lady'). She was the first person to hatch the idea, recently renewed with loud persistence by Patricia Cornwell, that Walter Sickert was the original Jack the Ripper. Overton Fuller's repeated theme was Buckmaster's cynical sadism when it came to sacrificing women in a man's war.

Maurice's response was that the women had volunteered to face the same dangers as the men. He never made light of the sufferings of any of his people, although he did hint that some of them, once armed with SOE funds, had become profligate in the wine and women department. Buck's admiration for his most famous female agent, Odette Sansom, was nuanced by the fact that, so he told me, smiling, she had been arrested in a hotel in bed with Peter Churchill only because 'they did what they were doing so loudly that they failed to hear the look-out's warning whistle that the Gestapo was on the way up'. Odette was tortured with sustained brutality, gave nothing away, and was later awarded the George Cross.

Churchill, whom she later married (and divorced), was treated leniently by the Germans on account of the surname, which, it was clear, he had the wit not to conceal from his interrogators. They assumed – and Churchill did not deny – that he was a more or less distant cousin of Winston's, although it was not true. In the early 1960s, we rented a cottage in Le Rouret, inland from Grasse. There was no hedge between us and a soft-stepping neighbour who found it amusing to surprise me, while I was reading, with some polite, proximate observation. He introduced himself as Peter Churchill. Since he was fly enough to dodge torture, he had had to make do with the DSO.

Few of Buck's agents displayed Jacques Doneux's capacity for strict observation of the training manual. If more had done so, fewer would have been captured and less might have been achieved. Men such as Harry Rée, originally from a Danish Jewish family, showed initiative and leadership that outflanked the rule book with positive results. Brave both physically and morally, he sabotaged French factories working for the Germans and dared to question the effectiveness of Allied bombing, which, he had observed, was alienating French civilians from the Allied cause. One of Buck's best people had been a drag queen and employed his seductive skills on German officers. What he did, for patriotic reasons, in occupied Europe would have landed him in prison in England. Alan Turing might have fared better under Buckmaster's command.

Buck obtained permission to insert the authentic log of a *réseau* in the south-west at the back of *They Fought Alone*. It mentioned a little place called Siorac-en-Périgord, where the château was cavernous enough to conceal a clandestine armoury. There is now a supermarket on the other side of the road from the château. We shop there twice a week in the summer months. I only once spotted someone reading *They Fought Alone*. It was on a tourist bus, on the way to Chichicastenango, in Guatemala, in 1974. He had left it, face down, on the seat during a comfort stop. When he returned I told him that I had written it. He said, 'Are you Colonel Buckmaster?' 'No, no, but I helped him write the book. My name is Raphael.' 'Really? So is mine,' he said. 'I'm a doctor in San Diego. I run the Raphael clinic. We do all kinds of operations, head to toe. You ever need one, stop by. Need two, I'll give you a rate.'

Just before *They Fought Alone* was published, Buck was pleased to tell me that he had sold an option on the film rights to his friend Sidney Box, for £1. No film was ever made. Was David Tutaev right to suspect that there was some dark aspect to Buck that he was expert at camouflaging, a duplicity that gave an Old Etonian smoothness to both sides of his character? He had done his best to honour Churchill's command, back in 1941, to 'set Europe ablaze', and if that involved making mistakes, or even blunders, he had fought a winning campaign. His good conscience was of a piece with his callousness. Despite Tutaev's dark intuition, I suspect that I should have been glad to obey Buck's blue-eyed orders and, if possible, to have been thought well of by him. In the same spirit, for whatever added reasons, I should prefer to be thought good company by Simon Raven than by any of Tom Maschler's angry young or youngish men. Not long ago, *They Fought Alone* was cited in the *TLS* as a documentary source. It has just been reissued as a classic of secret warfare.

After Lucienne Hill had used her mature flat iron on my juvenile jokes, *Lady at the Wheel* went into production. Anxious to avoid nastiness, Leslie invited me to attend an audition at the Prince of Wales for a leading lady. One likely candidate was a good-looking young woman called Jean Brampton, who had already played second leads. She came on in a strapless dress with a flared skirt and began to sing, rather well. As she took a deep breath for her final effort, the zip at the back of her dress burst open and her fine breasts tumbled forward. She caught them, one-handed, as she finished the song. 'Nearly showed the lot,' she said. Leslie and Billy Chappell thanked her and said they would be in touch. She was not cast. A short while later, disappointed in love, so the papers said, she committed suicide.

Lady at the Wheel opened at the Lyric Theatre, Hammersmith. Beetle and I went to the first night, but did not attend the party. Leslie had meant no harm, nor had he done any; he chose to belong to a world that, for all its glamour, had no appeal for me; but it would be untrue and ungrateful to say that he brought me no worthwhile rewards. *Bachelor of Hearts* was not the kind of movie that I should ever have wanted to write, but it furnished me with that vital commodity, a credit, without which no film career was likely to proceed. For all Miss Hill's cosmetic expertise, *Lady at the Wheel* closed after a short run.

Leslie and Yvonne's wedding feast took place in the new, smart, red-carpeted Panton Street offices of John Redway and associates, of which Leslie Linder was a joint managing director. I happened to talk to George Baker, then a fashionable young movie actor. He asked me what the party was all about exactly. Leslie had bumped into him in the street and invited him to come. He had no idea what we were celebrating.

When Paul was a few months old, we drove up to inspect a ground-floor flat in Highgate. Grange Road was wide and unpaved. The flat was in a large, red-brick Victorian house owned by a grey and respectable Miss Pearce. She was keen to have a child around the place. There was little more than a year remaining on the lease, which the outgoing tenants were willing to assign only if we were prepared to buy their furniture. Since we had little of our own, we did not object. It would take most of our money, but we agreed to pay for the rump of the lease, after the nice Miss Pearce promised that she would extend it by several years as soon as it lapsed.

My blond Heal's desk fitted handsomely in the window overlooking the rose garden and the slope of wide lawn where Paul moved himself around in his idiosyncratic way. He never crawled, he scooted: one leg under him, the other crooked, he propelled himself like a crab with one hand. I arranged our books on a set of planks supported by bricks (something I had first seen in Jonathan Miller's Gloucester Terrace house). We settled to a proper, modest life.

Cassell's had had no signal success with *The Earlsdon Way*, but my new best friend, Tom Maschler, who had recently been head-hunted by Allen Lane, made it his business and pleasure to have it accepted as a paperback by Penguin Books. Two years my junior, Tom had a rage to succeed not unlike Leslie Bricusse's, but he was driven by serious demons. Having fled Berlin with his parents when he was three years old, Tom carried an abiding sense of the horrors he had escaped. His idea of a great writer was Franz Kafka. He was determined to become the most important publisher of serious books in London. He remarked with scorn that the only con-temporary writer dealing with Jews in England was C. P. Snow, whose recent novel, *The Conscience of the Rich*, featured a caricatural eccentric somewhat resembling my great-uncle Jessel. Someone had to do better than that. Inspired, in part, by Tom's enthusiasm, I bought a wide, spiral-backed notebook and began a novel that would have something in common with the jejune effort I had begun in Ramatuelle, in homage to Maugham's *Of Human Bondage*.

I associated Jewishness with isolation. Beetle's large family had both insu-lated her from any such apprehensions and given her keen reasons to escape any demanding community. She saved me from loneliness and dared me to be happy. Paul was the proof of her belief in life. We never considered not having him circumcised; it was done by the Dr Snowman who performed the same service for the royal family. Although I had no sense of obligation to the rites of Judaism, to raise an untrimmed Jew would be to accede to the shame of being one. Dr Snowman did his tailoring, dipped his finger in wine, comforted Paul with it and we all said *Mazel tov*.

Curiosity led me to go, several times, to Brick Lane and catch what was left of the air of the East End I was glad not to have come from. With wished-for nostalgia, I bought *challah* from Grodzinsky's bakery. On one occasion, I asked for it on a Tuesday. They looked at me, with justice, as if I was some kind of a freak. If so, I had a remedy: I resolved my contradic-tions and absurdities, in whatever high or low sense, by writing, alone, in all kinds of voices. The prattle of my contradictions and fears rode rapidly down long pages of manuscript dialogue. Willie Maugham's theatrical facil-ity may well have had a good deal to do with his stammer. Inside his head, he had no hesitation in giving voice to the contradictions and agonies that gagged him in public.

It is always difficult to continue to work on something with no title. I soon decided to call my new novel *The Limits of Love*, in homage to Wittgenstein.

That love also had its limitations was part of my point. Manor Fields stood for me as a bourgeois *Unité d'habitation*. Suburban morality, of which the bowler-hatted Mr Love had been the local custodian, was a form of communal cowardice. There had to be a more daring and vital way to live. I thought it was socialism.

One afternoon, in search of comradeship, I went to the newly opened Partisan Coffee shop in Soho, and sat with a workmanlike mug of coffee, reading *The Golden Bough* as an advertisement for intellectual company. I left without finding common cause or *causerie* with anyone. When Tony and Anne Becher came to visit us, I greeted her unguarded admission that she was a Tory with ferocious astonishment. I had, I told her, never before met anyone of my own age who was that much of an antique. She burst into tears. I was sorry, but not chastened.

When Paul was eight months old, my mother agreed to look after him while I gave Beetle a deserved holiday. Irene was to be a patient and loving grandmother. Whatever had gone cold between us was put right, it seemed, by the affection that she gave Paul, and he her. For the rest of her life, she made the occasional Freudian slip of calling him 'Freddie'.

Beetle and I headed for the Riviera. Parenthood and lack of money made us unadventurous: I booked a full week, with *pension complète*, at the hotel Florida (two-fronted in the *Michelin Guide*) in Beaulieu-sur-Mer. The food was not as good as our fat cook's in Lucca, the ambience petit bourgeois. Monsieur Hulot might well have taken a holiday there. One night, a young woman wheeled a paralysed man into the dining room. They went from table to table with a deck of small watercolour paintings, laying one on each. There was an attendant printed notice. The artist was an ex-inmate of a Nazi concentration camp. The pictures had been painted with a brush held in his mouth. When the tour was completed, the girl came round to collect whatever people were prepared to offer. Several of the diners handed back the cards. I gave the girl a couple of thousand old francs. That night, we went to the casino and won twice as much at *boule*.

Beetle was glad to get home and retrieve Paul from Manor Fields. On entering 12 Balliol House, I always developed a bad, and worsening, headache. When first we visited my parents, Beetle had been surprised by Cedric's habit of picking an argument with me. It irritated him that she almost always sided with me. Cedric was having a miserable time with the stricture that, from time to time, he never knew when, would prevent him from pissing. Within an hour or two, he could be in agony. Various West End specialists affected to know what to do; it was usually painful and provided only temporary relief. No one could cure the condition until my parents went to Sweden, where a Dr Johanssen contrived an operation that excised the scar tissue and set the two ends of the re-severed urethra to grow together naturally. After decades of dread and fear, Cedric was repaired, for a while.

I was sorry for my parents, but good manners had to cover for the small love I felt for them. I have never been interested in the reasons that analysis might have revealed to be behind my indifference. Might it be that I always resented the fact that my mother never gave me her breast? Or is it that I felt betrayed when she allowed me to be sent to boarding school, even though I know very well that she had little choice? I cannot remember ever being greeted with literally open arms. Cedric was patient in seeking to improve my golf swing, my play of the cards and my tango, but his long concealment of the existence of my half-sister gave his moralising a late whiff of hypocrisy. I did not blame him for his past (no one owes an account of his life to his children), but I might have been spared the advisory humbug. I shall, however, always be grateful for that extra year at Cambridge. I did not hold it against him that he lacked the confidence to guarantee my mortgage. By the time that he had the chance to buy the flat he and Irene had rented for over forty years and needed £1,500 as a down payment, I was making enough money in the movies to give it to him, gladly. As I wrote the cheque, he said, 'Make it two thousand, if you like.' I did not.

hopes and fears unite and reveal people, but strangely in the hollowness of his own hopes and fears Ben was privy to a world he had
never acknowledged; he longed to be answered, and in the ringing
of his own mind, the hopeless ring against which he pressed himself, the world grew glassy clear for him, so that he saw Susan with
someone, huddled outside that ring, and he saw his own life a mere
splinter, a freak. The Party would never come to power, not in his
manhood. He was a man, a man still muscled from the pits, a man
who did not give in. And because he was a man the axe that split him
had an awful edge; because he was a man who had been knit together in his manhood and who had been one, the knots in him like
knots of wood, hard arteries of strength, unsplittable, because he
had seen his life as one thing and exulted in that oneness, the axe
that split him cut in silence, in an agony of silence, so that he knew
what hit him, wishing that the bullet had come first, in the back of
the neck, before the axe fell. His mind was opened by the axe that fell
in the hollowness of the eight o'clock street, the axe edged with the
knowledge that his wife was perhaps with another man, and that it
mattered. It mattered that the only thing which had come to be for
him was being destroyed. He had expected so much, waited for so
much, and this was the only thing which had really come to be, his
marriage; his marriage alone gave him place and time and reality.
But now, aware of his divorce from Susan, released by the Party, his
mind slewed with greasy uncertainty across the surface of life and he
was ready for the bullet. He was ready for the bullet which did not
come and so he walked on in the unwanted hours of reprieve when
the deadline had been passed in silence. The line of death had been
passed through and he lived still, suddenly conscious of his own
absurdity.

3

Colin said: 'Can there be an argument against violence?'
   'Of *course* there can,' Paul said. 'The whole notion of justice
depends on there being an argument against violence.'
   'I don't see why if someone is stronger he shouldn't have his
way.'
   'Good old Will of the stronger,' Paul said. 'I never thought I'd
meet him again.'

The Limits of Love

XX

GEORGE GREENFIELD FOUND me a supportive sideline as fiction coach to Cyril Ross, founder and managing director of Swears & Wells, the Oxford Street furrier of choice. In the 1950s, success and the pelts of dead animals went together. Cyril was a small, seemingly mild, tough-minded Jewish entrepreneur with literary ambitions. Perhaps with a subvention to its publishers, he had already brought out one novel. *Pirates in Striped Trousers* denounced the tactics of a new generation of businessmen who built their fortunes not as Cyril had, on expertise and hard work, but by boarding other people's vessels and holding them to ransom. Once at the wheel, they stripped the assets, sold off what was left, and proceeded to the next buccaneering episode.

Cyril would send me his latest, never very long manuscript and I marked it up, circling the clichés, and suggesting improvements in red ink, like some scribal Professor Anderson. My didactic efforts were worth twenty guineas a time. To take delivery, Cyril bought me lunch at Grosvenor House, where my distant, unseen cousins, Sir Benjamin and Lady Drage (Etta) had an apartment. It was a rare opportunity for fresh asparagus and smoked salmon. We did not drink wine with lunch. Cyril told me that Charlie Clore had once threatened to move in on Swears & Wells. 'Offered me a price for my shares well below their value and gave me twenty-four hours to think about it before he mounted a public, hostile takeover. So what I did was, I issued enough supplementary voting shares to mean I retained a majority, however many Charlie managed to sweep up on the open market. He had to give me best.'

'Did he take it well?'

'Charlie? He doesn't bear a grudge, he just tells you to watch out. Which I do. Do you want a cigar? Personally I smoke a pipe. Cigars…' The silence left them to Charlie Clore and his kind.

Cyril made a habit of good works. 'Do you remember the Victory Services Club, Fred, in the Edgware Road, during the war?'

'I remember going past it on the bus,' I said. I had been with my father, who had just pointed out the old Edgware Road Music Hall where he had seen Florrie Ford and Marie Lloyd. Cedric was born in a mansion flat just around the corner. 'Did you go to the Victory Services Club yourself then, Cyril?'

'I founded it. So happened I owned the property, so I thought why not do something for the war effort? It was for officers mainly. Eisenhower used to go there sometimes, so did Montgomery.'

'And did you meet them?'

'Truth to tell, Fred, I don't much go for the *goyim*.'

The Earlsdon Way must have been remarked in some Jewish circles. I received an invitation to attend a midday Sunday reception, at an address within walking distance of Grange Road, in honour of the Israeli ambassador. Curiosity and vanity led me to the large, double-gated house with a gravel forecourt. In the wide, high drawing room overlooking the rosy back garden, people who seemed to know each other were having drinks and lox with cream cheese. No one spoke to me. I stood for a while and then moved to leave. My host headed me off. I must stay and hear what the ambassador had to say. As he spoke, he was locking the white door to the sunlit room in which we were gathered.

The ambassador reminded us of the brave work that was being done in Israel and of the gratitude that he felt, and hoped he would have further reason to feel today, for the generosity of people such as those present. Even my very slow coach arrived at why the door had been locked and why the comfortable company had been assembled. After His Excellency had won his applause, my host brought out a list of all those present. He asked each guest, in alphabetical order, how much he was prepared to pledge. Whether by chance or agreed design, the first sums promised were often several thousand pounds. None was less than a few hundred.

At last, the dreaded moment came when I was named. I lacked the wit to be anything but truthful. 'I am a writer,' I said, 'with a wife and a small child and no more money than we need to live on, if that much.' As angry as I was humiliated, I walked across the room to the door. My host unlocked it and let me out. It was easier to take indignant action among Jews than elsewhere. Five years later, this incident supplied the basis of a scene in my novel *Lindmann*, which had a more tragic–comic conclusion than my lame exit.

American 'egg-head' paperbacks had begun to appear in my favourite bookshop, Ward's in the King's Road. Stanley Edgar Hyman's *The Armed Vision* alerted me, with revelatory force, to how little I knew about the new criticism. Like some instructive hydra, his book had many heads. Kenneth Burke made the biggest impression, along with R. P. Blackmur and Maud Bodkin, the lady with the archetypes. I was so impressed by Burke's *A Grammar of Motives* that I solicited John Wisdom's opinion of it. My modest approach may have carried a tincture of the accusatory ingratiation not unknown among climbing intellectuals. A notorious literary instance was Rebecca West's assault on H. G. Wells. Her sparky, proto-feminist denunciation of his novel *Marriage* led, quite shortly, to a perhaps hoped-for sexual subjugation that supplied social promotion at the same time. If I hoped that Wisdom would ask what, in particular, I admired and draw me into some kind of conversation, I was disappointed. He returned the book with a brief note, saying that Burke had 'an interesting mind'; his tone was courteous, but distant. It was as if I had asked Ken Rosewell whether he would care to have a knock-up.

In recent ratings, Burke has been relegated to a bibulous curiosity. He never had tenure of an impressive chair and was too combative, and versatile, to attract disciples in whose later table of contents he might have had an elevated place. His anatomy of the articulations of philosophical ideas remains unique and suggestive. A performer himself, he read philosophy in a dramatic light, in which scenery and actors play against each other in accordance with the logic of the piece. Wisdom's posthumous fate has been little different from Burke's: he hardly rates a footnote from any of the cardinals on whom today's reputations depend.

When we saw Ben Gazzara as Jocko de Paris in *End as a Man*, I wrote a long meta-Burkean essay in which I modernised the notion of the 'scapegoat mechanism' of which René Girard has since become the most sophisticated exponent. To reinforce my credentials, I made learned reference to Jane Harrison's *Prolegomena to the Study of Greek Religion*, which I never read at Cambridge but which had been republished in an illuminating New York paperback. The Athenian festivals of the *Thesmophoria* and *Thargelia* treated selected victims as Calder Willingham did the diabolical and charming Jocko. I sent my double-spaced piece to *Forum*, a standard-bearer of the new drama, edited by Clive Goodwin. He responded with an effusive letter of rejection. My essay was too elaborate for his pages, but he would be happy to see anything else I might care to write. I did not test his generosity.

Reduced to becoming the favourite ghost of Odham's Press, I was glad to have the money that came from rewriting the memoirs of Captain Bill Fell, a small, lean, creased New Zealander who was a wartime submariner and then, with the casual versatility of the British in those days, became a salvage expert. The typescript of *The Sea Shall Not Have Them* gave a bald, self-deprecating account of his steady nerve as he manoeuvred a mini-submarine under the protective netting at the mouth of an Italian harbour in order to torpedo enemy warships at anchor and then escaped the way he had come. The publishers were more excited by Bill's role in the aftermath of the Suez operation. He had spent several months helping the French clear the wrecks that the Egyptians had sunk in the canal. The chief French officer was known to his British colleagues as 'Captain Arnchers', in honour of his comic way of saying 'anchors'. Bill had no solemn views about the merits of the Suez operation. He noted only that when it became clear that the whole thing was a humiliating fiasco, the French officers had wept tears of shame and rage. The British shrugged and got on with the job in hand.

Now a confident cosmetician of gallant prose, I supplied Bill's book with a leaven of nautical dialogue of the kind that first seasoned Noël Coward's *In Which We Serve* and was recycled in *The Cruel Sea*. 'Steady as you go' was a staple line. When Bill read my aerated rendering of his adventures, he said, 'I can't stomach it. I'd sooner not have it printed.' I quite understood, I told him; but that was the journalistic salvage operation I had been hired to do. He sighed, made a few corrective excisions and the book was published.

The Sea Shall Not Have Them was my last ghostly effort, although George Greenfield did persuade me to read the manuscript of a man whose name on the title page was a triply hyphenated mixture of aristocratic ingredients (Montagu and Scott among them). He arrived for lunch, at my invitation, in a blue suit and Old Etonian tie. Before becoming, among other plausibly improbable things, a Russian Orthodox monk (he claimed to have known Rasputin), he had been Anthony Eden's fag-master at Eton. He even claimed to have beaten him, as Quintin Hogg did the young Freddie Ayer. The prolonged ingenuity of my guest's life story might have furnished an entertaining picaresque novel, but it was soon established that he was, in effect, his own ghost. There was something almost heroic in the trouble he had taken over the costume and the cover story, which had secured him a mediocre lunch and a glass of club wine.

Tom Maschler called to say that he had tickets for Beetle and me to go and see the second play in Arnold Wesker's trilogy (the first, *Chicken Soup With Barley*, had warmed critical hearts). *Roots* was being premiered at the new theatre in Coventry. Tom suggested that I drive the three of us up there. We arrived in time to go to the cathedral to see the Graham Sutherland crucifixion, which graced the high altar. The figure of Christ, on a yellow background, if I remember rightly, was embraced in a set of elongated brackets, quite as if He Himself were somehow optional in the appreciation of the pictorial scheme. I saw the work as that of an artisan who had been commissioned to serve a myth in which he could not bring himself to believe. The restoration of the cathedral seemed to be part of a campaign, more rhetorical than faithful, to reinstate the Christian ideology that furnished the Holocaust with a warrant for anti-Semitism. The painting was a flamboyant advertisement for a faith in which no one could ever again honestly believe.

In Wesker's play, Joan Plowright, who had displaced Dotty Tutin in Larry Olivier's affections, played Beattie, the provincial, politically unfledged girl enlightened, uplifted and bedded by the young Jew who had the map that led to the new Jerusalem. The third play in Arnold's trilogy would indeed be *I'm Talking About Jerusalem*, not quite the same one to which I had been asked to subscribe in that big house in Highgate. Born in the East End, Wesker was the latest prodigy to be promoted by the Royal Court Theatre. *Roots* received an ovation. It seemed that the audience's applause wished for some kind of secular deliverance. Their craving led them to deny that history had no promises to keep. The tinkerbell of socialism was kept alight by bourgeois applause.

We went round afterwards and were introduced to Arnold's mother. She was the living, foreign-accented evidence of how far he had already come from his roots. Arnold himself paraded so earnest a mission to bring joy to all that it would have been graceless not to embrace him, even as one looked at one's watch. A messiah who encouraged rather than scolded, he offered revolution without bloodshed, renaissance without birth pangs, salvation without The Bomb. Marching hopefully, especially from Aldermaston, became a way of arriving, and hooking up, for many of his generation. I chose to walk alone.

We went to the Unity Theatre to see Brendan Behan's *The Quare Fellow*. Its success exemplified Joan Littlewood's method of building an ensemble of improvisations on original ingredients. Whoever the author, Joan directed the current piece in such a way that she put a Marxist mark and her own brand name on it. Like *Roots*, Behan's play had its roots in autobiography. Its author had been a teenage member of the IRA and was sent to borstal for his activities in the UK and later served a long term in jail in Eire. His play was anti-capital punishment (the Quare Fellow was the one in the condemned cell), anti-capitalist and anti-British. It found a ready audience of those who were ready to believe, as Wesker proclaimed, that there was a way of stepping free of one's shadow while still retaining one's roots. Brendan was food and, more particularly, drink for the press. My BBC producer was happy to issue the usual army surplus W/T (wireless telegraph) equipment for me to go and interview him. Tom Maschler, who had access to as many people, if never the same ones, as Leslie Bricusse, accompanied me to Blackheath. If we got to Brendan early in the day, there was a chance that he would still be coherent.

The Mill House, where he lived with his wife, who, like the heroine of *Roots* was called Beatrice, was a heavy white building behind a triangle of lawn. Behan, in unbuttoned shirt, baggy grey trousers, no shoes, was on the telephone, watching his pink toes as he talked about a lecture that Christina Foyle wanted him to deliver. 'What's wrong with this fuckin' thing? I can't understand a word the woman's saying.' Barrel-chested, with curly sandy hair, a sweet wet mouth, he resembled an inflated baby, just off the breast. 'Have some whisky. It's all right, it's embassy whisky, duty-free.' Beatrice, big-eyed and freckled, brought glasses and poured with a tried, tired hand. She had the put-upon dignity of Dylan Thomas's martyred widow, Caitlin, who had recently sold her 'leftover' life dearly.

Brendan proposed that we go first to the pub. 'We'll have a couple of drinks and then we'll do the interview, don't you worry.' He grabbed me by the genitals and gave them a friendly squeeze. 'Come on, boy.' On our way, he pressed half a crown into a neighbour's baby's hand as it lay in its pram. 'If she grips it, that's good luck. She gripped it! See that? She gripped it. That's good luck.'

Acquaintances called out, 'Good morning', as we passed. Brendan responded, '*Bonjour, bonjour.*'

The public bar in the Railway Hotel was a brown-black dust hole with sagging leathered benches. A Spaniard was waiting for Brendan. 'I waited from twelve to three yesterday. You arranged to meet me.'

'Couldn't make it.'

'You arranged to meet me.'

'Couldn't make it. Give me a drink, Rosie.'

Whiskey gents in green bowler hats came in and slapped Brendan on the back. A stranger bumped into him and said, 'Sorry'.

Brendan tugged down his sagging white sweater. 'We'll excuse it this time, but next time: WATCH OUT!'

Very pink and clean, he rambled and then said something perfect, if not often quotable. He gave obscenity a Yeatsian tang. We took a taxi back to do the interview, which he knew himself too well to believe I would ever get if we stayed in the pub. As we reached the Mill House, the other tenant was mowing the triangle of lawn. Behan said, 'Look at that cunt.'

He did his best to be coherent when I asked him questions he must have endured a dozen times. Afterwards, he gave me a copy of *Borstal Boy*. I asked him to dedicate it to Paul. The pen slurred across the paper. The words 'To Paul with love from his dad's friend Brendan' were encoded in dangling scribble.

Having parted from Leslie Bricusse and his promise of fame and fortune, I worked steadily at *The Limits of Love*. Beetle neither expected riches nor seemed to crave them. There we were, secure in Highgate remoteness, with Paul, and a garden. It did not occur to us that we might live anywhere but in England. We saw John and Dudy Nimmo and a few other people, but I made no purposeful contacts in the literary world. I took solace in the silent conversation of the authors whose works I collected from the London Library by the under-armful, before going to play bridge. Occasionally I would see Hugh Thomas in the Reading Room. One evening, as we walked along Jermyn Street, he looked in the window of the Cavendish Hotel. A white-whiskered gentleman was having tea. Hugh said, 'That's old Lord Sandwich! Let's go in and talk to him.'

I said, 'I can't. I don't know him.'

'Neither do I. Come on.'

We walked through bottle-glassed doors into the lounge. Sandwich looked up as if he had all but expected us. Hugh explained that he was a historian and would be very grateful to have an experienced statesman's view of the pre-war policy of non-intervention in Spain. Sandwich was amiably forthcoming. Perhaps he was glad of the company. He did not go so far as to offer us tea.

I did join the PEN club, where Celia Dale/Ramsey was a regular. What had appeared desirable and exclusive at a distance was revealed as a kind of women's institute for both sexes. The papers given at the meetings might have stocked the herbaceous border in a garden of prim remembrance. At the AGM, I proposed that the intellectual standard be raised. Angus Wilson, whose recent novel, *Anglo-Saxon Attitudes*, had been scathingly appreciative of the moral values on which the British continued to vaunt themselves, sided with me against Richard Church, for whom literary refinement and descriptions of wild flowers were indivisible. Church derided me, nicely, as 'our stormy petrel', but my storms were limited to teacups.

Angus and I concocted a list of more high-browed speakers. Among them was Andor Gomme, John Wisdom's star pupil who had defected sideways to Frank Leavis and was now an accredited academic. He arrived with a stack of flagged volumes and delivered himself of a long sermon, serviced with dry and laughter-free quotations. If he had been less thoroughly prepared, he might have been twice as effective.

Since we had little money, Beetle and I decided to have a shared holiday with her sister Joan and her now ex-Communist husband. In March, Baron Moss and I set off in his Armstrong Siddeley Sapphire to find a suitable villa to rent in September, when the prices came down. His period of unquestioning devotion to the party had come to an end when Khrushchev, taking advantage of the West's divisions over Suez, marched into Hungary, deposed and murdered Imre Nagy and installed János Kádár as the new face, or two faces, of Mátyás Rákosi. The recapture of Budapest dispelled the illusion of serious change that had been augured, optimists liked to think, by Khrushchev's 1953 denunciation of Stalin, whose pitiless legate he had been in Ukraine, during the punitive famine of the 1930s. In unproclaimed atonement, Khrushchev formally assigned the Crimea to Ukrainian administration, although it remained under the *de facto* control of Moscow.

Who imagined that it would ever be anything else? We were stalled in the era of 'containment'. Doris Lessing, John Berger and Lindsay Anderson, and who all else with their hearts on ostentatiously rolled-up sleeves, still had little doubt that the Soviet Union, with modifications, represented the desirable future of mankind.

Baron's decision to quit *The Worker* was not the result of political disillusionment. Joan had eased the limitations of their life on £6.10s a week by getting a job at J. Walter Thompson's in Berkeley Square and she had also served notice on him. Neither her ability nor her beauty passed unremarked at the office. She had endured Baron's ideologically justified infidelities with patient anguish. Now it was his turn to be anguished. Although Joan's admirer was a married Roman Catholic, with conventional scruples, the fear of losing her was enough to transform Baron from apparatchik to entrepreneur. Adopting his own new economic programme, he started an advertising agency. Backed mainly by East End old boys who had made good, the petrol station owner Gerald Ronson among them, Baron Moss and Associates prospered sufficiently for him to acquire the large black car in which he and I drove south.

There was no friction between us, nor any brotherhood. He had left the party but could not step outside its frame of reference, even for fun. He was reluctant to admit that Stalin could have acted other than he did. Since the Nazis had been the predictable incarnation of the last stage of capitalism, the Holocaust was as much a proof that Lenin had been right as that something uniquely appalling had taken place. The notion that history had an inexorable logic made him almost complicitous even when its laws had savage consequences. We never talked about his marriage and he showed small interest in what I knew or in what I was writing. Jews we might both be, or be said to be; I had no sense that we were two of a kind.

When Baron was at the wheel of his Armstrong Siddeley Sapphire,

I watched the road in quiet apprehension. Very early in our trip, he accelerated into some loose gravel and the big car swivelled right round in the empty road. After that, I took over as often as I could. It gave me a good excuse not to talk. We drove to Nice and then all along the Riviera. After a day or two of futile inquiries, we found a feasible flat-roofed modern villa to rent in Le Canadel, a village on the outskirts of La Napoule. There was direct access to a sandy beach. The rent was £100 for the month.

We decided to drive on westwards and loop north, on the narrow curl of highway through the depopulated Languedoc, notorious for swarms of summer mosquitoes. After getting lost on some short cut, we ran low on petrol. I imagined being marooned, like Evelyn Waugh's victim-hero in *A Handful of Dust*, and obliged to spend lonely days and nights trying to enjoy Baron's monotonous company. In imminent danger of running dry, we emerged on the main road, not far short of a Shell station. We stopped overnight in Carcassonne, which happened to be *en fête*. Masked crowds were hitting each other with playful cardboard batons in some dimly remembered printennial rite. We had the worst cauliflower soup I have ever tasted in a hotel in the walled city and then went up a sagging staircase to another joyless shared room.

Baron saw in the guidebook that our route north needed scant deviation in order to embrace a visit to the caves at Lascaux, On our way to Montignac, just before crossing the Dordogne, we drove below the château of Siorac-en-Périgord, where some of Buck's people had stored arms and ammunition. At Lascaux, in those days, visitors could take the wide, slow lift down into the original prehistoric caves that two boys, out with their dogs, had fallen into not twenty years earlier. No travel supplements had prepared us for the luminous darkness in which our small party of tourists walked the narrow walkway past the bright bent murals with their brown and yellow freight of arrow-pierced mammoths and deer. The restaurant at Sergeac, where Baron and I had lunch, was run by a farmer. He had a private museum of prehistoric relics. After *confit de canard, pommes Sarladaises*, he led us into one of his fields, scuffed the ploughed earth with his boot and handed me a fang from a sabre-toothed tiger.

On my return to Highgate, I thought it time to confirm that our landlady was ready to formalise our promised new lease. Paul's large dark stare had charmed her and we had been becomingly discreet in our habits. My only bohemian excess was to have painted the peeling kitchen door dark blue. I went upstairs with confidence and came down in dismay. Miss Pearce had no complaint about our tenancy, but her sister Mrs Knights had just been widowed. She could not evict the long-resident schoolteacher who lived on the top floor; we had to move out. I made bold to remind her that, taking her at her word, we had spent our savings on furniture we could not take with us, since we had nowhere to go and could not now afford to find anywhere else. She was very sorry. And, by the way, would I please paint the kitchen door its original colour?

Tom Maschler came one evening to babysit for us while we went to dinner with the Nimmos. He walked into the living room just as I was locking one of the drawers in my desk. 'What're you doing that for?'

'I don't like people reading my notebooks.'

'What makes you think I'd do anything like that?'

I said, 'What's the matter? Aren't you interested?'

I told him that we were about to be evicted and would soon have nowhere to live. I needed to make some money. He said, 'Success, what do you think about it?'

'I wouldn't mind some.'

'I've got this idea for a book.'

'You and Dale Carnegie,' I said.

'That was ... about how to get ahead by being nice, wasn't it?'

'And that's not your way?'

'Why are you like this?'

'Good question. The bad answer is, we've got to move out of here. Our nice landlady's broken her word. I don't know what we're going to do.'

'I can make a few notes. You can take it from there.'

'Take what?'

'This book about how to get on in today's world.'

'I wish I knew.'

'Follow me. You do know actually, you just don't think it's nice to do it. Have you thought about living somewhere else?'

'I just told you, we're going to have to.'

'Not in England. Spain. What do you think about Spain?'

'I like Spain. I don't like Franco. Not a hard club to get into, right?'

'Only, I know someone who has a house in the south, right on the sea. Costa del Sol they call it. Empty all winter. If I ask her, Anna'll be glad to let you have it for next to nothing probably.'

'I can probably manage that.'

'You can live down there on £10 a week, easy. And I can come and visit you. How's the new book going?'

'Fine. *The Limits of Love*, I'm calling it.'

'Until you think of something better. Do you want me to talk to Anna? You can write our success book while you're down there.'

'If I can't think of anything better to do.'

'Do it right and I can get you a bit of money.'

'We're going to the south of France in September. If your friend's place is free after that...'

'Everything's free at a price,' Tom said. 'Put that in our success book.'

'Roughly speaking,' I said, 'money and success are synonymous.'

'See what I mean?'

'The S Man speaks.'

'The S Man. There's our title.'

'My title.'

'Same thing, right? I'll talk to Anna, but I'm sure it'll be OK.'

back to him from the blonde girl; the humour did not stay in her face as her husband poured wine into her glass, as it would have in Betsy's, for whom nothing went on but the present. Uneasily, Ian sensed that there was more to Josie: he couldn't get an equal response from her with a quick show of white teeth, as he could from Betsy. Of course she was quite a lot older—what, twenty-eight, nine?—and she wasn't pretty like Betsy: he'd have Betsy every time. He looked quickly at his wife. How different she was from the other woman, with her fragile prettiness, the blue innocent—he had hardly dared touch her sometimes—eyes and the white, unripe hands with their chipless nails (at a glance, Josie's hands were heavy, nails torn like cardboard), and the bob of neat auburn curls tight about shell white ears. There was such an *area* to Josie, such a volume of flesh, though she was not fat, that the slim pillar of Betsy's whiteness was as different from her as the vertical from the horizontal. Josie pushed away her hair with the back of her hand, while Betsy touched hers up with her palm, fingers out. Josie was impatient in the light, Betsy careful. Betsy was suited by the white light of the dining-room. It would have been quite proper if she had been sitting there naked, her little breasts— the right one with a tiny blue vein down to the pink nipple —peeking out above the line of the tablecloth. She was suitable for the light, but not so Josie: her nakedness would appal, clashing with the light, so that Ian did not care to imagine it, which was what made her woman, not girl. Betsy in the darkness was not the Betsy he knew, so that since they had been married—some thirteen months—a lopsidedness had come to their relationship, complicating Ian. He had brought her from virgin to what she now was, a girl capable

10

XXI

I N THE EARLY summer of 1959, Tom invited me to a meeting, in
Berwick Street, with some of the modish young people from whom
Granada TV wanted to cull ideas for a discussion programme with
a controversial edge. Doris Lessing, Arnold Wesker, Ken Tynan,
Stuart Holroyd, Lindsay Anderson and other candidate iconoclasts from
the index of Tom's *Declaration* were supplemented by Karl Miller, Nick
Tomalin and Edna O'Brien. We sat at a long shining blond table in a beige
room, as if for a game of verbal poker. People established their outspoken-
ness-for-hire by saying 'fuck' a lot. A few years later, Ken would come out
with the 'f' word on television and a terrible repetitiousness would be born.

The occasion was supervised by a Granada producer whose ambitions
and anxieties were buttoned in the same lightweight grey suit. Although
many of those present were, or had been, married, the going view was that
sex was the one form of free enterprise in favour with the company. Having
just finished the first draft of *The Limits of Love*, I had the nerve to confess
that my new novel advertised the merits of marital fidelity. Doris Lessing's
Circean smile was kind enough only to suggest that I could not be as callow
as I made out. Karl Miller allowed it to be known that, when first married
to Jane Collet, the beautiful girl at whose leopardskin tights Tony Becher

had pointed a shrieking finger on King's Parade, he had been surprised to discover that a married man could feel sexual desire for another woman. The indication was that he was now disposed to put Leavisite maturity behind him. I left the meeting with no great wish to go over the top with the up and coming.

John Sullivan invited me to come up to Oxford and dine in Lincoln College, where he was now the Dean. His duties included supervising the moral welfare of the college's undergraduates. He introduced me to W. W. Robson, an English don with small respect for the new fiction. 'One thing you can say for Wain and Amis,' he remarked (not for the first time, perhaps), 'they do have quite a good sense of humour; except for Wain.' Trust a don to allow for a semi-colon in his dialogue. Robson added that Amis had lifted two of his best jokes and put them in *Lucky Jim*. Perhaps because twice bitten, he cracked none in my presence.

Academic mimesis had impelled John to mantle his Liverpudlian accent in Oxonian overtones. The panelled and candlelit setting conditioned dialogue and manners. If Robson (in those days, initials were more commonly remembered than first names) was radical in politics, he was polite in society; he too admired Kenneth Burke and the New Critics. I suspected that, while my conversation might make him smile, my fiction would be met with severity. Emulation and odium often go together among intellectuals. The two classical scholars whom I knew best, Sullivan and Peter Green, had a certain mutual esteem, but no true friendship. In those days, reviews in the *Times Literary Supplement* were unsigned. When one of John Patrick's early books was favoured with a long, not wholly laudatory article, he was convinced that Peter was its author. As a result, he was not wholly displeased by Peter's decade-long failure to secure any tenured position. In truth, Peter assured me, the article at which Sullivan took durable offence was not his work at all. The *TLS* abandoned the principle of contributors' anonymity in the 1980s, though with little diminution of the resentments they were liable to excite.

I acquired an admirer in Robert Gutwillig, an American editor who happened to be in London and wrote to me after reading *The Earlsdon Way*. Under flattering pressure, I gave him a chunk of the typescript of *The Limits of Love* to read. His response was that, with suitable editing, it might well have a future in America. He was going back soon, possibly to a commanding chair as fiction editor of *Playboy*. Hefner was eager to expand his magazine's readership beyond those who opened it only to the double-breasted centrefold. Bob's four-sided, single-spaced letter promised that he could help me to be a better writer.

Tom Maschler reported that Anna Freeman-Saunders would be happy to let us have her beach-front cottage in Fuengirola, a few kilometres west of Málaga. We bought a roof-rack in preparation for loading all our portable goods into and onto PLD 75. Confident that he would be able to extract the fat advance we needed, I gave George Greenfield the revised manuscript of *The Limits of Love*. George had been a pupil and admirer of Frank Leavis at Downing, where he got a double first in English. His lengthy, single-spaced scrutiny of *The Limits* ended by saying that, despite many good scenes, he had to be honest: in his view, the book had 'not quite come off'. Agents often feel that they must prove their critical acumen, as much for the sake of their own vanity as with the expectation of being listened to. I asked George to send the manuscript to Cassell's as it stood.

Like George, Desmond Flower had won the MC in the war. He was grown up. Cassell's was a family business; Desmond was as much a solid merchant as any kind of a literary man. He said right away that he liked the book very much; it had the makings of a bestseller. He had only one practical comment, which he hoped I would take seriously: it was a bit long.

I said, 'I'm not cutting anything about the things that really matter to me and need saying. About the Jews, I mean.'

'Why ever should you?'

'And I don't think the sex is overdone either.'

'No more do I. I could have done with more of it if anything.'

'What is it that you're objecting to exactly then?'

'Six hundred and twenty pages,' he said, 'this manuscript.'

'Because it says what I became a writer to say. At last.'

'Here's what I suggest: take it home with you and cut ten words from every page. You'll be surprised how easy it is to do.'

It was the best advice that any young writer is ever likely to have been given. Hemingway's hints to other writers are often self-inflating, but his trim example still stands: what lasts best has the least fat on it. The lean shaft goes in deepest. After I did as Desmond Flower requested, the book was put into production, to be published in the summer of 1960. I avoided triumphalism when I told George Greenfield of how things had gone. He seemed genuinely pleased by Desmond's enthusiasm. It might well get a £200 advance. After I suggested that I might write a thriller, if he could get me some money, he came up with another offer from Odham's, my ghostly second home. They were updating a perennial bestseller, *Tales of Tragedy and Horror*. If I was willing to do some 2,000- or 3,000-word pieces on things such as the Nazi treatment of the Jews, the Tay Bridge disaster and the sinking of the *Arandora Star*, it would put some money in my pocket. I armed myself with a skimpy library and added it to our baggage.

Not long before we were due to quit Grange Road, Bernard Levin wrote an article in *The Spectator* in which he was happy to declare that there was no longer any anti-Semitism in Britain. Renown had converted yesterday's Taper into today's Doctor Pangloss. I sent him the cuttings that Beetle had culled during her spell at the Appointments Board in Cambridge a few years earlier. His secretary called and asked me to come and see him in Gower Street, where *The Spectator* then had its offices. In person, Levin was small, with black curly hair, tallowy white face, thick glasses and an unpromising handshake. He regarded me with more suspicion than solidarity. I told him that Beetle was uneasy at having the cuttings published (she had liked Jack Davies), but that the prejudice was so blatant and so systematic that she had agreed that Levin should see them. He asked me what I did and, only somewhat belittled, I informed him that I had written a couple of novels. He seemed to suspect that I was more trouble than I was worth. I left 69 Gower Street composing an involuntary account of Master Levin in the style of the Appointments Board's Philip Sinker: 'An unattractive, indoorsy sort of chap with, I fear, the rather oily black curls one associates with Talmudic scribes…'

Once Levin had read the cuttings, he became fiercely engaged with the scandal, and more friendly: he wrote to me that Lord Rothschild 's'intéresse' and that secretarial heads were likely to roll in the wake of his polemic in *The Spectator*. He would keep me posted. And so he did; until he did not. Journalists rarely persist with causes that turn out to be lost, however just they may be. More than fifteen years later, Levin was at a party given by Jack and Catherine Lambert, at the time when my television series, *The Glittering Prizes*, was causing a stir. It was the first invitation of any kind from Jack and Catherine since they had stayed with us five years before. Levin came up to me and said, 'What does it feel like to be the most talked-about person in London?'

I said, 'I was just going to ask you, Bernard.'

At the same party, John Vaizey was kind enough to tell me that he had been at a party of our one-time neighbour, the publisher George Weidenfeld's, the previous week. Eager to see the next episode of my series, he made an excuse to leave Chelsea Embankment early: he had work to do. Weidenfeld said, 'I know exactly why you're going home. If you really want to see Freddie Raphael's play that much, it's on in the bedroom.'

As an agent, Leslie Linder was always warm, optimistic company, but tenacity was never his first quality: he went from one thing to another, eager for jam, less happy when expected to cut bread and butter. I had a call from his young assistant, Richard Gregson. A couple of old Hollywood hands were in town and they wanted someone to rewrite a script entitled *Damon and Pythias*. Since it was based on an old Greek story, I was a natural to do the job. Richard had been in the Merchant Navy and was, for a while, a tea-taster in Borneo. His brother was the handsome young actor Michael Craig, whom the J. Arthur Rank publicity department often portrayed stripped to the waist. He had had to change his name because there was an established British movie actor called Michael Gregson. Richard's brother made enough of a splash as a movie actor to be summoned to Binkie Beaumont's presence as a possible theatrical leading man. Binkie was sitting at his desk, in shirt, tie and jacket, when Michael was shown in. They talked for a while and then Binkie stood up to reveal that he was naked from the waist down.

John Redway had a new young assistant, Gareth Wigan, who had been one of our hosts when *Out of the Blue* was in Oxford, before we opened at the Phoenix Theatre. Not many years later, Gregson and Wigan parted company from John Redway and associates. Representing John Schlesinger, Brian Forbes, Leslie Bricusse and others, they became the most energetic and influential film and TV agents in London.

Vestigial virtue drove me to check scholarly sources for the original story of Damon and Pythias. My *Oxford Companion* disclosed that Damon was a Pythagorean philosopher in the time of the fourth-century BC tyrant of Syracuse, Dionysius. When his best friend Pythias (more properly Phintias) was condemned to death, Damon stood surety for his friend while the latter left Syracuse to settle his affairs. Pythias returned to the city and redeemed his friend's pledge. Dionysius was so moved by the mutual trust of the two men that he pardoned Pythias. It would be nice to suppose that he then made friends of them both.

Sam Marx had been the long-serving script consultant for MGM. He had figured, in no prominent position, in the credits of any number of lion-ised movies. Now that he was retiring, the grateful management had given him a picture to produce, along with his friend Sam Jaffe, who had been an executive and then became a successful agent. His clients included Stanley Kubrick. I went to see the Sams in their suite at the Dorchester Hotel. Sam Marx would never have tolerated any screenwriter composing a scene that involved three people of whom two had the same name. One Sam apostrophised the other with repetitive rapidity. They were polite and they were friendly. They had little doubt that I was the man they wanted. I had even been to Sicily.

The fat screenplay was handsomely duplicated. They already had their deal to make the movie, but both Sams considered that the script needed some work. I should take it to this room they had booked for me at the Grosvenor House, read it, and tell them what I thought. They would fix for me to have coffee. I said that I should as soon take the script home with me, sooner. The thing was, the Sams said, they had a schedule, and the Grosvenor House was not far away. 'Nor is home,' I said. 'I'll call you in a few hours. Promise.'

As I stood up, Jaffe said, 'Fred, one thing we want you to be clear about. This is the story of two friends, the greatest friendship between two men the world has ever seen, that's our story, that's what we want to tell: two guys who'd do anything for each other, don't let's lose sight of that for one moment.'

Sam Marx said, 'And listen, Fred, one more thing before you go, we've been doing some thinking about our two characters, so: one thing to bear in mind when you're reading the script: the way we see it today, where it says Damon, that's Pythias...'

'And where it says Pythias...'

'That's Damon. Bear that in mind, Fred, will you, please?'

'Oh and Sam, we had one more thing, Fred: our two guys, yes, they're friends, and yes, they're Greek, but they absolutely must not be, you know what I'm trying to say ... Greek friends.'

I had already had some small experience of rewriting a script. When

I was working with Leslie, a Pinewood producer called Jo Janni was about to go into production with a script entitled *The Big Money*. We were solicited by Olive Harding, the script controller who had given us that two-picture deal, to put some late ginger into it. Ian Carmichael was the star. He drove to Chelsea Embankment in his olive-green Ford Consul convertible, the badge of his 1950s success, and told me the sensible things that he thought needed doing. I remembered seeing him in drag in a West End revue. He sat at the piano with an arm full of bangles that kept slipping down over his fingers as he played and he had to raise them, one after the other, and shake the bangles up his arm again.

Leslie Bricusse must have been busy elsewhere (he was a juggler who would be ashamed to have only one ball in the air) when I was deputed to go and see Jo Janni in his flat in Burton Court, across from the Royal Hospital in Chelsea. Some years later, when we were working together on *Darling*, he asked whether I remembered the first thing I ever said to him.

I said, 'Probably, good morning, sir.'

'No,' Jo said, 'the first thing you said was "What do you want to make this piece of shit for?"'

'And what did you say?'

'I don't know. But I do know that I agreed with you.'

Leslie and I had done our best to put some new old jokes in the script, which was to be directed by the perky John Paddy Carstairs. His knockabout inventiveness had been exercised to good box-office effect on Norman Wisdom movies. J. P. C. had a sideline as the British mutation of Raoul Dufy. Leslie showed the diplomatic taste to add one or two of Paddy's daubs to his collection. Our cosmetic work on *The Big Money* was received with pleasure by Ian Carmichael and with dismay by the picture's production manager, who said it was unprofessional: by changing the scene numbers, we had dislocated his budget. Did we not know that if a scene was cut, you had to preserve the numerology by marking it as deleted? One lives and learns in the movies, often things of very small interest.

Damon and Pythias was trite, witless and overlong. Experience proves that there is one infallible way of being hired as a rewrite man. You make a damning list of the places where a script does not work, but you emphasise that, if your prescribed course of treatment is followed, a good idea can be brought to fruition. After I had chopped the script with a constructive hatchet and suggested a few unsubtle ways in which it might yet be a hit, I was clutched, like any life-saving straw. Sam and Sam offered me a ten-week guarantee of £200 a week for ten weeks. It was more tempting than a round-table discussion with Karl Miller and kindred cultural monitors, but I declined the commission.

The offered rate rose to £300, then to £400 a week. Even then I could not bring myself to cash in on the skill with which I had made myself delectable to the two Sams. Despite our poverty, I was set on going to Spain and doing only, or almost only, the kind of fiction I had always intended. I threw away my long spoons and made a silent resolve never again to sup with celluloid devils. *Damon and Pythias* was eventually made and released, to no recorded ovation, in 1962. It is not only the mills of God that grind slowly.

Until Miss Pearce broke her word, I had assumed that when what my father called 'Christians' gave their word they would keep it. We left Grange Road for the south of France in a heavily loaded car, but without heavy hearts. Paul, never slow to be displeased, was always happy when we were on the road. Before we set out, I sent the complete manuscript of *The Limits of Love* to Bob Gutwillig. He told me that, if I adopted the radical changes he was planning to propose, he might find me a good publisher in the US.

I cannot recall how much money, in traveller's cheques, we had with us. Penury did not inhibit us from making our rendezvous with Joan and Baron at the classy La Petite Auberge at Noves, not far from Avignon. It had three stars in the Michelin, but dinner cost only £3 or so. Baron was now keen to give Joan the luxury that Marxist austerity had denied her. While we were having drinks, M. Lalleman, the young *patron*, brought us menus in the garden. Beetle and I had been together for almost ten years, so I was careful to ask whether certain dishes contained garlic, to which I knew her to be allergic. Lalleman chose to tell me that I would never keep my wife if I sought to impose my tastes on her diet. I responded as Aeneas did, when abused by Dido, by stammering and being prepared to say many things. I could wish that I had risen to Guy Ramsey's 'Remember which side of the counter you're on', whatever the French for that might be, but I merely glared at him. I have never known any other restaurateur, of whatever starry status or bold address, talk to a customer as Lalleman did to me that bright evening.

La Petite Auberge was the first place to announce its luxury by serving a flower and the morning newspaper on its breakfast trays. Perhaps in part to demonstrate to Monsieur L. that we were still together, we returned a few times in later years. The décor became more and more elaborate and the prices with it. The *moment de déclic* came when, as we were shown to our table, the hostess took Beetle's handbag from her and hung it, officiously, on a little hook affixed to the underside of the table, quite as if smart people would have known that it was there. I was not wholly sorry when Lalleman lost one of his stars, and then another.

Eizabeth David's *French Country Cooking* in hand, I did most of the cooking during our month at the Villa Tethys at Le Canadel. It was no memorable pleasure to sit on the beach with Joan and Baron, who wore a snap-brimmed trilby. They were still together, but otherwise apart. Their fourteen-year-old daughter Jenny stretched, beautifully, on a flat rock. Eight-year-old Alan scowled and fretted and did not want to play cricket. Beetle looked after Paul, who scuttled around the sand, while I went and shopped for my evening culinary performance. When no one was up at the villa, I sat on the terrace and typed a few more pages of *The S Man*.

Baron had celebrated his new affluence by buying an 8mm camera. It happened to be running when, without having previously adopted an upright stance, Paul got to his feet on the marble floor and walked fifty-three steps. Baron had to go to London in the middle of the month. On his return, he presented me with a white chef's *toque*, with a light-blue flash on it. The weeks went slowly. We seemed to have less in common with Joan and Baron by the end than when we met them at Noves. We have never again gone on holiday with other people.

I thought it would be quicker and cooler, and romantic, to drive to Spain through the night. The daytime roads would be cumbered with returning holidaymakers. We arranged a foam rubber mattress on the back seat of the Ford Anglia and set off in the early evening to drive first below Montpellier and Narbonne and then along the north side of the Pyrenees, past Pau, before reaching the border at Hendaye. The Guardia Civil at the deserted Irun crossing regarded us with unwelcoming suspicion. It seemed that they could not imagine anyone having an innocent reason for visiting Spain. In Franco's kingdom, time seemed to have stopped in 1939.

The narrow *carretera* was pitted with pot-holes and loud with snorting, bald-tyred pre-war lorries. The bulbous green hillsides carried tall cut-outs of black bulls with dangling football-sized *cojones*. Pairs of glowering Guardia Civil, in shiny black helmets that looked like portable typewriter cases, patrolled – one on each side of the road – swinging their green woollen capes, antique Lee-Enfield rifles on their shoulders, the Caudillo's occupying force. Since Paul was wide awake, we drove on through the day, exhausted and ill-humoured. The fragility of what I took for granted was abruptly evident. After a night's sleep, I felt more exhilarated to be out of England than ashamed to be in a Fascist country. Driving the long road south with its many bumpy detours, I decided that I should never again work in tandem with anyone or think about money, no matter what Dr Jan van Loewen had to say. Spain might be in bondage; I was free.

Anna Freeman-Saunders's house was in a dusty fishing village called Fuengirola, beyond loud Torremolinos on the way to Gibraltar. Calle Tostón *Diez y seis* had two bedrooms and a living room opening onto a patio blazing with geraniums and draped in purple bougainvillea; beyond the patio wall, the sea. The Calle Tostón was a long, tight row of one-storey houses with a three-storey apartment building at the end, just before the grey beach.

The day after we arrived, I started a new play. *The Roper House* was based on some of the things that Judy Birdwood had told me about her wayward, now dead, husband Rudolph. Nearly everything I have ever written has been based on what I have seen or heard. I have had little shame at using things I have been told. Something seems to impel people to tell writers their secrets, even when they can guess that they will make use of them, perhaps because of that. The novelist's mind had better be full of the rags and bones of other people's lives. It can take years for incidents to grow into a story. Some remain memorable, however trivial, but never germinate. I recall sitting in a flat in Girton House, Manor Fields, belonging to a man called Harry Matthews. I have no memory of how I came to be there. I had never spoken to him before and never spoke to him again. I was nineteen and proud of being in love with Beetle. Mr Matthews told me that he was very unhappy. He was sure that his wife was unfaithful to him with some young person who lived in Manor Fields. She liked young men. He was sure she would like me. Did he suspect me of being her lover? Why did he ask me to stay and talk to him about Beetle? Why did I feel that I was his soft prisoner, both wanting and not wanting to be free of him?

I finished *The Roper House* in less than two weeks. Its main character was an amalgam of Oswald Mosley and an architect of the same arrogant genius as Frank Lloyd Wright. I named him Stephen Taylor, after a menacing boy, and a fast runner, whom I had feared, for the usual reason, when I was at prep school in north Devon. Alone in the patio in the Calle Tostón, I did not give a thought to the Royal Court Theatre or to the playwrights who had eclipsed me in Ken Tynan's *Observer* play competition. As a writer, I have never imagined myself to be competing against anyone.

The day after *The Roper House* was done, I started a new novel, *The Trouble with England*. I typed ceaselessly until lunchtime, whenever that was. Beetle went to the beach with Paul. Tom Maschler had passed on Anna's instructions to pay our cook, Salvadora Martin, 300 pesetas a month, never more. A widow with four girls to raise, Salvadora always wore black. Her husband had been a fisherman, killed in an accident at sea. There was no compensation. She arrived, all in black, in the morning either late or later, carrying a black bag containing what she had found at the market for our lunch. She lit the charcoal stove and fanned it into flame with a wicker-work paddle.

On sunny days ('*oy so*' she would say, for '*hoy sol*'), Salvadora sang songs with a lot of *corazón* in the lyrics; on glum days, '*que lastima, que pena!*' was the theme. Between two o'clock and three, she would call, '*Señorito, la comida!*' Our diet included *lenguados, ritsoles, boquerones, tortillas, tomates relleños, gambas, paella, almondegas con arroz, berejena y judías*, an edible Spanish lesson that covered the long concrete patio table. The absence of many of her teeth compounded the effect of Salvadora's Andaluz accent. '*Lenguados no hay en mercado*' (there are no soles in the market) became '*Langwa-o no hay en mercow*'. As we ate, Salvadora would say, '*Todo!*', quite as if she really meant us to eat it all. *En verdad*, she cooked enough to be sure that black bag of hers left the house plump with what was left. It eased our consciences at paying her so little. She might be moody with us, but she was unfailingly, if teasingly, affectionate with Paul. 'Pablo, *niño guapo, niño feo*', her incantation had something of the contained heat of flamenco.

Fuengirola's fishermen had to haul their boats up the beach because Franco persisted in denying their request to build a jetty. Early in the Civil War, the villagers burned the church and chased away the priest. No one talked about those days. Salvadora promised us that everyone appreciated the *tranquilidad* that Franco had imposed. Anything was better than the disasters of war.

Several of the other houses in the Calle Tostón were occupied by *estranjeros*, expatriates, with artistic pretensions. Our neighbour to the right was a painter called Larry Potter, a graduate of Cooper Union and the first American black man we ever met. Slim, smart and glad to be out of the States, Larry admired Juan Gris before all other modern painters, and Herman Hesse more than Ernest Hemingway, who had been in Fuengirola that summer. Papa was writing up the series of *mano-a-mano* bullfights starring the rival *toreros* Luis Miguel Dominguin and Antonio Ordoñez. Larry's neighbours were German, Hans and Juliana Piron. Professional translators, he was Jewish, she was not. They had come to Fuengirola from primitive, sparsely inhabited Ibiza. It was cheaper to live there than anywhere else in Europe.

Hans was about to go to Frankfurt for the book fair. He hoped to pick up enough work to feed him and Juliana and their children, Claudia and Juani, for the next year. Juliana told Beetle that work was not the only thing he picked up; he also had his 'flirts'. She seemed philosophical about it; it did not occur to me that perhaps it suited her. Not yet forty, Hans had a heap of arty grey hair, boss eyes that bulged behind thick glasses and a prompt aptitude for laughing at his own jokes. Juliana *was* forty, just, blue-eyed and beautiful enough for age to worry her, a lot. Softening breasts hung loose under a dark-blue cotton dress. Claudia was eleven, blonde and had her mother's blue eyes; Juani was more like his father. Juliana's father lived with his money in Buenos Aires. He did not approve of Hans, but he did send expensive presents to Claudia. Hans had survived the Nazi occupation in Holland, where, he soon told us, he had been 'in the Resistance'. Larry Potter said, 'What it comes to is, he stole coal.' Juliana cherished a receding dream of visiting the isles of Greece.

Larry Potter and Juliana were both asthmatic; they understood each other. While Hans was in Frankfurt, they got together. Larry had a lot of charm. He even charmed a certain Miss Anson, the holidaying chairman of the Conservative association in Hemel Hempstead, into coming to a party he was giving. When he kissed her hullo, the matronly Tory lady said, 'Imagine if the Blues could see me now!' I was drinking some *anis seco* when a freckled woman with big brown curly hair, wearing a green knitted dress, came and pulled at my orange turtlenecked sweater. 'What's this?' Her name was Charlotte Gordon and she was a sculptor, she told me.

Further down the street lived Paul Hecht, the poet son of a New York hack-driver. He had saved for his trip to Spain by working for three years on building sites in the Bronx. Now he was learning to play flamenco guitar and living with a good-looking black American called Joan. I asked Larry Potter what she did.

'Joan? She sleeps a lot.'

When I told Larry that I had finished a new play, he suggested that I should read it to the 'community'. I said I had only one copy, so I should have to read all the parts myself. 'Who better?' I was afraid that *The Roper House* would be too British for a mostly American audience, but it held their attention pretty well. Larry surprised and flattered me by being able to quote or paraphrase several of Stephen Taylor's speeches after a single hearing. I told him that until I met him I had not believed the story, retailed among classicists, that ancient Athenian audiences could actually recite large sections of a tragedy after it had been staged only once. 'The work's good enough, why not?' Soon after my one-man play-reading, Hans came to the door with news that some German TV station was offering a prize of 800 Deutschmarks for a television play. 'I sink we do it,' he said. But I sought differently: Larry's enthusiasm made me keen to get my new play to my fan Betty Judkins in Dr van Loewen's office.

nothing. Now that the fever or whatever it was had left him he was aware for the first time of the seriousness of the theft he had suffered. He was without identity. He could prove nothing about himself. And yet he was safe—safe with the knowledge that Bruce and Jessica could testify for him— and yet, again, he was beyond them. He had passed beyond the point at which he had intended to stop; he had quit Jessica's house, like a fool, and couldn't go back. He smiled. He was really in trouble. Of course it was possible to go back and ask the Indians for his passport, but there must be a good market for British passports and even if there weren't, they were too stupid not to think that there might be. He was really in trouble. He had the leverage neither of money nor of nationality. He was the perfect man on whom they might pin Chatita's murder and because of the perfection of the role he was inclined to play it. It was not altogether impossible to believe that he had killed her. He had very little recollection of the crisis of his sickness and he might well have spent time with her. He remembered looking for her. It would not take long for him to convince himself that he had done it and once the conviction took root, the first policeman would be able to drag it out of him. How did they execute murderers in San Roque? The most sensible move would be to go to the British Consulate and tell them that he had lost his passport, but then they would ask him whether he had reported the loss to the police and how could he do that without giving them the details of how he came to lose it? That would lead inevitably to revealing that he had been out all night on the night of the murder, or the night when he assumed the murder to have taken place, and that would be to lay himself open to further inquiries which were almost certain to incriminate him. It was no longer fanciful to imagine himself being indicted for murder; it was no longer an amusing conceit. It was as near as could be a certainty. He was a fool to have left the security of the Villa Pinta. The obvious thing was to represent himself there, but he knew there was no future in so doing: sooner or later he would have to return to

194

A Wild Surmise

XXII

HARRY AND CHARLOTTE Gordon rented a big house in the Avenida José Antonio Primo de Rivera. The street does not carry the same name in today's democratic Fuengirola, which has a summer population of a quarter of a million. José Antonio was the Falange leader, killed by the Republicans in 1926. The Gordons had made enough money on Madison Avenue to take a year off to paint and sculpt in Spain. We were soon told that Charlotte had been the youngest art editor ever of *Seventeen*; she had been 'let go' because of temperamental differences with the magazine's managing editor.

Harry's cool first-floor studio was big enough for the large canvases on which he did his hard-edged stuff. Top New York galleries were keen to give him a show when he got back, but there were very few he was willing to go with. Not yet thirty, he had the aspect and bow-legged trudge and furrowed frown of a man braving undisclosed sorrows. He did like to tell jokes, though. The one I remember was about the Lone Ranger and Tonto. They're riding down a canyon when they see 5,000 Indians at the far end; they wheel round and there are another 5,000; the Lone Ranger looks up and sees ... 5,000 more on the skyline. The Lone Ranger turns to Tonto and says, 'Well, old timer, looks like we've finally had it this time.' Tonto says, 'Where'd you get the "we" shit?'

The Gordons had been art students together in Philadelphia, where his father, now dead, was a policeman. Harry told us that one day, when his father was on point duty, a man who had had a few drinks came over to him and said, 'Officer, is my fly undone?' Harry's father said, 'No, it's not.' 'Then how come I'm pissing?' Charlotte's father Leopold was an Austrian refugee and an inventor of genius, somewhat like Gordon Pask. He was employed by RCA. Some eighty patents for his many inventions belonged wholly to the company.

Harry's face would change when he told funny stories, of which he had a good number. The creases changed from vertical to lateral when he smiled. His laugh promised that he might easily be happier than he was. He had been raised as a Roman Catholic. When Christmas approached, we invited him to a communal roast turkey, baked in the village oven. Harry claimed not even to know which day it was.

Hans and Juliana owned an elegantly boxed mahjong set. Once the children were settled, they came to our house, carrying a suitable table, and taught us how to play. The game proved to be a picturesque form of rummy, with oriental tiles instead of cards. Hans's commentary added a little spice. 'Now I sink I finish it quickly,' he would say. His English was as fluent as it was foreign. His parents, Max and Else, lived in Málaga. Max was an enlarged, much louder form of Hans, who was already larger than the kind of life I was used to. Max wore a black cape and a black beret and pretended to amorous rights over his 'daughter-incest'. Juliana suffered more than she welcomed his embraces.

Every Tuesday, Beetle and I wheeled Paul up to the next village, Los Boliches, to catch one of the few copies of the *Sunday Times* on sale along the coast. On the other side of the *carretera* was a big villa with a high wall around it, facing onto an empty lot. Pink and black pigs rootled among the garbage. The villa's stone-arched wooden gates were always shut; the shutters too. The property was said to belong to '*El Alemán*', the German.

Soon after we settled in Fuengirola, we saw in someone else's newspaper that Harold Macmillan's Conservatives had won the general election. We never listened to the radio. There was no television. Macmillan's winning slogan 'You've never had it so good' seemed to promise that England's best hope was to remain in a state of faltering complacency. 'Supermac' was its woebegone miracle-worker. I had no wish to go back.

I wrote at least five pages of my novel every morning, often more. The unceasing clatter of my typewriter keys dismayed Paul Hecht and amused Larry Potter. I stopped briefly, in mid-morning, when the *cartero* opened the little gate on the beach side of the patio, and unloaded the mail onto the tiled table. I gave him the usual peseta for his trouble. If the letter was one I craved (from George Greenfield, for instance), I made it two pesetas.

One day, as Christmas approached, Hans came to our house. After asking, as always, 'Did you get letters?' he wanted to know if we meant to have a Christmas tree. It would be nice for the children. Where might we find a Christmas tree in Fuengirola? 'On ze way to Marbella, on ze right, there's a whole forest of them. We go one night wiz an axe and … why not?' I was too prim to relish the prospect of rustling conifers, however many there might be of them. Imagine if the Guardia Civil happened to come by. I announced a fortunate cold. Hans was displeased at my lack of nerve, but he did not go and cut a tree for himself.

After doing my Trollopian quota of work on *The Trouble with England*, which had been sparked by the paralysed man who came into the *pension* Florida and left his mouth-paintings on each table, I gave an hour or two to playing the honest hack. In John Prebble's style, and – in the chapter on the Tay Bridge disaster – with the help of his book, I compiled breadwinning chapters of tragedies and horrors. I wrote the segment on the murder of six million of Europe's Jews using as a crib Lord Russell of Liverpool's catchpenny paperback, the sales of which had been enhanced by the photographs of naked women being paraded before grinning SS men. In the course of my commissioned drudgery, I was philosophical enough to say that the so-called 'Jewish question' was not a genuine question at all; hence there was no call to answer it. Wittgenstein's *Philosophical Investigations* stood in its light-blue jacket on the chimney-piece.

In the afternoon, I craved exercise. Harry Gordon and I got in the way of kicking a soccer ball around on the patch of land adjacent to the *carretera*, beside *El Alemán*'s shuttered villa. Now and again, a large American car would drive past with off-duty GIs in it. Its licence plate announced: USAAF MORON. One day, the judas door in one of the big brown wooden gates of the villa opened and a trio of Spanish boys ran out and joined us. Pretty soon, we had enough regular players to make up two sides.

Gene Masson, a professor of painting from Miami, Florida, joined us occasionally. He had never played soccer before so I suggested that he go in goal. One day, Esteban, one of the Spanish boys from the German villa, hit a shot so hard that Gene, making a casual swipe at it, broke the little finger on his left hand. He held it up and laughed and said, 'Guy just broke my fucking finger. He broke my fucking finger, see that? Lucky it's not the one I paint with.' Gene had been a war artist in the Pacific with the US Marine Corps. He did not think that Harry was really a painter; 'hard-edge' was a style that was convenient for designers: they didn't have to know how to draw. Harry's pictures were all different and all the same. Harry's view of Gene was that he was a typical sun-belt, old-style artist who couldn't ever interest a progressive New York gallery.

Another black American painter called Clifford joined us on the football field, usually when we were just about done. He had connections in Morocco and was well supplied with hash. It made him sleepy, even when awake. With a cry of 'Time to get the lead out!' he would watch the ball roll past him with the frowning attention a zoologist might give to a rare, spherical beast. Clifford lived with a small, fair, English girl called Valerie. She told me he was the best lover a girl could dream of having. He beat her from time to time, but the bruises were a price worth paying to have a real man.

When I went to the Massons' house, down on the harbour beyond the Casino Bar in the middle of town, to see how his finger was, he was working on a big painting of goats spilling down a hillside. The floor was littered with charcoal studies he had made with, it looked, infallible spontaneity. A canvas on the wall was of three naked girls rolling on a set of cushions. 'Braniff air hostesses, they volunteered to pose for me, so I thought why not? They took their clothes off like they did it all the time. Why? Probably because they did it all the time.' Gene's wife Helen was dark, talkative and devoted. Although outspokenly Jewish, they had children called Robin and Leslie.

After our football games and a Pepsi or two at the casino bar, Harry Gordon and I went and talked in his studio, smoking big cheap cigars imported from Fidel's Cuba. I was British enough to be surprised at how Harry seemed to be on first-name terms with pretty well everybody: Andy (Warhol), Jack (Kerouac), Dick (Avedon), Jack (Kennedy, this time), and of course Marilyn. I never greatly enjoyed cigars, but I felt at one with Ernest as I puffed my Fidel y Julieta. We had been in Fuengirola for a few months when I felt a small lump at the back of my throat. The local doctor was called Verdugo, the Spanish for executioner. I did not feel the urge to consult him. I thought the lump would go away, but it did not.

Every few weeks, we would drive along the coast, past flat-faced Estepona and heaped San Roque, to Gibraltar where we could stock up on provisions unobtainable at Cayetano's in Fuengirola: Lipton's tea, crisp Peek-Frean biscuits and unrancid butter. The lump in my throat was bothering me enough for Beetle to insist I find a doctor while we were in Gib. I was directed to a throat specialist called Hamish Macpherson. A brass plate at the door, opposite Lipton's said that he was 'late of Guy's Hospital, London'.

His surgery was a large, bleak room on the first floor. He looked down my throat and then at me. 'You think you've got cancer, don't you?'

I said, 'It had occurred to me.'

'Well, you haven't. I know what's wrong with you and I can cure it.'

'Well, that's … that's … encouraging.'

'Where did you have your tonsils removed?'

I said, 'New York, when I was … five years old.'

'I might've guessed. American medicine! What you have is a post-lingual tonsil, composed of scar tissue. Result of inept surgery.'

'What … what does one … do about it?'

'It's a simple operation.'

'Operation! We're … we're only in Gibraltar for the day…'

'That's all right. We can do it right away. Do you have ten minutes?'

He had already opened a cupboard and taken out a large battery to which he now attached two leads from an instrument with two metal arms that tapered to a point. It would not have looked out of place in a Spanish inquisitor's tool kit. As I watched the point began to redden.

'It's quite a simple operation,' Mr Macpherson said. 'But it does require three hands. And, as you may have observed, I have only the two; so one of them will have to be yours.'

'What exactly…?'

'When my … instrument is red-hot, the tip, I shall insert it, carefully, so that it reaches down into the back of your throat and cauterises your supposed tumour. As the lump is composed entirely of scar tissue, it has no nerves; as long as you keep perfectly still, you will feel nothing whatsover. You may hear a slight … seething noise, but that's all.'

'What about, um, an anaesthetic?'

'Not necessary. I told you…'

'I know, but…'

'If you insist, I can always give you a swab of cocaine.'

'Please. This third hand…'

'I want you to take these two pieces of gauze and hold your tongue, maybe not your favourite activity. Stick the tongue well out, keep still, open wide, and ready when you are.' I swallowed. The lump was still there. I opened very wide and held my tongue. Mr Macpherson directed the red-hot iron to the back of my throat. There was a therapeutic sizzle and out came the iron. 'There y'are, you're cured. Let go your tongue, man, and have a swallow.' I did. I felt nothing.

I said, 'Well, thank you very much. What do I … owe you?'

'Normally, that would be three guineas. But since you assisted with the operation, we'll make it three pounds. What're you proposing to do now?'

I said, 'Go and find my wife and have a cup of coffee.'

'Typical! You'll drink it when it's too hot and you won't notice because of that completely unnecessary swab of cocaine and you'll give yourself cancer of the stomach.' I never smoked a cigar or a cigarette from that day onwards.

We arrived back in Fuengirola to find a letter from my mother (always a lively and fluent correspondent). Guy Ramsey had died. In an article in *Bridge Magazine*, Ewart Kempson, one of the 'Aces' in his classic handful of master players, reported that he had invited Guy to play in a weekend match in Norwich. After a 'black tie' dinner, he charmed the team, and their ladies, and won the pairs competition, partnering Kempson's wife. On the Sunday night, Guy again played 'with considerable skill' and then sat discussing the hands they had played until 2.30 in the morning. Kempson ends his piece: 'He died a few hours later. The doctor who was summoned found him writing to his adored wife. I shall always think of him as Guy Ramsey Sahib Bahardur. He was a gentle, kind, generous and extremely brave person. His end-play was a very happy one.' As I transcribe Kempson's dated words, my eyes fill with tears, as they did when I wrote to Celia fifty-five years ago.

Guy left no blazing mark on the world, but he is among those minor figures of whom friends and colleagues (Peter Green among them) continue to speak with affection and admiration. Perhaps too vivid a performer to be a novelist, he devoted all his energy to impersonating the urbane *flâneur* that indeed he was. As a journalist, he had flair and style, but he was too genial, perhaps too lazy, to be a careerist. He had small interest in politics and rejoiced in the England where the chivalry he had applauded in Ewart Kempson was commonplace. He loved to make a fine impression and tell a good story. The bridge world was salted with jealousy and backbiting. Guy had no time for cliquish rivalries; he took everyone on their merits, as English gentlemen always did, or were supposed to do.

Celia asked whether she might come and visit us in Fuengirola. I never wondered why she hoped to find us more of a consolation than her close friends E. Arnot Robertson and Marghanita Laski. She brought her young son Simon and stayed for a week. In her late forties, she seemed at once brave and somehow desirous of something that we could not, or would not, give her. She told me, meaningly, that if I was going to write many novels, I needed to have more experience of life than monogamous domesticity could supply. Perhaps she imagined herself as Colette's Léa to my Chéri. As we waited in the rain for the bus that would take them to catch the plane in Gibraltar, she said, 'I can feel the drops trickling between my tits.'

Harry and Charlotte Gordon went to Madrid to look at the pictures in the Prado and elsewhere. When they came back, Harry told us that the Academia Real had just made the last sets of eighty-four prints from Goya's original etchings of the *Desastres*. The quality was still good, but they would never make any more. He had a spare set, if we wanted them. The price was just over £100. It was a lot of money, but a chance that we chose not to miss. I have two of the prints on my wall, but not in my eyeline. Goya's unblinking eye furnishes images too demanding to be kept in constant view.

Franco's cruel Spain suited us. We were indeed passing rich on £10 a week. I finished *The Trouble with England* on a Friday and started *A Wild*

Surmise on the following Monday. On Saturday mornings, we left Paul with Salvadora and went to the big covered market in Málaga where they sold *chirimollas* (custard apples) and fresh strawberries in March. After doing the rounds, we went to Antonio's bar on the waterfront, where we refilled wicker-covered flagons with *fundador*, *vino tinto* and *agua aguardiente*.

Antonio tethered his donkey among the casks in the shadowy depths of his sawdust-floored *bodega*. He was a lame widower. His ambition was to emigrate to Australia. To get a visa, he had to go to Madrid with his small son. He could not afford to stay in a hotel. They arrived at the Australian embassy in the morning, in the clothes they had been in for thirty-six hours. The boy had soiled his pants. The Aussie official sniffed as they came in and that was that.

Fuengirola's American population was not all artistic. Two of them were veterans on disability pensions. One was an ex-Marine with whom I played poker a few times. His pet phrase was 'Up yours with a hay-rake, Jack!' The other was called Chuck; he had only one lung and seemed resigned to lonely decline. Then he surprised everyone with the announcement that he was getting married. His bride was a young whore from Málaga. He had no illusions about why she agreed to the wedding: she would get a good percentage of his pension after he died. Chuck had already been married and divorced in the US. When his son sent him a Christmas present of two pairs of socks, he refused to pay the few pesetas duty on the package. 'Spain, I don't need socks.' He married his *puta* in the new white village church (the 'loyalists' had burned down the old one) and lived for a while as happily as he knew how.

I read Lorca and Juan Ramón Jiménez. To improve my everyday Spanish I relied on paperback translations of Agatha Christie ('*Desde luego, señor Poirot…*'). I rarely looked at a Spanish newspaper. One day, on my way to play football, I saw that the rooting pigs, and the garbage, had been cleared from beside the *carretera*. The whole village was being spruced up with whitewash and happy flags. *'Porqué?' 'Porqué? Porqué mañana por la tarde viene el Jefe del Estado!'* Francisco Franco was coming to Fuengirola.

On the day itself, traffic was banned on the *carretera*. FRANCO was inscribed, again and again, in large whitewashed letters on the tarmac. The villagers lined the street, the children in their tight best clothes. The rein- forced Guardia Civil scowled. Just before Franco was due, a tall, slim old man in a straw hat, wearing an open, floral waistcoat, pointed white leather shoes and carrying a long polished cane, sauntered into view from the gypsy encampment to the west of the village.

In front of the *alcaldía*, the town hall, he came to the first FRANCO in the roadway. He tilted his head and put a careful toe in the O of FRANCO and did a little pivot. The Guardia scowled more than ever, but the king of the gypsies paid them no heed. He walked on, to the next whitewashed FRANCO and now he put that pointed toe into the eye of the A, never touching the whiteness, and did the same pivot. The tilt of his head seemed to ask what FRANCO was doing in the middle of his road.

The king of the gypsies sauntered to the side of the road only as the first motor cyclists came blaring into sight. They drove fast through the village and on towards Los Boliches ('Lo Boliche', Salvadora called it). Then came the first black limousine, then the second, then the third and the fourth and the fifth. In each of them sat a stiff, plump figure with a nasty moustache; uniformed acolytes beside him. Without slowing down, they came and they went, Franco and his four facsimiles. *'Con mis ojos le he visto!'* Salvadora said, with my own eyes I saw him; but which was the real one, neither she nor we will ever knew.

A few days later, I went to collect Harry Gordon to play football and he said he didn't feel like it. So what was the matter?

'You haven't heard?'

'Heard what?'

'Hard-edge is dead. It was in *Time* magazine.'

'I never even knew it was sick. So what?'

'So what? So every single one of the fifty-something paintings I've done since we got here is hard-edge. I had promises of interest from all kinds of galleries, including Sidney Janis. Now no one's even going to look at my stuff. Looks like I wasted a whole year.'

Could a genuine artist choose to do what he did only, or even principally, because there was a market for it? I was not, of course, indifferent to cash, but I never wrote a novel for a mercenary motive and I have never changed a word in order to please or appease some putative reader. I made it a habit to rely on the movies and television to subsidise what really mattered to me. While we were on the Costa del Sol, I had the luck, engineered by Richard Gregson, to be hired by Fritz Gotfurt to improve an Associated British Pictures script that was about to go into production. Dickie Todd was not happy with his lines. There is a rule as immutable as the laws of the Medes and Persians that the closer a movie is to production, the higher the fee for remedial script surgery. I made three times as much as my advance on *The Limits of Love* in as many weeks.

Gotfurt was one of the earliest of many refugees from the German cinema. The best, Fritz Lang, Billy Wilder among them, headed for Hollywood. Emeric Pressburger was one of the few who stopped in England, where he teamed up with Mickey Powell, whose career was fatally blighted in 1960, when he made *Peeping Tom*, a more truthful erotic myth than prudish British critics (voyeurs by trade) cared to countenance. Too cynical to advertise his cynicism, Fritz Gotfurt had been shrewd enough to quit Germany as soon as Hitler came to power. He had no pious hopes, as Wesker and others did, that man was redeemable. He had technical acumen, but no illusions about cinema as an art. Many small cigars had kippered and creased his complexion. He admired Dickie Todd more for his amorous adventures than for his heroic war record.

When Dickie announced his delight in the new lines I had given him,

Fritz promised that I should never be short of work as long as he was around. The next job he offered me was to adapt his wife's play, *Little Ladyship*, for the screen. I elected to stay poor and go on with *A Wild Surmise*. Not long afterwards, the *cartero* brought me a neat letter in which George Green-field said that he had read *The Trouble with England* and thought it too slim to be published on its own. Would I consider writing another novella to furnish a doublet that he could propose to Cassell's? They would want to follow *The Limits of Love* with a 'booky book' rather than a squib. For-tunately *A Wild Surmise* would be ready to supply it.

Its plot was based on a recent scandal in Spain. A large number of people had been poisoned, and a few had died, allegedly by the use of industrial oil, from Morocco, for making canned tomato sauce. In the end, which took some time to come, it was proved that the oil was innocent; Spanish tomatoes had been overdosed with toxic spray before they were cooked. I embellished the story and transferred it to San Roque, a fictitious South American country whose capital closely resembled Málaga.

The novel's anti-hero was Robert Carn, based on my Charterhouse friend Robin Jordan, who had indeed emigrated to South America. The name Carn was dredged from my memory of my prep school in north Devon. I can hardly recall its bearer but even his pre-teen personality had the sin-gular aura that distinguishes the maverick. Having said my piece about anti-Semitism and Jews, at length, I was determined not to be cornered into being a Jewish writer. At least half my books and stories contain no Jewish characters. I like to live, and write, in what my friend Joseph Epstein calls 'the middle of my tether'.

Tranquil Fuengirola suited me very well. My stacks of pages proved it. We made trips to the pottery in Coín and to Ronda, high in the sierras, where we sat in front of a coal fire at the Hotel Reina Victoria and were served with a full British tea by a red-haired waiter. Ronda had the oldest wooden bullring in Spain. A deep ravine cuts the town in two. It is said to have been the real-life location of a scene in *For Whom the Bell Tolls*, in which republican loyalists threw captive Fascists off the high scarp into the rocky abyss, unless it was the Fascists who did the throwing.

When my parents came to stay for a few days, we drove them to Granada to see the Alhambra. Larry Potter and the other Americans called my mother 'Irene' without hesitation. Larry gave her a little etching, of a reclining woman. He had nothing and he was very generous. Later he gave me a sketchbook thick with gouache cartoons in the style of Juan Gris. I have it in my desk drawer. Larry went to Paris soon after we left Fuengirola in 1960. I recognised him, under another name, in Jimmy Baldwin's novel *Another Country*, when I reviewed it in 1963. His asthma made him vulnerable and he was, he later wrote to Harry Gordon, 'flat on his black ass'. Larry died in 1966; he has since gained a measure of deserved fame as an artist.

someone else's business. It is in a position to be bought off and you, as its chief, are in a position to profit from the Law of Triple Vacancy.

The Law of Triple Vacancy is this: for every two employers who will employ a man because they want him to work for them, there is at least one who will employ a man to prevent him working for a rival. The dangerman is never out of work.

In a reasonably secure state where neither lawlessness nor revolution threatens, it is the man who threatens the security of others who is himself most secure. The boss who feels almost entirely safe from disaster will spend endless money to close the last gap through which danger might come. He cannot be expected to know that by employing you he has welcomed to his innermost counsels the very danger he seeks to avoid.

The human being longs for loyalty. He never finds it, but let him always imagine that he has found it in you.

A minute ago, you will say, I had an organization and now I am accepting employment. We say: precisely.

What about my old associates? The simple fact is this: they have begged you to accept the job. You have told them that you do not want to go. You have asked them what you should do. And they have all told you to take the job. If you phrase your dilemma correctly – as if it were they who were being offered the job – there is not one of them who will dare to accuse you of deserting them.

But – but – but—

No buts. Everything is taken care of.

But

(1) Why have I been offered this job and not any

XXIII

EARLY IN 1960, Beetle was again pregnant. She was not disposed to have the baby in Spain. I now had hopes of making enough money to afford the rent of somewhere in England, even if it meant doing things I did not want to do. Our prospects changed with a telegram from George Greenfield. *The Limits of Love* had won the Lippincott Prize, which guaranteed an advance of $2,500; the same sum would be devoted to publicising the book. Confident that he would share my pleasure, I wrote to tell Bob Gutwillig about the Lippincott Prize. He responded that if I was going to be a success, there was no point in continuing to know me. I took it that he was congratulating me. Perhaps he was. I never heard from him again.

Life in Fuengirola had been a liberation. I worked harder and better than I ever had before. I did not have to be anything I did not want to be; nor was I aware of what my contemporaries and supposed rivals were doing. My idea of being a writer has never had anything to do with social or careerist ambition; revenge is the sharpest spur. I wanted only to write the books I wanted to write and have them published. I might be a prig (no ignoble condition), but I was never calculating; I had no wish to please, although I am always pleased to do so. I took my chances, perhaps too many, but

I never schemed to obtain them; nor did I belong to any artistic or political group. Larry Potter's favourite character was Steppenwolf and I understood why, even though I have never much admired Hermann Hesse. Kipling's lonely cat is more my style.

In early May, we loaded the Ford Anglia with all our belongings and set off for Gibraltar, slowly; PLD 75 had developed a tendency to boil if I drove at more than 25 miles an hour. We decided that Beetle should fly home from Gibraltar with Paul. I would drive our lame and rusting motor back to England, where we could now afford to change it for something better. Beetle hoped that my parents would allow her to have her summer baby at 12 Balliol House. My mother suggested a good nursing home in Wimbledon.

I cannot remember having any thought or emotion as I trundled northwards. Is there really such a thing as the stream of consciousness? Alone, I neither dreaded England nor looked forward to it. My slow, loaded progress attracted no hitch-hikers. As I drove the long, straight road between the pine forests of Les Landes, the fumes from the car contributed to a blinding headache. I had to pull in and lie down in a dry ditch, where I slept almost literally like the dead for nearly three hours. That evening, at a restaurant in Vendôme where the *Michelin Guide* promised a generous meal for less than a pound, a large gentleman sat at an adjacent table, a white poodle on a chair next to him, a napkin as its supplementary collar.

I stayed a night or two in Paris and loitered, as usual, at the stacked tables at the Librairie La Hune. Scanning the Impressionists at the Jeu de Paume, I bumped into Julian Jebb and a party of friends, including Gillian Tindall. Julian had performed a number of mine in Brian Marber's Footlights show: 'Willie, Willie Somerset Maugham / You're at the top of the literary form / You'll be going on fine / Till you're ninety-nine / Willie, Willie, Somerset Maugham'. Julian was good casting for the Old Party; he was prematurely aged, small, clever and homosexual.

I expected it to be a relief to have congenial company in Paris. I resumed, with reluctant readiness, a more English persona than I had inhabited in Andalucia. I am not sure whether Julian was, as they used to say, a 'Roman', but la Tindall (an expert in French matters) certainly was. She was good-looking, fair and not amused by my patter. Years later, a novel of Ms Tindall's came to me for review. I did not much admire it, for spelt-out, objective reasons. She wrote me a letter accusing me of personal animus because she had not fancied me when we met in Paris. I had not been aware that I was a candidate for her favours. I have never met her again, though I have admired some of her non-fiction, and have said so in print.

Back in England, luck took the ladylike form of Dudy Nimmo's Newnham friend Anne Moore, who owned a furnished cottage in East Bergholt, Suffolk, and was looking for a tenant. Her tall, cadaverous husband Richard had been a lank-haired Liberal committeeman in the Cambridge Union. He now worked at the *News Chronicle*. When, to check some detail about our tenancy, I called the paper and asked to be put through to him, he picked up the phone and said, 'Leaders'. Beetle, Paul and I moved into the Old Mill House, East Bergholt, soon after my return to London, where my first move had been to trade in PLD 75, for whatever Beetle's cousin Geoffrey was genial enough to give us. We acquired a new, spacious, grey Standard Ensign with red upholstery.

I sent a freshly typed copy of *The Roper House* to Betty Judkins at Jan van Loewen's office. When I went to see her, she told me that, in the unlikely event that the play even got into rehearsal, it would be only a day or two before it was found to be unperformable. I took one more look at the polka-dotted tart still on patrol on the far side of Shaftesbury Avenue and left the office for good. I never showed *The Roper House* to anyone else. Fifteen years later, Stephen Taylor and his long-suffering, overweight wife became characters in the third of my television series *The Glittering Prizes*. Eric Porter, not the least critical of actors, did not have any problem saying my lines.

The Limits of Love was due to be published in mid-June. Richard

Gregson's confidence and range as an agent had grown in our absence. He arranged for me to meet Wolf Mankowitz, who was looking for a writer to adapt a novel entitled *Memoirs of a Cross-Eyed Man* into a vehicle for Peter Sellers, whose life and appearance had been transformed by being cast opposite Sophia Loren in *The Millionairess*. Pudgy, pasty-faced, bespectacled Peter, for whom Roy Speer had said the radio might have been made because no audience would ever choose to look at him, fell so thumpingly in love with Sophia that he had willed and dieted himself into being handsome. Vocal versatility was transmuted into facial refinement and tailored elegance. He wore slick glasses and went to Dougie Hayward for his suits ('clobber' as Leslie Bricusse would say).

Mankowitz too had been an East End boy. Clever enough to get into Cambridge, he was quick to become a follower of Frank Leavis. In his single precocious contribution to *Scrutiny*, he followed the Downing party line in lambasting the incoherent vatic verbosity of Dylan Thomas (had Richard Burton known of this disparagement of Welsh genius, his diaries might have been less admiring of Wolf's 'poetic' strain). If the graduate Mankowitz ever considered an academic career, he lacked patience for its small increments. Like the scholarly George Engel, Wolf had the intelligence to make himself the master of a somewhat abstruse subject, Wedgwood china, on which he wrote what remains the standard monograph.

In 1953, he had published *A Kid for Two Farthings*, a brief, pseudo-folkloric novella in which he revisited Spitalfields and turned the Jewish East End into London's version of Sholem Aleichem's Pale of Settlement. By the time I went to his office, above his Wedgwood store in Piccadilly arcade, Wolf had revised his accent backwards. It chimed with that of a rough, tough, street-wise businessman. Who would guess that the other side of his coin carried the image of a Downing man of letters? Wolf had the mimic's contempt for one-track minds and singular ambitions. My unmitigated accent led him to say that he wasn't buying any bloody Cambridge crap. Desert-booted feet on the desk, he played with an oversized matchbox which he slid open to reveal rubber-banded rolls of £5 notes. He was seeing a lot of people who were likely to be better qualified to do this script for Peter than I was, but he would let me know. I had the feeling that I had been summoned in order to witness how a clever Cantab East Ender, with a few bob, could work both sides of the street and still have time to write a show-biz A-Z for the *Evening Standard*. What we had in common emphasised the difference between us. Boasting of his photographer son's rampant sexuality, he spoke of him being 'stalky', a locution I have never heard elsewhere.

The Old Mill House had been built by John Constable's father. It was a grey stuccoed cottage down a hedged lane, a few hundred yards outside East Bergholt, near the Manningtree Road. Our only neighbours, in a cottage further down the lane, were Tom and Molly Cheale. Now a gamekeeper for the local land- and orchard-owning Eely family, Tom had survived being a prisoner of war after the capture of Singapore. He never complained and he never ate rice. I worked in a glassed first-floor conservatory, overlooking the lawn, which I had promised Anne Moore that I would keep mown. The vegetable patch outside the red-tiled kitchen was thick with asparagus and red-buttoned with raspberries.

Beetle was determined to have her new baby at home. Nurse Bray was a seasoned midwife, recommended by Dr MacBride, who would be available if needed. I made my last flannelled appearance on a cricket field, playing for East Bergholt. I made seven not out and bowled a couple of loose overs. I even persuaded Beetle that we should be better integrated if she went to a meeting of the local Women's Institute. She did so just once. Mrs Jenkins and Mrs Smith came for two hours twice a week and Miss Ireland when asked, to do the ironing. Miss Ireland, who was scarcely five feet tall, drove a large old Morris eight. On its way up the lane, it appeared to be empty. As it got closer, Miss Ireland's eyes could be seen looking out from under the brim of the big steering wheel, her hands higher than the top of her head.

East Bergholt had two famous living inhabitants: Randolph Churchill, who lorded at Stour House, a large pink Regency building facing out over the rolling pasture down to the river for which it was named, and Paul Jennings, who lived with his wife and six children adjacent to the Franciscan priory. Jennings was the weekly author of the *Oddly Enough* column in *The Observer*. His whimsical wit was collected in a Penguin entitled *Jenguin Pennings*. Another collection had been called *Oddly Bodlikins*. When I went into the village shop-cum-post office, I was glad to see packets of typing paper on one of the shelves. The shopkeeper was sorry but they were reserved for Mr Churchill. He had an undeniable need of instant supplies. When I dared to say that, in a democracy, shops should not withhold goods on display, I prevailed, just.

Randolph had a purple temper and was no respecter of the lower orders. When he called at one of the local garages for petrol, he lowered the window as little as possible and thrust a suitable bank note through it. The garageman, Arnold Handley, who became a friend of ours, was a red-haired ex-Communist ex-schoolteacher. When he brought the change, in coins, he posted them back through the crack in the window so that they fell all over the floor. Churchill said that he need not expect to enjoy his custom again. Arnold said, 'You got the point then.'

Randolph was not only a regular journalist but also in charge of the many volumes of his father's biography. He supervised and depended on a series of, so to speak, galley slaves who were quartered in the partitioned dormitory floor of Stour. Daylight reached them through Georgian windows which were rarely centred in the walls of their gimcrack accommodation. Some of the bedrooms had only a share of a window to themselves. Martin Gilbert, who later achieved fame as a historian, especially of the Holocaust, was one of Randolph's most reliable, and relied upon, assistants. When Randolph died, Gilbert ceased to be a ghost and became the accredited author of the last six volumes.

Martin told me, years later, that we must have been neighbours in East Bergholt at much the same time. He was, in effect, Randolph's social secretary as well as amanuensis. When overtures were made, by the producer Jack Le Vien, for an American TV series of Winston's life, Randolph determined to entertain him in style. Having summoned his oriental cook (his English ones had all left within a week), he demanded that, for once in his life, he produce something edible for their distinguished guest. The cook rose to the challenge by packing his bags and walking out. Randolph asked Martin to book dinner at the best local hostelry. There happened to be an excellent restaurant in nearby Stratford St Mary.

Jack Le Vien arrived and was primed with champagne before the three of them repaired to Le Talbooth. The thatched Tudor building pleased the guest. The sedulous attention of the owner, Gerry Milsom, brought out Randolph's most amiable aspect. After the meal was ordered, the wine list was proffered. Randolph said, 'What would the sommelier suggest to give delight to Mr Le Vien?' The wine waiter indicated one of the listed bottles. 'This one is very popular, sir,' he said. Randolph said, '*Popular?* What leads you to presume that I should ever want to drink anything POPULAR?'

One evening, I shared a third-class compartment with Paul Jennings on the train from London. Since I had heard him to be a piously uxorious Catholic, I remarked on the enlivening uses of adultery in making the marital world go round. Making oneself obnoxious to famous persons is not an unknown form of self-introduction, but I did not have much success. Some time later, I happened to buy the new Penguin pocket dictionary. Whether through sly intention or comic chance, the pairs of words that showed the first and last entry on each page had generated comic hyphenates: 'corkscrew-cornetto, fruitless-fuck' and so on. I sent word to our neighbour Mr Jennings, as a sort of apology perhaps, alerting him to the fun that he might have with these and other conjunctions. A few weeks later, his *Observer* column made protracted and witty use of them. He sent me neither a copy nor a word of thanks. There was no obligation to do so; that is what might have made it stylish if he had.

I finished *The S Man* and delivered it to Tom Maschler. A sustained piece of wilful cynicism, it merited the pseudonym, Mark Caine, that we clapped on it. A typical passage read 'The success believes in the team. (His team.) The success believes in the loyalty of the team. (To him.) He believes that the team should stick together. (Until he wants to dissolve it.) He believes that the company comes first. (As long as he is first in the company.) He believes that if everyone can come up with just one more good idea, final success is inevitable. (For him.)' I left the business of selling to Tom. He reported that Ian Hamilton at Hutchinson's was enthusiastic, although he accused Tom of 'bargaining like an Armenian'. A profitable deal was closed; the book would be out in time for Christmas.

Richard Gregson sent me to meet Stella Richman, who had been put in charge of drama for Lew Grade's Associated Television. The best TV plays were generally agreed to come from the stable of writers put together for ABC TV's 'Armchair Theatre' by Sidney Newman, a Canadian dramaturge with modish left-wing connections and ambitions. Expecting sceptical interrogation, I was greeted with immediate enthusiasm by a small, dark-haired woman. At once confident and unassuming, she was sure that *The Limits of Love* was going to be a big success, although she cannot have seen a word of it.

The ex-wife of Alec Clunes, Stella had been an actress and was alert to the prime importance of dialogue. She had a weekly drama slot to fill, directly after *Sunday Night at the London Palladium*. Lew had left the choice of material to her; we could do whatever we chose, as long as the ratings didn't dive. The first thing she offered me was a treatment by Truman Capote, entitled *Answered Prayers* (he later applied it to another work altogether). Set in New York, its plot featured a prototypical S Man who gets his comeuppance from a woman who, when we went into production, was played by Maggie Tyzack.

To be in at the creation of TV drama and to have Stella for impresario was to join the happiest school I ever attended. She commissioned one play after another and they were usually in rehearsal no more than a few weeks after delivery. Since those early pieces were performed live, in the studio, in front of cumbrous cameras, the stories depended on the words and on expert playing. It became my habit to start a new 48-minute play on Monday morning and finish it by Wednesday afternoon. I revised it on Thursday and posted it to Stella on the Friday. She or her script editor, Lew Griefer, whom it took no great wit to label 'the script-griefer', made brief comments, to which I responded promptly and I then had the fun of going to rehearsal. Lew was an ex-Communist, now in analysis; either Marx or Freud supplied the maquettes on which all his proposed emendations were based. Stella did not insist that I bend with his predictable wind. There was, I soon discovered, nothing so educational as hearing actors saying one's lines. It made me instantly alert to false quantities in the text and often able to interpose solutions before there was a problem. Rehearsal was, as Americans used to say, the best fun you could have with your clothes on.

One day, a youngish actor came up to me, as we were having a break, and asked whether I would mind if he asked me something. I imagined that he wanted a cut line restored or another added, but his question was 'Do you seriously think that thermonuclear war is likely to break out in the near future?' Not displeased to be taken for a pundit, I delivered a reasonable account, on the one hand and on the other, of why I thought that neither we nor the Russians had anything to gain and hence … etcetera. He attended to my lecture with the blinks and nods of a serious pupil and thanked me very much. As I finished my cold coffee, young Carmen Silvera touched me on the shoulder and said, 'Darling, do you mind if I tell you something?'

'Of course not.'

'When an actor comes up to you and asks you if you think that humanity can survive or whether strontium 90 is poisoning the water supply or the dictatorship of the proletariat will be good for the arts, there is one answer and only one: you put your hand on his arm and say, "Before I say anything else, let me tell you that you are giving a *fantastic* performance."'

The Limits of Love was published at the beginning of the summer. I woke up and found myself very well noticed. Peter Forster, in the *Daily Express*, devoted most of a broadsheet page to proclaim me 'a really remarkable new talent'. The characters in my book were said, in Graham Greene's words, to 'walk off the page into life'. Desmond Flower announced a reprint of my 'considerable achievement' almost as quickly as Victor Gollancz.

My feeling was more of relief than of exhilaration. In my callous innocence, I had no apprehension that any of the people on whom my lively characters were based might take offence. In fact, Beetle's sisters were dismayed by what I took the liberty of saying about quite recognisable versions of their marriages. I was embarrassed but, in truth, indifferent. Graham Greene had written of the sliver of ice in every genuine novelist's heart; if I must choose between a telling portrait and its subject's good humour, I seldom hesitate.

I had dedicated the novel both to Beetle and to Paul (*absit omen*, since my leading character bore his name) and I thanked St John's College for the money which the reverend Harper Wood had allowed them to bestow on me. It did not occur to me that Renford Bambrough, who had been my benefactor, would read my book or that he would take the character of Thornton Ashworth to be his portrait, although in many regards it was. Renford never mentioned the book to me, which is the only way, apart from his cool courtesies, that I knew that I had hurt him. I had assumed, conveniently, that scholars were above petty resentment.

I had a quick call from Wolf Mankowitz: if I was going to be some kind of a success, we should talk again. I was vain and subservient enough to honour his summons. He gave me the job, preceded by a few hints on what he and Peter wanted. The *Memoirs of a Cross-Eyed Man* began with its hero on the Rock of Gibraltar. Wolf had the idea he should throw a banana to one of the Barbary apes. 'The ape catches it, looks at it and throws it back. You take it from there.' And so I did, for fifteen hundred quid.

By the time I delivered the first draft of the screenplay, Wolf's association with Peter Sellers had broken up. There was no point in going any further with the script. I was paid off and went back to working for Stella Richman on an original idea of mine entitled *A Well-Dressed Man*. Three or four years later, I bumped into Wolf at the bar of the White Elephant Club in Curzon Street. Then the smartest showbiz hang-out in the West End, it was run by Stella Richman and her husband Victor Brusa. Wolf told me that he had just signed a three-picture deal to write and produce for Columbia Pictures, whose executives were not the smartest people he had ever met. He had found in his files this old screenplay that he had paid some donkey or other pennies to write for Peter Sellers. He had just sold the whole idea to Columbia and he was getting $150,000 for what amounted to some nipping and tucking on this old piece of junk, which was not actually as bad as he remembered.

Since I was busy with other things, I contrived to look impressed at the way in which he had fooled the fools. Something in my expression must have given Wolf pause. He looked at me and said, 'Freddie, listen, when you're free, if ever, I've got a project I'd like to talk to you about. For proper money this time.'

Wolf's shamelessness led me to assume that he must have an accountant capable of the kind of legitimate cunning that would enable one to circumvent the current punitive rates of income tax. He recommended a man called Cyril Glass. He took me on as if he were doing me a favour and seemed to have clever ideas about offshore tax havens and all the rest of the devices that, in the 1960s, were not deemed disreputable. A learned judge had ruled that honest citizens had a perfect right to avoid tax, but not to evade it. The implication was that, as in the case of death duties, one was either a fool or a saint if one did not take evasive action. Cyril put me into various schemes, commonplace for big earners in showbiz, and I made no objection. Later, one of them was adjudged to be more like evasion than avoidance, but I escaped public whipping by paying up. Cyril told me that he had a girlfriend, of the venal kind, who liked him to fuck her from behind. It was not that she enjoyed it more that way, but it allowed her to smoke a cigarette and look at a magazine while Cyril did his stuff.

A Well-Dressed Man told the story of a lonely man who hears an appeal for a witness to come forward to save a man accused of murder from being hanged. My Little Guy cannot resist being the Alibi Ike to whom, he imagines, an innocent man will be eternally grateful. He commits generous perjury by vouching for the guilty man's presence far from the scene of the crime, just for the grace of really mattering to someone. He then goes home, to resume playing chess by correspondence with a pen pal in Australia. Then the door bell goes and there is Mr Tattooed, shaven-headed Beefy who says, 'Hullo, friend.' End of Part One. In Part Two, the little man is so cruelly used by his parasitic tenant that he does him in. When I attended the first rehearsal, the two actors – one Peter Sallis, an old pro still at the receipt of custom, and big, bald Kenneth J. Warren, who died several years ago – were so hilariously straight-faced that their author literally fell off his chair and took several seconds to compose himself.

In time, the piece was sold to a number of foreign countries. One day, I was telephoned by a French producer lady, who wanted to tell me how well it had played. I asked her how long it had run in translation. 'We did it in three half-hour episodes,' she said. I said, 'That's twice as long as when we did it.' 'We had a very imaginative translator,' she said. 'Tell me,' I said, 'did people laugh at all?' 'Excuse me?' 'Did it get some laughs, *quelques rires*, the play?' '*Rires? Mais pas du tout*. Mr Raphael, you need not worry. We took your work as seriously as it deserves.' 'If not more so,' I said.

A Pinewood producer called Leslie Parkyn had seen Peter Forster's

review and my name on the bestseller list. He and his partner, Julian Win-
tle, would appreciate it if I would come to Pinewood and talk over an idea
they had. I hoped that they wanted to do a realistic movie based on *The
Limits of Love*, although I guessed that they were attracted more by the title
than the content. The project for which they thought me suitable was to
be a vehicle for Cliff Richard, about a Butlin's camp. They were planning
to have about sixteen songs in the show and they needed a storyline that
would link them together. I went back to writing plays for Stella Richman.

Sarah was being born while I wheeled Paul around East Bergholt. After
a longish labour, Nurse Bray panicked calmly and called in Doctor Mac-
Bride. I did not go upstairs until I heard Sarah cry. Then I cooked green
beans for lunch. Before she left the Old Mill House, Nurse Bray handed me
a brown-paper parcel, doubled knotted with strong string. 'The afterbirth.
You might like to bury it in the garden.' I dug a deep hole at the back of the
now overgrown asparagus bed and put the package into it, as if it contained
contraband. We had bought Paul a scooter, which was now revealed. When
he spoke to my mother, he said, 'Got a sister, got a cooter.'

I often took Paul shopping with me in the Ensign. There was a wide red
leather divider between the front seats, on which he sat to be able to look
through the windscreen. One evening, coming back from Dedham, a cat
ran suddenly in front of the car. Like a good BSM graduate, I emergency-
braked and avoided hitting it. I looked across and Paul was not sitting next
to me. The car seemed empty, except for me. Paul was under the dashboard, in an unhurt huddle. I put him back on the divider and we drove
home. From that day on, whenever I braked whatever car I was driving,
until we became accustomed to seat-belts, I tended to put my outstretched
arm across in front of the passenger.

The S Man was reviewed in the *Daily Telegraph* by Peter Green. Having
no idea that I was any part of the pseudonymous author, he denounced its
endorsement of opportunism and took it as a symptom of the sickness of

Harold Macmillan's materialistic England. In her review, in some glossy print, Elizabeth Jane Howard perceived the glittering lineaments of Laclos's *Liaisons Dangereuses*. One of my naughtinesses was to advise the S Man to take care to hang his school cap in the hall when he was in bed with his boss's wife. Despite the limited experience to which Celia Ramsey had drawn attention, I have never found it difficult to imagine a life unlike the one I have lived or to anatomise the kind of careerism on which I was too fine, or too squeamish, to embark.

A Spanish girl came to live with us in the Old Mill House as an *au pair* girl. Cristina Baselga came from a comfortable family in Zaragossa; she had never had to do any domestic work. We suffered her indolence for a while and then I did what had worked with my house platoon: I told her that we all had our parts to play in the house and, although I knew she was principally concerned to learn English, she had to pretend to be of help or she would have to go home. She took direction without complaint. When the *Tonight* programme came on the television set that Beetle's mother had passed on to us (it had decorous doors that could be closed over the screen), Cristina watched and listened to Fyfe Robertson and Cliff Michelmore before he moved on with Derek Hart and she went to give Paul his supper. Cristina and my fat brown volume of Lorca reminded me of how much I missed Spain.

Mrs Jenkins brought us pheasants for two and sixpence each. We were instructed to hang them by the claws until they fell to the ground. We were too squeamish to wait that long. People sometimes drove down at the weekend, Tom Maschler more often than most, with a succession of girls. My old headmonitor, Jeremy Atkinson, wrote to ask if he and Janet and their two children might come by and stay the night. Somehow we accommodated them. When Beetle proposed the same menu for her children as she was giving Paul, Janet said, 'That would be all right.' We were not asked if we ever came north (they were living in Harrowgate, where Jeremy worked for ICI) and should not, in any case, have imposed ourselves on them. In principle, we drive for pleasure only in a southward direction.

Beetle relished our rustic seclusion. She had the children and she had the garden. Country life was without stress and without loud incident. I worked all week, went to London to rehearse, when I was needed. I was glad to take the opportunity to play a few rubbers of bridge before driving home. There was no speed limit, except in built-up areas. After rush hour, I could drive the 70 miles back to 'dear old Bergholt', as Constable called it, in under two hours. There was only one thing wrong, from my point of view, in living in an English arcadia: during all the time that we lived at the Old Mill House, I produced many pages of script, but never a line of fiction.

into what you want. Believe me, you would not regret becoming my mistress.'

Joyce said: 'You're making yourself utterly ridiculous.'

'I don't think so. If I were utterly ridiculous you would tell your husband and your friends of this incident, but the fact is you will not do so. Ever. Hence this is not merely a conversation; it is an experience. Which is also, by the way, why we made nothing further of our little—fracas, shall we say?—through the open window. I am a very wealthy man. What I say is not ridiculous. The settings alone guarantee the play a certain run.'

Joyce said: 'Why should I ever want to—have a love affair with you?'

'For no reason. I did not say love. I notice it cost you an effort. Love is quite superfluous here. It need not form part of our calculations. It is nothing to do with what we shall do for each other. I can recognize the trapped and to release you would excite me very much.'

'I find you quite repulsive,' Joyce said.

'That is part of what excites me. I have a certain grudge against you. I admit it—an experience of very small public importance is responsible. I don't speak of it. So you see, we have a certain need of each other which can only be gratified by accident. The joy of it is that I expect nothing of you and you need hope for nothing from me. I shall give you presents, of course, that goes without saying, but nothing else; I shall not hope to have achieved anything with you. We shall take it and leave it, to put it crudely, though in public—in the narrow public life we shall have—I can promise you complete deference and the kind of luxury which, in the first place, made you want, so to say, to run into me. Anything that you want I shall do my best to gratify, in that

The Graduate Wife

XXIV

WHEN SARAH WAS a few months old, Beetle and I left the children with my mother and went to Paris for a few days. Being alone together, and out of England, made us lovers again; but not the same lovers who lived in those cold rooms in Crimée. We hurried to retrieve what we did not quite admit to each other that we feared we were losing. In the list of films in the *Semaine de Paris*, I saw one which was synopsised as being about an engaged couple going, with a party of smart people, to an Aeolian island where the woman, Anna, disappears. *L'Avventura* was on, in *version originale*, in a small cinema off the Boul' Mich'.

Michelangelo Antonioni's world, in which couples could be more remote in the light of the desire between them, was unnervingly evocative. Caressed by her director's camera, Monica Vitti was a vulnerable goddess, tipped almost against her will into replacing her friend in the affection of a weak charmer whom she knows she would be, and then is, a fool to love. The uneasy and unhurried rhythm of the movie, Giovanni Fusco's pulsing music, the story's lack of resolution, gave the adventure an asymmetrical elegance that I had never before seen in a movie. Antonioni's art was so different from, and so indifferent to, routine cinema that it was both more acute and more enigmatic than that of any other director. We both fell in love with the movie, though not in the same way. I recognised and I feared what I saw in common between me and Sandro, the one-time visionary architect who had settled for an easy life; I also feared that I could see something in Beetle's beauty, not in anything she actually said or necessarily felt, that passed judgement on my facility.

During supper at the Acropole (red linen napkins extra), just off the Boule' Mich', another look at the *Semaine de Paris* told me that *L'Avventura* was showing, in a French version, at a cinema near the Opéra; we went to see it again. A single viewing had sealed the piece into my mind. I noticed that a small scene, of no great consequence, had been cut in the French version. As we were leaving, I approached the manager in the foyer with the righteousness of the convert and said, '*En coupant une scène clé, monsieur, vous avez mutilé un chef-d'oeuvre.*' He said, '*Ecoutez, monsieur, le dernier métro va partir dans deux minutes. Mes clients préfèrent respecter leurs horaires quotidiens plutôt que de voir quelques moments de plus d'un film qui, pour pas mal d'entre eux, traîne considérablement.*' '*C'est un crime contre l'art du cinéma.*' '*Vous avez le droit, peut-être les moyens, de rester sentimental, monsieur. Moi, j'ai mon métier à faire. Bonne nuit.*'

L'Avventura was a talisman of a kind of creative cinema in which John Paddy Carstairs and his Pinewood peers had no place. Antonioni seemed to be an artist who knew precisely what he was doing, although what it meant was somewhat concealed from the audience; that, I was sure, was part of his magic. *L'Avventura* defeated expectation, turned each moment into some part of a whole that was never disclosed. Why did Anna disappear on that Aeolian island and what became of her? It was a thriller without thrills, a love story with a sorry ending, at once incomplete and completely satisfying.

I should discover, in time, that Antonioni's project had been blown off its original course by a series of accidents, the worst being that the company was stranded on that bleak island by lack of funds. Lea Massari, who played the elusive Anna, had caught pneumonia and could not return to do whatever Michelangelo and the screenwriter Tonino Guerra had planned for her to do. What seemed an impeccable and seamless innovation had been, in large part, improvised and patched together; but it was a patchwork contrived by a master.

In the spring of 1961, Cristina Baselga went back to Spain. I envied her. She was replaced by a fair-haired Irish girl called Siobhan O'Malley. Anne Moore had set no term on our time in the Old Mill House, but she now wanted either to sell it or to let it on a long lease. I knew that Beetle was happier than I was, but I chose to think that she did not want forever to live in a Suffolk village with no life outside the house and the garden. Our trip to Paris had reminded me of what we were missing. I had corresponded with Harry Gordon. His regular script reminded me of a world elsewhere. One of his letters told me that there was a house to let for June and July, big enough for the four of us, and our new help, on the *carretera* opposite our football field. The Villa Antoñita (nominally reminiscent of the director whose film had rekindled my interest in cinema) had a large square tower with a secluded room where I could work.

Something prevents me from recalling clearly in what spirit, and after what discussion, we moved out of the Old Mill House. Beetle and I had unshared attitudes to leaving it. I had no regrets; she did. I was sure that, one way or another, I could make enough money, even when out of the country, to keep the family and I thought that that was all that could be expected of me. Beetle had her children; I wanted to be the writer I had been in Fuengirola and not since.

Stella Richman promised that being abroad need not prevent me from writing more plays for her. The last piece of work I did before we left the Old Mill House was an adaptation of a very short story by Stanley Ellin, 'The Best of Everything'. Set in New York, it featured a social climbing outsider who happens to share a table in a crowded diner with a disgraced playboy, to whom he offers a bed in return for instruction into how to pass for an Ivy League smart-ass. It took me the usual three days to transpose the plot to London, where Ellin's Jimmy became a West End estate agent's clerk and his tutor a remittance man called Charlie Prince.

Siobhan seemed excited at the prospect of going to Spain. She went on a short holiday to Ireland to see her boyfriend, but came back, slightly against our expectations, with his blessing. We put the furniture from the Old Mill House into storage. The removals man, who had seen us into the house a few months before, said, 'You've got itchy feet.'

I should have known that we could not step in the same Fuengirola twice. Even in 1961, the summer months on the Costa del Sol were thick with tourists. Traffic and crowded beaches dispelled the timelessness of Juan Ramón's *'Catedral pobre, al sur, en el trigo de estío / cuando el sol puro es miel de los rosetones…'* We were richer, for the moment, not happier. I worked up in the tower, the door shut, in a big room, but I lacked the fluency that I had taken for granted in the Calle Tostón. Salvadora was busy and came only a few times to cook us a meal. We had a full-time *muchacha* called Maria, a big, good-looking, unsmiling girl who worked because she had to and who made no pretence of caring who we were. Unlike Salvadora, she was not particularly nice to Paul or to Sarah. At the smallest hint of reproach, she would say *'Yo mi marcho a mi casa.'* We went into Málaga in the new car and, as before but not quite, we bought food and toys in the market before going to Antonio's bar. He was older and, it seemed, more lame.

I started a new novella, *The Graduate Wife*, to go in a twin-pack with *The Trouble with England*. It was set in a duplicate of the Old Mill House, but the couple whom I depicted as living there were based on the Atkinsons, whose condescending visit excited satirical accuracy. I imagined their doubles in a sardonic, very English tone which kept the author at a distance. I no longer had any inclination to self-portraiture in my work. I might be more sure of myself as a writer, but I was less sure of what I was, or should be. The less I thought about myself, the more mature, and the more English, my work seemed to be, and the more distant from Beetle and from myself. I did not hurry to show her my daily pages; a symptom, perhaps of Antonioni's '*incommunicabilità*', perhaps of a sense of no longer being as important to her as I was before we had children.

It was too hot for football. Harry Gordon and I played tennis on the tiled court within the walls of *El Alemán's* villa. After a sweaty hour, we could dive into its adjacent pool. Harry had digested the consequences of the death of hard-edge and concluded that he would have to go back to New York City and take a job in advertising. Our talks of the previous year had been full of the romance of the artistic life, remote and dedicated, but now the big city seemed nearer. Beetle had two babies and she wanted somewhere permanent to live.

One afternoon, walking home, with my tennis racket, from the Casino Bar in the centre of Fuengirola, I met a large man in a tracksuit who was carrying a meshed sack full of tennis balls. He seemed to fill the pavement. He said, 'You play tennis?' 'I play a little tennis.' 'I play with Jock Krommer on the West Coast. You want, I learn you. My name is Boris.' 'I don't really…' 'You play doubles?' 'Can happen.' 'I play you with my son Sasha.' Because he was in my way, I agreed that Beetle and I would meet Boris and his son on the German's court the following afternoon. She had not played recently, but she had a strong forehand. Competition brought out the best in her game and character. It must be admitted that Sasha did not have the best possible footgear for the fast tiled court: he wore heavy rubber-soled boots. Boris produced several aces but was unduly ambitious at the net. When Beetle did not pass him, I produced lobs that left Sasha stranded. We won 6–4, 6–3. No arrangement was made for a return match. When we got back to the Villa Antoñita, Beetle said, 'We learned them.'

Harry Gordon had a birthday in June. We left the children with Siobhan and drove the Gordons in our new car up to Granada to hear Andrés

Segovia give a solo concert in the Court of the Lions in the Alhambra. We stayed the night at the Alhambra Palace and drank gin fizzes on the long, narrow terrace that stood high above the plain. Somewhere out there in the haze was the village where Garcia Lorca lived and was murdered. The Granada Palace's many bedrooms opened off long, wide corridors that reminded me of the one along which Monica Vitti ran, with elegant awkwardness, when she realised, early in the morning, that Sandro was not in the room with her. She ran and ran until she came to the deserted public rooms. In the last of them, she saw Sandro with the call girl whom they had seen, and pitied, if not despised, in an earlier scene. Beauty was not enough for him, nor was happiness.

On the day Hemingway died, 2 July, several people, some I did not know, came to the Villa Antoñita as if they needed the comfort of some kind of informal formality. One was a guy who wrote pulp fiction short stories. Harry Gordon said that he had 'a problem with Jews and blacks': he didn't like them. Charlie Reiter drove up in a black VW with his beautiful blonde opera singer wife, Anne. He had written a stream-of-consciousness novella which he gave me to read. Barnie Rosset's Grove Press was almost certainly going to publish it. The story was about a man, in New York on business, who is treated to a black call girl by whoever he just closed a deal with. She is very good-looking, cool and articulate. They have dinner and he gets to know her, he imagines, a little too well for the occasion to remain a commercial fantasy. She comes back with him to his hotel, but he cannot bring himself to treat her like the sexual treat he has been promised. He tells her that he likes her too much to want to go on. She says, more or less, 'And how about what I want?' It was well done, although I could imagine Bob Gutwillig wanting work done on it. Harry Gordon liked Charlie less than I did; he regarded him as some kind of a 'reproduction Ivy League dude'. Charlie and Anne looked like the perfect handsome couple, but she, it emerged, was more interested in her career than in being a wife. Like many opera singers, she was disciplined, dedicated and implacably self-involved.

Porter Sneyd also brought some of his work for me to see. He had a wispy beard, like a cashiered mandarin official, and wrote very short, 'experimental' stories; part of the experiment appeared to be that they dispensed with grammar, plot and characters. Porter's wife, whom he called 'Mitch', was scrawny in appearance and even in voice. I had no idea what they lived on, perhaps a disability pension. 'Mitch' had some unspecified chronic debility. They rented a small house up in the foothills towards Mijas.

Later in the summer, Charlie told Harry Gordon that he went to call on the Sneyds and found that Porter had gone to Málaga to sign some papers. 'She was lying there on the couch, in some kind of a wrapper, and she told me how Porter never did it any more and she probably never would herself and that's what she was thinking about, if I really wanted to know. So I thought, why not do her a small favour? What harm could it do? I did it strictly for her sake, but you know what? It felt good.' Charlie's book got published, but I never heard that he wrote another. He went to live in California and became a union executive, edited the local magazine and became fat. He told Harry Gordon that he was very happy with the way things turned out.

There was an outbreak of smallpox on the Costa del Sol that summer. We asked Siobhan whether she had been vaccinated. She had not. We urged her to go to Dr Verdugo as soon as possible. She announced that she preferred to 'battle against it with my own resources'. She certainly looked very well. When my parents came to see us, my mother described her as 'blooming'. Siobhan told Beetle that she found Spanish food very fattening; she had had to let out her skirts. The obvious question had to be put: 'Are you by any chance pregnant?'

'Impossible. Out of the question.'

'Impossible in what sense?'

'There's no way whatsoever I can be pregnant.'

My parents' visit added tension to the household. Irene was only fifty years old, but her skin was too delicate for the beach. The days were long and very hot. We went out in the car and we came back. I persuaded Salvadora to come and cook the occasional meal of her remembered specialities, but Irene had small appetite. One evening, when we were at table, Paul leaned across and kissed Beetle on the arm. My mother burst into tears. If my father was embarrassed by our looks of amazed exasperation, he felt obliged to defend his wife. I cannot recall what was said to have made her unhappy, but it was not admitted to be jealousy. Was she distressed by Paul's show of spontaneous filial affection of a kind that I had never offered? The scene was charged with unsaid things. I had two small children and I was about to be thirty years old. When, in his terse, tight-lipped way, my father made it clear that Beetle and, more particularly, I had not welcomed them as warmly as they had wished, I heard myself say, 'Why don't you fuck off out of my life and leave us alone?'

A Wild Surmise was published that summer and received even better reviews, in smarter places, than *The Limits of Love*; but it did not figure on the bestseller list. When Tom Maschler came down to Fuengirola to visit us, he promised, with aggressive candour, that I needed a more forceful publisher than Desmond Flower and his son Nicholas, who preferred motorbikes to books. *The S Man* had been bought by Penguins, with a £750 advance. It seemed a lot, but my share was soon gone. Tom was about to move to Jonathan Cape and was able, and willing, to play the part of literary patron. With favours to dispense, he was invited to meals in the houses of all the so-called writers in Fuengirola.

By some means, Tom acquired a packet of hash from Morocco and proposed that we all get together, smoke pot and use the Gordons' tape recorder to preserve the consequent conversation. It was a kind of chaste orgy in which we were all expected to make raw revelations. We smoked the stuff and sat there, for quite a long time, trying to be daring, or not, and then we stopped. When the tape was played back, it proved only that people under the influence of marijuana were likely to be very slow on cue and deliver themselves, *peditentim* as the Latinists say, very slowly, of confessions of little or no interest. The only memorable event of the afternoon was that Harry Gordon tripped on our doorstep and broke his big toe.

At the end of his week's stay, Tom asked the Gordons whether he might borrow their house and their cook, Pepa, for a big dinner with which he might return the hospitality of his various hosts. There were about ten of us at a well-loaded table. At the end of Pepa's feast, Tom leaned back and said, 'That's the first time I've had enough to eat since I got here.' I walked out of the house and into the village and down to the waterfront. Then I walked back again. I doubt whether Tom had remarked my exit.

As August approached, we had to leave the Villa Antoñita. Siobhan was now so prominently pregnant that, while never admitting her condition, she said that she had to go back to Ireland. We did not seek to detain her; but her fare had to be paid. So did the high-season rent for the Villa Sol, one of a tight trio of charmless bungalows at the west end of the village, not far from the tall tower of the Café Somio, where music thumped on till two in the morning. We parted from the sulky Maria and took on a smiling one. Needing money, I had asked the bank to send us money, as usual. The new manager replied that he would be happy to oblige as soon as my account was in funds. Selwyn Lloyd, now Chancellor of the Exchequer, had imposed a rigorous credit squeeze. When Beetle's father, who had been suffering from Parkinson's disease, died of pneumonia, Jonty Smulian, an American whom I hardly knew and who had fought in the Israeli Defence Force in the 1956 war, lent me money for our fares to fly home from Gibraltar.

Jonty was a friend of Aubrey David, an entrepreneurial architect who was filling the *campo* between Fuengirola and Mijas with more or less fancy villas. Aubrey liked clean lines and, at first, dispensed with banisters for the white marble staircases. Every architect, it seems, fails to take some detail into account. Aubrey discounted the quantity of liquor that a well-heeled *rentier* (and his lady) might be expected to swallow before lurching upstairs to bed and the heavy consequences of a missed step. On the sloping plateau between Fuengirola and Mijas, Lew Hoad, the Wimbledon champion of 1956, later opened a tennis farm. Aubrey's elegantly landscaped courts were divided by pools that might have been cadged from the Alhambra and into which loose shots regularly plopped.

For our few days in London, John Nimmo lent me his Austin A 40. He also offered me some money. He was a very kind man whose generous friendship I never properly honoured. He had a friend called Joe who had been a close friend of Ken Tynan's until Ken became too grand to acknowledge him. My financial problems were eased somewhat before we returned to Fuengirola. Stella Richman promised that there was no shortage of work for me when I wanted it. *The Best of Everything* had been produced, with Terry Alexander and Gary Raymond, and had been well received. I arranged to meet Stella in Sainte-Maxime in late September, when we should be driving back to England, to work out the timetable for my new ATV contract. Meanwhile, she advanced me enough money to repay Jonty Smulian.

I had written *The Graduate Wife* in a state of nervous unease, fearful that Beetle thought of me less as an artist than as a husband who was failing to provide a home for his family. She denied that what I feared was true; her patient vexation confirmed it. Nothing of my dismay was reflected in my new, cold, very English book. Whatever the confusion of my emotions, my brain stayed clear. I moped, but I also worked: whatever their state of mind, writers have to write. I allayed my own dreads with the precision with which I spelt out the complacency of my Oxonian characters.

Desmond Flower declared the finished novel too good to be one of a pair. He proposed to publish it and *The Trouble with England* separately. What was needed after that was a big book to match *The Limits of Love.* Tom Maschler's replacement at Penguin had been appointed too late to abort its paperback publication, but Tony whatever-his-name-was let it be known that he had no appetite for what he chose to call 'intellectual' fiction. *Majoresque cadunt altis de montibus umbrae*, as the new top man would never tolerate anyone to say.

In mid-September, we left the Villa Sol and the insistent nocturnal beat of music from the Somio. For a few thousand pesetas, Harry and Charlotte Gordon had bought a high plot of land that jutted out, precipices on three sides, a burly buttress at the base of the mountains that rose above Mijas. On the narrow neck that connected the property to the road, there was a little church dedicated to San Anton. Otherwise, the site was unapproachable. Harry proposed to build a house with two studios. He needed masons to do the basic structural work, but he would design the place himself and make the doors and windows. I envied his practical competence and his piano-playing. To fund construction, he and Charlotte were going back to work in New York. He had small hope of selling his paintings, but he had been offered a 'creative' job in an advertising agency at almost $20,000 a year.

I lacked the means or the appetite to continue living in Spain, but I dreaded our return to England. We would have enough to keep us, but I had small prospect of earning sufficient money to provide anything that would please Beetle as much as the Old Mill House had. She was willing to find a job, but that solution was also, it seemed to me, a criticism. I had to hope, and prove, that it was not really what she wanted. The children kept us together, and apart.

We crossed the border into France late on a Saturday night. On the Sunday morning, Beetle woke with a temperature and a fierce sore throat. I cannot remember in what hotel in what small town we had stopped. I can, however, see myself, as if on a spool of film in my mental cutting room, running down a long, straight street of shuttered houses and shops in search of a *pharmacie*. I found one that was open and pleaded for an antibiotic, as if my marriage depended on it. Whatever they sold me proved effective. By the time we reached Sainte-Maxime, Beetle was well enough to face

Stella and Victor, who were holidaying with their small son, another Paul.

I had sent word to Richard Gregson of where we would be staying, so that he could tell Stella. There was a message at the hôtel Chardon Bleu to call Gareth Wigan at the John Redway agency. I suspected that Stella Richman was not, after all, going to be in Sainte-Maxime; it augured ill for the promised contract. It took some time to get through to London. Beetle took Paul and Sarah to the beach. When at last we were connected, Gareth told me that Richard was out of town on business. He thought I would want to know that a producer called David Deutsch had seen *The Best of Everything* on television and wanted to buy the film rights and commission me to write the movie script. Was I willing to come back to England to talk to him? He assured me that David Deutsch was a very nice man, the son of Oscar Deutsch, the founder of the Odeon cinema chain. He worked for Anglo-Amalgamated, which had agreed to back the project. I could rely on the terms being fair and, more important, the film was likely to be made. Oh, and did I have a pencil? Stella Richman had rented a house in Sainte-Maxime; she had asked him to give us the address and phone number. She had agreed that I should do three more plays for ATV. She could pay me a little more than she had before.

I could imagine Karl Marx's ironic smile. Had he not said that economic circumstances determine the consciousness? My fears of inadequacy were purged. It was shameful and it was exhilarating to have the prospect of giving Beetle what she wanted and what I wanted to give her. What I have always least liked about myself, the urge to self-abasement, was banished. For whatever less than Lawrencian reason, I was restored to virility and self-assurance. Fiction might be what mattered most; the movies were my salvation. I told Beetle that we would go back to England, see Mr Deutsch, collect his money, get a new station wagon, in which Paul and Sarah would be able to stretch out and sleep, and then drive to Rome and rent somewhere where I could write the script. We spent a couple of easy days with Stella and Victor Brusa, who was pleased to compile the best picnics ever eaten on the sands of Sainte-Maxime, and then we drove up to Calais.

he is having to spend very much money. Now all Germans
are having all the time to spend very much money and my
father is not exceptional, you see. I don't know how much
this meal is costing us, but he is very angry because I will
not eat what he is ordering for me and the less I eat the
more he is ordering these expensive things. It is really
quite a scene, I think. The whole table is covered with
these things I have not seen in many years and the waiter
is all the time bringing more and all the time I am eating
nothing and my father is drinking bottles of wine, you see,
and getting altogether red in the face and telling me that
I cannot marry this terrible man who is never working and
all the time hiding from the world and so and I am telling
my father about Europe during the war and then he is
telling me what he has heard about me having a love affair
with a Nazi, you see, and how this will be the final
disgrace, marrying this terrible Karl, who is not a proper
person. Then he is telling me how clever he is and how
much money he is making in South America during the
war and how it is all quite safe and no one will take it away
from him and how he is now this important personage
with the Americans, you see. He is even asking me, I
think, to come and work for him as his secretary, you see,
because he is going to pay me so much money per month.
Now he is drinking big glasses of brandy and I have a plate
of cold *Crêpes Suzette* on my plate in front of me and he is
getting so angry! Finally, of course, he is telling me that if
I marry this refugee, you see, he is not going to leave me a
single penny and I am going to have to find my way in the
world all by myself without any help from him, whereas if
I am working for him, he is giving me a car and a big
allowance and when I am marrying someone he is finding
for me from a good family with a great deal of Von and
land and money and reputation, then he is giving me a big
dowry and so.... He is treating me, you see, like a little girl
just coming out of school with pigtails and so. Well, of
course, I am not now any longer a little girl, so I am telling
him that I am in love with Karl and we are marrying each

98

Lindmann

XXV

DAVID DEUTSCH ASKED us to celebrate our deal (I was to get £3,000 for the screenplay) by having dinner with him and his wife in their flat in Park Royal, a tall new block off Melrose Avenue. When she opened the door, I saw that Mrs Deutsch was the same beautiful Clare who had whispered admiration of my performance in 'Joe and the Boys' when she was married to Raymond Stross. She was – she told me quietly – much, much happier now. David's enthusiasm for our project led me to presume that the initiative was wholly his. It is at least possible that Clare had something to do with the fact that they watched my little play on television. David had no objection to my writing the movie in Rome. I assured him that I wrote better when I was near the Mediterranean. We would come back, if he wanted that, after he had seen the first draft.

Our new car was a Standard Vanguard, more powerful, as well as more commodious, than the Ensign. Before we left England again, we found time to drive down to Colchester and look at a few properties in the area. My mother was glad to take care of Paul and Sarah. It was as if what I said in Fuengirola had never been said; nor did it ever need to be repeated. I was about to be paid more in the next year than my father, who had just retired from Shell, had ever earned in a similar period. I did not think it important, but there it was. He and I never again had a sour discussion of the kind that had so embarrassed Beetle.

I had no urgent wish to return to East Bergholt, but nice houses with gardens were cheaper on the unfashionable Essex–Suffolk border than in Sussex or Surrey. After one quick visit, we made an offer of £4,000 for a whitewashed brick Georgian farmhouse behind a garage in Marks Tey, on the London side of Colchester. Now that I could flash the simulacrum of a steady income, we should be able to get a mortgage, but it depended on a favourable survey. I had done enough, I hoped, to convince Beetle that, in due time, we should have a permanent roof in England. I was in no hurry to live under it.

The big new car impelled me to drive eastwards across France in order to enjoy the *autobahn* down into Italy. I felt a twitch of triumphant transgression in crossing the frontier from which my grandfather Max had escaped fifty years before. Our one German night was mildly disturbed by rowdy voices in the street: French soldiers who had had too much too drink, but wanted more. We stayed in Heidelberg, where Willie Maugham went to the university, long enough only to allow a radio to be slotted into the car and then we headed south. Memories of the war in which I never had to fight led me to bypass Rome and head for Anzio, the site of an Anglo-American amphibious operation intended to outflank Kesselring's defensive line in front of Monte Cassino. The landing took the Germans by surprise, but the cautious American general Lucas failed to press on inland. The Germans regrouped, contained the bridgehead and inflicted heavy casualties on the soldiers pinched within it. Post-war Anzio turned out to be a rebuilt town of shuttered and charmless seaside houses and chalets of the kind to be seen in, as the Linguaphone had indelibly put it, '*centinaia e centinaia di stazioni balnearie*'.

We drove back to Rome. The most suitable and affordable flat was on the ground floor of the 6,000 block on the Via Trionfale, at the top of Monte Mario. Its owner, a contessa of indeterminate age, arrived to vet us in a black Fiat *Millecento*, no very grand motor, driven by a chauffeur in brass-buttoned black livery, wearing a peaked cap. Both might have been characters in flight from Alberto Moravia's novel *Il Conformista*. La Contessa regarded three-year-old Paul and fourteen-month-old Sarah with indulgent smiles and handed us the keys.

What and whose triumph over whom our street celebrated, I never discovered. It led down to the Milvian Bridge where, in 312 AD, the battle between the upstart Constantine and the incumbent emperor Maxentius ended with the victory of Constantine who had, for opportunist motives, united his soldiers under the sign of the Cross. Their success confirmed the Christian God's official and enduring tenancy in Rome. Constantine's theology was his own: conversion did not inhibit him from approving the building of a temple to celebrate his own family's divinity. Evelyn Waugh wrote a poor, pious book about the emperor's Christian mother, Helena. We regularly crossed the Milvian Bridge to go to the almost deserted 1960 Olympic village, which continued to flaunt a well-stocked, never-crowded *supermercato*.

Although Rome was thronged with tourists and what the rest of Italy regarded as bloodsucking bureaucrats and venal politicians, it was possible, if not always permitted, to park in the *centro città*. We were advised, by our Australian doctor neighbour Bob Singer, never to pay the marked price in the shops. The trick was to ask, '*C'é un sconto diplomatico?*' Is there discount for diplomats? 'But we're not diplomats,' I said. Bob said, 'Who said you were? All you did was ask!'

David Deutsch's bosses, Nat Cohen and Stuart Levy, made only one stipulation before backing our movie: they wanted the title to be *Nothing But the Best*. *The Best of Everything* sounded too cold. It was another small piece of evidence that in the movies anyone can have a good idea. Nat and

Stu left the rest to us: they preferred going to the races. Their greatest ambition, eventually achieved, was to lead in the winner of the Grand National. David encouraged me to be bold in 'opening up' the action; I was to make the piece as daring as the usual proprieties would allow. Thanks to the lively garrulity of my characters, I accumulated enough pages in the mornings for us to spend every afternoon going, with Paul and Sarah, to a gallery, a church or an archaeological site. Life and art were old neighbours in Rome.

Federico Fellini's film *La Dolce Vita* had been a shameless and scabrous hit a year earlier. We followed in the shadow of Anita Ekberg, in her ecclesiastical hat, as we climbed the tight stairs around the dome of St Peter's and onto the roof with its wide view down to Hadrian's Tomb and its sugary heaps of marble cannon balls. Jo Janni, whom I met again a few years later, thanks to David Deutsch, told me that the Vatican had been outraged by Fellini's episode depicting the venal and superstitious exploitation of two slum children's supposed vision of the Madonna. The appropriate cardinal announced that he was proposing to instruct the faithful to boycott the movie. Fellini was sufficiently alarmed to go, in penitential mode, as it were to Canossa. On his knees, he explained to the cardinal that he was a poor sinner, anxious only to show how degraded Rome had become and how simple people could be manipulated by the freemasonry of the media. Federico could scarcely restrain his tears. The cardinal promised that he now understood the sincerity of the film-maker's motives. The maestro could rest assured that his visit had not been in vain. With one more realistic sob, the director kissed the cardinal's ring and went, shaking, from the room. Back on unholy ground, in St Peter's Square, Federico slammed his left hand against his right biceps in a crude *abbraccio*, the 'fuck you' gesture of the Trastevere working man.

To amuse Paul and Sarah, I dusted off the stories about ancient Rome that ruins or place names recalled, from the Horatii on the bridge to the cackling of the Capitoline geese, from the murder of the divine Julius to the accession of the clumsy C-Claudius and the fiddle-playing Nero. I tried to emulate Guy Ramsey in never talking down, even when talking downwards. At the weekends, we took the *autostrada* to Assisi or Urbino or Civitavecchia, where Stendhal had once been the French consul. D. H. Lawrence had explored the low-domed Etruscan tombs at nearby Cerveteri and made out the Etruscans to be his kind of dark, instinctive people.

In Italy one can suffer from a surfeit of uplifting refinement. The comic and the grotesque come as a relief. We feared that the Garden of Monsters at Bomarzo might give the children nightmares, but they ran cheerfully into the stone ogre's mouth and gazed without a blink at the lichened muscular Hercules, poised on the point of ripping the inverted giant Cacus in half. Prince Pier Francesco Orsini built his little park of horrors in the 1570s, to vent his rage against fate after the death of his wife, Giulia Farnese. His counter-cultural parade of horrors was commissioned from the same architect, Pirro Ligorio, who finished the remodelling of Saint Peter's in Rome after Michelangelo died. On whatever *piano nobile*, Renaissance artists were also the hirelings of show business, erotic, pastoral or sanctimonious, uplifting, morbid or brutal, as their paymasters required.

Ligorio also designed the Villa d'Este at Tivoli, some 30 kilometres from St Peter's. With its surging fountains and tumbling man-made waterfalls, Cardinal d'Este's summer place was adjacent to a restaurant with a wide terrace where the children could run while our *abacchio* was turning on the spit. Nearby, the Emperor Hadrian's suburban retirement home embraced a country estate and a miniature town for the mournful emperor's staff. Hadrian neither liked Rome nor trusted Romans; he preferred Greece, and Greek love. His elderly blues were induced by the death of Antinous, the comely Bithynian ephebe drowned in the Nile in 130 AD. Did he jump? Was he pushed? Rumour promised that Antinous was dismayed by the onset of hairy maturity. Fearful of losing the emperor's affection, he soaked his cheeks in milk in the hope of staying Hadrian's baby-faced darling.

Perhaps, like Narcissus ('that plain boy', someone called him), he looked at his watery reflection too closely and fell into his soft mirror. By the side of the pool in Hadrian's Tivoli retreat crouched a marble crocodile of the kind that inhabits the Nile.

Rome was an immovable feast. Tacitus, the most stylish of sourpuss historians, said that his countrymen had made the world into a desert and called it peace; Petronius was no less scathing and scarcely less of a prig, though a more outrageous writer. As a result of its legions' conquests, Rome became the finest repository of stolen property in the world. The Vatican museum was the most sumptuous in the city. Its double helix of staircases confounded Heraclitus by ensuring that the road up and the road down were never the same road. Our favourite museum was the Villa Giulia. The most memorable sculpture in the Villa Giulia is of a man and his wife lounging, close together, on top of a terracotta-coloured sarcophagus. Known as 'The Happily Married Couple', they wear the perpetual, enigmatic smiles of those with the wisdom to keep the lid on their uxorious secrets. 'Don't never tell' is a good conjugal rule.

On our way home, whether from Ostia Antica – the least visited, most businesslike of all wide Roman ruins – or from the Baths of Caracalla (an allegedly monstrous emperor who did the Roman people a monumental favour), we would stop at the Gran Caffe Giulio Cesare for *capuccini* and *coppe Olympia* (tubs of chocolate-chip ice cream) or the savoury rice-balls known as *supplì*. We found no accessible expatriate society of the kind we knew in Fuengirola; nor did I miss it.

Now that we had some money, I encouraged Beetle to buy Ferragamo shoes and gloves and to have stylish outfits made for her by a dressmasker recommended by the smiling Ella Singer. In the evenings, we often left Paul and Sarah asleep, under the supervision of the janitor's agreeable wife, and drove across Rome to whatever restaurant featured in the Michelin looked appetising. I relished the overacting of the Alfredo renowned for his *fettuccini*. When they were ready to go to table, the lights were dimmed and the *padrone* came dancing in, purple flames leaping from the oval dish where the pasta writhed in creamy loops.

We saw the new movies (none funnier or more untranslatable than those starring Alberto Sordi) and we shopped on the Via del Corso and up the Via Condotti and on to the Via Veneto. No one questioned our right to a *sconto diplomatico*. I read Moravia, Pavese, Carlo Levi and Italo Svevo. I even began Manzoni's *I Promessi Sposi*. Writing *Nothing But the Best* allowed me the closet pleasure of impersonating the kind of heartless, double-dealing bounder whom I have always been, in practice, too squeamish to emulate. My script was, in some measure, a displaced homage to Ben Hecht and Charles MacArthur's film, *The Scoundrel*, which I had seen, between kisses, in company with Mary Jane Lehman in New York City ten years before.

Within a few weeks, I was able to send the first draft of *Nothing But the Best* to Richard Gregson. He responded, very quickly: it was the best script he had ever read. David Deutsch was eager that I come to England to discuss the second draft with his chosen director, Clive Donner. It seemed no trouble to get in the big blue Vanguard, cushion Paul and Sarah in the back, and drive north with the certainty that we would not be away for long. We went to stay with Joan and Baron Moss. They had moved into a handsome house, with a large garden, in bourgeois Woldingham, Surrey. Baron's Bentley convertible was in the drive.

Clive Donner had just directed *Some People*, a worthy piece with Kenneth More, sponsored by the Duke of Edinburgh, about a boy band redeemed from delinquency by musical success. Clive's reputation was based on his having edited the 1953 hit *Genevieve*, starring Kay Kendall. Based on the annual Brighton Rally of vintage cars, it had something in common with *Lady at the Wheel*. Leslie Bricusse had been appearing in *An Evening with Beatrice Lillie* at the time when 'sexy Rex' Harrison was having a flagrant affair with Kay Kendall while he and his wife, the delectable Lilli Palmer, were starring, as they had on Broadway, in John van Druten's *Bell, Book and Candle*. It had required no great wit to emend the title to *Bell, Book and Kendall*. Kay Kendall was now dead.

Clive Donner came from the same part of north-west London as Beetle. Bernard Levin was his cousin. When *Nothing But the Best* was eventually made, Bernard played the very small part of a drama critic. Since Clive had gone into the movie business as an apprentice, his ascent had something in common with that of my script's James Brewster, who – like the S Man – was bent on mounting the slippery pole of modern success. Clive was garrulous, friendly and imprecise. He wanted the plot to be expanded, but he had no clear ideas. I listened, I sighed and sometimes I saw, and sharpened, his point. In Stanley Ellin's plot, which I had had no call to amplify in the tight television version, Jimmy Brewster enrols Charlie Prince, an upper-class remittance man, as his social tutor and then, having graduated as a plausible toff, murders him, puts his body in a trunk in his landlady's cellar, and takes possession of his income. It then emerges that Charlie was the disgraced brother of the woman on whom James had fastened his purposeful affections. His daughter's impending wedding leads her father to seek to recall her scapegrace brother from the wilderness. The TV version ended with a trunk, which the viewers knew to contain Charlie's body, being delivered to the family house. Clive and David thought that the film needed an extra twist or two, which I promised to supply. Once again, arrogance and servility worked easily in tandem, the mark of the classicist.

We returned to the Via Trionfale, where I pinned a quick new tail on the script. There was still enough time left on the Contessa's lease for me to begin a new novel. Raul Hilberg's *The Destruction of the European Jews* had been sent to me for review by David Pryce-Jones, who was on the staff of the middle-of-the-road *Time and Tide*. The magazine's life was abbreviated by more fashionable journalistic traffic coming at it in both directions, but I have been glad to have David's lively and unflinching friendship ever since.

Hilberg's book had a programmatic callousness: his scope was limited by the cold determination to look solely at the means and machinery by which the Nazis and their acolytes, whether conscripted or enthusiastic, contrived to kill some four and a half million men and women and a million and a half children while engaged in a many-fronted war against enemies who made no conspicuous effort to deter them. Hilberg's book, followed by Adolf Eichmann's trial in Jerusalem, put an end to a decade and a half of – to put it decorously – reticence concerning Hitler's genocide.

I began *Lindmann* with no precise scheme, but with an urgent verve which had nothing to do with my own petty experiences of English anti-Semitism. My main character was a duplicitous, conscience-stricken impostor. That Lindmann was not the Holocaust survivor he claimed to be gave me licence both to be and not to be the chronicler of events of which I, like my main character, had in truth no first-hand experience. Lindmann was an alter ego whom I could inhabit and satirise at the same time. The characters who surrounded him in his London boarding house were drawn from diverse sources, not least from Hans and Juliana, our neighbours in the Calle Tostón. Juliana had told me little about her father or her life in wartime Germany, but enough to furnish my imagination.

My experiences in TV and, more recently, in conversation with Clive Donner and David Deutsch had been enriching in several respects. They also gave me a sense of how commercial considerations trumped all others. Not least the fun of writing scripts lay in arming actors with words they were happy to say and impressing directors with one's ingenious speed, but I was truly a writer only when alone with the page which, in my case, rarely stayed blank for long. *Lindmann* was an apology for having played the glad mercenary. The turning point in the plot came when the opportunist Milstein, whom I graced with the thrust of Tom Maschler, appropriated what he thought was Lindmann's life in order to write a commercial movie about the sinking in the Black Sea of what I called the SS *Broda*. The first long-playing record we ever owned was of Nathan Milstein playing the Beethoven violin concerto (the second was of Amalia singing *fado*).

The script within the novel tracked the true story of the *Struma*, which had sailed from Constanza, in Bulgaria, in 1943, overloaded with desperate Jewish fugitives. Its passengers were denied visas to land in Turkey because the British refused to allow them to enter Palestine. Perhaps of their own volition, more probably under pressure from London, the Turks required the unseaworthy *Struma* to leave their territorial waters with all its passengers on board. A night or two later, it sank, or was torpedoed, in the Black Sea. There were said to be two survivors, though neither, so far as I knew, had been traced or told his story. In the case of the fictional SS *Broda*, I postulated one survivor, the eponymous Lindmann.

David and Clive were delighted with the work I had done on *Nothing But the Best* and promised to begin the process of casting. It seemed likely that our scoundrel-hero would be Alan Bates, who was about to star in *A Kind of Loving*, directed by John Schlesinger. A screenwriter can always recognise when he has done a good job: he becomes superfluous. The producer and, in particular, the director are likely to assume his work to be theirs. However amiable, they now want the attention of mechanicals and actors to be directed only at them. There might yet be more work for me to do on *Nothing But the Best*; meanwhile we had a period of grace. We also had the slender means to go to Greece and tempting proximity to it.

XXVI

IN MARCH 1962 we yielded her keys to the Contessa and drove down the Via Appia and across to Bari, where we stayed the night in a big modern hotel. I woke the next morning with a savage sore throat and a high fever. I took aspirin and whatever else the hotel doctor suggested, but I feared we were stalled in limbo. Bari has its charms, but not many. Beetle took Paul and Sarah out and came back again. I sweated and I slept. The next morning, when I took my temperature it was 101.5. I shook the thermometer down and told Beetle that I was normal. We packed and left. By the time we drove onto the dock at Brindisi, the fever was gone. We drove the Vanguard onto the ferry and set sail for Igoumenitsa on the north-eastern coast of Epirus. The Latin term for the Adriatic figured in the Gender Rhymes, which I learned at the age of eleven, appended to Kennedy's Latin Primer: 'Masculine will always be / Things that you can touch and see / Masculine will also be Hadria, the Adriatic Sea'.

I began to study ancient Greek – starting with *luo, lueis, luei*, I let go, you let go, he lets go – when I was ten years old. Not one of my teachers at any stage recommended going to modern Greece. As Byron put it, 'Fair Greece! Sad relic of departed worth / Immortal, though no more, though fallen, great!' The only period worthy of prolonged academic attention was the fifth century BC, in which the Attic language and the Athenian empire had the double flowering that would be matched by that of England under Elizabeth I.

The eclipse of Athens in the Peloponnesian War was famously said to have 'taken the spring out of the year'. In fact, the city recovered much of its prosperity, if never the communal vanity that made the theatre, comic and tragic, both a civic embellishment and the crucible in which ideas and vanities were dissected in imagery and dialogue. In the post-classical Greek-speaking world, expanded by Alexander the Great's bloody crusade, there were many clever Greeks and more clever Greeklings. Writers who lacked Hellenic blood could become, as the Syrian Lucian proved in the second century AD, at once insolent and brilliant in their second tongue.

Like the English language, first mangled and then renovated by fast-talking immigrants into the US, Greek had an elasticity often made snappier by non-native speakers. Traditional classicists pursed their lips at such iconoclasts. Lucian was notorious for deriding the great statue of Zeus that Phidias enthroned in his temple at Olympia (it was said that if Zeus were to stand up, he would take the roof off the building). Lucian's contemporary, Dio Chrysostom – the man with the golden mouth – said, piously, that a single glimpse of the statue would make a man forget all his earthly troubles. Lucian, the emblematic jobbing journalist, had to think of something less deferential to say. He compared Phidias's sublime image to that of a listless old man in whom no one any longer had serious faith. In this, he was the predecessor of Stephen de Houghton, whose blasphemous squib procured the decline and rise of Mark Boxer.

Byron visited Epirus when it was a Turkish province. As he rode into Joannina, he saw a human arm and hand hanging from a gibbet; all that remained of a Greek patriot called Evtinnio, who had been tortured for three months, before being hanged, drawn and quartered at the orders of the Turkish governor Ali Pasha, who asked Byron to dinner and admired his 'fine white hands' and small ears. 'I'm very partial to Englishmen,' Ali told him. 'I particularly love English sailors.' Byron, like many British travellers, was appalled and beguiled by ruthless tyrants, even though he was willing to risk his life to unseat the Turks who had out-Xerxesed Xerxes.

We took the steep, zigzag road up to Dodona, greenest, most ancient and most remote of Greek oracles. Shepherds huddled under shaggy fleeces – some dyed saffron, some blanched – knees to chin to keep the warmth in. Long white crooks posted question marks in the cold air. Dodona's ancient priests were said never to wash their feet. Greek versifying may well have begun with oracular pronouncements; not, however, with those at Dodona. The rustling leaves of its sacred oak tree, duly interpreted by those chthonic priests, yielded divine responses to pilgrims' questions. One inquiry that survives, inscribed on a lead tablet, asked whether a man's current wife would give him children; another whether it was a good idea to keep sheep. Dodona was still a numinous site, but it offered no rustling hint as to which of the isles of Greece we should visit.

We drove south, via the paramount oracular site, at rug-draped Delphi, to Athens. We walked down Stadiou Street and tried to decipher what was on at the cinema on the façade of which was advertised, in capital letters, NTONALNT PTAK. The image of Donald Duck, on a billboard lower down, supplied a crib.

A travel agent called Thalia Taga had been recommended, in a recent *Sunday Times* article by Dilys Powell, the film critic and Hellenophile. Playing the petty impostor, I allowed Thalia to believe that Dilys was known to me personally. As it turned out, eighteen months later I was Ms Powell's junior colleague on the *Sunday Times*, when I became a fortnightly fiction reviewer under the distant aegis of Dilys's husband, Leonard Russell, and the immediate tutelage of Jack Lambert, whose handwriting and editorial tact equalled Guy Ramsey's.

Thalia Taga sent out for coffee for us and sweets for the children. She was advising us to go to Skiathos, when the telephone rang. The man at the other end was an ex-Minister of Marine, Artemis Denaxas. He owned most of a remote Cycladic island called Ios. Like Ali Pasha, Denaxas had a soft spot for the English. He wanted us to discover Ios before the French and the Germans. It was, Thalia promised, 'a sign'. If we sailed to Ios, Denaxas would come soon and, meanwhile, she would ensure that he sent word that we were to be well received. As guileless as Croesus, when he took Delphi's word for it that, by crossing the Ilissus, he would 'destroy a great empire' and never considered the grammatical duplicity which allowed that it might be his own, we relied on the benign patronage of the unseen Denaxas.

Viewed at a distance, Greece had seemed to be a small, jagged adjunct to the Balkans. Once there, it stretched in all directions. Lacking more specific or alluring advice, we honoured Thalia's oracle. On the following day, we went down to Piraeus, garaged the Vanguard and, with most of our belongings, boarded an obsolete English Channel ferry, built on the Clyde, now renamed the *Despina*. A fourteen-hour trip would deposit us, between three and four in the morning, at Ios. Before we had left the placid waters of Piraeus, the shrilling of the hooter cued old ladies in black to be neatly sick into grey cardboard boxes.

As we sailed under the lee of Poseidon's temple at Sounion, where Byron felt entitled to carve his name, in big letters, two bearded priests, in their tall black hats, were standing by the rail in soft conspiracy with two army offic-ers. Five years later, the army – backed by the church – would send young King Paul and his hated German mother Frederika, into exile and impose an officious tyranny on the country. We were uneasily asleep in our tight, brown, airless *prote thesis* cabin when the cry came, 'Ios, Ios!'

We took our possessions up on deck and stared into the lapping dark-ness. *Despina*'s lights glistened on toothy rocks. A red-eyed beacon blinked on a metal tripod. *Despina* turned and slid into the black goal of Ios bay. Below us, the breathing glow of cigarettes spotted the purple night. Invisible oarsmen were pulling out to meet the *vapore* as her anchor was unravelled into the Guinness-dark sea. The oarsmen scrambled up the rope ladder and grabbed our things, like helpful pirates. We were the only foreigners to disembark. Beetle carried Sarah down to the bobbing boat; and I carried Paul. Hands reached up and took us and our things into the boat. On shore, no one had heard of us. We put up in the only hotel in the harbour, the *xenodocheio Denaxas*, which was named in honour of '*ho plousios*', the rich man, perhaps because he or one his ancestors had fathered the hostelry's founder.

The next morning, Beetle's birthday, we looked up through the clear air at the starch-white village, high-shelved cubes topped by the church tower, 150 metres up the zigzag path with its up-and-down traffic of doleful, neat-rumped donkeys. There were no wheeled vehicles, no paved roads. Beetle was tired and wanted somewhere, anywhere, to unpack, get food for the children, set up Sarah's portable cot and be immune to the inquisitive stares of the islanders. More than anything, I wanted to resume work on *Lindmann*.

At breakfast (coffee, bread, vitam and honey), we were approached by a French-speaking Romanian who promised to find us a house. If it was a trap, I was glad to fall into it. He led us to a three-roomed *spiti* – the modern Greek for house comes from the Latin word *hospitium* – in the *campo*, the wide valley behind a long sandy beach adjacent to the harbour. There may have been other houses available. Some may even have had a bed more comfortable than a cotton palliasse, stuffed with straw, laid on five pliable planks on a rusty metal frame. Niko's cottage had a kitchen, with table and chairs, and a single deck chair. There was a terrace in front of the *spiti*, with a concrete table under the metal frame for the summer's vine. Too dispirited to care to traipse any further in the heat, we settled, as we often do, for the first plausible thing we came to. The rent was £2 a week. Judging from the Romanian's expression when we agreed to it, we were being overcharged.

I walked back to the hotel where we had dumped our possessions. Donkeys stood, like vacant taxis, under a rusting placard which announced, in festering white capitals, that Ios was the site of HOMER'S TUMB (scholarship somewhat confirms the claim). As I came out with our heavy blue suitcases, one of the donkeymen limped over and took them from me. Before I could argue or ask the price, he was roping them onto Phryne, one of his two neat, blue-beaded donkeys. Yorgios Galatsios appointed himself our island cicerone and was not to be denied. He already knew where we intended to live. When we got there and I asked him how much he wanted for his welcome attention, he said, '*Oti thelete seis*', whatever you want; a form of demanding generosity to which I became accustomed. The speed with which it was pouched suggested that five drachmae was too much; if so, it was not a great deal. The last thing I wanted was what the Greeks call *fassaries*, complications; they are a national sport, not infrequently a bloody one.

The islanders had their quarrels (loud voices cataracted down the jagged hill from the village), but their paucity and their isolation insured civility. If anything was lost, or dropped, it was always returned almost before anyone had time to look for it. The illusion that we were living in an idyll was sustained, by contrast, when we listened to the news broadcast, in very slow Special English, from the American airbase at Akrotiri in Cyprus. The announcer's educational tone was at cruel odds with the stories that he measured out of assassinations, bombings and massacres. The last phase of the war in Algeria was reaching its bloody climax in the savage activities of the French ultras' OAS (*Organisation de l'armée secrète*). Its self-righteous thugs committed conspicuous atrocities, such as murdering victims, French 'traitors' and Algerian wounded, as they lay in hospital beds.

Niko's cottage sat below a round, terraced hillock where, three decades later, the ancient city of Ios would be excavated. There was no electricity and no plumbing; the roof consisted of strips of bamboo, laced tightly together and laid across wooden beams, with a foot of rammed earth on top; our toilet was an earth-closet across a field. That one deckchair, reminiscent of

Wittgenstein's in his rooms in Whewell's Court, was our only luxury, apart from the German radio, which we had detached before abandoning the car. One night, there was a thunder storm. The piercing rain drilled straight through the roof and into the middle of our three rooms, where Paul and Sarah slept. In the morning, the earth floor was badged with black puddles. Only the corners in which the children were sleeping remained dry. Local gods, whimsy might claim, are kinder than the almighty.

We drew water from the well next to the terrace. Simplicity was not as simple as all that: it required an acquired knack, a timely twitch of the rope, to tilt the tin bucket so that it took on its first gulp of water and then sank down to be filled. We had to be careful always to replace the plank lid on the well. I worked at *Lindmann* in the mornings, sitting under the empty grape vine. If the sun was very bright, I opened and dangled our big black British umbrella from the trellis. The work went well. Our landlord, Nikos, would come by and watch me typing. He had never seen a typewriter before. Paul and Sarah improvised toys from the roots and stones on the island's floor. The beach was littered with fist-sized lumps of pumice, small change from the great explosion of the volcanic island of Santorini three or more millennia before. During our afternoons on the sand, we looked up from castling at the Kolynos-white church of Aghia Eirene, Saint Irene.

The islanders were poor; yet you never passed one without him giving you something, if only the flower from behind his ear. Panaiotis, the father of our landlord Nikos, came by each morning with a can of sheep's milk. It had fresh hairs floating in it. Properly strained, it made delicious rice pudding. One day we met a handsome man holding a very young calf around his neck, a modern *Moschophoros*. He and his partner (perhaps his lover) were the island butchers. He promised to keep some *sêkoti* (liver) *ya ta pethia*, for the children. I hoped, like any squeamish humbug, that it would not be that of the calf he was carrying. Meanwhile, he offered a slab of cheddar cheese, the product of a dairy that *ho plousios* Denaxas had funded.

We did most of our shopping on the harbour. The kiosk in the centre of the quay sold ION chocolate and small plastic toys. Paul collected beer bottle tops. It was easy to be happy. A smiling, smelly lady ran the Shell concession, supplying fuel for the local *caiques* and the few yachts that put into Ios, and also sold more or less crisp Papadopoulos cream sandwich biscuits. Their name did not yet carry sinister overtones. The sea was full of fish, but Captain Adonis, who sat with his seldom empty glass on the quay-side, was as deeply suspicious of Poseidon as any of his ancient ancestors. However calm the water, he could find good reason not to put to sea. The village postmaster, Michalis, who wore two pairs of glasses as improvised bifocals, doubled, in the late afternoon, as a more regularly daring fisherman.

Since no one spoke English, I matched my ancient Greek to what I was learning from my grammar and from the islanders. I had had the idea that we would spend some time in Greece and then go on to Israel. I bought a Hebrew textbook when we were in London, but I lacked the will to commit myself to its study. The alien script defeated me and the text, in translation, set no seed. I can envy those who master the mirror-reversed, vowel-free calligraphy, but Greece held and holds me captive; I have never felt any strong desire to escape. Greece became my Zion. In Athens once I had my hair cut and, since my demotic Greek was fairly good, the barber asked if I came from a Greek family. How else did I have so much black hair? I said, '*Ebraios eimai*' (I am a Jew). He said, '*Ellenes, Ebraoi, miadzouni*' (Greeks, Jews much the same thing). I said, '*Isos*' (perhaps). Always proud, often debased, divided among themselves yet roped together by loyalties and antagonisms, ancient and modern, clever and foolish, Greeks and Jews are the enduring incarnation of Mediterranean duplicity, answering yes and no to the wide world's invitation to abate their distinction.

Like Epirus, Ios bore traces of the centuries of the Tourkokratia; the Turkish occupation ended only in 1828. Many of the older men, like Niko's father, wore Turkish-style baggy trousers. More than a few of them had called

their fathers 'effendi'. They smoked hookahs in the café under the eucalyptus trees in the village square, while their tethered donkeys nodded and
nodded and never quite agreed. Life was hard and hardly different from the
old days. The only fresh vegetable, apart from potatoes, was broad beans.
When we asked the shopkeeper on the port whether he had any eggs, he
almost always rolled his eyes to the heavens, the unspoken way of saying
no. Yet when Easter came, everyone had celebratory red eggs to give us, *ya
ta pethia*. In Greece, children are the best passport.

One of Heraclitus's most frequently quoted apophthegms is 'the road
up and the road down are the same road'. The old Ephesian grouch can
never have taken the steep path up to Ios village; it was nothing whatever
like the same road down. The shops up there were better stocked than on
the harbour. After we had been on the island for a few weeks, one of the
shopkeepers asked us to his house for a meal. In his living room were the
framed reproduction of two large paintings, of King Edward VII of England and Queen Alexandra. I tried to express to Yiorgos how touching it
was to see such icons in a Greek house. He ducked his head forward and
dropped his chin. The pictures had belonged to his parents. He had no
idea who the ermined aliens were.

When we had eaten our *dolmades*, stuffed vine leaves, and our *arnaki
tou fournou*, roast lamb, and thick lumps of yoghurt, Yiorgos disclosed the
reason for our invitation. My Greek struggled with his, but I gathered that
he wanted me to become his partner in the chicken business. It was common knowledge we had come to Ios because we were friends of *ho plousios*,
the rich man, Artemis Denaxas whose absent presence lorded it over the
island. Yorgios imagined that we too must be rich.

Exorbitantly grateful for lunch, I heard myself agree to lend him several
thousand drachmae, but I declined to become a poultry farmer. Yiorgos
proposed to repay me, *siga, siga*, bit by bit. The first bit was a large tin of
island honey. When we poured some out to sweeten our daily rice pudding,

it was thick and dark brown and appeared to contain a large number of plump raisins. Closer analysis revealed them to be candied bluebottles. Next day, we again took the road up. Yiorgos shrugged, took the tin back and gave us another. We retrieved the rest of my loan, *siga, siga* indeed, in tinned milk and corned beef.

Yellow daisies and black-eyed, blood-banded poppies were soon springing from the fertile roof of Niko's cottage. A fig tree displayed green-nailed buds. The arthritic grapevine sprang to life and began to mount the trellis over the stone table where I was finishing my novel. On the long culminating day, I typed thirty pages in a frenzy of what I could believe was a gift from the local muse. Lindmann's stream of consciousness seemed to converge and flood with my own. I have never been a practising believer in inspiration but, as I hammered out those climactic pages, I might have been taking dictation. At last, I was writing as a man should, with no thought of the market or of the charm of what was appearing on the page. I said what I felt had to be said. I had no rivals; I cared nothing for what any critic might think. The phantoms of Alan Maclean and Auntie Marge might shake their heads, like some bicephalic crone, but I was free of fettering discretion.

As Easter approached, Artemis Denaxas, *ho plousios* himself, arrived on the island. The yachting season was beginning and it pleased him to parade, with his dogs Dick and Rover, on the Ios dockside. He had a white carefully upturned moustache. His uniform as honorary admiral of Ios consisted of white trousers, a blue blazer with gilt buttons and a flat cap. He greeted us warmly and invited us to lunch at his residence, which stood on a green hill above the harbour. We had been eating fried eggs and *koukia* for many weeks and were happily seduced by a generous lunch, wine from Santorini (of which Kiria Denaxas was a native) and cushioned chairs.

When Sarah grew restive, Mrs Denaxas opened the doors to the stone-flagged terrace adjoining the dining room. It had a low wall, she said, so the children would be perfectly safe playing out there. As Denaxas was pouring glasses of Metaxa cognac, Sarah climbed onto the white wall and then, suddenly, she was not there any more. Mrs Denaxas said, 'She's gone!' We ran out and looked over the wall. There was a drop of three or four metres. Sarah lay on top of the only green bush. There were large stones on either side of it. She was frightened but not badly hurt. Luck, it seemed, was on our side.

London was calling: my film was going to be shot; the director who would take all the credit needed my help. There was a certain lure in the news, which came in a telegram from my mother, that *The Graduate Wife* had had very good reviews, especially from Jack Davenport in *The Observer*. The ranks of Tuscany were, it seemed, opening their arms to me. A few days later, we made an excursion to Mykonos to meet Tom Maschler and his latest lady. I saw that the woman ahead of us as we disembarked from the ferry had a copy of *The Observer* in her wicker basket. I asked if I might have a look at it and explained why. She handed it to me, saying 'Don't apologise. We know very well how it is.' She was Elaine Steinbeck. The author of *The Grapes of Wrath* gave me a bleak smile, but had no appetite for writerly comradeship. Jack Davenport said that I wrote the best dialogue he had read in many years; I should try my hand at a play.

Tom's companion, Martha Crewe, had left her two children in London and had no wish to talk to ours. Tom and she left the hotel into which he had booked us and we scarcely saw them again, except at a distance on a trip to the island of Delos, where the statue of a slave dealer stands in for Apollo. Mykonos was famous, in those days, for the 'king of *pantalonia*', a tailor who promised to cut, fit and complete women's trousers, from a choice of bright materials, in twenty-four hours. On a secluded beach, we saw Soraya, the ex-empress of Iran, who had failed to give the Shah the son he needed as his successor. Soraya was with a female companion and seemed heavy with the child she had never had.

Several weeks before we were due to leave Ios, I asked Yiorgos Galatsios, whether any of the abandoned farmhouses was for sale. He came back with a list of properties. Nudging my heels against Phryne's flanks, I went house-hunting. The island was much bigger than we knew and there were many abandoned, often seductive properties. There were many sellers, it seemed, and no buyers. When I asked for a price, it was often very little, at first. As soon as the owner knew of our interest, the price went up. If I winced and agreed the new one, it went up again. The dream of living in wonderland receded every time we approached it. On a visit to the post office, Michalis looked over his two pairs of glasses and handed us a letter which announced that a survey of the property at Marks Tey had shown structural defects that made it impossible for the bank to grant us a mortgage. It was a smaller disappointment to me than the prospect of leaving Ios without a small plot to call our own.

A sadly smiling young woman called Flora came down to help Beetle with the washing. Her husband, Paniotis, was Yorgios Galatsios's rival for our chicken business. To denigrate him, Yiorgos made the traditional gesture, a thumb for the spout, his fist for the bottle, to indicate a drunkard. On the day before we were due to catch the *Despina* for Piraeus, Flora said, '*Thelete akrivos na agorazete ena spitaki?*' (Do you really want to buy a little house?) I said, '*Veveos, alla nomidzo pou then boroume.*' (Indeed I do, but I don't think we can.)

She led me up to the village and down the bouldered path on the other side to the uninhabited bay of Mylopota, which I had never seen before. At the far end, above the long, wide scimitar of golden sand, at the top of a quartet of terraces of olive, almond and fig trees, a green-shuttered cottage looked out over the Aegean facing the neighbouring island of Sikinos (which Solon once derided as the place for people who cared only for a quiet life). The roof of the little house was the cropped skeleton of a eucalyptus tree, with bamboo slats across the branches, not unlike Odysseus's bedroom on Ithaca. The only well was down on the beach level.

Flora wanted money in order to be able to send her children to school on Santorini, a place of black, once toasted beaches. The island is hooped around a great lagoon where the volcano's crater was, and is. Early in the second millennium, its eruption split the island open and spewed lava over the Aegean and, so they say, suffocated the bright Minoan civilisation that some people think was the fabled Atlantis. On a clear day, if you stand on the heights above Mylopota, Santorini is visible, hull down, on the horizon.

Going up, I asked Flora how much she wanted for her house. She said, '*Dtheka pente chiliades*'. Fifteen thousand drachmae; in those days, roughly £150. I feared that she would raise the price, if I agreed; but I did; and she did not. As we walked back down to the beach, we crossed a field with a broad frontage directly onto the beach and a well in one inshore corner. Flora said, '*Afto einai dthikosmou, an to thelete*' (This is mine too; if you want it). '*Poso einai?*' I said: 'How much is it? '*To ithio,*' she said; the same. I said, '*Tha to paro.*' (I'll have it.)

That afternoon we went to see the *eirenodikes*, the justice of the peace (more literally the peace of justice) and the transfers were formalised, in longhand. Sarah wept as *Despina* sailed past the white church of Aghia Eirene and out of Ios harbour; but I could now promise her that we would be back. Sarah always called Ios 'that place'. It mattered to her more than anywhere else. She painted images from it, big and small, again and again. Her ashes are scattered on the terrace below our renovated house up on the hill. Fifty years later, we and our sons and Sarah's daughters have built three houses, directly on the beach, facing Solon's lazy Sikinos.

Since I was now officially an American citizen, when we arrived in England I had to fill in the usual form. Having no other address, on the line labelled 'Permanent Residence', I wrote, 'Ios, Cyclades, Greece'.